Acknowledgements ix

Fiction

Rejoice! & Other Stories
KssssS
Burning Worm
Pax: Variations
Druids Hill

Acknowledgements

I would like to thank: the International Writers' and Translators' Centre of Rhodes for their gift of peace and quiet; Mariola Żychowska of Kraków Polytechnik; Mary Niesłuchowska of the American School of Warsaw, Evgeny Dobrenko and Natalia Skradol of Sheffield University, Michael Fleming of PUNO, Martin Hurcombe of University of Bristol, Julian Preece of Swansea University, and John Flower, editor of the *Journal of European Studies*; Judit Polgar, Cathie and Tony Gard, Brian Wasileski, Linda Pawłowska, Shirley Franklin, Yvonne Lyon, Corine Ferry, Nigel Jenkins, Alice Pepper, Maggie Kajiyama, Bill Brand, Mick O'Rourke, Chris Binns; my colleagues at Derby University: Moy McCrory, Simon Heywood, Jerry Hope, Adrian Buckner, Raymond Greenoaken, Matt Clegg, Neil Campbell, Sam Kasule, Robert Hudson, Christine Berberich, Carol Arijoki, Ian Barnes, Bali Sihota, and Maggie and Tim Shields. As always I thank Star, Luke and Madeleine Rose.

The author and publisher have obtained permission and would like to acknowledge two articles previously published by Carl Tighe and on which chapters 6 and 7 of this volume are based:

> Tighe C. (2010) 'Poland translated: the post-communist generation of writers' *Studies in East European Thought* (vol.62) 169–95
> Tighe C. (2016) 'Lustration – the Polish Experience' *Journal of European Studies* (vol.46) 338–73

Other titles by Carl Tighe

Non Fiction

Gdansk: National Identity in the Polish-German Borderlands
The Politics of Literature: Polish Writers & Communism
Writing and Responsibility
Creative Writing @ University: Frequently Asked Questions
Writing the World: Writing as a Subject of Study

Contents

	Acknowledgements	*viii*
1	Introduction – Spooks, shadows and unfinished business	1
2	Kundera's 'Kidnap' revisited	26
3	Polish writers and tradition – Partition and independence	50
4	Polish writers and tradition – Nazism and communism	84
5	Hungary – Writers in Transition	122
6	Poland translated – Post-Communist writing	141
7	Lustration – The Polish experience	162
8	The end of history, return to Europe, and rise of illiberal democracy	193
	Bibliography	*238*
	Websites	*255*
	Index	*257*

First published 2021
by Routledge
2 Park Square, Milton Park, Abingdon, Oxon OX14 4RN

and by Routledge
52 Vanderbilt Avenue, New York, NY 10017

Routledge is an imprint of the Taylor & Francis Group, an informa business

© 2021 the estate of **Carl Tighe**

The right of **Carl Tighe** to be identified as author of this work has been asserted by him in accordance with sections 77 and 78 of the Copyright, Designs and Patents Act 1988.

All rights reserved. No part of this book may be reprinted or reproduced or utilised in any form or by any electronic, mechanical, or other means, now known or hereafter invented, including photocopying and recording, or in any information storage or retrieval system, without permission in writing from the publishers.

Trademark notice: Product or corporate names may be trademarks or registered trademarks, and are used only for identification and explanation without intent to infringe.

British Library Cataloguing-in-Publication Data
A catalogue record for this book is available from the British Library

Library of Congress Cataloging-in-Publication Data
Names: Tighe, Carl, 1950–2020 author.
Title: Tradition, literature and politics in East-Central Europe / Carl Tighe.
Description: London ; New York : Routledge, 2021. | Series: Routledge histories of Central and Eastern Europe | Includes bibliographical references and index.
Identifiers: LCCN 2020037730
|Subjects: LCSH: East European literature--21st century--History and criticism. | Politics and literature--Europe, Eastern. | Europe, Eastern--Intellectual life--21st century. | Political culture--Europe, Eastern.
Classification: LCC PN849.E9 T54 2021 | DDC 809/.88917--dc23
LC record available at https://lccn.loc.gov/2020037730

ISBN: 978-0-367-63471-1 (hbk)
ISBN: 978-1-003-11928-9 (ebk)

Typeset in Sabon
by SPi Global, India

Tradition, Literature and Politics in East-Central Europe

Carl Tighe

LONDON AND NEW YORK

Routledge Histories of Central and Eastern Europe

1 Hungary since 1945
Árpád von Klimó, translated by Kevin McAleer

2 Romania under Communism
Denis Deletant

3 Bulgaria under Communism
Ivaylo Znepolski, Mihail Gruev, Momtchil Metodiev,
Martin Ivanov, Daniel Vatchkov, Ivan Elenkov, Plamen Doynow

4 From Revolution to Uncertainty: The Year 1990 in Central and
Eastern Europe
Edited by Joachim von Puttkamer, Włodzimierz Borodziej, and
Stanislav Holubec

5 Identities in-Between in East-Central Europe
Edited by Jan Fellerer, Robert Pyrah and Marius Turda

6 Communism, Science and the University: Towards a Theory of
Detotalitarianisation
Edited by Ivaylo Znepolski

7 A Nation Divided by History and Memory: Hungary in
the Twentieth Century and Beyond
Gábor Gyáni

8 Historicizing Roma in Central Europe: Between Critical
Whiteness and Epistemic Injustice
Victoria Shmidt and Bernadette Nadya Jaworsky

9 The Macedonian Question and the Macedonians: A History
Alexis Heraclides

10 Politics and the Slavic Languages
Tomasz Kamusella

11 Tradition, Literature and Politics in East-Central Europe
Carl Tighe
https://www.routledge.com/Routledge-Histories-of-Central-and-
Eastern-Europe/book-series/CEE

Carl Tighe was the author of *Gdansk: National Identity in the Polish German Borderlands* (1990), *The Politics of Literature: Polish Writers under Communism* (1998), *Writing and Responsibility* (2004), *Creative Writing @ University* (2009) and *Writing the World: Creative Writing as a Subject of Study* (2014). He was also the author of several works of fiction and taught at universities in Manchester, Swansea, Wrocław and Gdańsk, and at Kraków Jagiellonian University. He was Professor of Creative Writing at the University of Derby. Carl Tighe died in 2020.

Tradition, Literature and Politics in East-Central Europe

Milan Kundera warned that in the states of East-Central Europe, attitudes to the West and the idea of 'Europe' were complex and could even be hostile. But few could have imagined how the collapse of communism and membership of the EU would confront these countries with a life that was suddenly and disconcertingly 'modern' and that challenged sustaining traditions in literature, culture, politics and established views on identity.

Since the countries of East-Central Europe joined the European Union in 2004, the politicians and oppositionists of the centre-left, who once led the charge against communism, have often been forced to give way to right-wing, authoritarian, populist governments. These governments, while keen to accept EU finance, have been determined to present themselves as protecting their traditional ethno-national inheritance, resisting 'foreign interference', stemming the 'gay invasion', halting 'Islamic replacement' and reversing women's rights. They have blamed communists, liberals, foreigners, Jews and Gypsies, revised abortion laws, tampered with their constitutions to control the justice system and taken over the media to an astonishing degree. By 2019, amid calls for the suspension of their voting rights, both Poland and Hungary have been taken to the European Court of Justice and the European Parliament, who have begun to explore ways to put conditions on future EU funding.

This book focuses on the interface between tradition, literature and politics in East-Central Europe, focusing mainly on Poland but also Hungary and the Czech Republic. It explores literary tradition and the role of writers to ask why these left-liberals, who were once ubiquitous in the struggles with communism, are now marginalised, often reviled and almost entirely absent from political debate. It asks in what ways the advent of capitalism 'normalised' literature and what the consequences might be. It asks whether the rise of chauvinism is 'normal' in this part of the world and whether the literary traditions that helped sustain independent political thought through the communist years now, instead of supporting literature, feed nationalist opinion and negative attitudes to the idea of 'Europe'.

1   Introduction
Spooks, shadows and unfinished business

I view writing as an intervention in the world, an attempt to insert a personal point of view and angle of opinion into ongoing cultural and political debate. In my academic writing I have engaged with the interface between politics and literature in what Penguin Books used to call 'the Other Europe' – specifically, I have engaged with the PRL, by which I mean not only *Polska Rzeczpospolita Ludowa* (People's Republic of Poland), but what I call the Polish Republic of Letters – the writers, their opinions, struggles, influence and careers. I have been trying to fathom Polish literary culture, what shapes creativity, what made the modern Polish mind-set, what made Polish literary culture so different from that of the West, what made East-Central Europe the place it is.

I have written three books about Poland (this is the fourth), each in its own way a personal attempt to get to grips with Polish literary culture and ask what shaped the modern Polish mind-set, what made East-Central Europe the place it is and what it is that drives creativity. A great deal of my writing on this topic appeared first in *The Journal of European Studies*, where editor John Flower consistently and very generously opened up a space for my ideas and encouraged my writing on what Penguin Books used to call 'the Other Europe'.

I read and write about East-Central Europe in an effort to understand and order my experience. For me, the years 1973–94 were dominated by Poland – by visiting, residence, work, reading, research, Solidarność, Martial Law and the transition to democracy. These were years of tremendous change – physically difficult, politically confusing and very, very stressful: the weather was severe, queues were endless, food was scarce, toilet paper was a fantasy, vodka was cheap, political jokes were grim, denim was 'in', a plastic carrier-bag was a status symbol, everyone smoked and the backing track was Abba. My time in Poland was a formative, life-shaping experience that introduced me to the astonishingly rich cultural life and literary legacy of East-Central Europe. I have always said I gained my qualifications in the UK, but I had my education in Poland. This has been a kind of long, on/off love affair, my unfinished business.

2 Introduction

My Cold War

My first encounter with the Cold War came on a wet evening in the late autumn of 1956. I went with my father to the gloomy parish hall of Saint Francis' Church near Villa Cross in Birmingham to find it filled with rows of camp-beds. Several bus-loads of Hungarians had just arrived. They had been travelling for three or four days and a couple had bloody bandages. The remnants of the lives they had abandoned – clothing, boots, rucksacks, quilted jackets, fur hats, toys – lay where they fell. I had no idea what had happened or where Hungary was, but I remember the silence, the stink of exhaustion, shock and utter despair.

At that time the more run-down parts of Handsworth were where newly arrived immigrants and refugees settled on their way to something better. At Catholic junior school I was mainly with other Irish kids, but there were also Italians, Poles, Palestinians, Iranis, Jordanians, Greeks, Cypriots, Hungarians and Ukrainians. At my secondary school in Erdington the demographic changed a little with Caribbean, Pakistani and Indian kids, but there were several Polish kids – Popliński, Szpotański (Sputnik), Twardowicz, Smójkis (Smudger), Kamiński, Giery and Bach. They taught me a few words of Polish and introduced me to lemon tea, *ogórki, kompot, barsczcz* and *wódka* (pickled gherkins, compote, beetroot soup and vodka). Their parents had arrived in Britain after epic journeys via Romania and France or via the USSR, Iran, Palestine and Italy. I later came to realise that, judging by their accents, they were mostly from the *kresy* – the eastern borderlands annexed by the USSR as part of the Molotov–Ribbentrop Pact and retained after 1945. At the end of the war their homes were in the Soviet Union, Poland was a communist satellite and they were a stranded embarrassment to their erstwhile allies.

As wartime austerity faded and the culture of deference receded, I went to study English Literature at University College Swansea, where the '60s hung on into the late '70s. I became interested in recent translations in the Penguin Modern Poets series, where I 'discovered' Herbert, Rózewicz and Miłosz, then moved on to Borowski and Mrożek. Their irony and the idea of the audience these writers assumed appealed to me: the experience and tradition out of which this writing had grown were very different from the kind of writing I was studying at university. I wanted more.

I first visited Poland in 1973. I spent a month in the tiny village of Szczedrzyk, near Opole, teaching on an English Language summer-school run for UNESCO by the Central Bureau for Educational Visits and Exchanges.[1] This old German village – the local reservoir had been called Hitlersee and the nearby town had once been Oppeln – had been ceded to Poland in the post-war border shift: on the streets the kids went without shoes and a horse-drawn cart was the main form of transport. The simmering resentments Germans and Poles still had to negotiate – a great many Germans who wanted to leave after 1945 had been designated as 'autochthonous Poles' and forced to live on among the incoming Poles – meant that on more

Introduction 3

than one occasion we stepped over blood and teeth in the doorway to the local bar.

A year later I returned to Poland to take up a 'local contract' at Wrocław Technical University. At night I sat in my room high above Wrocław (I thought my address at 19/84 Plac Grunwaldzki significant) and, in the absence of TV, I listened to the lions roar in the nearby zoo and copied Herbert's poems into my notebook. This was a labour of love, a way of engaging, working out the internal structure of the poems, pushing past the language to read the experience that drove it.

In 1975 I moved to the University of Gdańsk, which had opened the previous year, and where I was their first foreign appointment. Every six months I had to register with the *milicja*. In Wrocław they quizzed me about my inherited wealth, university study, my father's occupation and which party I belonged to. That my mother was a classroom assistant and my father was a van driver for the Post Office puzzled them enormously. They lost interest completely when they I realised I was not a rich capitalist, did not own a car, had no land or huge inheritance, did not represent some decayed element of the aristocracy and had not attended Oxford or Cambridge. In Gdańsk, however, the *milicja* asked the same questions and then tried to recruit me as an informer.

'There are some very pretty students there, yes?'

'Yes, I suppose so.'

'And the staff have lots of affairs.'

'I wouldn't know.'

'So, just tell us – who is fucking who, who is ambitious, who wants promotion, who brings vodka to work in their briefcase, who has parties, who is planning to go to the West. You know, just the latest gossip.'

'I am sorry,' I said. 'But I don't speak much Polish and I have very little social contact with staff or students.'

'What are you, some kind of *cholerny pustelnik*?'

I had to look this up: 'bloody hermit', with just a hint of 'wanker'.

'But you will report to us if you hear something interesting...'

'If I hear of plans for robbery, rape or murder I will report it, just like any good citizen.'

That did not please them.

As a foreigner I was watched, but not very closely. Unlike BBC correspondent Tim Sebastian and other Western journalists I had no 'minder', and went wherever I pleased. I suspect several people – colleagues and students – were reporting on me to the police, but I never knew who for sure. And besides, there was little to tell. Normally the *milicja* leaned on

4   *Introduction*

the weaker students, offering to up their grades. But the weaker students could hardly report accurately on conversations in English. One student in particular failed repeatedly but was allowed back to continue his course. I checked the *protokoły* (student grade record) and yes, every fail-mark I had given him had been amended to a pass. The rumour was that his father was a close friend of local Party chief Tadeusz Fiszbach. In Polish they call it *wysokie protekcja* (high protection).[2] Inevitably the question arose: is my apartment bugged? The answer was: of course, but this is communist Poland so the bug is probably broken.

Unlike Wrocław, Gdańsk was a very tense and prickly place. There was an undercurrent of anti-Party feeling and one of the first buildings pointed out to me was Party Headquarters, burned out in the protests of 1970, but then rebuilt a provocative one storey higher. As a port city, the black market was very active and well developed, but that made those who ran it and those who depended on it very nervous. Being a foreigner in Gdańsk could be tricky. Several times I saw German tourists beaten up. Most weekends there were fights between the Finns and Swedes who were building the new North Port. It was possible to see both parties glowering at each other across the room, bandaged, splinted and stitched, at Sunday morning breakfast in the Grand Hotel, Sopot.

In my spare time I was researching the background to Günter Grass' novels. At that time very few people in Poland had heard of him and, wandering around the city, I continually had to make it clear – sometimes by showing my passport – that I was not a revanchist German, come to reclaim my family home. My first name did not help.

At the university I delivered courses on literature from the eighteenth century to the early twentieth century and I was instructed to focus closely on issues of literary structure and dialogue. But there were problems in the English department. Some of the younger lecturers were unhappy with our department manager. I thought of him simply as a manager, but in their eyes he was a figure of suspicion: what they suspected him of I could not make out. He was a pietistic Catholic, but my colleagues insisted that to reach this level of responsibility he must have come to an 'accommodation' with the Party. For some of these lecturers I suspect it was just envy – after his doctorate our manager had published almost nothing and chosen the 'managerial route'. However, the underlying pulse was that several lecturers nurtured an ambition to establish an English department in Suwałki, around which they hoped a new university would form.[3] They spent their time in tireless intrigue against our manager, questioning his decisions, undermining him, recruiting staff to teach at their fantasy university and trying to find someone in the Party hierarchy with the power to set it in motion.

In Gdańsk, as people became increasingly frustrated at shortages in housing, medicine and food, at dangerous working conditions in the factories and shipyards, and at proposed changes to the Polish Constitution, fliers and posters for Wolne Związki Zawodowe Wybrzeża (Free Trades Unions

Introduction 5

of the Coast) began to appear on the buses, trams, and the local blue and yellow coastal trains. As soon as posters appeared at the railway station the *milicja* tore them down. Tension was building to the protests of 1976 and the birth of Solidarność in 1980. The *milicja* had caught wind of something at the university, but they could not work out what. For them – and very few *milicja* were graduates – university was a baffling place. They probably connected unrest in the English department with the posters and fliers, and with the dissident Uniwersytet Latający (Flying University). In trying to recruit me as an informer they were looking for some kind of 'leverage', a way into the rapidly growing underground civic movement.

Eventually the atmosphere in the English department became so poisonous Party chief Tadeusz Fiszbach called a meeting at which attendance (even for the foreigners) was compulsory. This tall, bald man with enormous glasses and a disconcerting yellow and orange check jacket made it very clear that this discontent had come to the Party's notice and that the Party did not approve of constant jostling: there would be no further talk of a university in Suwałki unless the Party said so. He attempted to re-focus the staff with a pep-talk about responsibility, duty, the function of a university in People's Poland, and of course the leading role of the Party.[4]

I had been ill with a kidney infection over the winter and by June 1976, with my teaching finished, I wanted to return to the UK. However, the Gdańsk *milicja* refused me permission to leave until September. This was my punishment for not cooperating. Instead of arguing with them I asked for a permit to visit friends in West Berlin for a weekend. They said this would be fine, so I bought my train ticket, packed my few possessions and, clutching my guitar, I left. At the Polish border one of the passengers denounced me to the guards, saying I was carrying drugs – probably to distract from the fact they were carrying drugs. The guards took me away, strip-searched me and did a finger-tip search of my luggage. They were disappointed to find sugar, vodka and sausage in my bag. The border guard said:

'What is this for?'

'It is a thank-you to my friends in Berlin for offering me a bed.'

'Don't you have these things in the West?'

'Certainly, but they are expensive.'

'Your friends in the West are poor?'

'Most people I know are poor. That's capitalism.'

The guard looked at me as if I had just told the most outrageous lie. They let me go. I repacked my stuff and went back to my seat, eyeing my fellow passengers and wondering which one was the snitch. They all pretended to be asleep. In fact I was smuggling. I had Polish silver coins, black-market dollars and East German currency in my jacket pocket, but that was just too obvious – the guards did not look there. When I reached West Berlin the news on the radio was of protests, strikes and police action in Poland.

6   *Introduction*

Either I had got out just in time or I had missed all the excitement. I sold blood at a hospital, sold my guitar in a Charlottenburg squat, took my coins to a dealer and my *ostmarks* to a bank. I had just enough Western currency to buy a train ticket to London.

In the spring of 1980, after two years of teaching apprentice panel beaters, welders, bricklayers, miners and plasterers in 'twilight zone' evening classes at the West Glamorgan Institute of Further Education, I was delighted to be appointed Assistant Director of English Courses at the Jagiellonian University in Kraków, a British Council post. By the time I arrived the snow was thick on the ground, the shops were already empty and Solidarność was locked in confrontation with the Party.

Throughout that year Poland lurched from one crisis to another. The BC tried to pretend nothing out of the ordinary was taking place: to add to the difficulties, under instruction from Prime Minister Margaret Thatcher 'BC field staff' were not allowed to use the British Embassy shop. This was not just irritating but caused genuine hardship for all of us. The BC, we came to understand, dwelled in a diplomatic bubble and was very resistant to reality. For example, they called an early morning conference in Warsaw for all BC employees – a six-hour train journey for almost everyone – but failed to offer breakfast or even coffee. They had access to the Embassy shop. They seemed mystified that we were hungry, were not aware that there was no food available on the trains. The only advice they had to offer was, if the Russians invade, stock up with food, fill your bath-tub with water and wait for us to contact you. The idea of stocking up was a bad joke as the shops were empty or closed; our water supply was intermittent; and as for contacting us, most BC 'field staff' did not have a phone.

For the most part we were glued to the radio. From November 1980 until March 1981 I made transcripts of BBC World Service news broadcasts as a teaching aid. 'Listening Practice' was intense – everyone wanted to know what the world thought of events in Poland, and the BBC was often more informative than state-controlled Polish media. Solidarność thought of another use for these texts – they too needed to know what the world thought – and at their suggestion, when I had done with them in the classroom, I took the texts to our local Solidarność office. Over the spring and summer people slept in their cars to keep a place in petrol queues that stretched for miles, there were 'hunger marches' in Warsaw and other cities, and in Kraków there was a 'white march' of protest at political manoeuvring, indicating that patience with both the government and Solidarność was running out. Over the summer, after writing about Poland a little too frankly in *The New Statesman*, one of my BC colleagues had her Polish visa withdrawn.

By the autumn of 1981, although we could not have said what, it was clear something had shifted in the thinking of dissidents, the Party and the Polish military. My balcony overlooked the local train station and several times I was awoken in the early hours of the morning by the noise of trains loaded with tanks passing through; a large number of armoured vehicles

Introduction 7

and communications tenders were parked on waste land just two hundred yards from my apartment. The paratrooper barracks opposite my apartment block, which was normally used twice a year to induct conscripts, was full to bursting, not with paratroopers but with armoured corps troops in black overalls. Something was on the way. There were armed patrols on the streets – soldiers with fixed bayonets. After a tense, tough, very hungry year, the BC in Warsaw declined to discuss the idea that mine should become a 'hardship post' and, deeply frustrated, I left Poland shortly before Martial Law was declared.[5]

At the time, the threat of Soviet invasion seemed real. Poland had been awash with rumours to this effect since the Soyuz 81 military exercises in March 1980. However, we now know that while the USSR was conducting threatening manoeuvres on Poland's eastern borders and in the Baltic, rather than contemplating invasion the Soviets massively committed to war in Afghanistan and were leaning very heavily on the Polish leadership to solve its own problems. By December 1981 the Soviets had already refused several requests from General Jaruzelski for invasion and 'military aid'. On 10 December 1981, just three days before Martial Law, Andropov told the Politburo the Poles must find a way to deal with Solidarność and there were no plans to invade. On 13 December 1981 Jaruzelski declared Martial Law, claiming it was to prevent a Soviet invasion. The threat of invasion was designed to enlist Polish nationalist support to the government side, but it did not work (Kemp-Welch 2008: 326; Sebestyen 2009: 54–5).

After Martial Law I was refused a visa several times. Mostly my letters to Poland never arrived. The few letters I received from Poland were heavily censored, with long passages blacked out. I returned to Poland when Martial Law was suspended in 1983. By then little of my tiny social circle remained: several friends had lost their university posts, a few had been pushed into early 'retirement', a couple had gone 'underground' and several had spent time in prison. Two friends, in the ugly parlance of the day, had been 'emigrated' – that is, they had been given a choice: leave the country or stay in jail.

With Martial Law the Party had become irrelevant: large numbers resigned, burned their Party cards or simply ceased to attend meetings. The Party's terminal intellectual inertia, its lack of interest in ideology, inability to debate and negotiate, its failure to do anything beyond hang on to power led to a socio-political stalemate and the wholesale collapse of public life. Poles withdrew cooperation and participation: people became cautious, turned inwards, cultivated privacy, and relied on family and circles of close, trusted friends. The military tried assigning Party members to important positions, but the toll of 'collaboration' with the military meant they soon became socially isolated, fell ill, resigned, retired early or found other work.

I visited the housing estate in Azory where I had lived to find the phrase *TV kłamie* (TV Lies) spray-painted everywhere. Virtually everyone had turned the sound down and put their TV set out on the snow-covered balcony as a protest at military control: evening news-time saw the uniformed

8   *Introduction*

newsreader's head silently flickering from dozens of balconies through the freezing fog.

Communism in Poland had unravelled to an astonishing degree, but it had not collapsed or gone away. Still, there was more to come. The war in Afghanistan sapped Soviet morale, the price of Soviet oil was falling, industrial productivity was declining at an alarming rate and economic growth had almost ceased. On 26 April 1986, the Chernobyl nuclear power plant experienced a melt-down and a huge radioactive plume drifted away from the plant over Belarus, Russia, the Baltic Republics, and as far as the UK and Sweden. Suddenly it was abundantly clear that the un-reformed and inefficient Soviet system menaced what Gorbachev now referred to as 'our common European home'.[6] Whatever Chernobyl said about the USSR was underlined by the Armenian earthquake of 7 December 1988, which killed 25,000–50,000 people and injured 130,000 more: Gorbachev was forced to admit Soviet incapacity and request international aid. The need for *glasnost* and *perestroika* had become urgent and unavoidable. Massive Soviet military cuts were announced in 1988 and the Kremlin focused on unrest in the Ukraine, Baltic Republics and the Caucasus. Party leaders in Poland, Czechoslovakia, Hungary and East Germany began to understand that the USSR was not planning to come to their aid the event of 'unrest'. But even in April 1989, as Round Table talks in Poland started, power-sharing did not seem to be on offer.

By this time I had begun to understand I had been gifted with a subject for writing and research, and in October 1989 I began a PhD in the Department of Government at Manchester University. At the same moment, post-war certainties began a rapid dissolve. Within a few weeks, right across the former Soviet bloc, communism was almost completely un-done – only the USSR held on for a while yet. I headed back to Poland as soon as I could and watched the joyful chaos of the first democratic elections. In January 1990 the Balcerowicz reforms passed into law and immediately began to have an effect. One morning in April 1990 a friend of mine went to buy a loaf, which normally cost between four and six złoties. She had a hundred złoty note in her purse. She came home in tears saying the price of a loaf had risen to six hundred złoties. The disturbances of 1956, 1970, 1976 and 1980 had largely (but not exclusively) been about the government's attempts to remove subsidies on food and basic commodities. In each case the proposed withdrawal had been met by widespread unrest, civil disobedience and violence. People died in the protests. Capitalism, by removing subsidies regardless of the suffering, accomplished almost overnight what communism had been unable to achieve in the whole post-war period. But this had not been what people had fought for. A little later I stopped at the retail outlet of a small ceramics factory just north of Warsaw. The woman behind the counter had just five hand-painted egg-cups and one soup bowl for sale. The factory had closed some months ago but the woman said she was determined to keep the shop open until every last item had been sold. I bought the bowl and the egg-cups. She wrapped them in newspaper. From

Introduction 9

the car park I watched as she put on her coat, hung the *zamknięty* (closed) sign on the door and left.

It took a little while for the new reality to hit home. I was invited to a party in a smart villa in Natolin, just outside Warsaw. Our host (ex-Party) worked in the film industry and the whole interior was festooned with miles of cine-film. To everyone I met I said: 'You don't know it yet, but you don't want what we have in the West'. The general response was laughter and disbelief: 'You are only saying that because you don't want us to have what you have'. Communism had failed to deliver a more comfortable life to a spectacular degree, but it had redistributed opportunity and offered a very basic level of security. I came to understand that, for all their charm and sophistication, these people had very little idea about the reality of life in the West. They saw only the filmic wealth and ease: what it had taken to create these things was a mystery; the unevenness of wealth and privilege did not occur to them: the general feeling was that now they had got rid of communism, money would come to everyone.[7] The realisation that while communism had lied about most things – including the bright future that lay ahead – it had not lied about the nature of capitalism was still difficult to formulate or to accept. But there was no going back.

A lot of vodka flowed (inevitably), and late in the evening I wandered away from the dancing into a room where a man was sitting alone on the floor quietly drinking and crying. To me he looked like CIA, but he said he was an economic adviser. From his accent I thought he was from Texas. He said: 'I've spent the last six weeks travelling around these little mama-and-papa farms with just a couple of milk-cows to pull the plough, and you know they actually feed their animals grass and grain? I mean real grass and real grain. No animal feed, no chemicals, no antibiotics, 'cos that shit just ain't to be had and even if it was they couldn't afford it. And the quality of the beef is superb, beautifully marbled, absolutely superb... I've been in this business for more than twenty years and I've never seen anything this good. And it's my job to put a stop to it, tell 'em they gotta sell the farm to some agri-business outfit, so it can be run like in the West. I know communism was the enemy, but they had something good here and they didn't even know it. You see why I'm upset?' He said his name was Jim, but would not tell me his surname.

In the early summer of 1990 I visited friends in Berlin. Some of the border-guards at Potsdamer Platz, noticing that the wall was disappearing fast and reckoning their jobs in the *Grenztruppen der DDR* (Border-troops of the German Democratic Republic) would not last much longer, decided not to enforce visas: I cycled into East Berlin at the Potsdamer Platz checkpoint, only to be stopped at the Brandenburg Gate while attempting to return. Some border-guards were still enforcing the visa system. After a warning not to do this again (to which I readily agreed), the border-guards let me go. To celebrate my escape I bought an impressive *ushanka* (traditional fur hat) from a Russian sailor selling off his uniform piece by piece. By November Germany had been reunified and the wall was just a hindrance to ambitious building projects.

10   *Introduction*

As Poland's economic reforms got under way, *konto* (money change kiosks) began to spring up on every street corner; every second shop went bankrupt, became a private enterprise or declared itself a *hurtownia* (wholesale warehouse, paying less tax than a shop). But by the spring of 1991 the atmosphere had changed again: car theft was rife and it had become almost impossible to get car insurance for travel in Poland. Mugging, armed robbery, burglary, drug smuggling, people trafficking and organised prostitution reached what appeared to be epidemic proportions. Pornography and bloody horror films (mostly about vampires and/or zombies) seemed to be everywhere. As the *biurokracja* became more criminal and criminals became better organised, the *Milicja Obywatelska* (MO, Citizen Militia – the police) were revealed as effective at traffic duty and crowd control, but lacking the basic training or equipment to deal with actual crime, lacking even cars fast enough to chase the bad guys. Almost everyone I visited was installing reinforced steel front doors to their apartments. At the same time, Poland and Hungary were being fast-tracked for early entry to the EU, giving easier access to Western banking and money-laundering for criminal profits, and so became favoured destinations for Russian oligarchs, their money, their business and their henchmen (Glenny 2009: 25, 37, 91).

In Kraków in 1992 I saw blue graffiti Stars of David and slogans: 'Poland for Poles'; 'Jobs and Bread only for Poles'; 'Real Poles only'; 'USA-Zion = Cancer' (usually written right to left in imitation of Hebrew). In Lublin the graffiti just said: 'Jews Out'. In Warsaw the graffiti read: 'Here we are real Poles'. I saw a gang of *skinz* (skinheads) parading towards Marszałkowska behind a huge Nazi flag. The area in front of the Palace of Culture became a vast, sprawling bazaar, a tented encampment of 'independent' (black-market) traders, pickpockets, prostitutes and Russian soldiers selling off their equipment: for cash (hard currency only) it was possible to buy caviar, imported soap powder, pornographic videos, hand-grenades, perfume, assault rifles, condoms, flip-flops, a flame thrower, alcohol, jeans, hand-decorated crutches, embroidered pinafores, single slippers, samizdat books, even a BTP (Бронетранспортер, Soviet eight-wheeled armoured personnel carrier) complete with camouflage netting and 20mm canon (ammunition available but not included in the price). I was warned not to try taking pictures.

One of Adam Michnik's slogans around this time was 'Liberty, Equality, Normality'. But this last term was already proving tricky. Back in the UK in the autumn of 1992 I received a package in the post. Inside was a small plastic bag. It was marked in purple 'Poczta Polska – Uskodzone w tranzicie' (Polish Post – Damaged in Transit) and had taken some considerable time to catch up with me. Inside were more than a dozen of my letters from the Martial Law years – un-damaged, un-opened, un-censored and un-delivered – along with a compliments slip from the British Embassy in Warsaw. I do not know what role the Embassy played, but the return of my letters felt as if it was supposed to mark a small part of the transition to 'normality'.

Introduction 11

Writers and political science

Czesław Miłosz (1911–2004) wrote: 'It would be wrong to underestimate the subtle and hidden relations between poetry and politics' (Miłosz 1992: 78), while the poet Artur Międzyrzecki (1922–96) encapsulated the problematic relationship between literature, poetry, writers and political science very neatly when he wrote of political scientists knowing 'the latest trends' but not of 'desperation' or of the process of 'renouncing the game' or, tellingly, of 'an ability to wonder' (Międzyrzecki 1991: 59–60).

We can never make an entirely clean break with the past: while history never repeats itself, historical events echo, haunting the present just as experience haunts identity and permeates culture. At the time, those who fought in World War II were sure they did not know everything about it: black propaganda, censorship and military security made sure they did not. However, more than seventy-five years after the conclusion of the war the questions – about what was gained and what lost, the conduct and content, the meaning and results of the war – still linger. Inevitably, with the collapse of communism our perspectives on World War II, the Cold War and the idea of Europe have shifted. They continue to do so. And as perspectives shift and documents become available, a fuller picture has emerged. With time it is legitimate to look at the roots and assumptions of our world and to ask questions of the 'what if…' variety.

It is impossible to write about East-Central Europe without taking Germany into account. Historically, in spite of (or perhaps because of) its size and power, and because it was a latecomer to statehood, the dynamic German economy had great difficulty in finding a 'place' or penetrating the West European economy. Rosa Luxemburg (1871–1919) warned in her PhD thesis of 1898 that there would be serious consequences should Germany turn eastwards in search of economic expansion and new markets. (Luxemburg 1977) D.H. Lawrence (1885–1930) was one of the few people to grasp the changes taking place deep within the German psyche after 1918. In 1924 he wrote of life in Germany 'ebbing away' from the West, 'retreating' to the East, of 'strange things stirring in the darkness, strange feelings stirring out of this still unconquered Black Forest', of 'a sense of danger, a queer, *bristling* feeling of uncanny danger', of something that had happened but that had 'not yet eventuated' (Lawrence 1950: 175–9).[8] Neither Luxemburg nor Lawrence imagined that the ancient *drang nach osten* (drive to the East) or defeat in World War I would result in the Holocaust and the division of Germany. But what they both suspected was that the idea of Germany as *kultur-trager* (culture bringer), whether it was achieved or not, carried within it an aspect of menace.

Now we can ask: What is missing from European culture? Do we actually miss what is not there, and if so, how and why? We can ask what is present in European culture that we hardly notice and what should we still be wary of. We can ask if Nazism was really defeated or if the German military machine was just hammered into submission. We can ask what

12 Introduction

European culture (and the Middle East) would have looked like if the Jews and Gypsies had not been subject to the Holocaust, if Stalin had not massacred the Polish officer corps, if the East-Central European *inteligencja* had not been decimated by Nazism and then communism. We can wonder how a Europe of national minorities would have fared if the Nazis had not started a war. We can also ask what Europe would have been like if the Nazis had succeeded.

A successful Nazi Europe would almost certainly have been an intersection on the axes between the seething controls of East Germany and the bland but inescapable pressure towards the comfortable conformity of Switzerland: Nazi Europe would have been cosy, conformist and willingly ignorant. But could it have lasted? The more we know about the disastrous way in which the Nazis managed their economy – the incompetence engendered by duplication and internal rivalry, the reliance on inefficient slave labour, the Reich's cycle of conquest, plunder and expansion – the more doubtful it is that the Reich could have lasted for anything like a thousand years.

How can we assess the continuing impact of Nazism? The Third Reich lasted long enough to bankrupt the British Empire, provoke the rise of the USA and USSR as superpowers, make Europe virtually 'Jew-free' and locate German banks as a hegemonic force at the centre of the post-war set-up. The main aim of the USSR throughout the Cold War was to make sure Germany was never again in a position to attack it: after 1945 the dividing line between communism and capitalism ran right through Germany. Soviet priority was, as Khrushchev indicated to Kennedy, something like 'You look after your Germans and we'll look after ours'. West Germany largely came to terms with its Nazi past but fully embraced Europe, democracy and multi-culturalism only after the crisis created by the Baader–Meinhof gang and the 'German Autumn'. Germany is now locked into Europe as an economic powerhouse without need of war. For some this is a major achievement. However, in Poland and Greece resentment against Germany still runs high and the view is that instead of being threatened by the German military, Europe is now dominated by the German economy, its powerful banks and the burden of debt. Germany lost the war but won the peace.

Increasingly, populist politicians speak of 'Europe' as something outside themselves, something they are not a part of, as if it is something antagonistic to national life. This thought bubbles under the modern European identity and fuels the rise of the right. It indicates that while Germany may have over-reacted to the refugee crisis of 2015 to overcome guilt about a Nazi past, some EU members are not prepared to accept Germany's moral lead, resent the power of German banks, have not fully integrated European supra-national ideals into their psyche, have not substantially diminished nationalist opinion or begun to develop a cross-national, pan-European identity. On the other hand, the EU has not overcome its own complacency, become more flexible or less cumbersome, and (even after the refugee crisis and the Brexit referendum) has not moved swiftly to challenge the behaviour of the East-Central European states.

Introduction   13

In East-Central Europe something more mysterious, much less simple than the victory of democracy over communism and capitalism over communism, has been taking place. If we are to make sense of what has been happening there, we have to look into East-Central Europe's (and particularly Poland's) many-times frustrated social and political history. And by this I mean not only the development of its institutions and the experience of national history, but also the non-institutional evidence from deep within society. The roots of many of Poland's current social issues go back long before the communist years and even before the Nazi occupation. Since the collapse of communism, Poland has sought to re-establish continuity with an interrupted past and tried hard to resume pre-war nationalist habits of mind. This suggests very strongly that either the victory supposed by the Allies in 1945 was not clear cut, or that World War II was actually about something else. The legacy of doubts and questions is still there, even when they are not so very visible.

My writing on the interface between literature and politics has been an attempt to trace the outlines of this legacy. But I still have many questions. Given that civil society is still very weak in East-Central Europe, what do literature and the lives of the writers tell us about the 'inner life' there? And in what ways has the political and literary culture of post-war Germany been tested? What does literary culture tell us about politics and history? Can literature help to explain the mental contours of the past? Can it make the impact of the past on the present more understandable? Can it prepare us for the future? Because it is language-based, is writing always tribal? Does writing have any *real* power, or is it just hegemonic, ancillary, 'soft power', a vague kind of social influence?

These are political questions, but often they are reduced to the issue of whether writers merely reflect what they see around them and intuit changes on the way, or whether their analysis is more acute and they are, as Stalin insisted, the 'engineers of human souls'. Antonio Gramsci (1891–1937), who had a realistic grasp of these things, referred to the relationship between writers and society as a condition of 'mutual siege' (Gramsci 1971: 235). Writers do not have direct political power: even under communism they specialised in the steady drip-drip of hegemony, the slow formation of opinion. Post-communist Polish writers are neither required to deal with national themes nor required not to. The writers who have come to prominence since 1989 would probably be horrified at being identified as 'political writers', but they would find it difficult to deny the politicalness of their work or the freedom they enjoy to explore new, troubling, often personal themes. As post-communist Poland moved to the Right and the Catholic Church surged to exert moral authority, the politics of putting pen to paper, of making a public intervention, of breaching the wall of control that all societies construct, has continued but is less obvious.

Writers often see their work as a battle to understand what is happening to words and to reveal some of their hidden possibilities. For a writer to say what they hear, record what is happening in words, struggle to represent

14   *Introduction*

things accurately in writing, to be what novelist Elias Canetti (1905–94) called 'an earwitness', will always be characterised as an act of treachery, sedition, opposition or aggression by those who do not want their actions and ideas observed, recorded or dragged to light (Canetti 1987).

For writers, the creation of new work entails the choice of words, and that means dealing with two contradictory impulses. The first impulse is the temptation to use words as they are given by society and approved by politicians, to set down only words that are current, that do not cause problems, that can be easily absorbed, that do not challenge. This view assumes that writers envision their role merely as part of the entertainment industry and accept that they can make no meaningful intervention in the world. The second impulse, however, is to seek out and make use of words in ways that probe their meaning, make it obvious how words change, are changed and compromised in daily use, to reveal what is often hidden in words. A writer must always choose between these two possibilities, must always choose between 'servility and insolence' (Sontag 1982: 190). It is precisely in the world of words that writers and politicians clash. More people read novels than read political theory, but they don't necessarily read novels for the politics. Literature is a commentary on public life enjoyed in private, and for this reason it is difficult for political scientists to engage with it.

Political science, even as it shades into journalism or history, does not tell us much about feelings or what is in words, still less does it predict. It favours the study of power refracted through big ideas, theories, institutions, statistics, structures, organograms, speeches, the ebb and flow of party policy, manifestos, factions and changes of leadership. If we are lucky, political science as a kind of history tells us where we have been and how our thinking brought us to this point. In political science the life of artists and writers, their idiosyncratic cultural products, cultural life and the life of the mind are tangential to what drives the life of the polity. Yet politics and writing are linked. Fundamentally, both deal in words; both are products of the imagination, the collective psyche of a culture and its experience; both deal with the exercise of power in the development of an imaginative vision; both are part of a wider definition of culture as a process that creates morals and values – values, as the poet Zbigniew Herbert (1924–98) had it, that are 'worth living for' (Herbert 2010: 615).

Literature is a cultural activity, an instrument of societal self-awareness connected to various types of knowledge, social codes and forms of critical thought. It is a highly personal expression of identity, a living example of the history of a language, of what happens to meaning in language, of what is in words and how the content of words changes, of how social and national experience, consciousness and ambition are given shape. And in this politicians and writers are often at odds: while both share the medium of words and strive for an audience, their competing interest is to explain how they see the meaning of the past and the content of the future and explain the values they consider essential. It was no accident that as subsidy was withdrawn in 1989, publishing houses in East-Central Europe

Introduction 15

collapsed, piracy boomed and many writers went into politics. As they said at the time, after a lifetime dealing in words, this was the only career for which they were now fitted.

Yet, neither literature nor politics can provide an exact image of the human mind or precisely map its workings. Novels, poetry and plays, with their emphasis on introspection, imagination, personalisation, speculation and the inner life, all inhabit a political context and comprise a 'history of the psyche', which in itself constitutes political material. It is hesitant in its approach, uncertain of its effect, random in 'success' and unreliable in its reputation. And for all its observational capacity, literature is not necessarily more precise in its predictions than political science. However, because of the difficulty in theorising, codifying and interpreting the relationship of literature to politics, political science makes little use of literature.

The concerns of literature often intersect within institutions, but literature offers only an informal, hidden, disguised, oppositional and often illicit appreciation of political life. Literature is clearly a political activity, but there is no neat marrying-up of the political and literary spheres: literature approaches its subject matter in an oblique fashion, investigating the content of words, weaving a complex relationship between plot, characters and imagery, selectively creating a world that somehow connects to, and reflects on, the 'real world'. It is hard to imagine a society where human action did not meet some reaction invoking concepts of morality, responsibility, and social and political obligation. And among all the arts, this is particularly the case with writing.

During the lifetime of Solidarność, while Polish writers helped define what people were opposed to, they did not define the values they wanted to see in a new political system – there was simply no time and no forum to develop such ideas, and Poland as a political culture had very little experience of democracy in action (Witts 1985). I am aware of only one writer who identified the lifetime of Solidarność as *the* crucial moment, *the* vital opportunity, and who took Polish writers to task for missing it. The critic and essayist Andrzej Kijówski (1928–85) pointed out that for writers under communism the state had been the monopoly publisher, critic, censor, the sole arbiter of success and failure, the main literary agent, commissioning editor, reader, prize-giver and paymaster. The sudden removal of the state from the equation left writers adrift at a crucial moment, but this, he insisted, did not let them off the hook.

Perhaps he was too harsh. Polish writers, many of whom spent 1980–81 in endless meetings, readings, committees, debates and conferences, rather than in writing, and then spent time in prison under Martial Law, would probably disagree with Kijówski. Under military censorship and without a functioning publishing apparatus there was little that writers or 'literature' could have done. However, forty years on we have to admit that no long-suppressed literary masterpiece has emerged from the wreckage of communism. One way or another, it seems, with *samizdat* (self-published) and *tamizdat* (published abroad), Polish writers said everything

16 *Introduction*

they wanted to. However, as a populist definition of 'traditional' values has increasingly become the norm and the idea of Europe and the humanitarian values of the liberal-Left have come under pressure from ethno-nationalism, Kijówski's comment – particularly his identification of 'mental confusion and the degradation of everyday life' – feels like an accurate summary and perhaps even a prophecy.

Politics and literature – Careers in words

Although communism tended to blunt, supress, divert and hi-jack its aspirations, the creative *inteligencja* of East-Central European did not cease to exist after 1945. On the contrary, what was left of the *inteligencja* again shouldered an enormous social, political and moral burden in what Miłosz called the business of 'the nation and productivity' (Miłosz 2003: 196). Whether the Party liked it or not – and while they put a good face on it, generally they did not – writers were not only a kind of ambiguous state employee, they were also 'the unacknowledged legislators' of a poorly developed civil society and spokespersons for a very battered national identity (Reiman & Powers 1977: 508). However, communism may have unintentionally preserved and prolonged the life and historical role of the creative *inteligencja* by offering subsidy and employment within the expanding administration, protection from commercial pressures, and the extension of the *inteligencja* functions of protest and opposition (Janowski, Jedlicki & Micińska 2014; Konrád & Szelényi 1979).

Romanian writer Ghiță Ionescu (1919–96) referred to the first Polish attempt at de-Stalinisation in 1956 by paying tribute to a Polish and Hungarian 'creative intelligentsia' and pointing out that the resistance and critique put forward by Polish literary circles and publications was an example to everyone (Ionescu 1965).

Because they often defended 'traditional' values and often came out of a relationship with Catholicism, Polish literary judgements tend to be moralistic and to touch upon the 'national question'. Zbigniew Herbert, for example, regarded those who published under communism as positivist collaborators who besmirched national honour. The reality was, however, that unless writers held their nose and accepted some degree of Party control, they were not going to be published at all. In communist Poland a writer's career path was tortuous and uncertain, and their relationship to the Party was at best wavering. But after the 'thaw' of 1956, if writers drifted out of favour with the Party, the censor made sure they just did not appear in print: writers were not persecuted, imprisoned, killed or 'disappeared'.

Nowhere was the interface between literature and politics more complex, more intense and more revealing than in Poland. Poland is a sort of touchstone, and with hindsight we can see that of all the cultural seismographs available to us from the communist era, none was more telling than Polish literature. In spite of the Party's best efforts, Polish literature provided a

Introduction 17

substantial, critical meta-commentary on political life, marking each point on the post-war fever chart (1956, 1968, 1970, 1976 and 1980–81) with specific responses in poetry, drama, fiction, essays and film. Because daily life under communism often played like bleak, surreal fiction (in itself a criticism of the Party), writers could take the connection between literature and politics as established, even when they were not being particularly political (Kott 1990: 342).

This is very different from the situation of literature in Britain. In 1841, the English historian Thomas Carlyle (1795–1881) made the connection between literature and politics explicit:

> Literature is our Parliament too. Printing, which comes necessarily out of Writing, I say often, is equivalent to Democracy: invent Writing, Democracy is inevitable. Writing brings Printing; brings universal everyday extempore Printing, as we see at present. Whoever can speak, speaking now to the whole nation, becomes a power, a branch of government, with inalienable weight in lawmaking, in all acts of authority. It matters not what rank he has, what revenues or garnitures: the requisite thing is, that he have a tongue which others will listen to; this and nothing more is requisite. The nation is governed by all that has tongue in the nation: Democracy is virtually there. Add only that whatsoever exists will have itself by and by organised; working secretly under bandages, obscurations, obstructions, it will never rest till it get to work free, unencumbered, visible to all. Democracy virtually extant will insist on becoming palpably extant.
>
> (Carlyle 1993: 141–2)

Carlyle may have been overstating the obviousness of the connection. The reality of the connection – patchy and incomplete – shows through only intermittently. On the Left, the solidly bourgeois G.B. Shaw (1856–1950) and Beatrice and Sydney Webb (1858–1943 and 1859–1947) trumpeted their socialism loudly, ignored the imperialist Boer war, supported the Empire and the British effort in World War I, and failed to grasp the nature of capitalism. William Empson (1906–84), W.H. Auden (1907–73), Stephen Spender (1909–95) and Christopher Caudwell (1907–37) were all writers and activists on the Left, but the most famous British writer on the Left is, without doubt, George Orwell (1903–50). In his 1946 essay 'The Prevention of Literature' he wondered whether every writer was political and came to the conclusion that writers could not avoid being political since literature is an attempt to intervene in debate and to influence the viewpoint of one's contemporaries (Orwell 1968).

Raymond Williams (1921–88), though best known as an academic historian of literary culture, also produced three novels on political themes. In the 1970s, theatre was an important focus of political debate with playwrights like John McGrath, Trevor Griffiths, David Mercer, Howard Brenton, David Hare, David Edgar and John Mortimer on the Left. The

18   *Introduction*

novelists Lord Melvyn Bragg, Ken Follett and Barbara Vine, and the singer/songwriters Tom Robinson and Billy Bragg, have all been on the Left. Tariq Ali, though better known as a student-activist in the late 1960s, is also a novelist. Sunderland Labour MP Chris Mullin, who campaigned tirelessly for justice for Irish people wrongly accused of planting bombs for the IRA, wrote the political thriller *A Very British Coup* (1982), which became a very successful TV thriller (1988). Alastair Campbell, Prime Minister Tony Blair's spokesman and the party's main 'spin-doctor', wrote pornography before turning to politics ('Campaigns of a TV Stuntman' 2001: 3). Prime Minister Tony Blair admitted journalist Robert Harris into his circle of friends, but when the friendship cooled Blair found himself lampooned in *The Ghost* (2007). In June 2000 Beryl Bainbridge and J.K. Rowling, high profile Labour supporters, were both honoured by the Labour government. British politicians on the Left have sometimes (perhaps not often enough) employed professional writers to pen their speeches. Stephen Fry wrote for Neil Kinnock; Roy Hudd and John O'Farrell, along with Laurence Marks and Maurice Gran (creators of the TV series *Birds of a Feather*), wrote speeches for several Labour politicians; comedians Mark Steel and Mark Thomas were approached to write jokes for Labour Foreign Secretary Robin Cook.

On the Right, Winston Churchill established a reputation as an historian. Conservative writers who also happened to work in intelligence include Graham Greene, Charles McCarry, Ian Fleming (with his 'sex, sadism and snobbery') and Frederick Forsyth (whose novels were read and re-read by Mrs Thatcher, who herself appeared as a character in The Fourth Protocol). P.D. James had a seat in the Lords, courtesy of a Conservative Honours List. Ex-Shadow Home Secretary Anne Widdicombe, ex-Government Minister Edwina Currie and ex-Foreign Secretary Douglas Hurd have all written novels; Tory MP Rupert Allason wrote spy novels. After she sacked him, Mrs Thatcher's adviser Michael Dobbs MP went on to write the vicious House of Cards – a successful TV series in both the British and US versions. Ex-Government Minister Alan Clark was a military historian and a diarist; ex-Conservative minister John Selwyn Gummer had been a writer and a publisher before becoming an MP. Perhaps most famously, Lord Jeffrey Archer, though his publishers admitted providing him with considerable help in actually writing his books, nevertheless proved himself a remarkable fabulist. Sir Antony Jay, a Cambridge graduate with a career in broadcasting and public relations, co-wrote the award-winning series Yes Minister and Yes, Prime Minister (1980–88) with Jonathan Lynn, a contemporary of Michael Howard, John Selwyn Gummer and Kenneth Clarke at Cambridge. Prime Minister Boris Johnson wrote several books, including a biography of Winston Churchill and the raunchy comic novel Seventy-Two Virgins (2005). Oscar winning script writer Julian Fellowes (Gosford, 2002) was rumoured to write speeches for Conservative Leader Iain Duncan Smith. Ken Clarke, Chris Smith and Michael Portillo have all been judges for the Booker Prize.

Introduction 19

An interesting exception on the Right is novelist John le Carré (b.1935): he was once an intelligence officer attached to the British Embassy in Bonn, who on his own admission has become increasingly 'radical' over the last forty years, moving from the curmudgeonly 'old school' Right towards the frustrated Europhile Left. Le Carré was scathing about the Labour Government of Blair and Brown, which he described as a 'wastrel government that was for the people, by the people, except it was run by one bad Scottish piglet (Blair) and one unhappy Scottish hog (Brown), who emptied the piggy bank for the people while they were about it'. After the Conservative Party failed to win a majority in the general election of 2010 and formed a coalition with the Liberal Democrats, le Carré wrote of Etonians 'taking back the shop' with the assistance of 'B-list inexperienced liberals' (Flood 2018).

His comment neatly anticipated the response to the years of austerity that fuelled the Brexit campaign, which followed shortly afterwards and subsequently divided the Tory Party (Brown 2017). He later described Prime Minister Boris Johnson as a 'mob orator' and Brexit as 'an unmitigated clusterfuck bar none' (Banville 2019).

In spite of evidence to the contrary, the British 'mainstream' tends to prefer 'art for art's sake' and regards any connection to politics with a raised eyebrow. In general, an interest in politics goes against the grain and contemporary British culture, where it acknowledges the connection, views it as rather problematic: universities will take on the industrial novelists of the nineteenth century, non-white writers, writers engaged in identity-politics and the ramifications of literary theory before they willingly engage with issues of left and right. John Berger (1926–2017), for example, in spite of his literary achievements, is generally too openly leftist to be included easily in most university literature courses.

For the most part the British do not see literature as an important part of the civil, educational or political process. Art, of all kinds, is what can be purchased for entertainment, diversion and decoration. I suspect this is probably a hang-over from the Restoration of the Monarchy in 1660. After the Restoration, UK culture was dominated by London, and that in turn was dominated by the tastes and fashions of the court. Developing from this, 'taste' has been dominated by the social and political class that runs the money-market, financial services and insurance broking, and that benefits most from the 'following wind' of public school and Oxbridge connections. Because mainland Britain has not been successfully invaded since 1066 this 'natural order of things' has gone unchallenged, and as a result the culture lacks the instinctive feeling that literature has an important role to play in political life.[9]

However, while readers may feel English literature has little to do with politics, there have been numerous writers in Wales, Ireland and Scotland for whom this has not been the case. The 'Celtic fringe', Ireland, Wales and Scotland, do not generally consider themselves part of the British 'mainstream', emerging from a different literary tradition and experience of colonialism: they certainly do not share English literature's distaste for viewing

20 *Introduction*

literary culture as separate from political life. In reality, the connection would not have been mysterious to Shakespeare or his contemporaries, nor would it have been strange to Blake, Shelley, Byron, Wordsworth, Dickens and George Eliot, or to modern post-colonial writers like Chinua Achebe, Wole Soyinka or Ngũgĩ wa Thiong'o.

Unlike the *inteligencja* of East-Central Europe, largely the product of Partition, resistance and invasion, the British intelligentsia from the time of Daniel Defoe (1660–1731) onwards has largely been its own creation, predominantly commercial rather than cultural, utilitarian rather than spiritual.

As readers, we might note that the literary traditions of East-Central Europe are different from those of the West, but that is generally as far as it goes. How and why – these are not questions our culture encourages us to frame, and as a consequence those traditions and that literature are for the most part inaccessible and unexamined.

But even then, we are often too close to our own culture to see it clearly. The literary critic F.R. Leavis, for example, insisted rather ferociously that in English the 'line of tradition' was as much moral as it was literary, and literary judgement was an estimation of a writer's 'moral seriousness'. In English literature, he felt, there was an indivisible connection between literature and morality, and so after Shakespeare he identified only five writers in his 'great tradition': Jane Austen, George Eliot, Henry James, Joseph Conrad and D.H. Lawrence. That is, two women, an American and a Pole: the only English man admitted to the pantheon was Lawrence (Leavis 1948). Leavis made some surprising exclusions – the poets Pope, Blake and Wordsworth; the satirist Swift; the novelists Sterne, Fielding and the Bronte sisters; and all playwrights – but he later admitted Charles Dickens to his pantheon (Leavis & Leavis 1970). Nevertheless, in the UK, tradition is often associated with village greens, Parliament, royalty, maypoles, judges in wigs and gowns, Wakes Weeks, morris dancing and warm beer: the British appreciation of 'tradition' is distinctly ironic (Hobsbawm & Ranger 1983).

Harold Bloom said that American literary tradition is mainly concerned with being independent and self-reliant, without reference to Europe or the classics of ancient Greece and Rome. Its task has been to emphasise human dominion over nature and humanity's dominion over itself. Bloom saw tradition as a male-oriented struggle where psychological anxieties worked a rhetorical change by either avoiding or transforming the writing of preceding authors, to engage in a personal rather than historical process that is both competition and contamination. In this process, he thought, writers did not simply learn from and argue with preceding writers, but by becoming 'strong' they overcome their anxieties to supersede their rivals and gain access to the literary canon. In Bloom's version of tradition there is very little sense of writers contesting culture on behalf of the nation or in definition of the national identity: he would have us believe that in the USA tradition is merely personal (Bloom 1973, 2019).

In the 'West', the politicalness of literature and the act of writing are troublesome because they are not contained within a body of tradition and

Introduction 21

not easily housed within literary studies at contemporary universities. The growth of post-modern literary theory has promoted the idea that facts are not necessarily so, and that language itself is ineffably unknowable and inherently unreliable, thus confirming that the connections between politics, literature and identity are rarefied, remote and theoretical, and in unravelling them we are usually just wrong. Yet in spite of itself, academic writing on imperialism, colonialism, slavery, gender, race, identity and LGBTQ+ issues, in addition to talking to itself, has also from time to time offered oblique challenges to 'the mainstream'. Even so, in the 'West', serious creativity now goes where the serious money is – scriptwriting for video games, film and DVD – productions like *Boardwalk Empire*, *Madam Secretary*, *Billions* and *The Wire* – rather than into literature. That a contemporary writer might produce a political novel as influential as those by, say, J.P. Sartre, Upton Sinclair, Robert Tressell, George Orwell or Arthur Koestler now seems improbable. Even the writing of Joseph Heller and Philip Roth has very limited traction. Perhaps the closest we have come to real influence is the phenomenal success of J.K. Rowling's Harry Potter novels, and that interest in magic and fantasy as a reaction to monetarism and austerity is in itself significant. Generally, politics is present in recent writing for those who want it, but in the background, disguised, some would say made subtle almost to invisibility (Rosen et al. 2017; Lynskey 2019). In East-Central Europe, the connection – growing out of a sense of national tradition and identity – is much more direct, at times visceral. We have only to look at the work of a writer like Zbigniew Herbert and his debt to the Romantic tradition, or Günter Grass (1927–2015) and his relationship to Alfred Doblin (1878–1957), to glimpse very different sets of cultural relationships.

Writing and reading might not 'do' anything, but they make a difference: they operate to help form opinion and shape feelings and responses to the public world; they record and give voice to the opinions and feelings of the inner life. They offer private counsel and consolation. Writing and reading are internal, private experiences and it is in their nature to resist. They are very difficult for authorities to predict, monitor, shape or control. Not only is that part of their charm, it is also part of the threat they continue to pose. They are 'soft power', or as Gramsci would say, hegemonic.

About this book

The book takes its title from a series of BBC radio talks given by Arthur Alvarez (1929–2019) in the early 1960s. He opened his first programme with the words: 'Your first and last impression of Poland, as of all Eastern Europe, is of a shifting but utterly pervasive sense of trouble' (Alvarez 1965: 19). And Poland is still a good place to start.

The book comes at the interface between literature and politics from the East and left of centre and it comes mainly from my thinking about the nature of literary tradition. It is personal rather than theoretical, speculative rather than triumphal, questioning rather than conclusive. It looks at tradition, identity and writing through the prism of post-communist East-Central

22 Introduction

Europe and it treats the idea of tradition as 'rhizomatic' and not easily dragged to light. That is, tradition has a decentralised, adaptive structure. Its form and observance is that of diffused social knowledge consisting of connections between inherited attitudes, semiotic chains, organisations of power and also of resistance, which together inform collective struggle, political decision-making and artistic production. To say it is rhizomatic envisages not a hierarchic root and branch image of culture, but a model in which the micro-filaments of tradition spread into available space through fissures and gaps, to affect adjacent areas of human activity, by-passing or eroding what is in its way, but as a set of cultural givens and assumptions, leaving very little visible surface-trace of itself.

Literature and politics are cultural activities – that is, they are not entirely driven by the issue of earning a living, but rather what people feel compelled to make or do with their intellectual and creative capacities. These activities are part of the way humans organise and order themselves, and part of the way humans comment on the world around them. The division between writers and politicians is more or less arbitrary: there are writers in politics and there are politicians who write – even in Britain, where the connection may be less obvious, less discussed, less fashionable. In every culture the interface between tradition, literature and politics is baffling, diffuse, debatable, fugitive and difficult to pin down: it surfaces partially and fleetingly in loyalties, attitudes and opinions, now in literature, now in politics, now in military history... and nowhere is this more so than in East-Central Europe, and Poland in particular.

This book also looks at the interface between writing, politics and tradition to express a cumulative set of niggles, doubts and worries. It offers a sidelong glance at the unfinished business of the twentieth century, at the emergence of East-Central Europe from communism and at the complexities of Europe ever in the process of becoming. It assumes that literature, because it deals with experience, identity and personality, is a way of confronting the manner by which societies and cultures police the borders of community, define loyalty and express how society feels about itself. It does not take victory in World War II or in the Cold War for granted. It is part of my attempt to come to terms with the intense experience of witnessing the dying days of decaying Stalinism and observing its legacy of complications. This has been my experience to explore, part of my time on this earth, part of my understanding of what it is to be a European, and part of my understanding of what it is to be a writer.

It is odd to think I have been writing about East-Central Europe for more than forty years. I have to remind myself that the Berlin Wall (1961–89), which helped shape the world-view and politics of my generation, has now been down for longer than it existed. This is testimony to the 'wall in the head' about which Peter Schneider (b.1940) wrote (Schneider 1992). But while I am aware of the distortions of capitalism and commercial life in 'the West', and I miss the cheap, available, shared cultural life of the communist years, I do not share a sense of 'ostalgia' for the lost, cramped, contorted

Introduction 23

world created by communism. Certainly for the younger generation the Berlin Wall and the division of Europe are utterly remote, completely unimaginable and totally irrelevant. As John le Carré put it, communism is now 'a cause the world barely remembers' (le Carré 2017). Political life itself barely interests the younger generation – even in Poland – who feel politics has nothing to do with them, but nevertheless obsess about work, immigration, income and homes.

Nevertheless, by tracking tradition and the life and work of writers to identify some of the ways we arrived at this position, I hope I have made good some of the deficiencies identified by Międzyrzecki and recorded my respect for the writers of East-Central Europe. Time and again they have 'renounced the game' only to take it up again, faced 'irrevocable changes', demonstrated their natural resources and shown that knowledge of the venerated laws, an ability to wonder and a sense of humour – most of all this last – are essential for any writer.

Along with the writing of Sławomir Mrożek and Stanisław Lem, I have admired Zbigniew Herbert's writing for many years. As a young man I sat in my room at 19/84 Place Grunwaldzki in Wrocław and, in the absence of TV, while the lions roared into the night at the nearby zoo, I copied his poems into my notebook. This was my way of engaging with him, letting him speak to me, defining the content of his work, working out the internal structure of his thought.

As a 'barbarian', Herbert had been hungry to engage with the impressive historical artefacts that represented the culture of the West, and he tested the great monuments against his Polishness. As a 'barbarian' of a different kind I travelled in the opposite direction but, I would like to think, in much the same spirit. Poland, with a culture substantially different from that of the UK, gave me a great deal to think about. But instead of cave art and the great stone edifices of the past (Herbert's choice in the West), I settled on literature as the focus of my interest.

Herbert and I have many differences, not least those of talent. There are also the differences of East and West. And there is the difference in our experience: we belong to very different generations. Herbert insisted on tradition, but I did not always feel comfortable with what he claimed of Polish tradition and what he felt tradition should do. Additionally, he took his bearings from Catholicism and T.S. Eliot's sense of culture. He wrote as an East-Central European, always a Pole, but with one eye on the West.

As the son of an Irish immigrant, a working-class kid, a mongrel refugee from Catholicism, I was forced to find the elements necessary to construct my own tradition. This meant that while I could have gone in the opposite direction to become 'born again' Irish, in fact I could never be so directed, never so anchored to a viewpoint, and never as certain in my opinion as Herbert. My writing is more concerned with the 'other', with being inward, with finding my own intellect, with crossing boundaries and with being invisible: perhaps also with recognising my own personal Ireland in Poland.

24   *Introduction*

With its photographs, drawings, quotations and aching blank spaces I took the publication of *Notes Herbertowski* (Herbert 2014) as an invitation to look again at the context from which Herbert came. I also took it as an invitation to engage with tradition in Polish literature and to consider how the writers shaped by tradition to oppose communism had fared since its collapse. But I was determined to do this in my own way, to bring my own perspective to bear. I am an outsider, so regardless of what a specialist in Polish literary studies might make of it, this is *my* response: these are *my Notes Herbertowski*. Here, to paraphrase another Polish poet, a poor Westerner looks at the writers of East-Central Europe…

*

In August 1980, just as communism began its long, terminal wobble, I watched a TV report where seismologists said they had evidence of a huge tsunami in the eighteenth century that had devastated the eastern seaboard of Japan and ravaged the California coastline. There were no written records of the quake because at that time very few literate people lived in Japan and even fewer in California. The seismologists predicted another gigantic earthquake in the Indian and/or Pacific oceans: if it activated the San Andreas Fault, they said, parts of California might disappear beneath the sea and Nevada might well become attractive beachfront property. But asked when and where the next quake would take place, and how big it would be, one of them shrugged, pointed at the vast expanse of water and said: 'Out there… somewhere… soon… and very big… probably…'.[10] I cannot say how, over the next forty years, the political arguments in East-Central Europe will flow, how politics will influence literature or vice versa, or how tradition will shape literature and politics. It may be that illiberalism is 'just a phase'. But I doubt it. Illiberal nationalism increasingly appears to be the default position in that part of the world. But like the seismologists, I am pointing: 'Out there… somewhere… soon… and very big… probably…'.

Notes

1 Founded in 1948, the Bureau was absorbed by the British Council in 1993.
2 I suspect this phrase is deeply embedded in Polish culture. Joseph Conrad used it in 'The Warrior's Soul' in *Tales of Hearsay* (1925) (Conrad 1972: 6).
3 Suwałki, a town of about 70,000 inhabitants, located about thirty miles from the Polish–Lithuanian border. It has three high schools, but the idea it could support a university was fanciful.
4 I next caught sight of Fiszbach in newsreel of the shipyard negotiations with Solidarność. He was one of the signatories to the Agreement of August 1980. In 1981 he opposed Martial Law and was removed from all positions of responsibility and sent to Helsinki as Counsellor to the Polish Embassy. With the collapse of communism he was recalled to become deputy speaker of the *Sejm* (Parliament) from 1989 to 1991.
5 Happier experiences of working for the BC in Poland can be found in Conradi & Martin (1999).

Introduction 25

6 The Chernobyl accident wedded ecological concerns with national feeling, and with writers leading the charge, fed directly into the Ukrainian declaration of independence on 11 December 1991 (Plokhy 2019: 301–30).

7 The Soviet writers Boris and Arkady Strugatsky, in their sci-fi novel Пикник на обочине (*Roadside Picnic*, 1971), satirised communism with their creation of an alien artefact called the Golden Ball. It was said the Golden Ball would kill most of those who got near it, but would grant the in-most wish of someone who approached with a pure heart. Red Schuhart, the man who gets closest, wishes for 'Happiness for everybody, free, and no one will go away unsatisfied' (Strugatsky 1977: 153). These are the last lines of the novel, so we do not find out if he survives or if his wish is granted. Now we might see this tale not only as a satire on communism, but also on capitalism.

8 Lawrence's letter was written in 1924 but published in the *New Statesman* only on 13 October 1934.

9 The Dutch invasion of Britain in 1688 was a religious-dynastic spat intended to defeat Catholicism and restore the status-quo-ante, rather than a war of conquest: having beaten their foe, the Dutch withdrew.

10 Since then there have been two major earthquakes 'out there': the Indian Ocean on 25 December 2005 and north-east Japan on 11 March 2011.

2 Kundera's 'Kidnap' revisited

Milan Kundera was born in 1929 in Brno. In 1947 he joined the Communist Party: in 1951 he was expelled, then reinstated in 1956, in the brief thaw that followed Khrushchev's address to the Twentieth Congress of the Communist Party. Kundera began his studies at the Arts Faculty of Prague University in 1948 but had to leave after he was expelled from the Party. He resumed his studies at the Prague Academy of Performing Arts and graduated in 1958. He stayed on there to teach 'World Literature' and eventually became a professor at the Prague Institute for Advanced Cinematographic Studies.

Even though he was a member of the Party, Kundera was one of the first of the younger generation of Czech writers to react against the dreary socialist realist literature of the Stalin era, and his first novel *The Joke* (Czechoslovakia 1967, English translation 1982), a satire on the fake socialism of the Stalinist bureaucracy and the opportunists who thrived within it, was one of the first fruits of the Czech attempt to liberalise communism. In his collection of stories *Laughable Loves* (three volumes, Czechoslovakia 1963–9, English translation 1974), his story 'Nobody Will Laugh' traced the farcical tricks employed by a college lecturer to shake off an unpublishable, boorish author convinced of his own genius. The author's relentless pursuit of the lecturer results in his ruin. Most Czechoslovak readers, who sided with the freewheeling intellectualism of the lecturer, saw in the author's behaviour a lesson in the ponderous provincial philistinism and destructiveness of the Party.

In 1968 Kundera spoke out very openly at the annual Writers Congress to head off an attempt by the Party to stage-manage the event. He made it clear that the proposed reform of Czech politics was an attempt to create socialism without secret police, with freedom of the spoken and written word, where public opinion shaped policy, with a freely developing civic culture and a citizenry that was not fearful (Hamšík 1971: 44–5, 161). After the Soviet invasion, the Czech Central Committee took revenge on Kundera by opening disciplinary proceedings against him: his new work was denied publication, his books were removed from public libraries, he lost his teaching post and in 1970 he was again expelled from the Party. After the Party imposed this ban Kundera began to publish his books abroad, commenting directly on the repressive regime in Prague.

Life is Elsewhere (France 1973, English translation 1986) took its title from common graffiti of the student uprising in Paris in 1968. The novel follows the rise of a pompous lyric poet called Jaromil, an avant-gardist favoured by the Party, and his subsequent decline into police informer and, after many humiliations, his death from pneumonia. After this novel received the French Prix Médicis, Kundera and his wife were given an extended visa to travel abroad – in effect they were invited to leave the country. They travelled to France, where Kundera took up a post as lector in literature at the University of Rennes. They later moved to Paris. In 1979, in response to the publication of *The Book of Laughter and Forgetting* (France 1979, English translation 1981), Kundera was deprived of Czech citizenship. In 1981 he became a French citizen. *The Farewell Party* (France 1976, English translation 1977) dealt with events in a Czech spa town and satirised mothers, wives, jazz and contemporary mores in the manner of a farce. This novel was awarded the Italian Premio Mondello for the best foreign novel. In 1981 Kundera was awarded the American Common Wealth Award.

The Book of Laughter and Forgetting and *The Unbearable Lightness of Being* (1985) both dealt with reflections on human values and political life, particularly with the effects of Kundera's departure from Czechoslovakia. These novels were first published in Canada and then smuggled into Czechoslovakia, after which Kundera's name was rarely if ever mentioned in public by Czech officials. In émigré and domestic dissident circles there was some frustration with Kundera's philosophising: it was said he was now too out of touch with events inside the country to be able to comment on them effectively and he had no real understanding of the suffering of those who remained in Czechoslovakia after the invasion. Nevertheless, his books enjoyed considerable success in the West, where his cultural philosophising was perceived as the metaphysics of resistance, which his publishers and readers clearly relished.

Kundera's famous essay 'A Kidnapped West or Culture Bows Out' first appeared in 1984, the same year that his most successful book, *The Unbearable Lightness of Being*, was published.[1] In the eleven sections of the essay Kundera explored culture and politics, the culture of politics, the politics of culture and the connections between culture and issues of identity. His main theme, though, was the death of Central European culture and through that the death of European culture as a whole, perhaps even the death of Europe. Kundera wrote the piece as a literary essay rather than an academic piece: it is not overly concerned to nuance arguments, amass evidence or offer definitions. It might be thought that Kundera's essay was merely a writer's snapshot of a particular time, rendered irrelevant by the collapse of communism in 1989 and the collapse of the USSR shortly afterwards. However, Kundera wrote the essay urgently, as an obituary, as if the death had already taken place. It was designed to upset and provoke and it did just that, opening up a serious debate about the kind of place Europe was becoming in the Reagan/Thatcher/Kohl era. The essay also raised important questions about the nature and definition of Europe, its relationships with

28   Kundera's 'Kidnap' revisited

Russia and the USA, and what exactly had been at stake in terms of its culture as these relationships developed through the twentieth century.[2]

There are no sharp dividing lines: in one direction Central Europe shades off into Western Europe, but still it is not Western Europe. In the other direction Central Europe shades off into East-Central Europe, into Eastern Europe and then into Asia; and while East-Central Europe is not absolutely different from Eastern Europe, it is not Russia. Russian traditional military hierarchy, notions of leadership, the Orthodox tradition and the ideology of the state, along with the relatively poorly developed sense of civil society, mark out a real difference from the rest of Europe – but then Russia, while Asiatic in some respects, is not Asia. Kundera made no distinction between German-speaking Central Europe and non-German-speaking East-Central Europe: for him it was all Central Europe and the finer points of definition were not his concern.[3]

The most important thing about Kundera's Central Europe (West Germany, East Germany and Austria, but also what is sometimes called East-Central Europe – Poland, Czechoslovakia, Hungary and parts of Yugoslavia) was that it was not the West. But whatever it was called, this area of Europe had been the powerhouse of European culture before most of it, as Kundera writes, was kidnapped by the USSR in 1945. And if the Russian crime was kidnapping, the West's crime was indifference to that kidnapping. For Kundera the main issue was not particularly East or West, but a question of the difference between large and small nations. In his view, Central European states are small, conservative and relatively powerless, preoccupied with matters of tradition and culture, and particularly sensitive to the dangers of 'progress' and modernity and the effect these things have on identity and survival.

The idea of 'Europe' for these small states was not geographical, but was tied up with their participation in Christianity, democracy and civic freedoms, and with the spiritual idea of 'the West' (Kundera 1984a: 95). Kundera was aware of the danger posed to Central Europe by Russian communism, but also of the dangers posed by Western marketeering. He saw both as dominated by powerful, confident, brash, aggressive political figures who placed no value on culture because they were personally indifferent to it, because culture made no great profit and did not contribute much to effective political power, and because in neither Russia nor the West did it threaten national survival or the continuance of the ruling powers. Culture was a barely profitable enterprise or a mild political irritant. Kundera opposed much of what the West represented: in his opinion, the West paid for US dominance with a suicidal neglect of culture, seeking unity in commerce and identity in profit. But this, Kundera thought, in its own way mirrored the onslaught on identity within the Soviet bloc. For Kundera, the threat to his idea of Europe was more obvious from the East, in what he called the Russian communist 'Drang nach West' or drive to the West (Kundera 1984a: 101).

Kundera's 'Kidnap' revisited 29

Kundera was vague as to how a revived Central Europe might be restructured, preferring to concentrate on cultural and artistic concerns rather than on politics and strategy, but his thinking revolved around finding good reason to exclude Russia (and if possible the USA too) from exercising any real influence in Central Europe. Solzhenitsyn had claimed that communism was a disease afflicting Russia, but for Kundera Russia was the disease. Communism, he explained, was merely a symptom. Russia had been isolated from Europe for over a thousand years, and during that time had evolved a very un-European culture. Kundera saw Russia as intent on centralising, standardising and violently transforming all nations into copies of its own image. In contrast, it was important for Kundera to mark out and preserve cultural differences, but also to distance his ideas of East-Central European socialism from the history and practice of Stalinism. He asked: 'Is communism the negation of Russian history or its fulfilment?' For Kundera, Communism was both the negation and the fulfilment of Russian history (Kundera 1984a: 99).

Kundera was clear: while the West was culpable in not noticing that East-Central Europe had been kidnapped in 1945, the East-Central Europeans were themselves partly to blame for this by allowing pan-Slavism, a kind of sympathy or strategic common cause with Russia, to develop during their national awakenings in the nineteenth century (Kundera 1984a: 103). At that time the family of 'small nations', 'insulated, egotistical, closed off' as part of the great empires, realised that they shared a common experience and refused assimilation, but they had confused the Russian revolutionary struggle with their own struggle for survival.

The idea of East-Central Europe became popular on both sides of the Iron Curtain in the mid-1980s, mainly (but not only) in response to Kundera's essay. Political stalemate, SDI (the Strategic Defence Initiative, often referred to simply as 'Star Wars'), increasing economic difficulties and renewed Cold War posturing all marked the closing years of Reagan's period in office. The revival of interest in the idea of East-Central Europe allowed intellectuals to break through political deadlock and reassert a shared identity with the West in talk of common culture. In the West, the increasing trend towards 'Europeanisation' through economic integration had in a limited way helped to fill the intellectual vacuum left by the Cold War. While the rediscovery of Europe preceded the crisis in the USSR, the two were certainly related. After 1945 the USSR imposed on East-Central Europe its top-down version of society, with no independent civil element. For dissident writers and thinkers like Adam Michnik (b. 1946), Jacek Kuroń (1934–2004), György Konrád (b. 1933), Danilo Kis (1935–89) and Václav Havel (1936–2011) – many, but not all, ex-members of the Party – their struggle throughout this period was the struggle of memory against organised forgetting. That is, while aware of themselves as citizens in the wider world, they 'remembered' a different way of doing things, refused to accept the Soviet model of socialism or society and, in the face of Soviet

30 Kundera's 'Kidnap' revisited

attempts at totalitarian control, tried to reconstitute their own national civil society. It was against this background that the Western peace movement began to discover Eastern dissidents talking of Europe as a cultural entity threatened by both East and West.

Hungarian writer Gyorgy Konrád, in his book *Antipolitics* (1984), made it clear that the restoration of Central European independence was a precondition for the re-establishment of Europe itself. The debate about Konrád's book, which appeared at around the same time as Kundera's essay, showed Europeans on both sides of the Iron Curtain as seeking common ground and consensus rather than polar opposition and confrontation. But Konrád, unlike Kundera, also warned against Central European provincialism, Russophobia, xenophobia, anti-Semitism, anti-intellectualism and nationalism. In this – as Hungarian and Polish experience after 1989 was to show – Konrád was more of a realist than most dissident intellectuals.

To hark back to a mythical period of European cultural 'unity' was one thing; the reality of a divided Europe was quite another. For Polish, Czech and Hungarian intellectuals, the idea of Central Europe served to distinguish them from *Homo sovieticus* and link them to Western liberal intellectual traditions (Tischner 2005: 295). The notion that they were heirs to the West served to mark them out and discomfort the Soviets and it did so in a way that could not easily be policed. However, Kundera, like many East-Central Europeans with experience of Soviet communism, had a sneaking feeling, which underlies his whole essay, that Western intellectuals were dangerously naive.

Western civil disobedience in the 1980s, directed particularly at the deployment of US nuclear weapons in Europe, might have been a way of restoring the two halves of Europe to each other, but many East-Central Europeans saw CND/END, Western anti-nuclear campaigners like E.P. Thompson (1924–93), and particularly those in favour of unilateral disarmament as at best virginally foolishly in helping to undermine the West's stance against the USSR, and at worst as part of a communist front of unwitting Western stooges for the KGB. By attempting to remove nuclear weapons – even those targeted on Poland, Czechoslovakia and Hungary – CND/END was simply playing into the hands of the communists by disarming the West ready for further Soviet expansion (Thompson 1979, 1985; Thompson & Smith 1980). However, this assumed naivety may have been misplaced.

In fact, there had been an early attempt to create a European-wide nuclear-free zone long before CND/END, and it came from East, rather than the West. In 1956 the USSR attempted to open negotiations on the restriction and prohibition of nuclear weapons in Central Europe. The proposal was discussed at the UN and then dropped. Later, the Polish Foreign Secretary, Adam Rapacki, outlined to the UN a plan to outlaw nuclear weapons in Poland, Czechoslovakia and both German states: this was quickly endorsed by these states. NATO rejected the plan. In 1958 Rapacki returned with a revised plan to freeze the stockpiling of nuclear weapons and then bring in

Kundera's 'Kidnap' revisited   31

a phased reduction of nuclear armaments. This too was rejected. In 1962 a new version of Rapacki's plan was offered by the Polish government. This too was rejected. In 1957, 1968 and again in 1972 Romania proposed a similar plan for the Balkans (Thompson & Smith 1980: 235–40). In the West, at various times, Ireland, Sweden, Finland and Norway all proposed a nuclear-free zone in Europe. If anything, the threat of nuclear war was an urgent and unifying element in European politics. One of the first 'Westerners' to make contact with Solidarność in September 1980 was CND member John Taylor with a 'message of solidarity' from CND/END (Taylor 1981; Thompson 1985: 153).

After 1980–81 and the birth and suppression of Solidarność, the problems of the Eastern Bloc gave a great boost to the unification of Western Europe and its growing economic success. In addition, Reagan's aim in initiating SDI had been not only to provide a defensive shield for the USA, but to provoke an arms race he knew the Soviets could not afford. The strategy worked. The Soviets had already diverted scarce industrial capacity to maintain their military. They might have survived this situation for many years had they not experienced a severe, morale-sapping defeat in Afghanistan. Their response to SDI put the economy and their relations with their European satellite states under further stress. The eventual deployment of cruise and Pershing missiles under US command in Western Europe, and the resulting deployment of Soviet SS20 and SS22 missiles in Eastern Europe, was a blow to European pride and left both sides open to the possibility of a pre-emptive first strike. The peace movements (East and West) grew rapidly at this time as a belated recognition of the loss of political power, and as a protest at the all-enveloping rush of the US and USSR towards realising their global ideologies, political destinies and the maintenance of their superpower egos at the expense, if necessary, of the territories they were 'protecting'.

It was clear that if US nuclear weapons were ever used, they would be aimed at European and Soviet targets: if Soviet missiles were used they would be targeted within Europe too, since they did not have the range to reach the USA. However, it would not be possible to confine damage to east or west of the Iron Curtain: the whole of Europe would suffer. US territory would not be directly affected by the missiles. What made this even more horrifying in Western Europe was that both the USSR and USA clearly thought this 'foreign policy' should be acceptable to their allies. West Germany used the idea of a restored Central Europe to develop its standing within the European Union, to find further outlets for its dynamic economy, and to restore some pre-war influence in East-Central Europe and the Balkans. By stressing cultural kinship with East Germans they hoped to moderate NATO's nuclear stance and, if possible without necessarily removing US nuclear weapons, make West Germany less of a target for Soviet nuclear missiles. By stressing that there was no clear 'front line' for nuclear fallout, they indicated that weapons used against West Germany would also affect East Germans. This was a kind of politics without politics, challenging no

32 Kundera's 'Kidnap' revisited

borders, rescuing no minorities, threatening no one: it was a strategy that also avoided recalling previous German history in Eastern Europe.

With hindsight we can see that Kundera, in including East-Central Europe in his idea of Central Europe, had ignored the depth of resentment against Germany. Poles, Hungarians and Czechs had very good reasons for wanting to keep Germany (East and West) separate and at arm's length. In the past, Germany's economic imperatives in the *Drang nach Osten* (drive to the east) had made it oblivious to the feelings of its Eastern neighbours. Now those neighbours feared that any revamped version of Central Europe would not be the liberal assembly of small states imagined by the inter-war Czech leader T.G. Masaryk (1850–1937), but would be a German-dominated regional economy resembling Friedrich Naumann's (1860–1919) dream of Mitteleuropa (1915), or worse, a repetition of Nazi Lebensraum. They feared that, pulled out of the framework of cooperation with France and the other European Union countries, Germany's economic imperatives would again make it insensitive to its Eastern neighbours. But whatever their fears, the steadily collapsing Eastern Bloc economies desperately needed West German hard currency investment.

In Western Europe the Black Death altered medieval social structure by making the institution of serfdom unsustainable. In Poland and Eastern Europe, however, the Black Death did not have the same impact: social structures based on the muscle power of the peasantry remained in place much longer (Anderson 1984: 279; Ziegler 1970: 118). The problems of industrialisation complicated, but did not substantially alter, the process of nation-state building in the West. In Eastern and East-Central Europe, however, this was not the case. There, the penetration of foreign (mainly German) capital into multi-ethnic, largely peasant economies produced a steady reaction of hostility and suspicion.

In the late nineteenth century, the social order came under enormous stress and it became almost a reflex to see other ethnic and linguistic groups as responsible for lack of economic progress. To a very great extent the mixed settlement patterns of East-Central and South-Eastern Europe, the penetration of foreign capital and the insensitive power of the Russian, Prussian and Austrian monarchies had meant that many of the 'smaller peoples' lusted after their own state machine, if only to protect themselves from other nationalities. At the same time, the intellectuals of the mainly peasant societies of Eastern and East-Central Europe began to rediscover their native languages and literatures as a source of pride.

However, as the various (re)nascent nationalities became aware of themselves and each other, they began to clash at every point of contact. To a great extent, the establishment of a state to protect a given community could not be achieved without contravening the liberty of some other community within that state: these communities not only opposed the existing ruling powers, they were in competition with one another. Kundera's claim that the revolts of Central Europe, because they involved the culture of the

Kundera's 'Kidnap' revisited   33

peoples concerned, were 'far greater and far more decisive than they have been in any other European mass revolt' (Kundera 1984b: 2) is misleading.

Modern Europe developed not only within Christianity, but through the struggle to get out from under the power of the Church – Catholic and Protestant. Indeed, it was only with the French Revolution that Europe began to have a sense of itself outside a religious definition of Europe as Christendom. Revolts in Central Europe and the Balkans may have involved cultural identity to a far greater degree than, say, the English or French revolutions, but these revolts grew out of clashes within and between cultures and cultural ambitions. It is very hard to disentangle the war against Nazism from the many other cultural wars that World War II contained, but it is clear that the Nazi war on the Jews and the war on the Eastern front were fought with a merciless savagery on specific issues of culture and identity that had developed from a long history of religious intolerance of one kind or another.

Kundera's division of post-war Europe into Eastern, Central and Western Europe – 'three fundamental situations' (Kundera 1984b: 1) – was a massive simplification. Even when Kundera spoke of 'Geographic Europe', he ignored the vast differences contained within even Western Europe. He ignored the enormous divides between North and South, Protestant and Catholic, industrial and agricultural Europe: Eire, for example, has a great deal in common with Poland; Eire and Portugal are vastly different from Switzerland and Germany; Finland has a great deal in common with Eastern Europe; Sicily is very different from Norway. Kundera also conveniently forgot previous European empires – British history in Ireland, the Swedish and Polish conquests, the less savoury side of the Austro-Hungarian Empire, the unpleasant Prussian history of suppression in the East, and Germany's role in the creation of European nationalisms.

Kundera's image of the West as anchored in Christianity is a related simplification. Christianity certainly gave Europe a power system and sanctioned certain kinds of political rule, but the struggle to establish Christianity in its Roman version masked the political power struggles of institutional hierarchy and nation-building. When England converted to Christianity for the second time in AD 597, the Roman Church came into conflict with the older Celtic Church. The Synod of Whitby (AD 663) consigned Celtic Christianity, the Celtic languages, and Celtic culture and identity to a lingering death in obscurity on the margins of Europe. The Czech conversion (AD 860) and Polish conversion (AD 965) were initially military moves designed to help avert invasion by Germanic tribes. In Spain, the Christian re-conquest led to the persecution and expulsion of Muslims and Jews. The Prussian conversion of the Lithuanians in the fourteenth century was a long, drawn-out, bloody business that few converts survived.

The long history of European religious warfare, the politicking of the Papacy, the activities of the Inquisition and the long sequence of the Crusades are unifying in one sense, divisive in another, and their legacy is

34 *Kundera's 'Kidnap' revisited*

immense. In Britain, Catholic emancipation was not legally achieved until 1829, but in Northern Ireland and on the football terraces of Glasgow, Protestants and Catholics are still not fully reconciled to each other's presence. In nineteenth-century Germany, the primarily anti-Catholic *Kulturkampf* combined with the *Drang nach Osten* and fed directly into the Holocaust, the horrors of the Eastern front and the division of Europe in the Cold War.

The legacy of the Crusades has not been quite played out yet: in the Balkans, with the collapse of the Yugoslav state, Orthodox Christians and the desperate survivors of the communist elite joined forces against the Muslim population in 'ethnic cleansing'. In Chechnya, and later in Georgia, religious battle lines have been drawn. Europe and its various regions have been defined and divided as much as they have been united by Christianity. According to Kundera, Central Europe is very different from Russia, by virtue of containing the greatest possible human variety in the smallest possible space. In this it is a microcosm of Europe and the West. According to Kundera, on the other hand, the political regimes imposed on Central Europe by the USSR insist on the greatest uniformity of identity in the largest possible space.

Kundera made a passing attempt to cut the link between Russia and communism, but it is not very convincing. He may say that ordinary Russians do not want to oppress their neighbours and that it was Stalinist communism that made them do so, but Kundera believed communist expansionism was a part of the Russian imperial psyche, which, whether it was communist or not, is always and in every way Russian – a point also made by the Austrian novelist Joseph Roth (1894–1939) in his 1927 novel *Flight without End* (Roth 1984). Kundera claimed that everyone in Central Europe has been 'particularly sensitive' to the danger of the Russians. As proof, he cites the example of Poles who were 'Russianised' during the period of the Polish Partitions (1772–1918), and particularly after the Great Uprising of 1863. This is seen as part of a process of levelling-down Polish culture to Russian standards.

But Russianisation, though it was brutal, was a fairly haphazard business compared to the calculated and thorough brutality of the Prussianisation of Poles that occurred at the same time, or compared to the 'Germanisation' conducted by the Nazis. After 1918, the Hungarians and Czechs (who had no previous experience of dealing with Russia) were open to Russian influence in ways that Austria and Poland were not. When T.G. Masaryk, who wrote with great insight on Russian literature and culture, proposed a Central European Union of small states, he did this to resist German power, not Russian. In the same vein, when Friedrich Naumann offered his counter-proposal of Mitteleuropa it was so that Germany, building on the *Drang nach Osten*, could sever itself from the West, dominate the small states of Central Europe and expand its economic influence Eastwards.

Adolf Hitler inherited a dream of the domination of Europe aimed primarily at the traditional military, economic and ethnic penetration of the East. German efforts to dominate East-Central Europe have been far more consistent than Russian efforts. Communism was only one stage in Russian economic development: an attempt by other means to leap from late feudalism to the standards of liberty, citizenship, wealth, comfort and modern identity enjoyed in the West. Communism, as Khrushchev later said, was an attempt to catch up and surpass the West. This is the unavoidable historical baggage of the Russian Revolution.

Unlike Konrád and Havel, Kundera simply wanted to exclude Russia from Europe altogether. Its aim of world revolution and uniformity made it unacceptable. But in criticising the USSR – and there is much to criticise – Kundera ignored Central Europe's unique attempt in Nazism to create a modern identity for itself by denying and obliterating human difference. Nazi efforts to shape a standard European identity by dividing people into supermen and sub-humans, masters and slaves, those destined to rule and to be ruled or destined for work and extermination, barely figure in this idealised account. Yet Nazi genocide was, after all, a Central European attempt to deny the value of difference. If the Nazis had been successful, the illiterate sub-human slaves of the Reich would have been ruled by a new class of German-speaking, blue-eyed, blonde Central Europeans. The aims of the Russian Revolution and the Soviet Union were of an entirely different order. But while communism was a good enough reason for Kundera to want to permanently exclude Russia from Europe, he did not suggest that Nazism might be sufficient reason to exclude Germany and its allies.

Kundera's feeling that communism excluded Russia from Europe is understandable but slightly absurd. Along these lines he might also have asked whether, after 1492, the death of an estimated 100 million Native Americans at the hands of Europeans was the summation or the negation of Western culture. He might just as well have suggested that the Western European rationalism of Marxism (Marx and Engels were not Russians, after all) should be reason enough to exclude Western Europe (particularly Britain) from Europe. The implication of Kundera's argument is that there can be no peaceful coexistence between the East and West, not because of political ideology, but because their cultures cannot mesh.

Kundera saw Russia only as a brutal, primitive Asiatic, extra-European imperialist military power. But the West must, at least in part, answer for this. Russia was given good reason to fear the West in 1812, and the Soviets were given good reason to fear the West after 1917. It was not predetermined that Russian communism would develop in the way it did. If the Swiss had not sent Lenin to Russia in a sealed train, if Germany had not quashed the Spartacist uprising and Bavarian revolutions, if the Hungarian Soviet had survived, if Britain, France and the USA had not invaded revolutionary Russia, if the Poles had not gone to war with the Bolsheviks, there was a slim chance the Soviets might have taken another, gentler path; that Leninism and Stalinism might not have established the hold they eventually developed; that the reforming social democracy of Western Europe might have influenced the course of the Russian Revolution. As it was, the USSR came under Western siege from its first moments: accidentals, incidentals, maybes and might-have-beens.

36 Kundera's 'Kidnap' revisited

Kundera's claim that the peoples of Central Europe 'blew apart' the Austro-Hungarian, Russian and Prussian empires in 1918 is not entirely true. Rather, these societies imploded under the impact of prolonged war, modernisation, transatlantic cooperation and their own internal ethnic rivalries. In 1918 power dropped into the hands of the peoples of Central Europe. Yet the new states that resulted could not have come into existence at all, or have survived for long, without the connivance of the Western Allies. The societies that emerged from the wreckage of World War I gained enormously from the legitimation of the Allies, though the treaties of Trianon and Versailles left a legacy of grievances.

Cynically, the Allies saw a swathe of small states along the Eastern German borders as a way of buffering the Russian Revolution and at the same time of curbing German Eastern ambition. Kundera was certainly right, however, to emphasise that the collapse of the European empires in 1918 released a huge outburst of creativity in East-Central Europe – in literature, music, psychology and art. However, although we may now revel in the literary glories of East-Central European culture from this time, the economic collapse of the 1920s and 1930s, followed by the enormous disruption of World War II, meant that for many years much of what happened in these spheres went unabsorbed in the East and unnoticed in the West.

In his essay, Kundera mentioned a great many East-Central European writers, and their lives are instructive. Of the 'great trinity' of inter-war Polish writers mentioned by Kundera as having 'anticipated European modernism of the 1950s, notably the so called theatre of the absurd' (Kundera, 1984a: 106), it is possible to see that Kundera uses them slightly out of context in order to make his point, concentrating on their current status.

In the years 1918–39, Bruno Schulz (1892–1942), S.I. Witkiewicz (1885–1939) and Witold Gombrowicz (1904–69) were cut off from the traditional function of literary/political opposition acquired during the Partition era: they operated in an open market of ideas, and as a consequence exerted very little political influence. While Polish writers were freed of the burden of 'the matter of Poland', readers suffered confusion at the radical change this worked in what the writers had to say and the way the new literature functioned. Bruno Schultz was a provincial art teacher who published only two little-known books before the war. His work was intimately connected with sado-masochism, with the Jewish father figure and the impact of industrialisation on the rural identity of the tiny Eastern Polish town of Drohobycz. Schultz was found outside the town ghetto, shot and killed by a Nazi officer in 1942. His works remained almost unknown until after the thaw of 1956.

S.I. Witkiewicz was a drug-taking, anti-communist visionary who committed suicide in September 1939. His avant-garde artistic theories, novels and plays were little known until after the thaw of 1956 and did not begin to reach a wider audience until the 1970s.

Witold Gombrowicz's first two novels (*Ferdydurke* (1937) and *Possessed* (1939)) were entirely overshadowed by the outbreak of World War II: he

Kundera's 'Kidnap' revisited   37

spent the war in Argentina, refused to return to communist Poland and died in France. His works remained almost unknown in Poland until after 1956, when his novels and plays began to appear. Even then his three-volume *Dziennik* (Diary) remained unpublished, possibly because of his hostility to the Polish communist regime, but also because his description of his habit of 'cruising' for 'lower-class' young men did not meet with the approval of either the Party or the Catholic Church.

The Polish writers Kundera acknowledges were, in their own lifetimes and for many years afterwards, simply neglected. If the West did not discover these great modernist writers or note their passing until the 1970s, then communist Poland was hardly in a position to do so either. And had their work been better known in inter-war Poland, dominated by the military, the Catholic Church, the peasantry and the nationalist right wing, it is unlikely that the Jew, the junkie and the gay would necessarily have enjoyed much better success.

In inter-war Czechoslovakia, writers and thinkers benefited from an extensive Bohemian bourgeoisie, but nevertheless the situation for writers like Franz Kafka (1883–1924), Jaroslav Hašek (1883–1923) and Karel Čapek (1890–1938) was not greatly different from that of writers in Poland. The status of writers in Hungarian was not much different either. Although the writers Kundera singled out for praise now have an established place in literary history, in their time their contribution and achievement were far from certain. If anything, their work eventually achieved its current status in spite of everything that East-Central European history and culture had to offer – and possibly because the post-war regimes did not approve of them, which once known made them desirable. Kundera forgets (or at least chooses not to remember) that East-Central Europeans can conduct themselves as badly as anybody else.

Kundera rightly emphasises the Jewish contribution to Central European culture and thought, and praises the Jewish heritage as the 'intellectual cement' of Central Europe. For Kundera and many other intellectuals this is undoubtedly so, but for others it was not. Central European intolerance made an enormous contribution to anti-Semitism: German nationalism in particular provoked other nationalisms. Zionism was a form of nationalist response to the intolerance of German, Russian and East-Central European nationalisms (Kundera 1984a: 107). Nazism too was a Central European phenomenon and the state of Israel, as George Steiner has argued (Steiner 1983), is in this respect a European creation.

Kundera says it is difficult to draw the borders of East-Central Europe with any precision, but he also admits that all borders are imaginary and have to be redrawn for each new historical situation (Kundera 1984a: 107). This is so with time and experience too. We have to wonder whether his emphasis on these writers is not the result of the impact of communism. If communism and Nazism had not intervened, would these writers have achieved the same significance Kundera affords them, or would they have simply disappeared on the open market? Would other writers have done

38 Kundera's 'Kidnap' revisited

something different? Did World War II and the Cold War perhaps given these writers a significance they would otherwise have lacked? What is certain is that, for Kundera, the destiny of Central Europe anticipates the destiny of Europe in general, and that he sees the work of many of the writers of this part of the world as a series of 'long meditations on the possible end of European humanity' (Kundera 1984a: 109).

To a great extent, communism, an incredibly sluggish, conservative and contradictory entity rather than a revolutionary phenomenon, did much to preserve pre-war East-Central European societies. But it did so in such a way that it trapped their conservative mentality and their very specific cultural and literary moulds, their linguistic and ethnic grievances. It is with this legacy that the political class and the alienated, diminishing, almost invisible, post-communist intelligentsia of East-Central Europe now has to grapple (Kurczewska 1995). But the wider question is: did art and literature ever unify Europe, let alone its national cultures? Culture is far more negotiable, far more likely to mutate, than any other aspect of human existence. Culture is flexible, but culture in the sense that Kundera uses it is also class-bound. Was cultural unity ever a feature of European life in the way that Kundera supposes?

There were shared concerns, common interests, in the harshness and boredom of rural life and in the stresses of urban development, but beyond this there was little unity in minority ambition, language and literature, or national culture. Indeed, in multi-lingual empires like Russia or Austria-Hungary, language itself was a barrier. The national awakening of the nineteenth century did not remove this barrier, but operated to make it greater. In the visual arts and in music the situation was slightly different. It is surely significant that Gothic, Renaissance and Baroque styles touched only certain parts of Europe, and had almost no impact on the huge mass of Eastern Europe.

On the other hand, Stalinist art, music and architecture offered a unifying style and culture for Eastern Europe. Stalinism went further than any social force since feudalism in unifying Eastern European social structures, in moving peasants off the land and into factories, in making one town look pretty much like another, and in creating a fairly uniform urban peasantry. It is true that larger nations have little sense of their own fragility, and that small nations have a clear sense they may not be here tomorrow.

However, by insisting on East-Central Europe as a zone of small nations, Kundera by implication simplifies the situation in the West. Switzerland has a population of about 6.7 million; Eire, Scotland and Wales each have populations of about 3.5 million people; Basque and Breton populations are even smaller. These places have a very acute sense of their historical position and the compromises language and empire have worked upon identity and culture. The 'small nations' of East-Central Europe are much larger than the 'small' nations of the West: Hungary has a population of 10.2 million; the Czech Republic 10.4 million; East Germany had a population of 14 million; there are over 39 million Poles. It may be that it is not a question

Kundera's 'Kidnap' revisited 39

of numbers, but one of historical experience enshrined in culture. There are many experiences the 'small' nations of East-Central Europe share with the 'small' nations of the West. The history of the Jews and Gypsies in both halves of Europe also has correspondences. Polish and Irish history are remarkably akin. Protracted struggles in Ireland, Wales and the Basque Country surely indicate long-standing unhappiness at being confined within an alien empire. And as black militants often point out, there is no black in the Union Jack or in the French tricolour.

Kundera's idea of Central European innocence is nothing more than a myth. Both World Wars grew in the fertile soil of Central and East-Central Europe. World War I started with discontent at Austrian rule, and World War II started with an Austrian pining for the restoration of empire, but an empire that was ethnically 'pure', purged of the minorities that had plagued the Austro-Hungarians. Kundera displays sentimental affection towards the old Austro-Hungarian monarchy: when he refers to 'little Austria' he is romanticising.

It is true that some still regard the old empire as a kind of multi-lingual, multi-ethnic showhouse for Central European culture, and it is possible, even now in homes in Kraków, for example, to see pictures of the Emperor Franz Josef next to pictures of Pope Jan Paweł II. The empire was a powerhouse of culture in the late nineteenth and early twentieth centuries. But the writer Robert Musil (1880–1942) saw through this myth and regarded the Austro-Hungarian Empire as *'cacania'*: Austria-Hungary was the home of an empire that, while it was comparatively liberal, was still a repressive military power sitting on a large number of unhappy smaller nationalities. Austria-Hungary may have been a great cultural centre, but it was also the prison-house of nations and the birthplace of Adolf Hitler and a great many of his cronies.

Vienna and the Czech borderlands were a major factor in creating Hitler's mind-set. Though this area was not as volatile as other parts of Europe, it was nevertheless a place of anti-Semitism and racial tension. After Hitler's rise to power in Germany, Austria came to see the Axis alliance as a way of restoring its pre-1918 fortunes, and it was Hitler's first, and far from unwilling, victim. There are continuities that make it unwise to hanker after some golden time of cultural rectitude, to insist on a lingering cultural sensibility inherited from the old empires, or to blame the evils of post-war Central Europe on the communists. The dispossession and expulsion of almost fifteen million Germans from Eastern and East-Central Europe in the years 1945–9 was a brutal totalitarian act, accomplished locally, before the imposition of post-war communist regimes, and it underlines the point that East-Central Europeans could be as brutal as anyone else. The bad-tempered post-communist division of Czechoslovakia into two republics, genocide in the ex-Yugoslav republics, the rise of skinhead culture and attacks on refugees, Jews and Gypsies in East Germany, Hungary, Romania and Poland have all given the most powerful rebuttal to any cosy myths of a pure and benign cultural inheritance, and made clear the realities of

40 Kundera's 'Kidnap' revisited

ethnic tension that Nazism made use of and that communism once held in check.

Poles have long regarded themselves as the bastion of Western civilisation against the barbarian East. And there is a long tradition of Russian thinkers who see no advantage in looking to Europe. But is this unchangeable? Was Kundera making anti-Russian propaganda when, in the opening lines of his essay, he asserted that no Russian could think of dying for Europe (Kundera 1984a: 95)? Within two years of the essay's appearance, Kundera's analysis was challenged by events. The disaster at Chernobyl initiated or crystallised a change in Soviet thinking: on 26 April 1986 (nearly two years after the appearance of Kundera's essay) the atomic reactor at Chernobyl exploded, showering Europe with radioactive dust. Poles had to take iodine tablets for months; large areas of the Ukraine were evacuated; radiation hot spots were found in Finland, France, Spain and Sweden; Welsh lamb was contaminated for over eight years; the British were told not to go out in the rain; Muscovites were told not to go outdoors at all.

The Chernobyl disaster revealed what many Soviet citizens had suspected – that their nuclear industry was as inefficient as the rest of the economy. It was also massively dangerous. The competence of the communist hierarchy and leadership was called into question. Instead of declaring an immediate alert, the Party had delayed admitting to the accident for several days, during which time the nuclear cloud spread, affecting hundreds of thousands of people in the Ukraine, Belarus, Poland and Sweden. This was a terrible indictment of the Soviet mania for secrecy. Soviet failure to take adequate care of their allies put alliances under tremendous pressure.

Without a nuclear war, Europe had been contaminated. Soviet politicians, who had good reason to find some positive aspect to the affair, were not slow to see that the dozens of helicopter pilots, firemen and technicians who went to combat the fire at Chernobyl, many of whom were later to die of cancer, could be said to have sacrificed themselves not just for the USSR, but for Europe. Suddenly Europe – the whole of it – was a legitimate subject of debate. Soon afterwards Gorbachev began to speak of 'our common European home', and there was reason to believe he meant it.

Gorbachev's demand for openness and reform could hardly be denied after Chernobyl. A new sensitivity to ecology and the environment, underlined by Chernobyl, made it clear that no matter where the lines on the map were drawn, a nuclear disaster (or a nuclear weapons strike) affected everyone. It was suddenly imperative that Europe take back political control from the USA and the USSR, if only to get rid of nuclear missiles. The West had shown, over a period of forty-five years, that it would not take any steps to alleviate hardships in the East and, apart from monitoring the internal problems of the Soviet Empire, had shown little interest in the East.

The presence of US nuclear weapons in West Germany, Britain and Holland, an uprising in East Germany in 1953, the Hungarian uprising in 1956, the Soviet invasion of Czechoslovakia in 1968, serious unrest in Poland in 1956, 1968, 1970, 1976 and 1980, the suppression of Solidarność in

Poland (martial law had been imposed in 1981 and had not yet been lifted), the disastrous Soviet war in Afghanistan, the deteriorating Soviet economy and the continuing monolithic power of the Soviet Communist Party – all seemed to make the status quo appear absolutely fixed and unchangeable. However, after Chernobyl, at precisely the moment that his argument was directly relevant and his discussion clearly necessary, Kundera's lack of a political strategy and his unwillingness to credit the Soviet peoples with any spirit or desire for change (given the chance) undercut his essay.

Kundera's repeated question is: how could the disappearance of Central Europe have gone unnoticed? His answer is that Western European unity was once religious, that this eventually gave way to a cultural unity, but that now 'culture in turn is giving way'. Europe no longer sees European unity as cultural unity, says Kundera, and for this reason it has allowed Central European culture to disappear. Certainly Western Europe now sees its experience as very different from that of the countries that fell under communist control after 1945, but the 'Western experience' of the UK, France, Belgium and the Netherlands, for example, is also different from that of Austria or Switzerland, and different again from Scandinavia, Finland, Greece, Spain, Portugal, Norway, Denmark or Ireland.

Cultural unity is hardly a category that figures in Western thinking. Increasingly, Western Europe defines unity (so far as it debates the matter at all) in terms of a willingness to surrender sovereignty and enter into economic and commercial uniformity within the European Union and common currency and markets, and a diverse range of non-Western countries are queuing to join. But was it once different? The more cynical answer is that unity was not important enough, and was hardly ever an issue for the West. In particular, Western Europe could not solve the identity problems of Central Europe. Two World Wars offered evidence enough of this, and having fought them, the division of Europe in 1945 was the price the West was prepared to pay for peace and prosperity. In the 1980s, Margaret Thatcher does not seem to have known any more about Czechoslovakia than Chamberlain knew in 1938.

In addition, Central European folly and Western naivety about Hitler meant that by 1945 the power to wage war had in any case been virtually removed from the damaged and impoverished European states, whatever their language, culture and history. The power to wage war had been taken over by the US and the USSR: Europe became a set of client states. The squabbling, lethal European family was impotent to alter what, almost haphazardly, became the Cold War. In the late 1980s, as wealth and confidence returned to the West (they never did appear in the Eastern states), as Soviet military power felt the slow drain of Afghanistan and economic control began to wane, anti-Semitism, racism, xenophobia and anti-intellectualism promptly reappeared. It is not so much that the West had not noticed. It was simply that the cultural unity Kundera perceived hardly existed in the minds of anyone outside the liberal intellectuals of Central Europe. And increasingly, with the collapse of communism, they came to think that

42   Kundera's 'Kidnap' revisited

perhaps anti-Semitism, racism, xenophobia and anti-intellectualism was the real cultural unity of Central Europe reasserting itself.

Kundera confidently tells us that culture has bowed out, but it is not always clear what he means by culture: high culture or folk culture, daily life, or all these things? Whichever it is, Kundera has a point. With the exception of Eire, Scotland and Wales, the West has rarely had writers of the kind Kundera refers to – repositories of national wisdom, moral authorities, touchstones for the language, 'awakeners' of identity. And in general, with the exception of Scandinavia, the West is very suspicious of artists, art and culture. The Arts Council of England, for example, over the last forty years, while it offered massive subsidies to opera, ballet and arts administration, consistently refused to finance writers directly, supported very little new publishing, funded theatre inadequately, and barely funded new theatre writing. It never encouraged art with a direct political connection and, while it funded the living artists hardly at all, preferred to support the performance of safely dead 'classic' authors. In England, culture is a slightly risqué concept, a distasteful and possibly rather dirty word – particularly under Conservative governments. Under Labour governments the puritanical embarrassment and workerist philistinism that has haunted the left since Cromwell generally means that the arts have not done much better.

In a West that dreams of markets and profits, but where artists and writers cannot make a profit or survive in the market, it is almost inevitable that artists should be left-leaning and in need of patronage. The arts, since Shakespeare's times, have by and large been commoditised. The West can afford art and literature as part of its general consumption, but it does not like art or literature that is new or unfamiliar. And it does not like writers, art or artists unless they can be commoditised and marketed as 'classic' (i.e. dead) or, if still living, as 'successful media personalities'. The West recognises that literature and art are part of capitalism but remains scandalised by the cost of art – even though very little of that cost ever finds its way back to the artist in terms of the artist's earning power. In the West we confuse commercial success with artistic success and increasingly judge art and literature by the rules of the marketplace: appropriately, contemporary critical practice encourages us to believe that 'the author is dead'. It was only under communism that the social standing and political power of writing developed by the smaller identities trapped in the great nineteenth-century empires were preserved (in all their ambiguity) into the twentieth century.

The communists may not have understood it, but they loved culture, funded it and aspired to produce it and somehow to control it. They set about mass literacy campaigns; produced vast quantities of cheap books and newspapers; set up dance troupes, ballet companies, mime theatres and provincial repertory theatres; funded new universities, schools and teachers; and gave mass access to higher education. They were, however, keen on the more conservative aspects of culture and preferred folk culture rather than high art and the avant-garde. Their taste was for traditional forms with

Kundera's 'Kidnap' revisited   43

clear 'progressive' social messages rather than the experimental or the new. In spite of this preference, in post-war Poland, Hungary and Czechoslovakia a genuine national intellectual culture persisted, grew, changed, developed and informed daily life. But it often did this alongside, or even in spite of, official culture, not entirely because of it. And in East-Central Europe there were hordes of artists. Each state had its professional writers, supported by a union, with a decent income, a home, a pension, reprints and prizes, social status and standing, and a political function. By and large, they were troublesome only from time to time.

The collapse of communism in 1989 brought about the wholesale collapse of almost all the cultural, artistic and literary organisations of East-Central Europe and destroyed the idea of the 'professional writer'. Not through censorship, but through the pocket, the free market achieved for literature in a matter of days what more than forty years of communist censorship had failed to achieve: it silenced the writers. Not permanently, and not totally, but it deprived them of a readership and distracted them by forcing them to engage with politics and the business of earning a living in ways they had not previously experienced.

In the West, artistic silence matters much less than it did in East-Central Europe. This is partly because Western populations are ethnically, linguistically and culturally less homogeneous, because cultural life is more fragmented and because the political class engaged in such matters is much more divided and smaller. The West is a series of post-modern mini-communities, united only by accidents of geography and economics. In the material comfort of the West, the political silence of artists matters much less than their struggle to earn a living. The marketplace long since effectively silenced the role that literature might have played in Western society: literature is not edible. Kundera indicates that the disappearance of the revues and literary magazines from Western Europe – even those specialising in the literatures of the states behind the Iron Curtain – was a sure indicator that culture is bowing out.

For Kundera this indicated the power of commerce in the West and the collapse of identity in the East (Kundera 1984a: 117). He points out that, under communism, in Poland in particular, the review or small journal was often an underground publication and therefore important to political identity. In this communism unwittingly gave writers a special position in their war to preserve identity and culture. Kundera may well be right in that if all the literary and cultural reviews published in Western Europe were to vanish overnight, very few people would notice. But even in the West there is still a tiny, increasingly quaint bubble of literary engagement – writers still write, readers still search out food for souls. They are few in number, and the search may not be as urgent or near universal as in the former Eastern Bloc, but the writers are still there, scribbling away. If almost no one reads them, if the publishers will not publish them or the market does not judge them successful, it is hardly the writer's fault. Nor is a commercial judgement a literary judgement.

44 Kundera's 'Kidnap' revisited

It may be that, rather than culture bowing out, the market, with all its trash, has bowed in. Writers are powerless in a free market – until after their death or until political events overtake them, of course. Then they become marketable as tragic figures, unacknowledged prophets. Kundera hardly takes into account the continuity and the contradictory nature of US culture, nor does he acknowledge the changing nature of Western culture.

The marginal peoples of Europe created the US. Europe offered the North Americans a European notion of what was culturally central and unifying, and they wanted little to do with it, except to oppose it. Europe made marginal European people into American provincials. They made the US devoutly and creatively provincial by founding a state based on provincial anti-state values. The infant US repeated this pattern across the continent, making what was provincial and individual even more so, only further and further west, and with less and less of what Europeans recognised as culture. Why should we be surprised that this provincial individualism is reflected in US culture as a whole? Indeed, what they have achieved in this area is often what Europeans now accept and admire. Whichever way round we look at it, the relationship of the US to Europe, the outlying to the centre, the province to the capital, the marginal to the mainstream, it is problematic and constantly shifting: always and everywhere.

Kundera's attitudes are very much part of the Czech 'generation of '68': twice expelled from the Party, he was an ex-Party member who opposed Stalinism with his aspiration to 'socialism with a human face'. But disillusioned with socialism in its Soviet version, Kundera was soon appalled by the poverty of Western affluence and disillusioned with the culture of the open market. Trapped between these worlds, he benefited fully from neither the culture of East-Central Europe, nor the freedoms of the West. His democratic oppositionist ambitions cut him off from East-Central Europe, and his socialism and seriousness about culture, the failures of materialism and the false triumphalism of free market propaganda meant that even though his novels were successful, he could not be easily absorbed by, and did not feel at ease in, the commercial–cultural life of the West. His novels played with notions of memory and fidelity, but under the pressure of history and actuality he inclined towards a flippant, elegiac 'lightness' and painful forgetting.

Just as complex attitudes to 'modernity' produced conservative resistance in nineteenth-century Russia, so Soviet 'internationalism' produced a conservative reaction to the levelling-down of East-Central European intellectuals and non-Party leftists. In spite of his left leanings, Kundera, in the manner of the old intelligentsia, is also conservative and elitist in his own way. For Kundera, popular culture is probably either a communist-funded provincial folk-dance troupe or marketable Western rubbish: it is shorthand for fake, substandard trash. It is no accident that he sees modern, democratic, party politics as 'absolute opportunism', mere kitsch and cliché (McEwan 1984: 29).

Kundera's 'Kidnap' revisited   45

But mass culture, East or West, communist or capitalist, does not always represent a decline in standards. High art was a category of activity from which the bulk of the population were excluded: mass literacy, functional literacy perhaps, may make art and culture accessible to a wider audience, but if that is seen only as a levelling-down, it cannot make the situation more acceptable to a conservative intellectual. Mass literacy is something new in human society. It is altogether a new category of experience, and therefore cannot be a decline from high art. While the shortcomings of mass literacy in confusing good literature with commercial success and in its relationship to capitalism, to the nature of the market and to kitsch are all increasingly clear, the effects it will have and what kind of culture it will eventually lead to – especially with the speed of technological advance – we cannot say.

The Cold War and the Iron Curtain divided Europe for nearly fifty years. Historians argue as to who was responsible for creating these things. They also argue about why the Soviet Union collapsed rather than repair the gaps in the Berlin Wall and the Hungarian border; why it never moved to crush the opposition movements in Hungary, Czechoslovakia and Poland; why it did so badly in Afghanistan. Doubtless, after Afghanistan Chernobyl played a significant role, but for the moment these are genuine political mysteries. However, it is clear that communism was not defeated through the power of the Western military, the efficiency of the free market, the rightness of God-fearing Christians or the power of intellectual argument. Communism collapsed from its own inertia and inefficiency, its internal contradictions and corruption: it was bankrupt in every sense. That it was not defeated is something the triumphalist right has yet to acknowledge or fathom, and the fact that it cornered the brand-name of socialism has consequences for the self-image of all those East-Central European intellectuals who, like Kundera, opposed communism in the name of enlightened socialism.

It is not difficult to see Europe, the Cold War, and the old Eastern Bloc in Kundera's terms, especially since the new Europe, in its unofficial financial and military borders – which reinforce the old Christian/Orthodox/Muslim divides – bears an uncanny resemblance to pre-war Europe. Kundera was not alone in thinking that after 1945 East-Central Europe had been attached to Soviet Asia and that the West was indifferent. Kundera's point about approaching these things from east of centre as well as left of centre is also valid. But given the level of material prosperity in the West and the level of deprivation in the East, it was easy for Kundera to demonstrate the implications of the division of Europe and the consequences of 'Sovietisation'.

Politically, both the denigration of Russian culture and the assertion of a Western culture in East-Central Europe could be justified – even if both were simplifications, even if both were misleading. Nor is it difficult to make Western liberals (who might at other times be safely dismissed) feel guilty about these things. That is not to say that Kundera's essay is either manipulative or naive. It was an attempt to reach out, shake things up, make contacts, insist on connections, continuities and discontinuities, and

46 Kundera's 'Kidnap' revisited

stress that something indefinable and massively important was being lost or ignored. It was for this reason that in 1989 Polish, Czech and Hungarian intellectuals began to speak of a 'return to Europe'.

Five years after Kundera's disconcerting essay appeared, Europe went through massive changes with the collapse of communism. And a great deal more has happened since then. Germany has been reunited; Western Europe has drawn closer to an economic union and at the same time the prospects of that union have been subject to massive revision; the Soviet Union has disappeared; Poland, Hungary and the Czech Republic have joined NATO and the European Union. But beyond that, the ethnic hatreds of the ex-Yugoslav states continue to boil, and the collapsed economies of Romania, Bulgaria and the former republics of the USSR have been left pretty much to their own devices. Russian politics has lurched towards banditry, corruption, kleptocracy and dictatorship.

The united Germany, still paying for reunification, its fingers burned dabbling with the collapsing rouble, is currently too preoccupied with re-establishing the euro to reflect on its contribution to the Balkan wars of secession or the impact its economy is making throughout Eastern Europe. Yet reluctantly, and without apparently fully understanding why or what the implications might be, Germany has been tied ever more firmly into a key role within Europe by becoming the banking power at the centre of the European Union. It is always the writer's task to undermine, criticise and oppose whatever is – be it politics, literature, culture or even the way of the world. But that cannot be the only measure of Kundera's essay.

It is of its time and place, certainly, but from its fractured, partial, partisan, East-Central European perspective, the essay outlined problems that writers of all kinds continue to grapple with. The issues it raises – the traditional East-Central European concerns: culture, politics, art, identity, the place and function of literature, the responsibility of individual writers, the overwhelming power of kitsch and the market, the impact these things have on democracy – are still with us, revealed, restored, refurbished, made urgent, if only we knew it, by the collapse of communism, the premature triumphalism of the 'End of History', the uncertainty of the European Union and the abrupt revelation of casino capitalism and its attendant bankocracy.

Neither the free market nor its opposite has been a great joy to Kundera (Hughes 1988: 28–31). For him, the pressures were twofold. On the one hand, the dynamic West had the successful marketisation of the psyche, the commoditisation of the arts, the privatisation of its products, and the accompanying devaluation of writers, universities and intellectual life begun by Thatcher and Reagan. On the other hand, the stagnant East suffered from the almost complete failure to develop the economy, a massive material and organisational failure, political insensibility, communist control and stagnation in the arts – except for the work of émigré, oppositionist, dissident, underground samizdat and tamizdat writing.

Civic society, so long sought by the opponents of communism, is in the West seriously compromised by commercialism. In this Kundera is

Kundera's 'Kidnap' revisited 47

undoubtedly right. Political dissent in the West cannot be equated with dissent in the old Eastern Bloc, but the advent of the internet, blogging, self-publishing, e-publishing and the opportunities opened up by Twitter and Facebook, while they may not be exactly the same thing as the Flying University, the Jazz Section or the University of the Air (the old dissident civic information and education networks of the communist times in Poland, Czechoslovakia and Hungary), and certainly lack intellectual input, nevertheless perform some of the same function in contradicting commercial self-censorship while getting round established opinion and the main blocks to free expression to establish independent civic connections.

The Cold War held so much in check that it is still too early to say with any certainly that the outcomes of World War II have been fully appreciated. Likewise, we cannot say that the collapse of communism necessarily means the defeat of the entire range of left-wing opinion, or that the results of the Soviet implosion can be contained, or whether the newly found banking power of the reunited Germany can be controlled. The consequences of Soviet intervention in Afghanistan and the Western support for the Taliban are likely to be with us for many years to come.

And, as a tiny part of the Western intellectual world worried about post-post-modernism, we were suddenly brought face to face with the fact that Islamic fundamentalism is in violent reaction against the idea of the modern – all of it. At the same time, we find ourselves embarked upon a transition to a global economy for which we have not fully prepared and in which much of the world cannot fully share. And while we are launched into the complexities of post-communism, the ideas of the left stubbornly linger, refuse to go away and still offer tantalising half-solutions.

When contemporary observers from Western Europe visit Warsaw, Kraków or Prague they often note with wonder that there are now McDonald's, Marks & Spencer, Benetton, Laura Ashley, Starbucks and a host of other retail outlets. But they also remark that 'over there' universities 'still maintain standards'; lecturers and professors enjoy considerable social standing; there are still enormous outdoor book markets, public libraries with actual books and thriving bookshops; literary journals are still widely read; 'old-style' café culture still exists; writers and intellectuals still have some respect, and a role (though diminished) to play in cultural and political life; and apparently some writers still have something to say and an attentive readership. In observing these things, visitors are noting the anachronistic differences between Europe's East and West, between two or even three time zones, two rates of economic and social change, two (of many) styles of being European. Their surprise at these things is a measure of how the West, rather than the East, has changed. What they are noticing is the past-ness of their past, their difference as Westerners. These things are nothing less than echoes, traces and confirmations of Kundera's observation that the lingering respect for the idea of the intelligentsia and the life of the mind enjoyed in East-Central Europe were not significant aspects of contemporary Western culture and that in the West, under pressure from

48 *Kundera's 'Kidnap' revisited*

America, culture has to a very great extent bowed out, or has at least ceased to be a concern for politicians, and has been largely removed from political debate since, where it has not been successfully commoditised, in the UK it has become part of the charity industry through the national lottery. In short, whatever tragedy Central Europe faced, the real tragedy was that in Western Europe culture no longer had a role in intellectual or political life, that 'Europe itself was no longer experienced as a value' (Kundera 1984a: 118).

The focus of Kundera's snapshot has certainly changed. We might now see the world not as divided into East and West, communist and capitalist, but into North and South, the Haves and the Have-nots, those with access to water, oil and finance, and those without access to these things. We might now see Europe as united by its economic and financial disorganisation. We might also prefer to think of Europe in relation to China, Africa and the developing economies of South America, rather than in relation to the declining powers of the USA and Russia. But the subject of Europe and its attempts to redefine itself – now in response to the crisis of the Anglo-American banking system, the euro currency crisis, the changing fortunes of Germany and the abrupt rise of bankocracy – has not faded.

Kundera's central questions and observations about the nature of Europe, the relationship of its various parts, and the layers of its culture and identity remain unchallenged, consistently troubling, contradictory and unanswered: but in this essay and in his novels his insistence on a cultural diversity capable of resisting commercial trash is clear. Although it did not appear so at the time, Kundera's 'sudden unfurling of the banner of nostalgia' now looks exaggerated, slightly hysterical, a way of side-lining Russia (Herling 1987: 179). But that is to underestimate what lies at its heart, to take it only for its surface concerns.

The essay caught up and recast in a more urgent way many of the themes that he had been turning over in his novels and which he was later to develop in his essay collections (Kundera 2007, 2009). His myth of Central Europe may appear strained to us now – a pastoral idyll – but his concern is not so much with politics itself, but with the impact of politics on culture, and what he highlights is that if the culture of post-communist Europe is to be more than a collection of the great figures of the past, minus national rivalries, but plus the ghosts of the Holocaust, it will have to find a way to encompass the history of totalitarianism in all its varieties, along with the struggles to oppose it. Developing a broad consciousness of the remaining threats to European culture includes the task of revealing and tracing the history of the many threads and pathways of error, diversity, jealousy and fear that led to the disaster that overtook Europe in the twentieth century, unravelling the many ways in which totalitarianism operates and unmasking its many guises.

It is precisely because Kundera comes to these problems from left and east of centre that he sees them with such clarity. Just as the political legacy of the failure to integrate Germany into Europe and the resulting World

Kundera's 'Kidnap' revisited   49

Wars are still with us and haunt the changes to Germany's role since the fall of the Berlin Wall, so the cultural questions raised by the Cold War, which are implicit in Kundera's essay, are likely to remain an awkward and unresolved gift to the future of the West from the past of East.

Notes

1 The essay first appeared as 'The Tragedy of Central Europe' in *The New York Review of Books* (1984b). Kundera's title for the essay was 'A Kidnapped West or Culture Bows Out', as published in *Granta* 11 (1984a).
2 Responses to Kundera were many and various. For example: Ash (1989); Dussen and Wilson (1993); Keane (1988); Rupnik (1989); *Writings on The East* (1990)
3 Elsewhere (Kundera 2007, 2009) he was more specific. For example, he defined East-Central Europe as Bohemia, Poland and Hungary, which along with Austria had never been part of Eastern Europe, and which, he said, had taken part in the 'great adventure of Western civilization, with its Gothic, its Renaissance, its Reformation' (Roth 2002: 91–2).

3 Polish writers and tradition
Partition and Independence

Tradition

Tradition is an ongoing conversation about how the habits, style and achievements of the dead shape the behaviour, attitudes and opinions of the living. Tradition is also the picked-out experience or way of doing things that over time a culture decides it is useful to preserve (Hobsbawm & Ranger 1983). Language is a tradition, but tradition is also a kind language carrying its own philology, grammar, vocabulary, tenses, aspects, cases, genders, syntax, categories, exceptions, and markers of experience and identity. Indeed, Karl Marx thought the unconscious, embedded, unrecognised power of tradition was capable of derailing or diverting revolution and modernity (Marx 1967).

The word 'tradition' derives from Latin *traditionem*, a composite from *tradere* (*trans* + *dare*, dare to cross). In English, as in Latin, the word includes ideas of trade, handing something over, handing on to succeeding generations or changing one thing into another, but it also includes lying and betrayal. This is the root behind 'tread' (follow a path), 'trade', 'trader', 'traitor', 'betray', 'traduce' and 'translate'. Raymond Williams said the word tradition 'moves again and again towards *age-old* and towards *ceremony, duty* and *respect*', but at the same time, considering how little has actually been handed down to us intact and how various the survivals are, each example of 'tradition' is in its own way 'both a betrayal and a surrender' (Williams 1976: 269).

George Steiner emphasised that tradition is not fixed, but involves constant reinvention, 'substitution, permutation and inter-animation [...] a sequence of metaphoric relations and possibilities of relations'. Tradition cannot convey an unchanged past into the present and is always and inevitably a reinvention, an adaptation and betrayal of the past. The 're-write rules' of tradition may vary from period to period and from genre to genre, but the present always translates the past (Steiner 1998: 484–5).

Each culture experiences its own tradition as 'natural', but Polish ideas about literary tradition are very different from English language ideas on the subject. In Polish the word *tradycja* (tradition) has been part of the language from about the sixteenth century and relates to 'views,

Polish writers and tradition 51

norms, conduct succeeding from one period to another and transmitting to the next' (Długosz-Kurczabowa 2018: 667–8). Although it comes from the same Latin root, the content is not the same as in English. None of the derivative words – 'tread', 'trade', 'trader', 'traitor', 'betray', 'traduce' and 'translate', which in English give it an ironic quality, are etymologically connected in Polish.[1] *Tradycja* signals authentic, original, unchanged, undiluted and pure to the extent that as a synonym only 'time-honoured' seems adequate (Stanisławski 1970: 1186). It is not unusual to read un-ironic assertions such as, referring to Polish cuisine: 'an unbreakable thread of tradition that links the most distant events with the present' (Lemnis & Vitry 1981: 9).

The assumptions behind tradition in Polish are often both nourishing and subversive. Usually the word is understood as a function of Polishness, connected to identity, religion and the family, and in politics it is often connected to opposition. Catholicism, which regards itself as handed down from ancient authority, is a form of traditionalism that, combined with the Polish language, encourages and reinforces popular beliefs about Polish identity. In Polish literary culture, tradition is not about adherence to a particular historical line of development in literary forms – the sonnet, sestina, short story or novel – but about the subject matter: tradition is likely to be defined as fidelity, patriotism, a relationship to the *naród* (nation). There is little sense that to stay the same a tradition must change, and the idea that tradition might be contested contradicts popular usage: for some not to be Catholic is to be outside tradition, not to be Polish.

Romanticism and positivism

During the partition of Poland (1772–1918), relentless 'Russification' and the Prussian *Kulturkampf*, designed to convert the 'bad Polish stuff', put Polish identity under extraordinary pressure. Only in the Austrian partition was limited national expression allowed. In the Russian and Prussian partition areas, Poles had no national institutions and little or no access to government, education, banking, the military or the civil service. A sense of nationality barely existed for the peasantry, who were conscious of speaking Polish (mostly local dialect) and of being Catholic, but only in relation to the immediate geographical area they knew, rather than in any wider national sense. Consequently literature, theatre, music and art performed a vital, unifying national function for Polish speakers, particularly for the slowly developing middle class and the *inteligencja*. The effect of partition was to shape Polish politics not along the lines of left and right but to divide along the lines of response to invasion, occupation, repression, failed insurrection and the ongoing fact of partition.

Polish romanticism first emerged in the writing of Adam Mickiewicz (1798–1855), starting with his 'Ode to Youth' (1827) and developing with *Konrad Wallenrod* (1828), *Księga narodu polskiego i pielgrzymstwa polskiego* (Paris 1832, Book of the Polish Nation and Polish Pilgrimage) and

52   Polish writers and tradition

his epic poem *Pan Tadeusz* (Paris 1834), the opening lines of which lament and invoke the lost paradise of the old Commonwealth: 'Litwo! Ojczyzno moja!' (Oh, Lithuania! Fatherland of mine!). This indicates that from the start Polish romanticism was bound up not only with indignity, rural nostalgia, the loss of independence and the loss of colonial holdings but also, to put it another way, with what was to become the problem of minorities. In the third part of his drama *Dziady* (1832), Mickiewicz followed the spiritual transformation of the solitary, romantic figure of Gustaw into Konrad, the mystic seer who transforms poetry into national feeling and totally identifies with the national cause.

The other notable romantic 'bards', Juliusz Słowacki (1809–49), Zygmunt Krasiński (1812–59) and Cyprian Norwid (1821–83), looked to traditional *szlachta*[2] society, thought of themselves as patriots and saw the function of writing as the protection of the nation. Apart from ending partition, they were conservative and did not like the idea of social change. Krasiński in particular, an arch-conservative who favoured the resurrection of the *szlachta* as ruling elite, was particularly averse to the idea of revolution. Also, while romantic tradition favoured heroic sacrifice and brave deeds, and viewed the poet as *wieszcz* (bard, seer, prophet), Słowacki, Krasiński and Norwid did not accept without question Mickiewicz's 'messianic' view of Poland as the sacrificial 'Christ of nations'. Nor did Słowacki accept Mickiewicz's view that the *szlachta* – whom he saw as responsible for the partition – were Poland's natural rulers or that they had any substantial role to play in the restoration of independence.

Still, the expectation was that writers, as 'the conscience of his nation', would do more than merely create entertaining books. Writers 'stood in' for political life: they were the 'renewers' of the national community, maintainers of the national language, interpreters of the national will and 'awakeners' of the national conscience. The romantic tradition – variously described as 'nationalist', 'conspiratorial', 'idealist' and 'insurgent', and of necessity often written in exile – was summed up in a formulation by Prince Józef Poniatowski (1763–1813): 'God, Honour, Fatherland'. Arthur Alvarez, seeking the equivalent of the Polish romantic writers in English literature, said that lacking political parties, civil society and open debate, the effect of partition on Polish literature was 'as though the finest flower of the Great Tradition were Rudyard Kipling' (Alvarez 1965: 21).[3]

Critics of Polish romanticism accused the movement of mysticism, emotionalism, irrationality, fantasy and provincialism, and of placing the feeling of the collective above developing a social and individual sense of responsibility: although romanticism dominated Polish literature, painting and music, and clearly helped sustain national identity, it did not promote mature self-knowledge, but instead engendered a sense of frustration and legitimised a sense of alienation. Given that long years of exile were a major experience for Chopin, Mickiewicz, Norwid, Słowacki, Krasiński and a great many other Polish intellectuals and potential political leaders, perhaps this was inevitable. On the other hand, because the romantic tradition

Polish writers and tradition 53

defined itself through the experience of partition, which affected Poles, Jews, the ethnic minorities and relations between them, Polish romanticism, while socially conservative, was ethnically inclusive and allowed self-identification.

The failure of the Polish Uprisings in 1830, 1848 and 1863 and the revolution of 1905 – said by some to be the fourth Polish Uprising – were widely seen as a failure of the romantic mind-set and led to its antithesis in positivism. While romanticism was often guided by exilic views, positivism was a distinctly 'home-grown' development, designed to find a way of accommodating the occupying powers without actually collaborating. The movement looked to Comte and the English utilitarians, Bentham, Darwin, Spencer and Mill, for ideas about social, political and economic development. Within positivism, romanticism was viewed as an important strand of national literature, though 'fragmented and selective'. The positivists, residing in Poland rather than Paris, saw themselves as realists and regarded the romantics, many of whom were in exile, as hopelessly self-sacrificing and mistaken: not only that, but they felt the romantic messianism had led Poles into uprisings that stood no chance of success. They stressed that under political conditions that could not be successfully challenged, where opposition was a crime and censorship made criticism impossible, education, important practical social work and social improvement, coupled with a policy of conciliation with the Partitioning powers, was the only option. In its extreme form, followers of positivism wanted to avoid all contact with the occupying powers and construct an alternative, parallel state.

While the romantic writers generally had a favourable attitude towards multi-ethnicity – particularly towards Poland's Jews – positivists often favoured a policy of assimilation for the Jews and Polonisation for the other minorities. But the divide was not simple and it was possible to find writers who managed in varying degrees to combine aspects of both positivism and romanticism. The novelist, bookseller and publisher Eliza Orzeszkowa (1841–1910), often spoken of as a Nobel Prize contender, lived a life of semi-seclusion in Grodno but was watched closely by czarist spies because of her writing on 'social themes' and her strong sense of 'national duty'. In her novel *Nad Niemnem* (*On the Niemen*, 1888) she insisted on the survival of Polish identity, viewed a sense of belonging to a local community as of paramount importance, saw romantic notions of resistance to Russian rule as unproductive and felt that a precondition of independence had to be the strengthening of specifically Polish culture, mainly through education. In her Catholic spirituality and her unhappiness with the immorality modernism seemed to require, she stood slightly apart from the mainstream of positivism, but while she campaigned for Jewish rights, like most positivists she favoured assimilation.

Bolesław Prus (1874–1912) had been badly wounded and imprisoned by the tsarist authorities in the 1863 Uprising, so even though he became a noted positivist, his romantic credentials were impeccable. His novel *Anielka* (1880) criticised the vapid, spiritless life and politics of the *szlachta*,

54 Polish writers and tradition

and his novels *Faraon* (Pharaoh, 1896) and *Lalka* (Doll, 1890–96), though rooted in romanticism, constituted a decisive break with the idea of the poet as insurrectionary national leader. Prus observed Polish society – he wrote regular newspaper 'chronicles', which form a rich seam of observation on daily life in Warsaw (Prus 1956) – read Spencer and studied ancient Egypt in an effort to understand the nature and workings of 'the social organism', civic, social and national responsibility, the roots of political power and the process of nation-building. Like many positivists he believed the Jews in Poland should assimilate (Kott 1990: 222–35). Although many lost patience with his ideas of 'total artistic freedom' and interest in 'capitalist prosperity' under the protection of Tsarist Russia, he was often said to be the ideal positivist.

Henryk Sienkiewicz (1846–1916) was born of an impoverished *szlachta* family in Lithuania. In his *Trylogia* (*Trilogy*, 1884–8) of epic adventure novels dealing with seventeenth century Polish history, in *Krzyżacy* (*Teutonic Knights*, 1900), in the Biblical tale *Quo Vadis?* (*Where Now?* 1895) and the adventure story *W pustyni i w puszczy* (*In Desert and Wilderness*, 1912), Sienkiewicz continued the romantic tradition by inviting sympathy for the slaughtered, persecuted and conquered, and admiration for those who resisted. However, he also criticised romantic attitudes. In his story '*Latarnik*' (Lighthouse Keeper, 1876) a lighthouse keeper, an exiled Pole, rapt in memories of home as he reads romantic Polish literature, forgets to light the lamp and causes a shipwreck (Sienkiewicz 1931: 194–208).

The complex relationship between romantic and positivist world-views was certainly an issue for Joseph Conrad (Józef Teodor Konrad Nałęcz Korzeniowski, 1857–1924). On both maternal and paternal sides his family had *szlachta* roots. In 1861 Conrad's father, Apollo Korzeniowski (1820–69), a distinguished and revered poet and translator, conspired with the 'Mierosławski Reds' to found the Underground Warsaw City Committee: he was denounced by an informer, arrested with his wife and the four year old Joseph, his lands were forfeit and he was exiled. Two years later, in the 1863 Uprising, Apollo's older brother Hilary (d.1873) was arrested and exiled, and his younger brother Robert (d.1863) was killed. Conrad's Grandfather, Teodor Korzeniowski (d.1863), had served in the army of the Grand Duchy of Warsaw but died on his way to join the partisans.

Tadeusz Bobrowski (1829–94), Conrad's maternal uncle, regarded the Korzeniowskis as irresponsible romantics, seriously misguided, inclined to frivolous gesture and debt. He sided with the positivists, did not agree with the 1863 Uprising and posed his own family as a model of efficient management, good sense and balance. In 1900, Bobrowski's *Pamiętki* gave us a telling description of Conrad's father and the romantic scheme of things. According to Bobrowski, Apollo Korzeniowski had only a vague understanding of politics and an exceedingly soft heart, hence 'his great sympathy for the poor and oppressed' and that was why he 'thought he was a democrat'. But, Bobrowski said, 'these were only impulses of the heart and mind inherent in a member of a good family of the gentry; they were not truly democratic convictions'.

Polish writers and tradition   55

Bobrowski felt Korzeniowski's political and social ideas amounted to nothing more than 'a hazy inclination towards a republican form of state incorporating some equally hazy agglomeration of human rights as set out by the Constitution of the Third of May' (Bobrowski 1900: 362).[4]

However, the difference between Conrad's maternal and paternal lines was not as clear as Bobrowski liked to think, and several members of Bobrowski's own family held attitudes and opinions almost identical to those of the Korzeniowskis. Bobrowski's uncle Mikołaj (b.1782), like Conrad's paternal grandfather, had joined Napoleon's army to fight for Poland's freedom: he saw action at Leipzig and in the retreat from Moscow, worked his way up to the rank of captain with the title of *chevalier* and was awarded the *Virtuti Militari*, the highest Polish military honour. Bobrowski's brother Kazimierz (d.1868) was arrested and imprisoned at the start of the 1863 Uprising and that same year his near-sighted brother Stefan (d.1863), who was politically active in the 'Red Faction', was killed in a pistol duel with a member of the opposing 'White Faction' (Stape 2008: 9–15).

Issues of fidelity, patriotism and identity haunt Conrad's writings. In his earliest letter to his maternal grandmother, Conrad described himself as *polak-katolik* and *szlahcic* (Polish-Catholic and nobleman). Given the impact of the 1863 Uprising on his family life, Conrad probably found the atmosphere of his childhood joyless and rather stifling. Many of Conrad's stories rehearse clashes of loyalty, competing claims on identity and ideas about the role of work that grew out of his childhood experience and the inter-relation of the romantic and positivist traditions. Conrad insisted on the distractive and redeeming power of 'work', but he also paid tribute to the 'continuity of tradition', which he defined as 'the work of men' creating a 'simple ideal of conduct' (Conrad 1970: 201). It is no accident that Conrad, though he was well read in romantic literature, particularly Mickiewicz, was also very fond of the positivist writings of Bolesław Prus (Najder 1964: 24, 262).

Stefan Żeromski (1864–1925), perhaps the best known of Conrad's Polish contemporaries, supported Conrad's insistence on a non-didactic identification of social problems and saw this as a legitimate source of fiction: he championed Conrad as a Polish writer who had to leave partitioned Poland in order to write freely (Czapski 2018a: 54–5). This was in strong contrast to Eliza Orzeszkowa, who in 1899 wrote an article entitled 'The Emigration of Talent' in the magazine *Kraj* (Country) that portrayed Conrad as a traitor who had deserted Poland, 'jumped ship', a shameless careerist who wrote for bread, betraying his country and his language (Najder 1964: 22–3, 1983: 187–8). Conrad was aware that Orzeszkowa's comments referred to his novel *Lord Jim*, which had been published that year, telling the story of a very un-heroic man who abandoned his ship. Conrad wrote of Lord Jim, the man who 'jumped ship' in the novel, saying: 'He is romantic – romantic [...] And that is very bad – very bad... Very good, too'. In this Conrad expressed his ambiguity towards the contradictory demands of romanticism and positivism (Conrad 1968: 165).

56 Polish writers and tradition

It is interesting that towards the end of the nineteenth century, after the failure of the 1863 Uprising, as a great number of leaders and writers went into exile or were exiled, when industrialisation and the movement of population from rural to urban settings gathered pace and Jewish assimilation began to increase – developments that put *tradycja* under pressure – the word *ekstradycja* (ex-tradition, literally outside tradition) emerged (Jedlicki 1999).

At the end of the nineteenth century, the idea of *tradycja* inevitably became entangled in debates about Polish culture: modernity, change, improvement, civilisation, identity, religion, hierarchy, loyalty, duty, 'right conduct', industry, economics, citizenship, democracy, political opinion, freedom, sexual orientation and attitudes to minorities. As Eva Hoffman pointed out, culture – understood, in its broadest sense, as a system of meanings through which we perceive the world – 'is an undeniable, if pliant shaping force. Culture *does* mold our subcutaneous perceptions, as well our overt beliefs; it influences forms of feeling and even the very structure of desire. It sometimes also shapes ideology and political phenomena' (Hoffman 2004: 130–31).

The failure of the Polish Uprisings meant that by the end of the nineteenth century any lingering power the *szlachta* possessed had been broken and romanticism experienced a set-back. But, by a strange cultural metamorphosis, in the years that followed the elite values and orientation of the *szlachta* became much more general throughout Polish society. For both the *inteligencja* and the Polish peasantry, the *szlachta* represented an ideal lifestyle (Wat 1990: 2–3). The culture of the *szlachta* spread through the Polish speech-community to become a quest for democracy (but in a much wider sense than the *szlachta* had enjoyed it) and to include the idea of nation-building.

At the same time, the stubborn *szlachta* dislike of authority and their bristling independence, which had contributed to both the partition of Poland and the failure of the Uprisings, transmuted into a strong sense of Polish identity and the dream of independence. Poland was 'still not lost' because, by the end of the nineteenth century, increasing numbers who had previously been part of the vast featureless illiterate peasant *hołota* (rabble), the tiny *inteligencja* or the nascent middle class, now, as in Sienkiewicz's story 'Bartek the Conqueror' (Benecke 1915), felt themselves to be heirs to *szlachta* culture and saw themselves as Poles. Andrzej Walicki described the emerging mentality at the end of the nineteenth century as that of a 'working-class *szlachta*' (Gomułka & Polonsky 1990: 21–39).

1   Unlike Western Europe, the Polish *inteligencja* was often barely educated and typically not a part of a commercial middle class; it included not only the few who had professional qualifications bzsmen, and those who made a living from non-manual labour (writers, scholars, teachers, artists, clerks, civil servants) whether or not they had been formally educated. This was an economically very insecure group, yet by the end of the nineteenth century it had become central to national

Polish writers and tradition   57

identity and had begun to play a pivotal role in national politics. And yet, its importance derived from the crucial role it had played during the Partitions when, blocked from any other outlet, it engaged in 'the rule of souls' (Plach 2006: 11).For Poles, class consciousness and sense of national identity arrived simultaneously at the end of the nineteenth century and both operated to contradict and extend notions of tradition. As industry impacted on the rural economy, Polish peasants moved into the rapidly expanding cities of Poznań, Warsaw and Łódź. From the 1880s onwards it became increasingly apparent that Poles (mainly rural, peasant, poorly educated, usually illiterate, conservative and, apart from the Church, lacking in civic leadership) saw the promise of independence mainly as an opportunity to remain as they were, but as Poles. Inevitably they were unsettled by modernity: the traditional moral authority of the Church was challenged by democracy, proved hostile to bourgeois-liberal commercial values and did little to improve the lot of the peasants; though powerful, the growing feeling of national identity contributed little to economic progress but a great deal to resentment and a sense of victimhood.

2   By the end of the nineteenth century the Polish Left was split between the *Międzynarodowa Socjalno-Rewolucyjna Partia 'Proletariat'* (International Social Revolutionary Party 'Proletariat', 1882–1909) and the *Polska Partia Socjalistyczna* (Polish Socialist Party, PPS 1892–1948), both of whom believed that socialism and independence went hand in hand. The only other possibility on the Left was the *Socjaldemokracja Królestwa Polskiego i Litwy* (Social Democracy of the Kingdom of Poland and Lithuania, SDKPiL, 1893–1918), a party that felt independence could only be achieved after a successful revolution (Eve & Musson 1982: 129–61). For the *PPS* and most liberals, the existence of a Polish state meant the dominance of Polish language and culture and demands for loyalty from, and a tolerant suspicion of, the minorities (Jedlicki 1999).

Against this background, in the years 1890–1918 the movement known as Młoda Polska (Young Poland) developed. This was the start of the modernist movement in Poland and it incorporated several very different elements of literary style and tradition – decadence, neo-romanticism, symbolism, impressionism and art nouveau. Conrad's modernist contemporaries in Młoda Polska still found themselves pulled between romanticism and positivism as they sought to re-assess and revive their romantic heritage and at the same time to introduce West European cultural norms. While they recognised Mickiewicz's achievement, they found him rather preachy; Krasiński they found too conservative and shallow; only Wyspiański found favour. Their impulse was mainly liberal and they tended to emphasise literary judgement over political engagement or commitment. However, they were hampered by Poland's social structure, particularly by the low levels of literacy and by the tiny middle class.

58 Polish writers and tradition

These tensions were present, for example, in the writings of Stanisław Wyspiański (1869–1907), perhaps the most significant of the Młoda Polska writers. His play *Wesele* (The Wedding, 1901), which recalled an actual wedding between a poet and a village girl, explored the idea that Poland could somehow be made whole again by a union of intellectuals and peasants. In the play the Poet, in conversation with the Bride, defines Poland as her beating heart (Peterkiewicz & Singer 1970: 65–6). The hope that intellectuals will refresh themselves by immersing in rural tradition and the peasants will find a way to express their patriotism in this union is short-lived. The play ends by suggesting very powerfully that there is a kind of paralysis afflicting Polish society in the closing years of partition. In the final scene of the play the wedding guests hide the scythes and sabres they had planned to use in an uprising and instead move in a languid dance to the fiddle of the *Chochoł* (Strawman), whose music 'puts the soul to sleep', keeps them entranced and thus prevents them from achieving independence. The play ends with the admission that 'the golden horn' (the possibility of calling the populace to insurrection) has been lost: the *inteligencja* have failed to lead the peasants. The play is still a popular, ambiguous and important part of the Polish theatre repertoire.

While *Wesele* captures some of the challenges facing Polish identity, this way of thinking and writing did not satisfy everyone. Many criticised Młoda Polska for failing to keep pace with the revolutionary changes taking place throughout Europe and for divorcing cultural issues from everyday life and the impossibility of a political action: the poor still lacked jobs, the standard of education was appallingly low, and 'tradition, gentry prejudices, snobbery, dreams of the trappings of office' still dominated the life of the inteligencja (Jedlicki 1999: 182). Probably the worst that could be said of Młoda Polska was that it attempted to preserve a kind of naivety about what was needed to revive and maintain an independent Poland long after real innocence had been lost in the Uprisings (Mikoś 2006: 243). For many writers and readers, romanticism was still a substantial and demanding legacy, a kind of self-explanatory ethical norm that could not be contradicted and required no validation. Eva Hoffman later summed up the romantic tradition as embodying a much sought-after effect called *polot* (visionary, lofty, inspirational, soaring) and she listed the poetry of Mickiewicz, Polish cavalrymen and Chopin's A-major Polonaise as prime examples (Hoffman 1991: 71).

Stanisław Brzozowski (1878–1911) said the choice was still between seeing the writer as 'the soul of the nation' or the idea that the writer was part of 'building life in Poland', which meant 'the working class educating itself for autonomous work at the level of today's technology' (Mikoś 2006: 323). Brzozowski rejected romanticism in its entirety in an effort to blend modernism, Marxism and positivism in the creation of an individualist 'philosophy of labour'. He believed all national life would be dependent on 'labour' but still could only be understood through 'national tradition' and 'culture' (Kołakowski 1981: 215–39). In Brzozowski's most influential

Polish writers and tradition 59

book, *Legenda Młodej Polski: Studia o strukturze duszy kulturalnej* (*The Legend of Young Poland: Studies in the Structure of the Spirit of Culture*, 1909), he accused Młoda Polska of returning to romanticism, pseudo-mysticism, nationalism, provincialism, decadence, immaturity, narcissism and impotence.

Because the 'organic work' of the positivists often meant not only educational development and economic activity but a break from the *szlachta* idea of sovereignty and abandonment of conspiracy, romantics – particularly those in exile – often saw the positivists as sell-outs, collaborators and traitors. For the most part history has judged the positivists worthy but dull, but in their own way both traditions encouraged writers to see themselves as 'bard and tribune' and to 'place their talent at the service of the nation' (Kijowski 1983: 41). But while they did this in different ways, these traditions were not entirely separate: they vied with each other, flowed into each other, intertwined and argued, and there was movement between them. Both helped form the basis of what is often called 'Czarnolas literature', the classic works of Kochanowski and the Polish romantics, some of which Poles learned by heart.[5] However, it could be said the sanctification of romanticism over positivism hampered the 'crystallisation' of other intellectual currents. Jedlicki complained: 'In Poland one was hardly allowed to define oneself and one's own values against Mickiewicz; one could only annex him and ascribe him ideologically to oneself. It was therefore necessary to create a Mickiewicz who was a positivist, as well as one who was Catholic, socialist, conservative, nationalistic, mystical...' (Jedlicki 1999: 210).

The failure of the 1905 revolution hit what remained of Polish ambitions for independence very hard and the wave of pogroms that followed were a foretaste of the pressures that now lurked. In the restructuring of relationships and attitudes that followed, romanticism and positivism still cut across the left–right political divide. However, the Right began to gravitate towards *Stronnictwo Demokratyczno-Narodowe* (SDN, National Democratic Alliance) and the opinions of the Endecja movement.[6] At first, Endecja simply wanted an improved relationship with czarism, did not support armed struggle, saw Russia as a protector against Germany, was a supporter of free enterprise and burgeoning (but still very uneven) industrial capitalism, and offered no challenge to partition. At the time these ideas were not so very far from those of the positivists. As a response to 'Russification' and 'Kulturkampf', Endecja had at first seen the minorities as potential allies in the protection of the Polish language but, when the minorities failed to offer support in this, had moved away from the romantic view and had begun to favour forced assimilation. After 1905 Endecja shifted towards ethno-nationalism and was to shift much further with independence.

Polish independence

Although fighting in Western Europe ended on Armistice Day 1918, over the next three years Poland had to fight to establish its borders. As in the other

60   Polish writers and tradition

neighbouring new states to emerge from the collapse of the great empires, the Polish military tried to grab as much territory as it could before peace talks began. The Versailles Treaty (signed June 1919, effective from January 1920) recognised Poland's western border but left the eastern border undefined. What followed was war with Germany over the Poznań area, three Silesian uprisings, the Greater Poland Uprising, a series of Polish–Czech border clashes, the Polish–Ukrainian War, two Polish–Lithuanian Wars and the Polish–Soviet War. While Piłsudski's troops maintained discipline, others, including those of General Haller, often ran wild: most of the troops seemed to treat the *kresy*, with its intermingled populations, cultures, languages and religions and its fluid identification markers, as if it were enemy territory. In many of the key battles on the vast East-European plain, Polish cavalry played a major role.

Piłsudski dreamed of re-creating Poland *międzymorze* (between the seas), stretching from the Baltic to the Black Sea. This was the old Polish Commonwealth at its greatest size, including parts of Lithuania, Latvia, Estonia, Belarus, Ukraine, Hungary, Romania, Yugoslavia and Czechoslovakia. The central belief behind this federation of languages and nationalities was that Poles should dominate and take the political lead. However, this plan was not viewed favourably by anybody outside Poland and even within Poland did not find support from Endecja, which favoured Polonisation of minorities and a uniform Polish identity rather than a multi-cultural, multi-lingual federation.

By the Treaty of Riga in March 1921, Poland had not only proved it was nobody's puppet state but had alienated all its neighbours and drawn scathing criticism from French and British politicians. By 1922, when the violence slowly subsided, parts of Poland had been invaded several times and epidemics, starvation, deportation, atrocities, massacres, banditry, para-military actions and pogroms (Pińsk and Kijów, 1919) had become the norm, particularly in the *kresy*[7] (Böhler 2018: 157–86). From March 1919, the *Komunistyczna Partia Robotnicza Polski* (KPRP, Communist Party of Polish Workers, formed from a merger of SDKPiL and PPS in 1918) was an illegal organisation, but it organised a wave of strikes across Poland. KPRP believed Poland should remain a Russian province, did not support the creation of an independent Poland and sided with Lenin in the Polish–Soviet war of 1920 (Topolski 1986: 221–4).

The Poland that emerged after 1918 was not the old Commonwealth revived. Like the Commonwealth, independent Poland was mainly rural, multi-ethnic and multi-lingual, but partition had ensured it was not relaxed about this. The total population was about 31,915,900, but only sixty-eight percent were Polish, the other thirty-two percent were German (2.3 percent), Ukrainian (13.9 percent), Belarussian (3.1 percent), about 3.3 million Jews (about 8.7 percent) and there were also Russians, Lithuanians, Czechs and Slovaks. The dominant identity was Polish-speaking, Catholic and nationalist, but this majority was barely led, inexperienced, poorly educated and often illiterate, rural, parochial, massively suspicious of difference, surrounded by 'others' and increasingly intolerant.[8]

Polish writers and tradition 61

Poles rose unevenly to the challenge of independence. The collapse of the great empires that had held them in subjection was totally unexpected: it gifted the Poles with something longed for, fought for, but for which they were unprepared. In particular, independence proved to be a shock for the *inteligencja*. In effect, Polish society had been decapitated by the long years of partition, when the traditional political leadership, if it had not been arrested, executed, exiled or dispersed abroad, had retreated to distant country estates. Poland now comprised of three long-neglected, poverty-stricken regions from the edges of distant empires. The military, politicians, administrators, educators and creative *inteligencja* of the new Poland had to find a way to insert themselves into a notional country that had six currencies and three legal systems, a nascent and unintegrated industrial sector, a poor road and telephone network, no seaport and no unified railway – there was no train from Warsaw to Poznań. Politicians and administrators also had to find a way to govern a culture dominated by an illiterate peasantry that was determinedly *tutejszy* (local, literally 'here-ist', from *tu* meaning 'here') in its perceptions and which, for the most part, while it insisted on its Catholicism and Polishness, did not identify very strongly with the new state. The artist Józef Czapski (1896–1993), descended from the Polish *szlachta* and the aristocracy of Eastern Europe, who served in the Polish cavalry, recalled a long-suffering peasant soldier in the Polish–Soviet War of 1919–21, saying: 'All this for the motherfucking homeland'. The remark, he said, 'became common parlance' (Czapski 2018a: 16).

During partition every evil could be blamed elsewhere, but with independence Poles were forced into the realisation that their faults were their own. With independence the aim of the bulk of the population seems to have been to reap the benefits of the new state while remaining unchanged within a traditional Polish life. As they struggled to overcome the difference between their expectations of independence and the reality, with no agreed procedures about the content and style of government or even a way of deciding whether or not to move towards democracy, they experienced a kind of 'moral hangover': amid the sense of euphoria that followed independence, critics noted tendencies towards lying, indecency, cowardliness, a lack of sobricty and a general irresponsibility (Plach 2006: 77; Zamoyski 1987: 340).

In the years 1918–26, with over a hundred political parties, a weak presidency and a powerful *Sejm* (parliament), neither the parties of the Left nor Right could provide stable authority. No less than fourteen governments failed, and the hope that Poland might become a 'modern', liberal, cosmopolitan society began to fade. Gabriel Narutowicz, a leftist and Poland's first president, was accused of relying on the support of Jews and minorities, and a vicious campaign against him ended with his assassination by an Endecja supporter in 1922. A series of political assassinations followed.

Piłsudski, who had retired to his family estate after the assassination of Narutowicz, was shocked at the failure of Polish democracy, horrified by Endecja's ambition for Poland, determined to prevent them from forming

62 Polish writers and tradition

a government and equally determined to achieve political stability. In May 1926, after yet another government fell and the president turned to Endecja, Piłsudski led a march on Warsaw and, after a week of fighting, a military coup backed by the *Komunistyczna Partia Polski* (KPP, Communist Party of Poland)[9] and the unions and supported by many of the liberal *inteligencja* (including several writers) installed a military regime under the ageing Marshal Piłsudski. Piłsudski's regime was known as *Sanacja* (Cleansing), and harked back to the moral purity of the insurgents of 1863. He understood that an 'ethnically pure' Poland would be too weak and unstable to survive for long, and tried to find ways to align himself with the minorities, saying, for example, that it would probably be more effective to speak of the state, rather than the nation. The success of the Polish military in the border wars and in Piłsudski's coup transmuted martial valour – particularly the 'dashing' ethos of the cavalry – into a political virtue, but in government this was to prove a mixed blessing.

The coup split Poland not only into left and right, poor and rich, east and west, but into what novelist Maria Dąbrowska (1889–1965) called two 'Moral Nations'. One nation linked the idea of modernity with the resurrection of the Polish state, Polish ethnicity and Catholicism, felt there was a moral power in Polishness and the use of the Polish language, and feared that the socialists would turn the country into a Jewish Bolshevik federation. The other nation was rather more traditional, tolerant of Jews and minorities, secular, rather left-liberal, did not define Polish citizens by their religion or their language and feared that Endecja would rip up the constitution, dismiss Parliament and turn Poland into a fascist state.

Piłsudski's coup aimed to produce stability and played into the hands of the major landowners by representing their political interests and by favouring conservative tradition. But Piłsudski understood that Poland was neither the vast Polish Commonwealth of his dreams, nor the ethnically pure entity that Endecja craved. Piłsudski had flirted with socialism in his younger years. He had been leader and clandestine organiser of anti-Tsarist activities for the PPS and had been deported, arrested again, escaped, and robbed banks and trains to secure political funds. However, he had broken with PPS to form his own revolutionary socialist party, but later said he 'got off the streetcar of Socialism at the stop named Independence' (Piłsudski 1972). The Communist Party realised it had been mistaken in supporting him when, just after the coup, Piłsudski refused to amnesty thousands of political prisoners. After the coup the atmosphere changed rapidly and the national psyche began to shift. The poet Antoni Słonimski (1895–1976), a Jewish member of the Skamander group, wrote wistfully that 1918 had been a time when the words 'freedom', 'independence', 'Poland', 'communism' and 'revolution' had not signalled disillusion or failure (Słonimski 1926: 2).

Piłsudski was the product of a landed Polish–Lithuanian noble family from Wilno. In the *kresy* he had been brought up on the romantic classics (particularly Mickiewicz and Słowacki) and Sanacja was attached to the cult of the heroic leader. The regime supported the teaching of romantic

Polish writers and tradition   63

literature in schools, and in theory was committed to the idea of the broth-erhood of nations and the preservation of the multi-ethnic population inherited from the old Commonwealth. But in every sphere Sanacja lacked energy and vision: although it claimed to be interested in reform and renewal, Sanacja was a blank screen onto which all sections of society pro-jected their own interpretation of what this might mean. It became increas-ingly clear the regime was uncomfortable with change, had no intention of leading change and sought only to licence organisations that trumpeted modernity and reform. By destroying democracy, suppressing left-opposi-tion, installing a military regime and limiting the size of the ruling elite to the (mainly) military caste and the larger landowners, Piłsudski certainly bolstered a sense of Polish tradition, but he also inadvertently helped push Poland into a reaction against his regime, towards ethno-nationalism.

Opposing the unfocused and arbitrary Sanacja in a tame *Sejm* (parlia-ment) were the Peasant Party and the very focused and ambitious Endec-ja-inspired nationalist parties around SN, fed on the ideas of Roman Dmowski and operating in close alliance with the Catholic Church. After independence, Endecja rapidly evolved to see the minorities as rivals in reli-gion, competitors in business, unreliable pseudo-citizens and lurking ene-mies of the state. Endecja rejected the strand of romanticism that said a state could be built upon a shared historical experience and instead insisted on linguistic, ethnic and religious criteria for citizenship. For Endecja, the existence of the Polish state implied a dominant ethnicity and the exclusion of 'non-Polish' groups from the functioning of the state. Endecja looked for a homogenous Poland and posed the image of the 'pure', conservative, tra-ditional, Catholic Pole against the 'enemies' along its borders and the image of the 'Jews, Bolsheviks and Freemasons' who it said supported Piłsudski. An increasingly boorish SN railed against the Jews, opposed the legalisation of civil marriage and argued it was a Polish woman's Catholic and national duty to bring up her children to oppose the 'weakness' and liberality of Sanacja.

After a brief revival, rural Poland went into a steep decline. Land reform began but occurred at the same time as hyper-inflation and so made lit-tle difference to rural poverty. For much of the inter-war period, Polish currency was massively over-valued on the international exchange, making what little produce Poland could export very expensive. The integration of Poland's inherited railway systems and the construction of the new port in Gdynia were not completed until the late 1920s, but with the Wall Street Crash of 1929–33 the price of Poland's main exports – agricultural produce and lumber – declined massively and neither the railways nor the new port could mitigate this. Also, profits generated in Poland were not necessarily re-invested in Poland: roughly forty-five percent of Poland's industries were controlled by British, French, Belgian, German and US financial interests – eighty-nine percent of iron and steel, 56.8 percent of mining, 54.4 percent of chemicals – and they also had a representative on the Board of the Bank of Poland (Arnold & Żychowski 1965: 188).

64 Polish writers and tradition

Severe economic hardship rapidly became the norm. Fearing creeping communism, Endecja attacked attempts at protective labour legislation and loudly identified the minorities as problematic. Rising prices and falling wages led to decreasing production and factory closures; massive demonstrations became a regular occurrence across Poland. In July 1930, in response to attacks by Ukrainian nationalists who were resisting what they saw as enforced 'Polonisation', Polish cavalry and police 'pacified' the Ukrainians of Eastern Galicia: the damage to Polish–Ukrainian relations was enormous. In 1932 the government sent an infantry battalion, five hundred policemen and a squadron of planes to put down demonstrations in Berehy Dolne. That same year there was a wave of *Polskie strajki* (Polish strikes – factory occupations). Rural unrest continued until 1937. For all his military success, Piłsudski seemed unable to control Endecja. In 1932 he lost patience with opposition politicians and, claiming they were preparing a putsch, imprisoned them in the fortress at Brześć. Although public statements from all sides were radical, in general the political atmosphere was increasingly listless, self-serving, dizzyingly hedonistic and increasingly chauvinist; in the literary world utopianism, futurism, nihilism, catastrophism and all shades of communism lived side-by-side and interpenetrated each other. But the Great Depression worked relentlessly to transform what remained of the tolerant legacy of the old Commonwealth: the suspicious, defensive Polish identity that solidified around the Endecja movement in the mid 1930s was massively at odds with the minorities. In 1934 Ukrainian nationalists assassinated the Polish interior Minister and both Ukrainians and Byelorussians looked to the USSR for assistance. The large German minority of Silesia had never accepted inclusion in the Polish state and refused to acknowledge the border. In 1934 Sanacja repudiated the League of Nations Minorities Treaty, set up a camp at Bereza-Kartuszka and imprisoned a great many Polish and Ukrainian nationalists, along with Jews, communists, profiteers, oppositionists, minority leaders, communists and trade unionists. Understandably, as the regime became increasingly repressive, many began to feel it was operating for the benefit of the big landowners and that poverty and large-scale disturbances were to be Poland's permanent condition. It is probable that in the years 1929–37 about two million Polish citizens emigrated, mainly to the USA, Canada, Latin America, France, Holland and Belgium (Arnold & Żychowski 1965: 189).[10]

While Sanacja was reluctant to pass anti-Semitic laws, it was also reluctant to stand against popular opinion. After Piłsudski's death in 1935, power fell into the hands of President Mościcki, Foreign Minister Colonel Beck (an ex-legionnaire) and head of the military Marshal Śmigły-Rydz (sometimes Rydz-Śmigły, another ex-legionnaire). Śmigły-Rydz announced the formation of *Obóz Zjednoczenia Narodowego* (OZON, Camp of National Unity), an organisation designed to support the regime, but which fell into the hands of Boleslaw Piasecki and the *Obóz Narodowo-Radykalny-Falange* (ONR-Falange, Camp of National Radicals – Falange) and immediately became a noisy, violent, anti-Semitic rabble. Inspired by Mussolini's

Polish writers and tradition 65

Fascists, ONR had been formed in 1934 by members of the Endecja Youth Movement who felt that Endecja's anti-Semitism was not extreme enough.[11] However, Endecja, which had been moving steadily to the right, was unhappy at losing control, immediately banned ONR and absorbed much of its 'radical agenda' (Kunicki 2012: 25–6). Śmigły-Rydz then compounded his error by hinting he was thinking of a coup to install a fully totalitarian regime. Although the coup never materialised, the regime became increasingly authoritarian and bent to pressure from Endecja, which had begun to absorb the Falangist ambition of the radical ONR. Increasingly, politicians of the older generation felt set against the emerging young radicals. While the military regime was primarily concerned with maintaining its authority, Endecja renewed its push for a racially pure Poland – 'Poland for Poles'. Endecja particularly resented the Jews, whom they regarded as unwelcome strangers, and began organising Jewish benches in universities, large-scale boycotts, demonstrations and assaults.

Polish literary experience

Artistic responses to independence and to Sanacja varied considerably. After the Brześć affair, the regime bled liberal and left-wing support and was increasingly viewed as repressive and authoritarian, even by former supporters like novelist Maria Dąbrowska. Some elements of liberal opinion still clung to the vestigial promise of reform and rebirth. *Towarzystwo Odrodzenia Moralnego* (Society for Moral Rebirth) thought it imperative Sanacja should turn to artists, literati and theatre directors for ideas, and among the *inteligencja* there was a brief revival of interest in positivism. In spite of evidence to the contrary, the poet Kazimiera Iłłakowiczówna (1892–1983) believed in the hope offered by Piłsudski, continued as his personal secretary in spite of the Brześć affair and thought of herself not as a poet but as a 'civil servant working for her country' (Plach 2006: 51–7, 91).[12] The poet Julian Tuwim (1894–1953), a Jewish member of the Skamander group, revised his social contacts after the Brześć affair and put some distance between himself and the regime. On the other hand Tadeusz 'Boy' Żeleński (1874–1941), poet and pamphleteer, often judged to be the *infant terrible* of the Sanacja period, a supporter of sexual freedom, women's rights, abortion on demand and a staunch opponent of the Church, remained a Piłsudski supporter (Plach 2006: 72, 140).

Interwoven with the ongoing debate about the rival traditions of romanticism and positivism, and modifying it in various ways, there were now debates about the relationship to the West, the differences between Poland and the West and what Poles understood by 'Europe'. In general debate they are split into *narodowcy* (nationalists) and *zachodniofile* (Westernophiles), both intent on their definition of Polishness and their vision of the future. Even if the bulk of the writing community were opposed to the regime and did not support Endecja, they shared very little fellow feeling, cooperation or organisation. Some were later inclined to dismiss Endecja as a

66   Polish writers and tradition

bunch of 'simplistic obscurantists' and saw the inter-war years simply as 'a wasted opportunity' (Tyrmand 2014: 289). Czapski, for example, observed that the 'creative force' of Polish national identity had become 'a force for isolating oneself and pushing others away', and in dealing with other cultures a 'force of appropriation' had become a 'force of Puritan exclusivity' (Czapski 2018a: 236). Others felt it was a time of discovery and excitement. In spite of political uncertainty, these years saw an astonishing wave of creativity in philosophy, mathematics, anthropology, linguistics, economics, visual arts, music and architecture (Lesnikowski 1996). Literary life – largely confined to the towns and cities, often showing itself as a search for novelty in contesting the two main literary traditions of romanticism and positivism – flourished.

The Skamander movement, founded in 1918, was named after the river Skamander (modern Turkish Karamenderes), which, according to the *Iliad*, was where the Trojan War had been fought. Many of the movement's adherents at first supported Piłsudski and, while they followed literary developments in Russia, France, Italy and Czechoslovakia, sought to re-focus Polish literature on 'normality' after its long diversion into supporting the national cause during the Partitions. They constituted a kind of neo-romanticism, but sought to break the link between Polish history and Polish poetry and to insist on cosmopolitanism rather than nationalism. For the most part they did not share the general feeling of optimism that followed independence.

The leading Skamander poets Leopold Staff (1878–1957) and Bolesław Leśmian (1877–1937) had little interest in national matters and sought to de-politicise and de-sarmatise poetry.[13] However, other members of the group – Julian Tuwim, Antoni Słonimski, Jarosław Iwaszkiewicz (1894–1980) and Jan Lechoń (1899–1956) – were more engaged. Lechoń, one of the founders of the movement, in his controversial poem 'Herostrates' from the collection *Karmazynowy Poemat* (*Crimson Poem*, 1920), criticised what he saw as a Polish tendency to dwell on the injuries of the past. He urged resistance to any form of special pleading for national demands, saying: 'And in spring, let me see spring – not Poland' (Lechoń 2007). The Skamandrites saw themselves as liberal, leftist cosmopolitans, continuing Polish literary traditions in terms of literary forms, but with their own choice of subject matter: avant-garde without breaking with the continuities of the past. In general, they avoided semi-mythological Polish heroes to concentrate on themes about daily life, the inner being and ordinary people (Shore 2006: 22–4; Wat 1999: 6).

Czesław Miłosz (1911–2004), a young Skamandrite from the Lithuanian area of Poland, struggled with sexual and poetic experimentation under the combined burdens of military dictatorship; the lure of socialism and the threat of Bolshevism; the remnants of gentry-culture; and the traditional, inherited interpretation of Mickiewicz, as well as with the ideology of Endecja in the multi-ethnic *kresy*. For him independence was a 'sad period full of dark forebodings'. He noted that after independence many positivists, who if they were not on the Left did not think of themselves as on the

Polish writers and tradition 67

Right, who opposed revolution of any kind, defended the underdog and embraced progressive policies, now found their moral position increasingly compromised by political proximity to Endecja (Miłosz 1983: 286).

Juliusz Kaden-Bandrowski (1885–1944) had been a member of Piłsudski's Legions in World War 1, a staunch supporter of Piłsudski's coup, and afterwards the chief spokesman for 'official literature'. In his novel *General Barcz* (*General Barcz*, 1923), he showed the brutal internal struggles for control that took place after independence and later he documented the developing psyche of the newly independent Poland. His three-volume novel *Czarne skrzydla* (*Black Wings*, 1928–33), set in Zagłębie Dąbrowskie (Dąbrowa Basin) in the Silesian coalfield, was a gloomy flagellation of foreign capital, Polish management and socialist politicians, but was sympathetic to the miners. Even so, while his analysis was pointed and critical, he felt increasingly isolated and imprisoned by his loyalties.

Although there were futurists in Kraków and Warsaw, there was no substantial futurist movement in Poland. Futurism fed into literature, theatre and the visual arts, but writers associated with futurism were not taken very seriously. Probably most writers intuited that futurism opposed and dissolved the emerging identity of independent Poland, particularly cutting writers off from the tradition, history, literary culture and language that gave them their bearings (Adamczyk-Garbowska et al. 2016: 286–7). The futurists dismissed the Skamandrites as traditional because they had a neo-romantic programme of action. The Skamandrites (with the exception of Miłosz) regarded the futurists – particularly Aleksander Wat (1900–1967) and Bruno Jasieński (1903–38) – as 'programo-phobic barbarians' whose work led away from Polish literary tradition but only as far as anarchy and decadence. That it might also lead to communism did not at first seem likely, but after flirting with Italian futurism both Wat and Jasieński found its connection to fascism unacceptable and moved steadily leftwards.

While historical novels by Zofia Kossak-Szczucka (1889–1968) and Jarosław Iwaszkiewicz were popular, other issues now presented themselves as subjects for literature. By exploring identity and gender issues, the novelists Pola Gojawiczyńska (1896–1963), Maria Dąbrowska (1889–1965) and Maria Kuncewiczowa (1885–1989) struggled to break free of the stifling militarism and the male-dominated ideology of nationalism by challenging the traditionally assigned role of the *Matka-Polka* (Mother-Pole). Zofia Nałkowska (1884–1954), dismissed by some as a 'bluestocking', was an outspoken advocate of women's rights. Nałkowska was married to Jan Jur-Gorczechowski, a long-term associate of Piłsudski, a conspirator for PPS who had served time in prison for insurrectionary activities under the Russians and Austrians, and who with the struggles for independence rose to become commander of the Warsaw City Militia, director of the State Police, director of the Security Department at the Interior Ministry and then in the years 1922–7 became commander of a gendarmerie division in Grodno. Their marriage lasted from 1922 until 1929, but her proximity to power in independent Poland was a unique vantage point to observe the ethos of the

68 Polish writers and tradition

new state, the abandonment of socialist sympathies, the rise of Endecja and the position of women.

In *Romans Teresa Hennert* (1923, *The Romance of Teresa Hennert*) Nałkowska referred to partition as 'that other life', saying it was 'terribly unreal'. But in her portrayal of independence, against a background of war in the *kresy* and revolution in Russia, she showed the status-obsessed, frivolous, claustrophobic life of officials and their families in Warsaw, along with the corruption, pompous intrigues and deceptions of the military. She found the new state – particularly the limited role allowed to women – something of a disappointment. Amid the parties, entertainments and romantic manoeuvring, she showed independence as a restoration of Poland to 'Europe', explicitly contrasting even dancing style in Poland with that of 'Europe'. One of her characters says the idea of independence has 'fallen apart and been horribly crushed by post-war reality' and a young lieutenant remarks that Poland, which had until recently suffered the shackles of captivity, was now subjecting peoples on its eastern borders to the same treatment: 'Such is Poland. One shouldn't have expected anything different' (Nałkowska 2014a: 76, 98).

Nałkowska's novel *Choucas* (1926/7), set in a sanatorium in the Swiss Alps, explored the opinion of the assembled patients, who were drawn from all over Europe. Their various nationalisms are shown to be nothing more than fearful paranoia based on prejudiced stereotypes, and Nałkowska's suggestion is that nationalism in all its varieties is simply another kind of illness. She refers several times to the Irish War of Independence (1919–21), the Irish Civil War (1922–3) and the Armenian massacres (1915–17): the line, repeated several times, that 'one nation should not oppress another' is an ironic motif arising from these conflicts but also reflecting on Sanacja's attempts to forcibly Polonise the minorities (Nałkowska 2014b).

In Nałkowska's novel *Granica* (1935, *Boundary*) she took this idea further by providing an analysis of the progressive and socialist Polish *inteligencja* who, after 1918, gradually compromised their ideas about independence, allowed themselves to be side-lined and ignored by the prevailing national identity, and became complacent about the intolerant, hierarchical opinions of the right-wing. There are a great many references in the novel to boundaries and barriers, particularly social and sexual, but also those of Poland's disputed borders. There are also several ambiguous passages in the novel where it is not clear whether she is discussing personal or national independence. Although there is talk of land reform, breaking up the great estates, modernising farming methods and developing industry, Nałkowska shows the stifling effect traditional rural Poland had on Zenon, a budding intellectual returning from study in France. In France he felt 'everything was still possible, everything was beginning again from the start' in independent Poland. But in Poland he feels the 'deliberations in Geneva, pacifism, the Pan-Europa Movement appeared like menacing signs of modernity'.

In *Granica*, Zenon comes to dismiss his own ideas for change and improvement, developed by study and residence abroad, as 'exotic' and 'fanciful'.

He feels 'the culture of the west' is 'finished and petrified in every detail', that the 'scraps of the old postulates of liberty, equality and fraternity [have] fallen away'. The boundary of his moral resistance, 'the ultimate boundary of opposition', is 'moving imperceptibly farther and farther away'; he drifts into editing a local newspaper rather lackadaisically, and through his social connection to 'the best social circles' takes up hunting and finds himself appointed (without election) as mayor. He also starts unsatisfactory and overlapping affairs with two women, neither of whom is willing to criticise him simply because he is a man and that is how men behave (Nałkowska 2016: 39, 41, 83, 106, 195).

Nałkowska was famous for addressing the 1907 Polish Congress of Women on the subject of sexual equality, 'double standards', and a woman's 'right to a whole life'. She had specifically challenged attitudes to eroticism as part of the structure of 'morality' determined solely by a male hierarchy of values. She wanted to encourage a 'rational, even intellectual, approach to eroticism' in the hope that this would 'allow a consideration of eroticism in conjunction with other aspects of the life of the human community'. She was certain that eroticism was not a private, individual matter, but had 'ramifications in all areas of human life'. She said it was not possible to separate eroticism from other aspects of life 'through contemptuous disparagement in the name of morality, discretion, or even by demoting it in the hierarchy of subjects worthy of intellectual attention: it is not possible to isolate it by prudery or relegate it to science just because of its purely biological dimension' (Nałkowska 1932: 7). Her comment seemed designed to upset the traditional moralists of the Church. Her view was that without a fundamental revision of sexual roles, changes in the way women were treated and the opportunities open to them, there was little point to the masculine preoccupations of war, revolution or (it is hard to avoid the implication) the struggle for the restoration of the Polish state. For her there could be no national independence without women's independence.

Jarosław Iwaszkiewicz, who came from a *szlachta* family, suggested in his story 'The Wilko Girls' (1932) that independence, particularly in rural Poland, brought no great change and was a case of 'not doing anything special', 'just living, like everyone else'. But Iwaszkiewicz noted that independence brought with it a growing awareness that Poland was not like 'Europe'. In his story 'The Birch Grove' (1932) he repeatedly contrasted 'pictures of Europe' – the grand pianos, 'European tunes', good roads, hotels, sanatoria, the mountains and Calvinist correctness of Switzerland – with the flat landscape, endless forests, sandy roads, tuberculosis, promiscuity, folk tunes and accordions of rural, Catholic Poland (Iwaszkiewicz 2002: 21, 32).

The novelist Stefan Żeromski (1864–1925), who had been engaged with the cause of Poland for most of his life and many of whose heroes had been devoted to the idea of Polish independence, had at first plunged himself into journalistic work in support of the new republic. Poland showered him with honours, but he soon became disillusioned and began to feel little real social or political progress was being made. In his last novel *Przedwiośnie*

70   Polish writers and tradition

(1924, *The Coming Spring*) he observed the new Poland with a very critical eye, noting a lack of civic dynamism, growth of crime, fragility of social cohesion, patriotic complacency of the bureaucracy, elitist delusion of the military, self-satisfaction of the Warsaw middle class and the overwhelming poverty to be seen everywhere. He saw no great promise in the Russian Revolution and, while he had little hope for home-grown socialism, he felt this was probably the only way forward for Poland. Endecja accused him of being an apologist for revolution and terrorism and of holding 'un-Polish opinions' (Żeromski 2007). Looking back on Żeromski's life and work, Czapski commented: 'We have two traditions in Polish literature regarding treatment of historical themes. One serves the interests of national megalomania, and the other is the bitter tradition of reckonings, the tradition of Żeromski' (Kostrzewa 1990: 54).

Bruno Schulz (1892–1942), Stanisław Ignacy Witkiewicz (1885–1939) and Witold Gombrowicz (1904–69) were the founders of modernist prose in Poland; they were also the three 'bad boys' of the period. Their works hardly fit any established category of literature and for the most part they had little hope for the future of civilisation or humanity. As far as possible they turned their back on traditional national themes, shrugged off their roles as guardians of the nation's spiritual history and shifted the argument about the 'reality' of Polish identity towards grotesque, idiosyncratic, anarchic, surreal, satirical fantasy and overt criticism.

Gombrowicz, the longest lived of this trio of 'wild cards', was another *szlachta* descendant, an anti-clerical atheist from childhood, a provocateur and determined avant-garde novelist. He left Poland in 1939 as Cultural Envoy to the Polish community in Argentina but was stranded there by the outbreak of war. Although the publication of his writing was delayed for many years by exile, nevertheless his engagement with Polish literature – particularly that of the interwar period – remained intense. He pondered his relationship to literary tradition and, perhaps because of his long stay abroad, appreciated the Italian saying 'traduttore, traditore' (translator, traitor: to translate is to betray). In his novels *Ferdydurke* (1937) and *Pornografia* (1960) he railed against the authority of the 'great aunts' of Polish literature, and in his diaries he accused Poland of 'infantilism'. Instead of the vulgar word *dupa* (arse), Gombrowicz often used the more polite *pupa* (botty or bum) and the reflexive verb *upupiać się* (literally to bottify or bumify oneself) as a 'keyword' to indicate what he considered to be infantile opinion or less than adult judgement.

Witkiewicz had an electrifying and divisive impact on Polish literature, literary theory, painting, theatre and philosophy. In his vast surreal, absurdist, anti-utopian, catastrophist novel *Nienasycenie* (1932, *Insatiability*), he showed Poland ruled by a dictator known as Kocmołuchowicz (dirty face, almost certainly a reference to Piłsudski's enormous moustache). Europe is menaced by an oriental pill that saps the will to resist and, as a consequence, is in thrall to communism. Meanwhile the Chinese Army, driven by faith in the ideologist Murti-Bing, has already conquered Russia and is

Polish writers and tradition 71

approaching the Polish border. He dared to satirise the Church, intellectuals, Marxism, patriotism and the peculiar schizophrenia engendered by the 'hope' of nationalism, believing everything independent Poland put its trust in was, by definition, primitive, retrograde and outdated.

Inter-war Poland's steady move to the right solidified the very particular national identity, moral code, poetic tradition and political loyalty that Zbigniew Herbert (1924–98) later came to insist on. Herbert was to say: 'I was born and raised in the Second Polish Republic. For me, those twenty years are a yardstick with which I measure all that happened later, and not only matters of honor or duels'. His reference to duelling was not casual: duelling was a central part of the traditional code of honour that Herbert felt he had inherited. He claimed to have duelled twice in his youth (once over a woman he had never met), but insisted he could no longer duel with his contemporaries because according to the duelling code they did not come from a sufficiently 'honorable background' (Poppek & Gelberg 1994).

Joseph Conrad had written of duelling and the Polish military caste's obsession with 'the code' in the Napoleonic era (Conrad 1908). Duelling had been codified by Władysław Boziewicz (1886–1946) in *Polski kodex honorowy* (1919, *The Polish Code of Honour*).[14] The first edition had been reviewed unfavourably by Tadeusz 'Boy' Żeleński, who felt that only the most retrograde Poles still clung to this tradition. With independence and the elevation of the military, Poland was again beset by an outbreak of duelling. In his story 'The Chief Culprit' (1936), the futurist Jasieński caught the atmosphere this code engendered: 'Smiling arrogantly braided officers would saunter through the streets, striking the pavements with the dazzling scabbards of their long sabers that trailed behind them like trains'. Later in Jasieński's story the protagonist returns home unexpectedly to find 'a long saber in the hallway', his wife in the bedroom and 'a thickset officer, buttoning up his white summer uniform and adjusting his multi-strapped harness'. The officer expressed his readiness to 'give satisfaction', patted his holster, picked up his sabre and 'left the room in no particular hurry' (Jasieński 2014: 133–4).

Looking back over the period, Miłosz observed: 'Tradition, which speaks with redoubled power during a period of convalescence, imposes its own formulas, its own language' (Miłosz 1996: 85). The military saw itself as Poland's saviour, emphasised its role as protecting insurrectionary tradition, defended its status and kept democracy at bay. By 1939 Piłsudski's ex-legionnaires and Poland's military leadership had come to believe the slogan 'Polska – to My' (Poland – That's Us). Inevitably, we have to wonder how the Polish officer corps could become so boorish and so snooty. The answer is not that these men came from *szlachta* backgrounds, but that they came from relatively humble origins but aped and parodied *szlachta* behaviour and values – the very values that had brought about partition in the first place. With independence and the demise of democracy, military life and the sacred task of protecting Poland gave these people status by putting them in

72   Polish writers and tradition

line of descent from their insurrectionary ancestors (McGilvray 2013: 26). But this cherished notion hid the reality that their social status was illusory, their political power was temporary and the military edifice was unstable.

Polish-Jewish literary experience

Harold B. Segal wrote: 'Polish literature is a literature of Jewish experience: indeed it is the greatest European literature of Jewish experience' (Segal 1996: xi). This may at first appear to be a strange claim, especially given the often disturbing nature of Polish–Jewish relations. Historically, the cultural and linguistic autonomy of the Jews in Poland had a downside in that over time it impeded integration. For most of their thousand-year history in Poland Jews had spoken Yiddish, and while many lived in *shtetls* (small rural Jewish settlements), the bulk of the Jewish population lived in towns and cities. For the most part Poles and Jews lived parallel lives, their paths rarely crossed and the two societies did not mingle: they were strangers to each other. However, after about 1860 reform-oriented families like the Słonimskis, Toeplitzs and the Natansons began to assimilate and to play a significant role in Polish culture. As part of a response to positivism and the increasing Polonisation of the Jewish *inteligencja* in Austrian Galicia, other families lower down the social scale also began to see advantage in assimilation. At about the same time, rural Jews also began to migrate to the cities and the pain and uncertainty of the move was recorded in the Polish writings of Maurycy Szymel (1903–42), Stefan Pomer (1905–41?) and Czesława Endelmanowa-Rosenblattowa (b.1879/81) (www.yivoency-clopedia.org/article.aspx/Polish_Literature).

According to the 1931 census, forty-two percent of Poland's Jews were engaged in industry, mining and crafts; thirty-six percent were involved in trade; about three quarters lived in towns and cities; and about a third lived in the *kresy* (Fuks et al. 1982: 32). In an urban environment Jews were usually involved in workshop crafts – particularly handicrafts, shoe-making, leather-work, tailoring and textiles. Towards the end of the nineteenth century some Jews also began to enter politics, the unions, the teaching, legal and medical professions, bookselling and publishing. Although they were barred from many factories and banned from entry to the professions after 1937, they were a growing part of the industrial working class of Łódź, Poznań, Warsaw and numerous small towns. A small minority also began to enter the entrepreneurial class – industrial and commercial, great and small. Although Jewish finance had been massively important in the nineteenth century, by independence only a few Jewish banking enterprises survived.[15] Though they could hardly compete with the bigger state-backed Polish banks, their role as bankers, financiers and money-lenders – seen as financing competition for Polish enterprises – caused enormous resentment (Polonsky 1993; Sandauer 2005: 20).

In the 1860s Adolf Jakub Cohn (1843–1906) had announced a project to 'propagate Polish-Israelite literature'. Like many others he dreamed of

Polish writers and tradition 73

inclusion and integration, and hoped that by learning Polish the Jewish community would build a bridge into Polish life (Prokop-Janiec 2003: 3). While Cohn's project failed to materialise, integration, assimilation and the use of the Polish language grew considerably, to peak in the 1870s and 1880s. Up to this point Polish-Jewish literary life, such as it was, had centred on the weekly magazine *Izrealita*. In the years leading up to the turn of the century writing in Yiddish and Hebrew achieved something of a renaissance, with new journals, novels, poetry and translations from the Polish classics. However, in the inter-war years the Jewish literary scene developed rapidly, if unevenly, in newspapers and journals. While Polish journals rarely responded to material in Polish-Jewish magazines, a growing number of Yiddish language literary magazines began to respond to publications in Polish (Adamczyk-Garbowska 2016: 79–84, 153, 234–5). It also became increasingly common to find Yiddish novels and stories peppered with Polish phrases and transliterations, and Polish-Jewish novels peppered with Yiddish words followed by a Polish translation (Prokop-Janiec 2003: 50). As Deutscher was to point out, Jewish themes entered Polish literature, even if they sounded quite 'exotic and esoteric – perhaps even completely unintelligible' – long before they made an appearance in Russian literature (Deutscher 1981: 55).

In the interwar years the cultural influence of the *szlachta* lingered and, as the institutions of the new Polish state developed, the middle class grew and the civil service expanded, Polish language and identity acquired prestige. A group of Polish-Jewish writers began to emerge. In 1931 the Sejm passed a law against all forms of discrimination on the grounds of race, religion and nationality and around 1933 the concept of Polish-Jewish writers burst onto the Polish literary scene. Up to 1901, although there had been a number of Jewish writers in Hebrew, Yiddish, Russian and German, there had been almost no significant Jewish contribution to Polish literary culture. I.L. Peretz (1851–1915) and Sholem Asch (1880–1957) published successfully, and Israel Joshua Singer (1893–1944) and Isaac Bashevis Singer (1902–91) both began to publish in these years, but they all wrote in Yiddish. Their work appealed to the more conservative, traditional Jewish readership who, even if the themes of the novels they read were modern, preferred them mediated through a language in which they felt comfortable (Prokop-Janiec 2003: 7). However, in the early 1930s Polish-Jewish newspapers and literary magazines sprang up in Kraków, Lwów and Warsaw – among them *Nasza Opinia* (Our Opinion), *Chwila* (Moment), *Nowy Dziennik* (New Daily), *Nasz Przegląd* (Our Review), *Nowy Głos* (New Voice) and *Miesęcznik Żydowska* (Jewish Monthly). Young writers like Isaak Deutscher (1907–67) often submitted their work to several of these magazines. Increasingly in the mid and late 1930s, Polish-Jewish writers began to turn away from journals and to seek publication of novels and collections of short stories.

After independence rural Poland was a backward province of its former self, not even a distant part of empire, determinedly modern but at the same time still medieval in its anti-Semitism and increasingly uncomfortable

74 Polish writers and tradition

about its other minorities. Jewish merchants and traders had often been involved in local markets and distant sources – in Russia, Turkey, Greece and the north shore of the Black Sea. For them Russian and German had been the preferred languages simply because they gave access to a very wide area for commerce: the Polish language was the narrower choice not only in terms of trade but also in terms of cultural horizons. For most people language was identity and for many Jews assimilation was a leap into the unknown, the exchange of a fully formed and ancient tradition for another tradition that was not so ancient but fully formed. Changing language, culture and identity meant abandoning something well known and established, a diminution or dilution, and could be characterised as a kind of treachery. But even at its height, assimilation was not a simple process (Polonsky & Adamczyk-Garbowska 2001: ix–xlvii).

While Polish was becoming the language of social advancement and the route to a wider culture, these goals could usually only be achieved by abandoning religious, personal and family traditions to adopt national or supranational ideals, the dominant ideology, a new set of social relations and traditions and perhaps even a new identity. And even then the attempt might fail.[16] Julian Stryjkowski (1905–96) said the prevailing opinion among Poles and Jews was that 'a Jew always remains a Jew, even if he gets baptised' (Stryjkowski 1972: 193). Michał Głowiński (b.1934) said that although many Jews assimilated, this did not make them fully Polish in the traditional sense because most were indifferent to religion in any form and did not convert to Catholicism (Głowiński 2005: 130). Isaac Deutscher pointed out that, unlike Poles who found themselves outside tradition, the Jewish heretic who transcended Jewry to assimilate nevertheless still belonged (however distantly) to Jewish tradition (Deutscher 1981: 26). Even so, there were tensions between assimilated and orthodox Jews, tradition and modernity, life in the *shtetl* and life in the towns.

After about 1902, as Polish nationalism grew, assimilation began to slow. Even so, while the new Polish state was building itself, Jewish writers sought rationality in progress and modernity and felt socialism was still a promising prospect. In this changing and challenging situation, some of the most influential Jewish literary talents of the time – Bruno Jasieński, Aleksander Wat, Bolesław Leśmian (1877–1937), Julian Tuwim and Bruno Schultz, among many others – identified very strongly with Polish avant-garde literary culture. Słonimski, for example, a rationalist–pacifist, despaired of the future for Polish liberals, who he said were threatened at home by chauvinist nationalists, by communism from the east and Nazism from the west. Nevertheless, he maintained an interest in romanticism, kept pictures of Adam Mickiewicz and Stefan Żeromski on his desk alongside a photograph of Marshal Piłsudski, and until the Brześć affair openly socialised with leading members of Sanacja.

Writing in the early 1930s, Roman Brandstaetter (1906–87), a Zionist and orthodox supporter of Hebrew writing, acknowledged that many Jewish writers knew 'Czarnolas' literature very well.[17] He also acknowledged

Polish writers and tradition 75

that 'a kind of Polish-Jewish writer is slowly evolving who is unassimilated nationally and culturally, who sings in the Polish tongue his Hebrew yearning for the land of his fathers and who completely expresses in his works [...] the specific Jewish soul'. However, he saw the acquisition of Polish culture as a flaw, and felt that what some saw as a 'connection' to Polish life was actually a growing 'dependence'. Brandstaetter regarded Polish-Jewish literature as a 'necessary cultural interference', important to a tiny minority, but largely ignored by both Poles and Jews, and which would eventually be rendered irrelevant by the rise of a Hebrew national culture.

Nevertheless, in his poetry, Brandstaetter often revealed his own knowledge of, and attachment to, 'Czarnolas' literature (Prokop-Janiec 2003: 4, 27–8, 60–61). And he was not alone in his appreciation of Polish literature. Isaac Deutscher was familiar with the works of Mickiewicz, Żeromski, Orzeszkowa and Maria Konopnicka (1842–1910) (Deutscher 1981: 20, 55, 95). The revolutionary Hersh Mendel (1890/93–1968/9) was familiar with the works of Mickiewicz, Słowacki, Żeromski, Orzeszkowa and Konopnicka (Mendel 1989: 63, 100). Calel Perechodnik (1916–44), who became a ghetto policeman in Otwock, quoted from Kochanowski, Mickiewicz and Słowacki (Perechodnik 1996: 113, 153, 169). Perechodnik and his brother belonged to Bejtar – a 'Zionist organization that propagated the idea of creating an independent Jewish state in Palestine'. But this, he added, 'did not interfere at all with my feelings as a good patriotic Pole'.[18] He 'adored Polish poetry, particularly that dating from the loss of independence – and especially of Mickiewicz'. He said the reason this literature 'really spoke to my heart' was that he connected it with the history of the Israelites: 'I assumed that Poles, so long oppressed by their enemies, would understand Jews, have compassion for us, and help in whatever way they could'. He saw no contradiction in being a Zionist and a Polish citizen (Perechodnik 1996: xxii).

There seems to have been a kind of growing congruence between Polish and Polish-Jewish writers. By the mid 1930s, as the possibility grew that Poland might be absorbed by Germany or the USSR, there was a darkening of tone in poetry with nocturnes and elegies, and the recognition that humanity faced a common threat from nationalism in its varying forms. In Yiddish writing there was a conservative movement to preserve tradition, a condemnation of life in large towns, which was often seen as threatening tradition, and a desire to return to the simple traditional life of the *shtetl*. This was matched in Polish by a conservative and often sentimental regard for traditional village life, lamentation at the unsettling effects of modernity and a determined provincialism. The neo-romantic idea of a wedding between intellectuals and villagers was matched in Jewish writing by the romantic idea of the *halutz* (volunteer) working the land in Palestine (Prokop-Janiec 2003: 227–9).

The dilemma of Polish-Jewish writers was rehearsed repeatedly in the pages of the influential, liberal, assimilationist journal *Wiadomosci Literacki* (*Literary News*). In general Polish-Jewish writers sought a wide and

76   Polish writers and tradition

progressive urban readership, so while some chose to interpret Jewish culture for Poles or to sing of their 'Hebrew yearning', they realised that Jewish themes often cut them off from potential Polish readers. These writers felt they could function effectively only in a 'non-Jewish' language and yet felt responsible for shaping a modern Jewish culture. Consequently, many chose to explore Polish topics, but within that the problem of Jewish identity was often a central if slightly hidden concern. The main exception to this was Słonimski, who had been brought up as a Catholic, identified fully with Polish culture and felt free to criticise Jews.

While many Polish-Jewish writers refused to allow themselves to be defined and boxed-in by ancient problems, Endecja saw the massive and influential Jewish engagement with Polish culture as an invasion and, in a thinly disguised racial dismissal, the nationalists often charged Jewish writers in Polish with a lack of tradition. Sandauer recalled a lecture in which a critic said Tuwim might be a good poet, but his work was 'not Polish in spirit'. To this Sandauer remarked the critic clearly had not realised that 'non-Polishness of genius' could enrich Polishness: 'Blessed are writers as "non-Polish" as Tuwim and Schultz, of whom it can be said that they had in them elements not yet witnessed in our culture' (Sandauer 2005: 27). Tuwim, though born into an assimilated family, came to feel he had been rejected by Poland and that assimilation had failed him. He nevertheless insisted he had found a home in poetry and the Polish language.

Polish-Jewish writers as a group had a tendency towards the avant-garde in art and the revolutionary in politics, and as such they were something of a challenge to Polish literary tradition (Segal 1996: xi–xiii). Sandauer surmised that 'an individual who has torn himself from his native tradition and has not yet developed strong roots in another one tends to be anti-conservative. He is likely to support revolutionary movements because they promise him equal rights in the new society'. He felt this explained large-scale Jewish participation in the October revolution and why he, along with Julian Stryjkowski (1905–96), Adolf Rudnicki (1912–90), Stanisław Wygodzki (1907–91), Adam Ważyk (1905–82), Kazimierz Brandys (1916–2000) and Aleksander Wat, among others, became communists or fellow travellers (Sandauer 2005: 29, 37).

Wat explored modernism, Dadaism and futurism, before making connections with Russian communism. Although he was not a member of the Communist Party, Wat was probably best known in Poland for editing the influential left-wing journal *Miesięcznik Literacki* (*Literary Monthly*, 1929–32) before it was closed down by the regime. His foreign reading, un-Polish interests, political views, ethnic origins, avant-garde style and poetic fracturing of Polish grammar meant that whatever his eventual contribution to Polish literature, he was not generally seen as 'rooted in the tradition of Polish poetry' (Wat 1990: 3, 21). Wat was convinced that 'everything had been eroded, removed, cleaned out' in independent Poland, and that in choosing communism he was siding with the 'only faith that existed'. He felt driven by 'the malice of that time, that terrible obstinate malice' that came

Polish writers and tradition 77

from 'a sort of intellectual hoodlumism'. In the title story of his collection *Bezrobotny Lucyfer* (1927, *Lucifer Unemployed*), he showed Lucifer trying to market his talents in a world so wicked it had no need of them. In his story 'Long Live Europe! (From the Memoirs of an Ex-European)', Wat showed he had little hope in the idea of 'Europe' and offered a sarcastic hymn of praise: 'Blossoming endlessly, nihilistic and full of faith, revolutionary and orthodox and inspired: eternal, eternal, immortal Europe!' (Wat 1990: 80).

Writing in 1921, futurist Jasieński was open about the issues facing the inter-war writer. He identified the main problem as the struggle with a Polish 'national ego', and the fact of a 'hard, unbending, all-resistant national psyche capable of surviving'. He warned: 'A century and a half of political servitude has left a hard, indelible suture running down our physiognomy, psyche, and creative work. Our cultural consciousness has not been as free to develop as those of western states. By necessity all our national energy chose the path of most resistance, struggling for language, life, and self-organization' (Jasieński 2014: 2). Jasieński believed the 'virus of modernity' had fallen upon an unprepared Poland, causing a feverish struggle. He claimed partitioned Poland had never been interested in 'the riddle of contemporary European culture' because it had been preoccupied with 'its own affairs', that the 'red polish phlag has long been a red nosewipe' and that Poles believed their traditions were somehow undermined by independence. Jasieński said he was through with being part of a 'menagerie nation producing mummies and relics'. He wanted a 'great clearance of old junk… old traditions, categories, customs, pictures and fetishes' (Jasieński 2014: 10–18, 57–9). Possibly because Jasieński was already a noted *enfant terrible*, a Jew, and what was worse, a futurist, very few took him seriously. His poetry readings were often banned by the police and at one event the audience stoned him. He fled to Paris in 1925, but after the publication of his catastrophist novel *Palę Paryż* (1928, *I Burn Paris*), with its critique of Western culture and the destructive stresses of capitalism, he was deported (twice) before settling in Leningrad.

Perhaps the most startling Polish-Jewish talent from this period was Bruno Schultz, a writer and art teacher in the small town of Drohobycz in the Galician oil and gas field. In *Sklepy Cynamonowe* (1934, *Cinnamon Shops*) and *Sanatorium Pod Klepsydrą* (1937, *Sanatorium under the Sign of the Hourglass*), his strange, poetic, surreal stories reveal industry, modernity, anti-Semitism and the attractions of the wider world as major pressures on traditional Jewish life (Hoffman 1998: 159–200). This pressure was particularly evident in the lives of women, the wavering authority of patriarchy, the questioning of the hierarchy and the traditional life of the *shtetl* with its 'disregard of privacy, the indifference to the advantages of individual freedom, the tribal closeness' (Hoffman 2004: 87).

For Schultz, the challenge to Jewish tradition meant all kinds of possibilities had begun to open up – changes to diet and clothing, reading matter, urban rather than rural life, reform, assimilation, socialism, communism and

78 Polish writers and tradition

Zionism. In several of his books, but particularly in *Xięga Bałwochwalcza* (1920–24, *The Book of Idolatry*), Schultz's artwork reveals the clash between orthodoxy and modernity by repeatedly showing him, or traditionally dressed Jewish men, lasciviously eying nudes and fashionably dressed Polish women as if viewing them from the shadows of one world in the light of another.[19] Schultz, through a mixture of 'daring pride and artistic conviction', seems to have been determined to ignore the anti-Semitism of his workplace and hometown and, in his own way, brought these specifically Jewish concerns into Polish literature (Adamczyk-Garbowska et al. 2016: 336).

An exception to the increasingly polarised atmosphere was the poet Józef Wittlin (1896–1976). He had initially been part of the Skamander group and later became a theatre director and critic, publishing reviews and poetry in several Polish magazines, but particularly in *Wiadomości Literackie* (*Literary News*). While he did not challenge prevailing attitudes towards nationalist opinion of the Jews, he challenged accepted attitudes towards the ruling military caste. His novel *Sól ziemi* (1935, *Salt of the Earth*), based on his experiences in World War I, describes how an illiterate, bandy-legged railway-worker from a backward Hutsul[20] village in the Carpathians was drafted into the army for a war he did not understand and in which he had little stake. Given that a military dictatorship ruled in independent Poland, that militarism was a central feature of political life and Hitler had become Chancellor in Germany shortly before the novel was published, this was a bold move. But probably the novel proved acceptable because it was about a Hutsul in the multi-lingual Austro-Hungarian Army, rather than a Pole (or a Jew) in the Polish Army. Nevertheless, the novel struck a chord, was very well received, was translated into fourteen languages and won Wittlin a Nobel Prize nomination in 1939.

Jews had fought for Polish independence in the Uprisings and in Piłsudski's legions, and the traditionalist Agudat Israel Party (founded 1916) had declared allegiance to the new state as soon as it was founded. After the Balfour Declaration of 1917, however, Jewish leaders like Ze'ev (Vladimir) Jabotinsky, along with the Revisionist Party, Betar and numerous other Zionist organisations, promoted emigration to Palestine with increasing vigour.[21] While anti-Semitism had always existed in Poland, it had always been on an average. In independent Poland a nationalist narrative of Polish heroism that portrayed Jews as Poland's conspiring enemies came increasingly to the fore (Janion 2014b: 52). In this, Endecja drew support from across the social spectrum: the nobility, the middle class, the *inteligencja*, the professions, rural communities and the Church hierarchy. After Piłsudski's death, under pressure from Endecja, Sanacja began to restrict kosher slaughter, limit entry of Jews to the professions and make shop-owners display their name on shop fronts. He adopted a harsh 'citizenship law' and went from insisting on a 'Jewish bench' in universities to attempting to prevent Jews – particularly in the areas of law and medicine – from attending university. At least two professors who opposed the 'Jewish bench', the economist Edward Lipiński (1888–1986) and the philosopher, logician and

Polish writers and tradition 79

ethicist Tadeusz Kotarbiński (1886–1981), were attacked and beaten up. Endecja worked hard to remove Jews from the life of the state, from the civil service and from all public office (Rudnicki 1993).

By the mid 1930s, as tolerance of experiment, difference and the promise of socialism faded and Poland moved steadily towards the right, Polish-Jewish writers became much less prominent. Indeed, Polish-Jewish writers spilt into two factions: those who favoured assimilation in spite of the difficulties, and those who saw the Polish language as a way of revitalising Jewish national culture by targeting assimilated Jews with Zionist ideas. Jewish life in Poland was increasingly triangulated by tradition, assimilation and Zionism. In spite of poverty, emigration and the looming international crisis, by the end of the 1930s Jewish culture in Poland was involved in a slow social evolution and was 'rife with new energies and potentials' (Hoffman 1998: 257). Jewish opinion between the wars was shaped less by tradition and increasingly by 'the lay, liberal, rationalist and sometimes free thinking elite' (Polonsky 1993: 476). Led by rabbis the Agudat Israel Party – with its conservative, traditional approach of religious observance, loyalty to the state and life lived in expectation of the Messiah – felt that while Jewish emigration was encouraged by Sanacja, it undermined the standing and effectiveness of the party. Replacing the faith of traditional belief with the teleology of revolution was not an easy transition, but for many facing rising anti-Semitism the choice was not remain or emigrate, but between communism and Zionism.

There are no accurate records, but it seems that in the years 1919–42 almost 140,000 Jews left Poland for Palestine. In 1927–38 about 200,000 Jews left Poland: of these about 75,000 left for Palestine in the years 1933–6, but many headed for Argentina, Canada, Australia and the US. Of those who remained in Poland, as many as one million relied on 'relief' from US aid organisations (Fuks et al. 1982: 38–9).[22] As Agudat Israel's traditional authority weakened, it was gradually forced to consider the possibility of building a new home in Palestine. At the same time the socialist Bund, which had initially opposed Zionism on the grounds that emigration to Palestine weakened the forces of the proletariat, sought the dictatorship of the proletariat and fought for Jewish rights throughout the diaspora, began to feel that their notion of equality in work and their insistence on political organisation no longer sufficed to satisfy Polish-Jewish aspirations. In 1937 the Comintern (Communist International, 1919–43) decided to liquidate the KPP and ordered the death of all the members within reach of the NKVD – Stalin's revenge for their 'May error' in supporting Piłsudski's coup.[23] With this, Jewish trade unionists, Bundists, socialists and revolutionary communists now felt surrounded by enemies, and increasingly they too felt their only hope of building a socialist future lay in Palestine (Deutscher 1982; Mendel 1989: 315, 327).

It is possible that assimilation and changing attitudes to traditional authority, social structure and opportunity may have hampered understanding of, and resistance to, Nazism. As Eva Hoffman wrote: 'the war came at

80 Polish writers and tradition

a time when the *shtetl* communities were making the transition from ortho-doxy to modernity, and from the older modes of religious authority to still untested forms of modern, party-based politics – resulting in a temporary vacuum of power and of trusted structure' (Hoffman 2004: 273). Also, although the numbers were probably small, Zionism had begun to subtract from Jewish life in Poland, recruiting the most active, the toughest, the most independent, energetic and capable personalities into para-military groups like Haganah, Lehi and Irgun before assisting them to enter Palestine.

The Holocaust killed three million Polish Jews including Bruno Schultz and almost all of the Polish-Jewish writers of the inter-war period. It destroyed Jewish tradition in Poland, concluded the debate about assimila-tion and, even though a few writers continued to write in Polish in Israel, ended any substantial relationship with Polish culture. Only a few of the surviving Polish-Jewish writers, mainly those on the Left, stayed in Poland after 1945. Słonimski, for example, had no interest in Zionism and tried to persuade others to stay. Some Jews – among them Jakub Berman (1901–84), Adam Ważyk (1905–82) and Władysław Broniewski (1897–1962) – returned to Poland with the victorious Red Army as functionaries of the new regime (Shore 2006). But for most Holocaust survivors the hostility they encountered on their return from deportation, forced labour and the camps, and a series of post-war pogroms in Kraków, Kielce and Rzeszów, resolved their doubts about Zionism.

*

The complex inter-twining of romantic and positivist literary and political traditions, their rivalry, content, intersection with notions of left and right, and the growth of Polish-Jewish identity between the wars still confound easy classification. Czapski, for example, recalled meeting the political writer Adolf Bocheński (1909–44), who came from wealthy landowning family in the *kresy* not so very different from Czapski's family background. Czapski expected him to be an arch-nationalist and a reactionary, but soon found that he was an active supporter of mutual understanding between Poles and Ukrainians, 'and in the days when the worst clashes between the two races occurred, his lectures in Lwów were attended by both Poles and Ukrainians. That was rare in those toxic days of mutual hostility'. Fur-thermore, Bocheński was 'a consistent opponent of blind nationalism and nationalist chauvinism'. He dreamed of a Poland that was not ethnographic but federal, multinational, and truly liberal'. Czapski understood Bocheński to be a 'committed conservative' whose cult of tradition 'was so extreme that it sometimes seemed anachronistic'. But he had to admit that upon closer inspection, 'even staunch progressives were surprised by the boldness of his notions and the vehemence of his attacks on historical falsification, and on what he called obscurantism, which he exposed and condemned, whether it was on the left or the right. What he sought was a return to the great traditions of Polish statehood' (Czapski 2018a: 372–3).

Polish writers and tradition 81

The interwar literary and creative *inteligencja*, Polish and Jewish, though it was independent, non-conformist, often wildly experimental – itself a reflection of the rapidly fluctuating political and social situation – was for the most part oppositional but formed only a tiny, weak and rather wavering element of public opinion. Although Sanacja changed over time, sexual liberation, the challenge of modernity, the challenge to tradition, changing attitudes to the Church, excitement at the idea of national regeneration, the hope that the false expectations of independence might be realised after all and the conspiratorial opposition that Sanacja generated were all part of the fabric of political life. Partition had launched Poles into the process of consciously preserving Polish traditions and increasingly presented identity as a given for those who spoke Polish. With independence this became a circular argument that saw history as destiny and seemed to say: 'we preserved Polish traditions and we survived; therefore it is right to preserve the traditions that enabled us to survive: we will become what we once were'. Independence invited Poles to feel justified in their traditions without requiring any reconsideration of their place in the modern world or their relevance in a revived Poland. For most, the reality of independence did not challenge traditional identity before reinforcing it.

Wiskemann may have been right when she said that under Sanacja most people 'were not on the whole odiously humiliated nor grossly tormented nor completely silenced' (Wiskemann 1966: 79). In independent Poland collectivist, didactic and ecstatic national ambitions clashed with local, personal, sceptical and ironic modes of expression, and with identities that were simply not Polish (Anders 2009: xiii). The results were unpredictable. While the authorities of independent Poland promoted Polish patriotic traditions, they increasingly sought internal uniformity and aloof distinction from neighbouring countries and in doing so produced a bristling elitism, martial swagger, resistance to authority, obstinate independence and a tendency to haughty fragmentation. They also reinforced an exclusive sense of hierarchical, traditional, national identity that was often opposed and contradicted by the creative community.

For Czesław Miłosz, as he fled eastwards, the start of the war brought 'a mixture of fury and relief' as he realised 'the nonsense was over at last' and there was 'nothing left of the ministries, offices and Army' (Miłosz 1981: 204).

Notes

1 Tread – *krok*; trade – *handel*; trader – *kupiec*; traitor – *zdrajca*; betray – *zdradzać*; traduce – *oczerniać*; translate – *tłumaczyć*.
2 *Szlachta*: nobility or gentry: the historical landowning class; part of the ancient political leadership which up to the Partitions enjoyed legal privileges and whose members often owned vast estates. After the failure of the Polish Uprisings, the *szlachta* became increasingly dependent on the Partitioning powers. Those who thought *szlachta* legal privilege might be restored with independence were disappointed. Their special status was abolished by the March 1921 Constitution. However, *szlachta* mentality, attitudes and style are persistent elements in Polish culture.

82   Polish writers and tradition

3   The allusion is to F.R. Leavis (1895–1978) and his *The Great Tradition* (Leavis 1948).

4   The Constitution of the Third of May 1791 was designed to balance *szlachta* privilege – particularly the *liberum veto* (free veto) – by clearly demarking the powers of the executive, legislative and judiciary under the monarch. Probably, as Bobrowski indicates, this was too little too late: the new constitution provoked a Russian invasion, defeat of Polish forces and a further Partition.

5   Czarnolas: a village in east-central Poland near the town of Zwoleń, about 100 km south-east of Warsaw, famous as the home estate of the Renaissance poet Jan Kochanowski (1539–84).

6   Endecja is a blanket term for the National-Democracy movement and the various political parties that represented it. SDN was a secret organisation founded in the years 1886–97 by Roman Dmowski, Jan Ludwik Popławski and Zygmunt Balicki, as part of the Liga Narodowa (National League), a conspiratorial organisation active in all three partition zones. SDN was founded specifically to represent the National Democracy movement at elections. By 1918 Endecja was well known for lobbying the Polish cause abroad and, as *Związek Ludowy-Narodowy* (Popular-National Union), was offered a place at the Paris Peace Conference and found itself part of the transitional Polish Government. In response to Piłsudski's coup, ZLN renamed itself *Stronnictwo Narodowe* (SN, National Alliance) in 1928. SN was an umbrella Party representing the Catholic-nationalist right.

7   *Kresy*: Poland's eastern holdings in Lithuania, Belarus and Ukraine. The towns of Wilno and Lwów were major cultural centres and the focus of Poland's eastern defences. The loss of these cities and their hinterlands in 1945 had a lasting effect on the Polish psyche. For many Poles these lands were 'the real Poland' (Arciszewski 1956).

8   Joseph Conrad (1857–1924) had visited Poland in 1914 and was aware of a 'poisonous stream' of opinion suggesting Poland would be a danger to its minorities but, with no direct experience of the emerging state, he did not accept it (Conrad 1970: 121).

9   The KPRP (*Komunistyczna Partia Robotnicza Polski*, Communist Party of Polish Workers) changed its name to KPP in 1923.

10   Poland had been an exporter of people for some time. It is estimated that in the period 1875–1914 some 3.6 million (fifteen percent of the population) emigrated (Bobińska & Pilch 1975: 124–6).

11   ONR was led by Bolesław Piasecki, who in the post-war period did a deal with the communists to become leader of the PAX organisation.

12   Miłosz did not forgive Iłłakowiczówna her connection to Piłsudski: she is not mentioned in his history of Polish literature (Miłosz 1983) and she is not included in his anthology of post-war poetry (Miłosz 1965).

13   Sarmati: a nomadic Iranian people known to the ancient Greeks, thought to have invaded the Pontic steppe and Ukraine, expanding into Hungary and Poland in the fourth and fifth centuries before being absorbed into the ruling warrior elites of East-Central Europe, eventually in Poland to provide basis of the *szlachta* ethos. Agata Pyzik blames 'Polish melancholia', 'tedious sentimentalism' and 'political infantilism' on the traditional cultural influence of the Sarmati (Pyzik 2014: 149–54).

14   Although duelling died out at the end of World War II, the *Kodex honorowy* had a long 'after life', went through eight editions up to 1939 and was reprinted as late as 2012. In January 2011 politician Zbigniew Kozak criticised Premier Donald Tusk's handling of the investigation into the Smolensk air disaster by saying: 'Are you and your ministers familiar with Władysław Boziewicz's *The Polish Code of Honour*?' The implication was clear (Swan 2013).

Polish writers and tradition   83

15 By 1914 the number of Jewish banks still in private hands had diminished considerably. The management of the joint-stock banks conducted by Jewish bankers included the Dyskontowy Bank in Warsaw, the Warsaw Commercial & Industrial Bank, the Zachodni Bank, the Warsaw Commercial Bank and the commercial bank founded by Wilhelm Landau. Also, in the rapidly industrialising city of Łódź, Jewish bankers managed the Bank Handlowy and the Bank Kupiecki (www.yivoencyclopedia.org/article.aspx/Banking).

16 Some examples where integration to the Polish *inteligencja* failed are listed in Michnik and Marczyk (2018: 350).

17 'Czarnolas' is shorthand indicating Polish literary classics. Czarnolas, about 100 km south-east of Warsaw, was the estate of the poet Jan Kochanowski (1530–84), one of the founders of Polish literature.

18 Betar (Bejtar), founded in 1923 by Ze'ev Jabotinsky. The organisation was affiliated to Irgun Zvai Leumi, the military wing of the Revisionist Party. It adopted salutes and uniforms and was one of many Zionist organisations in Poland at the time. To aid Jewish emigration, the Revisionists and Irgun were supported with arms and training by the Polish military leadership, who were anxious to see Jews depart (Bethell 1980: 41). Israeli Prime Ministers Yitzhak Shamir (Yitzhak Yezernitsky) and Menachem Begin (Mieczysław Biegun) had both been members of Betar in their youth.

19 The German novelist Alfred Döblin (1878–1957), who visited Poland in search of his Jewish roots in 1924–5, observed the same pressure of sexual temptation on the streets of Kraków: 'But what can I do with the streets: I'm suddenly corrupted. What a world. On the ring, I see the powdered feminine beauty of Poland, in light-coloured stockings, the sharp, piquant, sexy faces, the full figures. They're not isolated although they're walking ten or fifteen feet from me: they head toward me though the air, the light carries all of them to me [...] this intrusiveness everywhere in the streets' (Döblin 1991: 201). The 'ring' is *planty*, a public park on the site of the Kraków city moat, still a favourite place for walks and fashionable display.

20 Hutsul (Ukrainian: гуцул; Polish: *hucuł*; Romanian: *huțul*): a distinct ethnic group located in the eastern Carpathian Mountains on the old Polish/Romanian border, now in western Ukraine and Romania.

21 Zionism had been founded by Theodor Herzl in 1897, but, while Polish Jews were at first rather unenthusiastic, a broad spectrum of political orientations gathered around it, including the Mizrachi (religious), radical Marxists of Poale Zion and the revisionists under Jabotinsky.

22 Palestine was a harsh, underdeveloped, uninviting, rural prospect and throughout the 1920s and 1930s Zionist leaders complained that even when the Jewish Settlement Agency secured immigration permits for them, Polish Jews did not use them. In 1925 the fourth Aliyah (wave) of immigration began after the Polish currency reform enacted by Prime Minister Grabski hit the Jewish middle class very hard. That year about half of the 35,000 Jews arriving in Palestine came from Poland: most refused settlement in a kibbutz and chose to live in Tel Aviv (Segev 2000: 237, 395).

23 By removing them from the reach of the NKVD, arrest and imprisonment in Poland inadvertently saved the lives of several communists including Bolesław Bierut, Władysław Gomułka, Edward Ochab, Stefan Jędrychowski and Alexander Zawadzki, who all survived to become powerful figures in the post-1945 government.

4   Polish writers and tradition
Nazism and communism

Although the Nazi and Soviet occupations were murderous from the start, even by January 1942, when Reinhard Heydrich, increasingly aware that Operation Barbarossa was failing, convened the Wannsee Conference to determine the exact mechanism for the extermination of the Jews, it was hard to imagine the full extent of the damage the war would wreak on Polish society. It was also difficult to determine the extent to which, even if it was on the 'winning side', post-war Poland would be dominated by the USSR. In exile the style, mind-set and assumptions of the Sanacja regime were highlighted; the contradictions and clashes within national tradition became excruciatingly clear; and events and personalities conspired to ensure the loyalties that inspired Poles to resist also hampered their efforts to unite and cooperate.

Tradition and rivalry in exile

While the legend of 1920 loomed large, Piłsudski felt comfortable surrounded by reliable 'yes' men. He systematically promoted officers from the untrained, enthusiastic, heroic Polish Legions, which had served Poland so well in the struggles for independence, but he ignored well-trained officers from the Russian and Austrian armies – many of whom had graduated from military academy and had experience of trench warfare. Instead of sending officers to military academy, he preferred to pick men of his own choosing for promotion.

Piłsudski's grasp of military tactics seems to have been poor and even though he thought an attack from the USSR was more likely than an attack by Germany, very little war-planning was undertaken. Piłsudski ignored the experience of the British French and German armies of 1914–18 and instead based his defensive preparations for war on large scale, Napoleonic style cavalry manoeuvres to occupy the enemy while the reserve mobilised. Śmigły-Rydz, who took over the leadership after Piłsudski's death, was an unimaginative traditionalist who resisted change. Although Poland had begun to purchase up-to-date weaponry, it was predisposed to protect the traditional ethos and was slow to convert cavalry to armour, invest in anti-aircraft weaponry, build defensive fortifications, develop a bomber

Polish writers and tradition   85

force or motorise the infantry, and the navy was hampered by having access only to the port of Gdynia (McGilvray 2013: 25, 27, 30–31, 35). The result was that by 1939, with the exception of figures like Anders, Sosabowski and Maczek, the bulk of the Polish military was decidedly amateur in its approach to war.

History had taught Poles that war was not only a matter of military glory, but one of national survival. However, they were to pay dearly for the tactical and strategic mistakes of their leadership. In September 1939 Germany attacked with forty-two infantry divisions, four motorised divisions, seven armoured divisions and one partly mechanised cavalry division (in total over 3,200 tanks). Poland opposed this with thirty-seven infantry and eleven cavalry divisions, a tank brigade and a half-formed tank brigade – a total of 313 tanks (Edwards 1998: 31; Garliński 1985: 12–13). Although the Polish Army was fighting on indefensible terrain with little in the way of natural barriers, and mobilisation of the reserve was incomplete, the Polish military performed well against the Germans at Mława, Ruszki, Kiernozia, Westerplatte and Warsaw. But the Soviet invasion two weeks later ensured Poland's defeat and prompted the writer Witkiewicz to commit suicide.

The usual explanation for the Polish defeat is an over-reliance on the horse and the attitudes of an old-fashioned cavalry officer class (Bethell 1976: 31), but defeat was not just a matter of a traditional mind-set. Modernisation of the Polish Army was also matter of cost. In the years 1933–9, half of Poland's national budget – 6,500 million złoty – went on standardising weapons, taking French advice on developing the air force, developing chemical weapons and the purchase of modern weapons, warships and tanks. This was a vast sum and a massive burden for a backward rural economy. But in the same period German investment in war materials – the equivalent of 200,000 million złoty – dwarfed that of Poland. Śmigły-Rydz had budgeted for further military modernisation at a cost of 574 million złoty, but this fell far short of what was necessary to counter a German attack, let alone an attack from both west and east (Forczyk 2019: loc 1013).

Antagonism within the Polish military became apparent even as the defeated Polish Army crossed the border into Romania. Politicians, elements in the Polish Army and diplomatic staff at the Polish Embassy in Bucharest collaborated with the French and Romanian governments to bring about the end of Sanacja rule. The Polish leadership, separated and interned at several locations, were put under pressure. President Mościcki, one-time colleague of Piłsudski in the Socialist Party, a leading 'moderate figure' in the government who had already decided to resign, was pressed to name a successor. He named Wieniawa-Długoszowski, a career diplomat who had once been Piłsudski's adjutant. However, the French found him hostile and simply refused to announce the change. Eventually Władysław Raczkiewicz, Mościcki's fourth choice, who had served in Piłsudski's legions and had been an Endecja supporter before joining the Sanacja regime to hold several government appointments, was sworn in. Raczkiewicz accepted the

86 Polish writers and tradition

resignation of the government and appointed General Władysław Sikorski – who was well thought of in France and had been meeting foreign ambassadors for some weeks – as prime minister to head a 'cabinet of national unity'. Though General Sosnkowski had not resigned from the role of commander-in-chief, he was still missing so Raczkiewicz appointed Sikorski. When Sosnkowski reappeared Raczkiewicz named him as his successor, much to Sikorski's annoyance.

Sikorski had been Polish Prime Minister briefly in 1922–3, then minister of defence. In November 1925 his obvious dissatisfaction with the government led President Wojciechowski to warn Sikorski not to attempt a military coup (Webb 2008: 142). Nevertheless, he joined Roman Dmowski in forming the secret Pogotowie Patriotów Polskich (Aid for Polish Patriots) and continued to plot the overthrow of democracy in favour of a military dictatorship. Their plans were pre-empted by Piłsudski's coup in May 1926. In 1928 Piłsudski relieved Sikorski of command of the Lwów Army Corps as a punishment for his refusal to support the coup. In the years 1928–35 Sikorski became a resolute opponent of Sanacja in the Sejm, but after Piłsudski's death Sanacja became increasingly authoritarian and in 1935 Sikorski was obliged to leave Poland for Paris.

In the autumn of 1939 Sikorski felt the behaviour of the Polish government after the German attack had been disgraceful and he saw the leadership of the regime – Foreign Minister Józef Beck, President Mościcki, Marshal Śmigły-Rydz – as directly responsible for defeat. Sikorski was determined to use this opportunity to push for change and, while he did not see defeat as the end of Poland, he saw the war as a chance to end 'a certain idea and a certain Poland'. In France he set about constructing a coalition government that was sworn in almost immediately. Neil Ascherson called these developments 'a discreet revolution to overthrow Sanacja masquerading as a constitutionally correct transfer of power' (Ascherson 1987: 91).

Inevitably, Sikorski's coalition suffered rivalry and division from the outset. Even amongst his allies in the coalition, Sikorski had little in common except that they all opposed Sanacja. Each of the political parties had at least two major factions and many would not sit at the same table. The coalition was made up mainly of 'second string' politicians, simply those who had managed to escape. It also included several high-ranking officers as ministers, vice ministers, deputies, adjutants and assistants who were still loyal to Sanacja and wanted the regime restored. On the left there were members of the Polska Partia Socjalistyczna (PPS, Polish Socialist Party), which supported democratic and progressive legislation, and Stronnictwo Pracy (Labour Alliance), a party so small it was sometimes described as 'the party without followers'. In the centre the coalition included members of Polskie Stronnictwo Ludowe (SL, Polish Peasant Party), which was reform-minded and had often supported Piłsudski. On the ethno-nationalist right the coalition had members of Stronnictwo Narodowe (SN, National Alliance), the largest and most vociferous of the opposition parties, inheritors

Polish writers and tradition 87

of the Dmowski's National Democratic mantle. SN was bitterly opposed to Piłsudski's coup and the Sanacja regime; they considered themselves to be 'pure Poles', were hostile to the Jews and wanted forced assimilation of all minorities. Many SN members refused to become part of Sikorski's government and cold-shouldered those who did (Koziński 2016: 99–102).

To make matters worse, the exiled Polish leadership was obliged to observe the 1935 Polish Constitution. Many SN members thought it 'un-Polish', 'undemocratic' and outrageously liberal; others criticised it as weighted towards the power of the President – it had been tailored to fit the demands of Piłsudski. The main objection was that the military had seized power illegally in 1926, overthrowing the legally adopted constitution of 1921, so for many the 1935 constitution was itself an illegal document. However, it was from adherence to the constitution that the Government-in-Exile derived its political legitimacy and they had no mandate to change it.

Sikorski was suspicious of everyone associated with Sanacja and wanted to settle accounts with those he deemed responsible for the military disaster. He also suspected about 1,500 officers were still loyal to Sanacja and wanted to neutralise them by keeping them away from the bulk of the Polish military and centres of power. Many of these officers knew Sikorski as an opponent of the regime, disliked him intensely, did not trust his attitude to the Soviets and resented his leadership (Garliński 1969: 33–5; Kochanski 2012: 212). Lacking troops for them to command, it was not difficult to separate them. At first a centre for 'redundant officers' was created at Cerizay in France: in reality it was a kind of open prison, and when Polish forces were evacuated to Britain these officers were detained in Douglas, in Broughton and at Glasgow Rangers football ground, then shipped offshore to the Isle of Bute in the Firth of Clyde, ostensibly tasked with guarding the coast. Within days of arriving in Britain, Sikorski set up a commission to investigate their behaviour.

From Bute, General Dąb-Biernacki, a leading agitator against Sikorski who had previously been arrested in France on suspicion of planning a coup, realised these officers had been isolated for a reason. In July 1940 he wrote a long and insulting letter to Sikorski, copied to Piłsudski's widow, President Raczkiewicz and Marshal Śmigły-Rydz, asking to be released from the Polish Army and claiming, amongst other things, that Sikorski was running a dictatorship, tolerating a party clique and using his 'unprecedented power' to 'negate and reject absolutely everything that was done before You' (Koziński 2016: 102). In October 1940 Dąb-Biernacki was found guilty of contravening the Polish Military Code and sentenced to two years and six months in prison. The following month he was dismissed from the army and at the request of the Polish authorities was detained by the British. This did not stop him agitating and in April 1941 he went on trial again, this time charged with directing a conspiracy against Sikorski's government. He was found guilty and sentenced to four years imprisonment. He served a year, was released due to poor health and went to live in Ireland where he became a beekeeper.

88 Polish writers and tradition

In July–August 1941, General Burhardt-Bukacki (another of Piłsudski's legionnaires) came into conflict with General Gustaw Paszkiewicz and General Izydor Modelski, both of whom were deputy ministers. Sikorski relieved Burhardt-Bukacki of his post. However, it was not long before Modelski, under secretary of war, was also in trouble. He had been dismissed from the army for opposing Piłsudski's coup and was a long-time rival of General Marian Kukiel, who had gone into the reserve after Piłsudski's coup but was now vice-minister of war. It was said that in France, where Modelski had been personnel and registration officer to Sikorski's cabinet, he had led groups of hooded soldiers in search of Sanacja officers interned at Cerizay in order to satisfy his political and personal animosities. In London, Kukiel accused Modelski of provoking political quarrels and poisoning the atmosphere.[1]

Raczkiewicz distrusted and disliked the Soviets intensely and felt Sikorski was 'soft' on them. He was not alone in this: ministers August Zaleski, Marian Seyda and General Sosnkowski resigned over Sikorski's July 1941 agreement with Maisky. Though the agreement freed thousands of Polish soldiers from captivity in the USSR, it angered army officers who could not forgive the Soviets for the invasion of 1939. Antagonism was not so clear among the rank and file, though the Polish military system put great emphasis on loyalty, so soldiers often felt obliged to follow their commander's lead. Sosnkowski's resignation was particularly important as he had shared a prison cell with Piłsudski and, while he did not support Sanacja, as erstwhile commander-in-chief he had the loyalty of the bulk of the Polish officers training in Scotland.

The Government-in-Exile was in a humiliating position. Not only was it suffering from military defeat and the pain of exile, it was internally divided and entirely dependent on the host country and Allied generosity for food, medicine, uniforms, equipment and accommodation. At Sikorski's insistence the Government-in-Exile promoted a liberal-democratic agenda with equal rights for Polish Jews and other minorities, but this view, supported out of necessity by some of the coalition who worried about offending their Western allies, departed from the beliefs of many Sanacja supporters and from SN's pre-war policies.[2] In particular, SN resented the two Jewish representatives on the Polish National Council of the Polish Government-in-Exile, Dr Isaac Schwarzbart, a leading Zionist, and Szmul Zygielbojm, a socialist-Bundist.[3]

No matter how liberal the official policy of the government was, it was difficult to overcome traditional anti-Semitic assumptions. From July 1940 onwards the British War Office and Foreign Office began to note an increase in anti-Semitic activities around the Polish Army (McGilvray 2013: 60). Possibly assuming it was simply anti-Semitic, international Jewish organisations had very little interest in the Government-in-Exile and it was at first very poorly informed and almost entirely indifferent to the fate of Jews in occupied Poland. David Engel has pointed out that even as information about the Holocaust began to filter through, 'demands' made on the

Government-in-Exile were often evaluated in terms of the high priority of 'the Polish community' and the low priority of Jews. It was also difficult for them to overcome the traditional perception of Jews as competitors who inhibited the development and prosperity of ethnic Polish commercial ventures; the established pattern of adverse treatment of Jews in the Polish Army, universities, the professions and in society at large; the claim that 'anti-Jewish prejudice' was really an example of 'ineluctable anti-Polonism'; the belief that Jews were 'ill-disposed' towards Poland and not prepared to defend Polish independence; and the stereotypical claim that Jews were conspiring with the USSR against Poland (Engel 1987; Engel 1993).

After 1942, as closer contact with the Polish Underground was established through couriers, evidence of the Holocaust began to leak out. Jan Karski, an emissary between the Polish Underground and the Government-in-Exile, was one of the first to deliver an eyewitness account of his clandestine visits to Warsaw Ghetto and the Bełżec death camp to Allied leaders in the hope of prompting a reaction. The Government-in-Exile made several public declarations exposing Nazi genocide and demanded the Allies find a way to intervene, and from December 1942 they supported the rescue work of the underground organisation Żegota (codename for *Rada Pomocy Żydom*, **Council Aiding Jews**).[4] Articles on the Holocaust appeared in *Dziennik Polski* (Polish Daily), *Żołnierz Polski* (Polish Soldier) and *Polish Fortnightly Review*, and in early 1943 the Government-in-Exile asked Pope Pius XII to condemn Nazis policies.

Some members of the Government-in-Exile barely managed to tolerate each other, and friction between Sikorski, Raczkiewicz, Seyda, Zaleski and Sosnkowski (plus many others) did not enhance coalition leadership or produce political equilibrium. Roosevelt and Churchill felt Sikorski was badly advised and urged him to make changes to his Council of Ministers. Stalin wanted him to remove the abrasive Professor Stanisław Kot (member of the Peasant Party, an opponent of Sanacja, determined build his party for the post-war era but also determined to pursue personal vendettas), President Raczkiewicz and Professor Marian Kukiel, claiming they were pro-Hitler, anti-Soviet and concerned only with browbeating Sikorski for their own political ends (Kochanski 2012: 344).

In September 1939 Sir Howard W. Kennard, British Ambassador to the Government-in-Exile, who was looking to find like-minded democrats to work with among the Poles, advised British Foreign Secretary Lord Halifax that after the defeat of the Polish Army and the retreat into Romania, Poles would be unlikely to trust their former leaders again.[5] Lloyd George, under the influence of the historians Sir Lewis Namier and E.H. Carr, considered the Government-in-Exile to be 'class-ridden' and thought the Soviets had done the Polish people a great service by forcing them out (Coutouvidis & Reynolds 1986: 74; Kochanski 2012: 343–8; Zimmerman 2015: 43).

While the Underground was an extension of the government and a legitimate part of the Polish state, courier Jan Karski (1914–2000) claimed it was a break from Sanacja and a return to 'the still older traditions of Polish

90   *Polish writers and tradition*

parliamentary democracy'. He felt the Underground had 'more power and freedom' to consult and organise than had been possible before. By this he meant that unlike the pre-war government, the Underground could try to make common cause with opposition parties and with the minorities.

Some parts of the Underground movement, particularly the elements run by PSP, and for different reasons parts run by SN, hoped that post-war Poland would not be a continuation of pre-war arrangements and saw the war was an opportunity to overcome social divisions and move beyond the confinement of military rule. Stefan Korboński (1901–89), one of the founders of the Underground movement, said the military disaster had made clear 'the bankruptcy of the pre-war regime' and that Underground activities would have to be 'directed by opposition parties, which had proved their loyalty to democratic ideals. The defeat should act as a cleansing fire' (Korboński 2004: 10).

Inevitably, the Government-in-Exile had difficulty controlling the Underground leadership in Poland. Some of the Underground groups wanted to see the end of Sanacja and have democracy restored, but some of the groups and many of the senior officers had served in Piłsudski's legions and were loyal to Sanacja. While still in France Sikorski had begun to fear that General Michał Tadeusz Karaszewicz-Tokarzewski's Służba Zwycięstwu Polski (SZP, Service for Poland's Victory), the military unit in Poland controlling the Underground, would be a focal point for Sanacja supporters and an attempt to revive the regime. Sikorski demoted Tokarzewski and ordered him to leave Warsaw for Lwów. Sikorski also replaced SZP with Związek Walki Zbrojnej (ZWZ, Union of Armed Struggle), run from London by General Sosnkowski.

From exile it was difficult to gauge just how far political opinion in Poland had shifted as a result of war, defeat and occupation. Many of the Sanacja officers expected a short war and the restoration of the regime as soon as it was over; some observers feared Sanacja officers, who had no interest in restoring democracy, planned to use the Armia Krajowa (AK, Home Army, formed in August 1942, the main umbrella resistance organisation linked to ZWZ and the Government-in-Exile) to seize power in a coup rather than chance their fortunes at an election. Following the end of the war against the Germans, even without a coup, liberals and leftists feared a civil war between Sanacja loyalists and SN, or perhaps even a three-cornered civil war with an alliance between Sanacja and SN against an alliance of Socialists and the Peasant Party (Lukas 2001: 59).

Like the Government-in-Exile, the AK was an amalgam made up of a wide range of political loyalties. On the left were the groups run by Gwardia Ludowa (People's Guard), loyal to the Polish Socialist Party, who regarded the AK leadership as a Sanacja clique, but nevertheless cooperated. Another large organisation of the centre-left was the Bataliony Chłopskie (Peasant Battalions). On the ethno-nationalist right of the AK there were various groups: Obóz Polski Walczącej (Camp of Fighting Poland), established by the Obóz Zjednoczenia Narodowego (Camp of National Unity); Narodowa

Organizacja Wojskowa (NOW, National Military Organisation), established by SN; and the Konfederacja Narodu (Confederation of the Nation), established by the far-right Obóz Narodowo Radykalny-Falanga (National Radical Camp – Falanga). On the far-right was Narodowe Siły Zbrojne (National Armed Forces), created in 1943 from dissatisfied NOW units. This was to become the third largest element in the Underground opposition, but it refused to be subordinated to the AK, was closely linked to the SN, repeatedly fought units of the AK, was involved in a series of anti-Semitic and anti-Ukrainian massacres and at the end of the war was accused of collaborating with the Gestapo against the Soviets (Lukas 2001: 40–60).[6]

Sikorski's relationship with General Anders, head of the Polish II Corps in the Middle East, did little to allay his fears of Sanacja. Both men certainly saw themselves as potential post-war political leaders. Although Anders at first supported Sikorski's efforts to maintain the Polish–Soviet Pact, Sikorski did not trust Anders and feared him as a rival. Anders did not purge Sanacja officers from his command and, as the relationship became increasingly fractious, he called repeatedly for Sikorski to resign. After two years in Soviet jails, Anders had the trust of most of his commanders and sensed that if Sikorski attempted to fire him there would be a mutiny. After their evacuation from the USSR, the officer class of the Polish II Corps rapidly became an arena of 'sharp political propaganda'. Churchill attempted to rein-in anti-Sikorski comment in the Polish press, but speculation about the Katyń massacre proved impossible to control. BBC broadcasts to Poland were censored, as was the Polish press in the UK and in the Middle East. However, Soviet outlets continued to criticise the London Government-in-Exile and make anti-Polish statements until, in April 1943, Churchill summoned Soviet Ambassador Maisky for a dressing down. The failure to address the issue of the Katyń massacre and Sikorski's apparent willingness to let the eastern provinces (where many of the Poles had their homes) be the price Poland paid for an alliance against the Nazis caused massive resentment within Anders' army. Among the many charges levelled at Sikorski, it was now said that, by not allowing collaboration with the Nazis, he had sided with the Soviets to escalate the 'horrendous biological and material losses' (Garliński 1985: 180).

Within Anders' II Corps, a group of officers had come under the influence of Captain Jerzy Klimkowski. He had fought under Anders in 1939 and later become a courier for the nascent Underground. Arrested by the Naródnyy Komissariát Vnútrennikh Del (NKVD, People's Commissariat for Internal Affairs), he had been in Soviet jail with Anders and was now his aid de camp. Klimkowski was 'fanatically anti-Sikorski' and his time in the USSR had served only to reinforce his extremely right-wing views. The Foreign Office and Special Operations Executive (SOE) had codenamed him 'Plague', and it was thought he aspired to become Minister of State for the Middle East in a post-war government – certainly he was someone with serious political ambitions. The officers gathered around him were rabidly anti-Soviet, anti-Semitic and anti-democracy, and believed Sikorski

92 Polish writers and tradition

had betrayed Poland, selling it 'to Russia and the Anglo-Saxons through his passivity and slowness' (www.pl.wikipedia.org/wiki/Jerzy_Klimkowski). They felt it was necessary to cooperate with the Nazis against Soviet territorial ambitions.

Klimkowski was convinced that Sikorski's proposed inspection tour of Polish forces in the Middle East in July 1943 was actually a disguised plan to sack Anders. Several senior Polish officers knew about Klimkowski's group and Anders, possibly flattered by their adulation but certainly sharing some political sympathies, seems to have tolerated their opinions. There were at least three other groups of anti-Sikorski plotters in Anders' II Corps, and Klimkowski is known to have warned Anders of a rival group's assassination plot against Sikorski. However, by the summer of 1943 the rumour was that Klimkowski was preparing to assassinate Sikorski as part of a political coup. The mood among Polish officers was very poor and Anders warned Sikorski an attempt on his life could not be ruled out (Garliński 1985: 214; Mulley 2012: 154).[7]

There had been an assassination attempt on Sikorski in March 1942 when a bomb was found on his plane. There had been another attempt in December 1942. Sikorski survived the inspection visit to the Middle East, but died in Gibraltar when his plane crashed at the start of the return journey. Officially his death was an accident, but conspiracy theorists see it as an assassination and usually blame the British or the Russians. However, Sikorski 'had enemies amongst his compatriots who would certainly have wished to see him dead' (Coutouvidis & Reynolds 1986: 88). Anders had promised to remove Klimkowski but did nothing until just after Sikorski's death, when Klimkowski was arrested and found to be in possession of missing materials from Anders' HQ. What he planned to do with these documents was never established: some surmised he planned to offer them to the Soviets, but it is equally possible he planned to offer them to the Nazis as a bargaining chip against the Soviets. Klimkowski was tried, convicted and jailed for a year and a week (McGilvray 2013: 90–92, 95–7).[8]

Even after Sikorski's death, when the role of prime minister went to Stanisław Mikołajczyk, the leader of the Peasant Party, and the role of commander-in-chief went to the staunchly anti-Soviet General Sosnkowski, conflict continued: these two leaders became bitter enemies, barely speaking for long periods, and spent a great deal of time and energy trying to restrict each other's powers, contesting control of the Underground movement and generally undermining and frustrating each other (McGilvray 2013). Mikołajczyk was determined to act correctly and continue Sikorski's policies, including reaching an understanding with the Soviets: he certainly did not want to allow Sanacja back into power. Sosnkowski, on the other hand, felt Sikorski had been weak in dealing with the Soviets, criticised Mikołajczyk's reluctance to stand up to them and was appalled that the Allies had failed to guarantee the restoration of Poland's pre-war eastern borders.

Sosnkowski opposed the AK plan to start an uprising in Warsaw in August 1944, but when the Allies did not support it he accused them of breaking their treaty with the Poles. It later transpired that Sosnkowski had not fully briefed the AK leadership: they were unaware that the Polish Air Force was subject to Allied strategic control, and so was not free to support the Uprising as they wished. The Polish Independent Parachute Brigade had also come under Allied command, but even so it was not possible to allocate sufficient aircraft to fly them to the aid of the insurgents.[9] Churchill exerted pressure on Mikołajczyk, and Sosnkowski was demoted from the role of commander-in-chief in September 1944 and left Britain for Canada two months later.[10]

The issue of anti-Semitic bullying within the Polish armed forces surfaced several times during the war. A Parliamentary Special Commission reported on this in February 1944, but with little effect, and there was a lengthy debate in Parliament on 6 April 1944, at a time when 30–50 Polish-Jewish deserters faced court martial. Previously, over two hundred Polish Jews out of a total of 850 had requested transfer to the British Army, which the Foreign Office had approved ('HC Deb (6 April 1944), vol. 398 cc2260-303'). Approximately three thousand Jews, from a total of four thousand, many of whom had been judged 'unfit for service' and tried to enlist three or four times before being accepted, had deserted the Polish II Corps while it was stationed in Palestine, presumably to join the British Jewish Brigade or one of the illegal Jewish military units then forming (Kochanski 2012: 197–8).[11]

While the Allies were sympathetic to the plight of Poland, they found the constant intrigues, animosities, rivalries, manoeuvring, resignations and accusations of treachery exceedingly bitter and difficult to negotiate. The Allies were utterly mystified by the behaviour of the Poles and could hardly credit that, when faced with national catastrophe, they failed to find unity of purpose. The Allies were not interested in the legacy of the Partitions behind Polish behaviour, traditional political rivalries or the reasons for Polish intransigence over their eastern border. In the end the Poles were right to suspect Allied pragmatism, but the competing aspects of tradition, the clash of military and political loyalties, and the power struggle they generated encouraged Polish officers to look down the wrong end of the telescope.

The possibility of Sikorski's dismissal, the threat of assassination and the possibility of mutiny all helped prevent the Government-in-Exile from realising that, squeezed between the demands of the British, US and Soviet governments, Poland may have been the first to fight, but neither Britain nor the USA had strategic interests in East-Central Europe. The Poles were junior partners in the Allied war effort: the Allies could beat the Nazis without Poland, but not without the USSR. The traditions, rivalry and ambitions of the Polish leadership hardly figured in end-game calculations. If Sanacja Poland was the price the Allies had to pay for keeping the USSR on-side, defeating the Nazis and bringing the war to an end, they were willing to pay it. By the end of the war the only thing that could be said with any certainty was that neither the London Government-in-Exile nor Stalin's Provisional Government in Lublin actually represented Polish interests or opinion.

94 *Polish writers and tradition*

Writers in war

Soviets and Nazis waged a relentless campaign to annihilate the Polish *inteligencja*, killing or imprisoning politicians, intellectuals and artists. In addition to the millions of Polish citizens murdered by the Nazis, between one and two million Poles were transported in conditions of extreme hardship for resettlement in Siberia or imprisonment in the Gulag system (Karol 1983; Zajdlerowa 1989). The experience of Siberia was already part of the Polish romantic mind-set. Gustaw Herling-Grudziński (1919–2000) said that after an NKVD interrogation in which he had been accused of spying for the Germans, he lamented he had been unable to find 'glorious sounding phrases from the catechism of Polish political martyrdom' when he was sentenced to five years forced labour in a camp at Yercevo near Archangel (Herling 1987: 3).

One of the most grievous blows of the war was Stalin's order to the NKVD to assassinate twenty-two thousand Polish prisoners of war, almost half the officer corps, at Katyń in 1940. The dead included an admiral, four generals, one hundred colonels, three hundred majors, one thousand captains, two thousand five hundred lieutenants and five hundred NCOs. Among the dead were *inteligencja* reservists: twenty-one university professors and lecturers; three hundred surgeons and physicians; two hundred lawyers, judges, prosecutors and court officials; three hundred engineers, and hundreds of writers, teachers and journalists. This was clearly an attack on the *inteligencja* traditions of independence and resistance to Russia these people represented. More leading *inteligencja* figures – including the poet Tadeusz Boy-Żeleński (1874–1941) – perished in the Nazi massacre of professors at Lwów University in 1941, and yet more in the camps, in the Underground and, like Leon Stroiński (1922–44), Tadeusz Gajcy (1922–44) and Krzysztof Kamil Baczyński (1921–44), in the Warsaw Uprising. In total Poland was to suffer six million dead in the war.

While most creative and artistic life came to a halt during the war, writers at least could continue in private, making occasional illegal forays into print as literary culture became part of the Underground and cyclostyled pamphlets and secret readings became a form of resistance. Even so, novels and theatre became impossible to sustain. The most popular literary form was poetry. Publication was always hazardous, but the Underground publishing operation was massive, providing newspapers, periodicals, political bulletins, general information and approximately one thousand book titles for Polish readers (Górski 2017). Herbert, who had identified with the AK, acknowledged the role of poetry in wartime national life, saying: 'One could [...] write a book about what we Poles owe to poetry. I refer to the recent past. During the occupation even the least sensitive people felt the true value of poetry. The partisan song was shorthand for rage, the camp poem an eye of hope, a few lines in a newspaper were a rhythmic pattern of our longing' (Herbert 2010: 556). Karski was to recall: 'There was not

Polish writers and tradition 95

an Underground paper which did not contain some poetry, verses of classic Polish authors or modern poets' (Karski 2019: 295).

Wartime experience encouraged writers to make writing into a kind of witness statement or a loyalty oath: Słonimski, Staff, Broniewski, Tuwim and others continued to write during the war, though their work shifted from personal themes towards national and Party issues. Konstanty Gałczyński (1905–53) managed to produce two clandestine volumes of poetry in a POW camp. In 1940 the Underground press produced forty-six copies of a poem by Miłosz, written under the pen-name Jan Syruć (Garliński 1985: 131–4; Topolski 1986: 253). In May 1945 the Underground published *Ocalenia*, another collection of Miłosz's poems. In the 'Przedmowa' (Fore-word), he asked: 'What is poetry that does not save / Nations or people? / A connivance with official lies' (Miłosz 1988: 78). Miłosz already had an eye to what was to come.

Adolf Rudnicki (1912–90), recounting a wartime conversation with Miłosz, recognised that in crossing over from literary to political tradition, ambiguities of loyalty and identity abounded, that tradition and national identity were still a kind of straitjacket, acknowledged that all notions of tradition were inherently conservative, and noted the difficulties of either breaking with tradition or the problems of trying to innovate within a tra-dition (Zagajewski 2007: 134).

Rudnicki's phrase 'correctly received tradition' harks back to the Polish romantics and implies that if tradition was 'correctly received' it could not avoid being revolutionary, but even if it was revolutionary it had to be policed to make sure it was 'correctly received'. And he catches the difficulty of the relationship – 'To be on good terms with tradition is to have it well digested', but it is also to 'have the courage to break with it'.

In the final year of World War II, in his poem 'In Warsaw', Miłosz saw the wind scattering the dust of Warsaw's rubble and with some sadness noted the continuing impact of the conspiratorial romantic tradition in the style, politics and behaviour of the AK (Miłosz 1988: 76). He felt that in the cir-cumstances neither the Underground writers (of which he was one) nor the AK had any choice but to act as they did, and that the Warsaw Uprising of August 1944 was both inevitable and disastrous.[12]

For more than two years after the defeat of the Nazis and the Soviet 'liberation' of Poland, the country was wracked by assassinations and civil war. The NSZ and others fought on. For them communism was not only a foreign ideology imported on the point of Soviet bayonets, it contra-dicted Endecja's version of tradition and ethno-national identity and had to be opposed publicly, resolutely, violently.[13] As Nina Karsov (b.1940) later commented: 'No-one trusted the real Poles, because how could you trust pre-war officers or Home Army and similar 'bandit' types' (Karsov & Szechter 1971: 255). A rigged election in 1947 meant the communist take-over was complete. Stefan Korboński (1901–89), who had played a major role in the AK, was arrested and then released, but afterwards, with

96 Polish writers and tradition

intelligence reports indicating the Soviets planned to assassinate London premier Mikołajczyk and other London-based leaders, felt obliged to flee Poland and concluded: 'The chapter in our lives entitled "conspiracy" was closed. A new chapter was opening' (Korboński 2004: 495).

Writers and communism

The experiences of war, the shape of the new Poland and reactions to communism were to be the main challenges facing post-war writers, and these issues – all of which intersected concepts of identity, loyalty and tradition – were linked in complex ways. In 1945 Poles found themselves in a new Poland, shorn of the *kresy* and the major cultural centres of Lwów and Wilno, located a hundred miles west of where it had been before the war and now incorporating the ruined German cities of Posen (Poznań), Breslau (Wrocław), Danzig (Gdańsk) and their hinterlands. Poland expelled millions of Germans from its new territories, while Poles forced out of homes within the USSR now arrived as settlers.

Post-war Poland had virtually no ethnic minorities and was, for the first time, almost entirely Polish-speaking and Catholic. The ethnic and linguistic purity so desired by the Endecja movement had been achieved by Nazism and communism. In addition to wartime casualties, massive wartime damage, boundary changes and population exchange, writers – where they were not still in exile – found they were now constrained not only by the language, culture and traditions reinforced by the war, but increasingly by the reality of censorship and 'the system' imposed by Moscow. Most Poles (those still in Poland and the émigrés too) felt that the Molotov–Ribbentrop Pact had been an attempt to partition Europe, but at the Yalta Conference the West had simply abandoned Poland. Communist domination meant Poles found themselves attached to an Asiatic rump and inevitably there was a widespread revision of hopes and orientations as opinions of 'the West' and the idea of 'Europe' were challenged by the 'new reality' and the shortcomings of 'victory'.[14]

Even though the new regime offered very favourable conditions for writers in terms of commissions, royalties, reprints and a captive readership, Zbigniew Herbert, for instance, who had seen how communism functioned in wartime Lwów, wanted as little as possible to do with it (Poppek & Gelberg 1994).

Some writers, like Adam Ważyk, Władysław Broniewski, Tadeusz Borowski (1922–51), Wisława Symborska (1923–2012), Wiktor Worosylski (1927–96), Tadeusz Konwicki (1926–2015) and a handful of others, felt communism really was the way forward and supported it willingly. For a while some writers even wrote in its praise. Many writers, like Jerzy Andrzejewski (1909–83) and Kazimierz Brandys (dubbed the neo-positivists by Leopold Tyrmand (1920–85)), whatever their misgivings about the USSR, felt they had no option but to accept communism and rather warily went along with the new regime. Some even joined the Party in the hope

Polish writers and tradition 97

they could function as 'loyal critics'. A few told themselves that if anything of Polish tradition was to survive then a moderate degree of cooperation was essential.

Up to the 'thaw' of 1956, opponents of the regime were at great risk from the security services. After that, while opposition led to 'unpleasantness' and was 'troublesome', it was very rarely fatal (Iwaszkiewicz 2002: xv). A critical message, even after 1956, was never advisable because in a system of near total control, while the writer might survive, they and their books could simply disappear from public view (Leftwich Curry 1984). If writers wanted to continue to publish, they had to develop strategies to get round censorship. They discovered that while it was not possible to openly criticise the Party, its policies or its leaders, it was possible to criticise the ways the policies were applied, to say mistakes had been made, that improvements were necessary. It was also acceptable (and strategically better advised) to criticise the Party's allies. But this approach had its problems.

In 1949 Paweł Hertz (1918–2001), a 'liberal' Party member who wrote for *Twórczość* (*Creativity*) and *Kuźnica* (*The Forge*), felt compelled to criticise *Tygodnik Powszechny* (*Weekly Universal*), the Soviet bloc's only independent Catholic newspaper. Hertz felt *Tygodnik Powszechny* 'was no longer interesting', and in a spirit that was patriotic, positivist and mindful of the Party, he accused the newspaper of 'promoting intellectual provincialism', of toadying to the lowest elements of the regime in 'false solicitude' in 'conformity with primitively conceived didactic aims'. In reply, a senior columnist at the journal explained to Hertz that by agreement with the censor the journal was limited in what it could say or discuss, even if this gave the impression it was concerned only with matters of religion: this was the price of its independence. Hertz realised he had reached the limit of his positivist cooperation and a short while later left the Party (Mayewski 1958: 136–8).

At first Leopold Tyrmand wrote for several regime-approved journals, including *Tygodnik Powszechny*, but as communist control tightened he found himself increasingly hedged in by political considerations. In 1953 his connection to *Tygodnik Powszechny* meant he found himself unofficially banned, without substantial work and unable to earn a living.[15] In 1954, instead of writing for the state publishing houses, which meant he would more or less have to promise to write what the Party wanted, he began a diary, writing for his 'desk drawer'.

The first generation to reach maturity after the war contained few young writers who had inherited *inteligencja* values from family, class and religion, and fewer still who had read enough to enable them to fully internalise these values. While the parents of this young generation felt that in comparison to war, occupation and the grim, grey world of communism, the interwar years seemed like a kind of lost paradise, the new writers were too young to have any real sense of what had been lost. The status quo was what they knew and it seemed, at first, that their future lay in their relationship with the Party and in Party approval, rather than in opposition: the

98 Polish writers and tradition

Party was simply a *pociąg sosu* (gravy train), an opportunity to be seized and manipulated because it was one of the few routes to literary, social and economic advancement. Initially these young writers embraced the upbeat, formulaic *socrealizm* (socialist-realism) of the 'Boy meets Tractor' variety when it was made the Party's preferred style in 1949. But they soon found themselves blocked not so much by the Party but by the limitations of *socrealizm* as a literary form, then by the *inteligencja* and its sense of tradition, and then increasingly by the flat contradiction of the reality that surrounded them.

One of the first literary challenges to the 'world view' the Party was trying to create came with the novelist Zofia Nałkowska's *Medaliony* (1946, *Medallions*). Nałkowska was well known as a novelist from the interwar period, but in 1945 the incoming communist authorities asked her to serve on the Commission to Investigate Nazi War Crimes. Whatever she thought of the new regime, she set aside her feelings to help document some of the effects of Nazism. As part of her work for the Commission she visited the camps at Auschwitz, Stutthof, Majdanek and Treblinka. Her report – seven short chapters totalling barely fifty pages, including witness statements, testimony, and her own descriptions of what she saw – is now considered to be a masterpiece of documentary reporting on the Holocaust. Her description of the process by which the anatomist Professor Spanner attempted to turn corpses into soap at the Danzig Medical Academy is a model of control and revelation. In this book there were no heroes, there was no martial glory and there was no sense of victory. By refusing to pass overt moral judgement and by letting witnesses speak for themselves, she managed to show the success the Nazis enjoyed in subduing the German intelligentsia and the incredible de-sensitisation worked by the Nazis as mass murder was incorporated into the economy.

Alongside Nałkowska's report, the stories of Tadeusz Borowski also took up the challenge of finding an adequate and appropriate style to discuss and describe what had taken place in the camps. Both Borowski and Nałkowska were aware that their writing challenged notions of morality, law, tradition and obligation (Borowski 1978: 110). Borowski had been arrested by the Nazis in 1943, sent to Auschwitz, transferred to Natzweiler-Dautmergen and then to Dachau-Allach, where he was eventually liberated by the Americans. After spending time in a Displaced Persons camp, he returned reluctantly to communist Poland in 1946. He was already sceptical about Polish martyrology and felt his experience in the camps demanded a style that was radically different from his poetry. His story collections *Pożegnanie z Marią* (1947, *Farewell to Mary*) and *Kamienny świat* (1948, *World of Stone*) appeared just as he joined the Party. His treatment of wartime street life and his experience of the camps in stories like 'A Day at Harmenz', 'The People Who Walked On', 'Auschwitz, Our Home (A Letter)' and 'This way for the Gas, Ladies and Gentlemen' was unlike anything that had gone before. He saw no point in making brutality, suffering and death into something heroic or beautiful and there were no longer any clear moral divides.

Polish writers and tradition 99

He made no moral judgement of the Nazis except to show how the cruelty of the camps created a new 'norm' of conduct where prisoners swindled and made other prisoners their victims. In the camps all distinction between good or bad behaviour, honourable or criminal conduct, were abandoned, reduced and rendered meaningless. For Borowski there were only survivors and the dead.[16]

At first Borowski was an enthusiastic Party member but, although he was not blocked by the censor, his style was not something the Party felt comfortable with. Indeed, the violence of the camps seemed to indicate a new angle on future human conduct that the Party had great difficulty in accommodating. The Party could applaud Borowski's suggestion that the 'culture of the West' had failed Poland. After the events of the war, Borowski was certainly not alone in this: in the pages of the magazine *Kultura* (Paris, 1947–2000), exiles and émigrés like Jerzy Giedroyc (1906–2000), Józef Czapski, Zofia Hertz (1910–2003), Zygmunt Hertz, Józef Wittlin, Gustaw Herling, Jerzy Stempowski (1893–1969) and Andrzej Bobkowski (1913–1961) were beginning to re-assess the nature of a 'victory' that left Poland a loser on the winning side, and through that to **chart the complex changes in Poland's relationship to the West, Western culture and to 'Europe'** (Kostrzewa 1990; Mikołajewski 2018). In Poland, the idea that the West had somehow betrayed them gave the Party a chance to insert their rival 'culture from the East'. Also, while the Party was seeking writers to produce literature that divided the world into fascists and communists, guilty and just, progressives and reactionaries, heroes and traitors, it did not see Borowski's nihilism and amorality as pointing the way to an inevitable, bright communistic future.

But it was not only the Party that was puzzled by Borowski. Polish literary expectation of wartime tales of suffering, martyrdom and heroic conduct was also contradicted. Readers and critics were affronted by his work and even those who were not indignant were made uneasy. The reading public found it difficult to see that his apparently amoral, passionless, relentless account was in fact an effective disguise for it's very opposite. Borowski believed that Western values had failed and the idea of Europe was no longer a valid proposition, but at the same time he offered only the 'antipode' of his desires: 'antiheroic, antimartyrological, antimoralistic, laical, provocative, derisory' (Drewnowski 2007: 6). As a result, while Borowski is admired by a few in literary circles, he has generally been neglected and even today is considered to be something of an exception, outside the mainstream of tradition, a strange literary 'case'.

But Borowski was not alone in challenging traditional views of wartime behaviour. In 1961, Kornel Filipowicz (1913–90) published *Pamiętnik Antybohatera* (*The Memoir of an Anti-Hero*). With its venality, opportunism, lack of patriotic feeling and its tale of low-level collaboration with the Nazi occupation (the narrator applies for citizenship as a *Volksdeutsche*[17] to improve his rations), the book was a catalogue of anti-heroic survivalism and a counterpoint to the idea that all Poles resisted the wartime descent

100 Polish writers and tradition

into the moral abyss. At the end of the book the anti-hero ponders why he is still not fully happy and concludes: 'Perhaps, deep inside, I harboured some hidden grudge against people and the world that I hadn't been forced, as is often the case in wartime, into some act of heroism against my will? Perhaps a life which emerges intact from such an adventure later holds some unusual, special value for a person?' (Filipowicz 2019: 70).

Marek Hłasko (1934–69), a rare, genuine, working-class writer, burst onto the literary scene in 1954–6 with two books that not only made him a favourite with the Party, but an instant pin-up for the rebellious younger generation. However, Hłasko found writing was hard work and felt the 'great labour' of reading the Polish classics was a waste of time: he just wanted to make money and be a celebrity (Hłasko 2013: 27–8). Hłasko described an encounter in the mid 1950s with the critic Artur Sandauer (1913–89), who tried to get Hłasko to grapple with the poetry of Miron Białoszewski (1922–83), probably the most private and least 'national' of the post-war poets. Sandauer read the poems aloud, but Hłasko, in spite of 'superhuman effort', claimed to understand 'absolutely nothing' until Sandauer 'took me to be a moron and threw me out' (Hłasko 2013: 147).

Hłasko resisted what *inteligencja* colleagues tried to teach and broke with writers who attempted to guide him: Władysław Broniewski, Jerzy Andrzejewski (1909–83), Andrzej Brycht (1935–98), Igor Newerly (1903–87), Marek Nowakowski (1935–2014), Arnold Słucki (1920–72), Jerzy Tyrmand and Kazimierz Brandys. These were some of the dominant personalities shaping Poland's post-war literature, and even where they initially offered qualified support for the Party but later broke with it, they saw themselves as 'quarrelling and contending with ideology, desperately defending endangered humanity' (Zagajewski 2004: 197). Like Hłasko, many Party members were a little afraid of the creative *inteligencja*. It is possible his antipathy to education, *inteligencja* values and learning in general was what the Party liked about Hłasko. However, Hłasko's brutal portrayal of Polish working-class life meant he soon ran up against the censor, fell out of favour with the Party and then defected. He summed up his failure by saying: 'They took me for a fool my whole life' (Hłasko 2013: 139).

The friction of the interwar years had shifted: in the post-war period the clash was between the collectivist, didactic and truncated ambition of communism, and the personal, sceptical and ironic modes of dissidents and oppositionists. But as always, relationships between these elements were complex and changeable. The communists needed the support of writers in order to legitimise themselves, yet inadvertently they made writers central to the preservation of pre-communist cultural values. Communism – particularly the Party's attempt to impose *socrealizm* as the only acceptable style in all the arts in the years 1949–56, the reversal of the gains made in the 'thaw' followed by the massive expansion of censorship after 1956 – steadily alienated intellectuals, created dissidents and again forced writers to consider very carefully their relationship to Poland, to Polishness and to *inteligencja* tradition.

The tensions within Poland were echoed in the Polish community abroad. In 1963 the Ford Foundation invited Witold Gombrowicz to Berlin to spend a year as writer-in-residence and he left South America for the first time in twenty-four years. He thought of himself as a 'Polish yokel' and regarded his diaries as 'the intrusion into European culture of a villager, of a Polish country gentleman with all the mistrust, the common-sense and the realism of a peasant' (Gombrowicz 1988: 35). Throughout his exile Gombrowicz had tried to 'stop being too easy a riddle', to break with any restrictive definition of his identity, to break out of 'the deadly mediocrity of my milieu' and to confound the expectations of Polish literary tradition by bidding for acceptance as a universal writer (Gombrowicz 1988: 91).

Gombrowicz was by this time an international success as a playwright and he anticipated the visit would mark his entry into West European culture, but he was to be disappointed. In Paris he visited the editors of the Polish émigré magazine *Kultura* (Culture), but they left him cold with their politics, their history and their 'Continental sophistication'. Paris suffocated him with its overweening self-importance and he began to regard Europe as 'a kind of death'. He was introduced to Günter Grass, Uwe Johnson and Peter Weiss, but they regarded him as an oddity, a provincial from Poland whose provinciality was compounded by the provinciality of exile. Afterwards Gombrowicz wrote that the real difference between Eastern and Western intellectuals was simply that the Westerners had not 'had a good kick in the a----' (Gombrowicz 1988: 13). He summarised his feelings about the visit: wondering if the failure was the fault of 'a certain anachronism peculiar to the Polish character' or 'intellectual idleness of the West, which shows a marked preference for worn-out formulas', he concluded: Poland's 'relationship with the world had something bad, something tainted about it, and I, as an artist, felt somewhat responsible for this fateful "Polish legend". It was essential to put an end to it. But how?' (Gombrowicz 1973: 103).

Gombrowicz fought not to be seen as a 'Polish writer', and struggled to break free of restrictive 'forms' of Polish identity and to present himself as a complex creative entity, but his diary was in fact a long, unconventional argument with Polish literature. His *Testament* showed that even with an international prize, a growing reputation and a lifelong dedication to not doing what was expected of him, the tradition of breaking with tradition had its problems. However, as his work was banned in Poland, most Polish readers were not aware of his achievements, his opinions or his struggle until much later, when heavily illegal copies of his work were smuggled in from Paris and when heavily censored versions of his works began to appear.

Neo-positivism

While those who were opposed to communism from the first did not change their minds, by the mid 1950s the neo-positivists – 'progressive Catholics', Catholic intellectual organisations, Party discussion groups within

102   Polish writers and tradition

universities, *Tygodnik Powszechny*, *Znak* (Sign) deputies to the Sejm and even the tame Catholic 'front' organisation PAX – began to feel that 'loyal opposition' was proving ineffective. By the mid 1960s the feeling was increasingly that cooperation was simply a waste of time, the Party was not listening. Stalin was dead but a decaying Stalinism remained in place, and the freedoms won in the 'thaw' of 1956 were slowly being recalled, but to no great purpose. One of the first writers to express this feeling was the young Sławomir Mrożek (1930–2013). He had begun to view the Polish literary cannon, particularly Bolesław Prus and the positivists, through the lens of communism.

In 1884 Prus had published a story called 'The Human Telegraph'. It is an early example of what we now call micro-fiction. On a visit to an orphanage, the Countess witnesses a fight among the children over a book. She is told that all the children in the orphanage love to read, but there is a shortage of books. That night she recounts her experience to a friend, who later visits a Mr. Z- 'whose entire life was passed in performing trifling services to such representatives of humanity as comprise Classes VII to III of the official hierarchy'. As a result of their conversation Mr. Z- decides to put an announcement in the local newspaper requesting books for the orphanage. A few days later, in the company of a professor of physics, the Countess arrives at the newspaper office to find a shabbily dressed chimney-sweep from the hat-factory waiting with his anaemic daughter. They have brought a few books for the orphans in response to the Countess' advertisement. The Countess asks the name of the chimney-sweep so that he might be thanked formally, but he refuses to give it, saying this is not necessary because he is 'only a poor working man'.

In this story Prus was satirising the well-meaning, progressive, aristocratic do-gooder and her inability to fully recognise the human dignity of the man donating the books, her mechanistic understanding of society, her failure to identify the real problems and her patronising, 'noble' attitude.

Mrożek viewed 'The Human Telegraph' in terms of its political tensions. Communist Poland had industrialised at an incredible pace. As the rural population shifted from the countryside into the rapidly expanding cities, the resulting issues – youth culture, industrial pollution, social adaptation, educational deficits, peasants in factories, the contrast of rural within urban, and a whole range of urgent social, political and medical problems – rapidly came into view. Yet at the same time the growth of censorship dictated that 'real problems' like Soviet military control, political prisoners, the legitimacy of the regime and the Katyń massacre could not be discussed openly. By the mid 1950s, when it became clear the Six Year Plan had failed, this refusal to acknowledge and debate mistakes had a massively negative effect on the Party membership, on the already poor standing of the Party and on the attitudes of those who up to now had worked with the regime. Against this background, Mrożek published a collection of stories called *Słoń* (*The Elephant*, 1958). This volume subtly challenged communist orthodoxy with anarchic humour and satire, putting neo-positivism under the spotlight.

Polish writers and tradition 103

One of the stories was 'On a Journey', which took up Prus' idea of the human telegraph.

Mrożek's are very much tales of the People's Republic of Poland, with its surrealist inefficiencies and shortages. He makes satirical use of Prus' story, updating and poking fun at its positivism. Mrożek inverts the notion of progress, using it to laugh at the Party's sense of totalitarian hierarchy and at its claim that the life offered by the People's Republic of Poland was genuinely humane and progressive, constantly improving, rather than increasingly surreal, bedevilled by shortages, absenteeism and alcoholism. In several stories in *Słoń*, Mrożek re-used and re-worked the romantic and positivist literary tradition handed down to him.[18] The critic Jan Błoński, noting the schizophrenic mixture of 'old' and 'new' in this collection, wrote: 'the modernists laugh at tradition while the reactionaries laugh at the progressives' (www.culture.pl/en/artist/slawomir-mrozek). Mrożek drifted away from the Party after 1956 and left Poland for Italy in 1963.[19]

In his play *Tango* (1964), Mrożek offered his most profound comment on revolution and its clash with tradition. Using the generations of a traditional family as his model, he initially viewed rebellion as inevitable and positive, but then wondered, once revolution had achieved its purpose, what the next generation could rebel against. In a revolution where traditional restrictions, rules and taboos had been successfully subdued and repressive standards had been destroyed, he supposed the new freedoms must eventually be overturned and a new sense of order and discipline established. In this play the trouble seems to have started with the revolution of 'nineteen fourteen... eighteen... nineteen... twenty two...' (Esslin 1970: 110). This is perhaps a suggestion that it could have been at any time, but it is also a sly reference to the date of Polish independence. Arthur, whose parents rebelled, 'broke with tradition' by making love in public and had only 'one rule: do as you please', has a problem in that he has no restrictions to rebel against (Esslin 1970: 111). However, he claims there is neither 'humility' nor 'initiative' in the current set-up and longs for the resurrection of the order, manners, discipline and hierarchy his parents overthrew.

Later, on the eve of his wedding, he realises theory is not enough: brute force will be needed to demolish the status quo entirely if his revolution is not to be overturned. The brutal, primitive Eddie, taken into the family as a kind of servant, has no time for or interest in tradition or theory, but he completes the logic of the revolutionary argument by killing Arthur and dancing the tango – a dance that once embodied revolution and liberation – over his body. The ending might be compared to that of *Hamlet*, where philosopher Hamlet dies and is superseded by the bustling Fortinbras, fresh from military conquests in Poland. But it is also likely Mrożek had Mickiewicz in mind. *Tango* stands Mickiewicz's *Dziady* on its head, seeing brutality and Falangism in Eddie's power, rather than liberation and restoration.

Mrożek was not alone in confronting tradition or in trying to re-set Polish literary culture. Most of the writers who took the neo-positivist route (whether they joined the Party or not) fell out with the Party either after

104 *Polish writers and tradition*

1956, 1968, 1970 or 1976. By 1980, writers who still supported the Party were very rare. Aleksander Wat, perhaps because he was outside the mainstream of Jewish, Polish and Soviet literary tradition, was able to reflect in a very individual manner on the nature of literary tradition. In his essay 'The Key and the Hook' (first published in *Kultura*, Paris, in 1963), he observed that in Polish literature conventionalisation was the principal stimulus to artistic renewal. By this he meant that when the 'tempo of history was slow', the writer's glory came from repeating and perfecting what had been done before, not out of a lack of inventiveness, but simply because there was no call for anything challenging. But when history 'accelerated', sharpening the contradiction between the tempo of life and the exhaustion of petrified forms, the writer became disturbed, anxious and keen to record 'subjective time'. Wat contrasted this with the evolution of literature in the West, saying the noise and confusion of the West 'in no way indicates agony' (Wat 2018: 236). By the late 1960s, Wat thought of Poland as a place 'where too many died for the country... a country of too much oppression and rebellion. A sick country. Poland' (Wat 2018: 75).

After 1968, writers like Jerzy Andrzejewski (1909–83), Tadeusz Konwicki (1926–2015) and Kazimierz Brandys (1916–2000), who had all been well disposed towards communism in the immediate post-war years, became increasingly critical of the Party. Brandys had never been favourably disposed towards unreconstructed Polish tradition and was only gradually persuaded from the hope that communism would help. In his diaries, published in Paris, he wrote that Polish literature was happy to remain 'provincial' and 'traditional'.[20] It lacked variety and range because it had not passed through the historical stages other European literatures had experienced and instead had become obsessed with itself. Polish literature, he said, had writing about the manor and the estate; as the gentry had no court to attend they decamped to their distant estates in the country, and so Poland missed the development of tightly plotted drama and court intrigue. Instead the gentry produced the *gawęda* – rambling, far-fetched, ornate, poetic tales, usually presented orally for the entertainment of noble neighbours.[21] He said because Polish society lacked a well-developed and numerous bourgeoisie, it lacked comedy of manners or satirical literature displaying the humbug and hypocrisy of middle-class ambition. Since its industrial working class had been tiny until the twentieth century, and then had been made up of peasants transferred into factories by communism, Polish literature did not represent poverty or working-class struggle. It lacked police stories because the police represented alien authority; it lacked crime stories because crime was generally defined by a foreign power.[22] Poland lacked colonies and so did not develop adventure stories. Polish literature, he said, avoided serious discussion of the Catholic Church, but instead offered the rhyme words *lud i cud* (nation and miracle) (Brandys 1984: 60–61).

With his multi-layered novel *Rondo* (1982), Brandys launched a fierce assault on the conspiratorial tradition, telling the tale of Rondo, a small

Polish writers and tradition   105

Underground unit in World War II. Tom the narrator, a part-time actor, is rumoured to be Marshal Piłsudski's illegitimate son and it is at the moment he starts growing a moustache that he decides to become a conspirator (Brandys 1982: 103). Tom may be seen by some as a representative of the 'old order', but he invents Rondo not out of patriotism, but simply to improve his standing with his actress girlfriend Tola – for whom 'conspiracy was an aristocratic perversion' – and he recruits his friends to protect them from becoming involved in real (dangerous) Underground work.

When Gombrowicz's *Diaries 1956-69* (1969, published first in Paris) were read clandestinely in communist Poland of the mid 1970s, it was clear his comments, though they took communism into account, grew out of his engagement with the literary scene in the interwar years. His quest to save Polish culture from its determined national-provincialism was judged by some to be a serious affront to patriotic tradition, deeply compromised by his open homosexuality and by his long residence abroad. For others, however, the diaries were a fascinating delight. He not only provided a deeply personal critique of the provincialism imposed by communism, but in considering interwar literature he challenged tradition, broke the cultural frame, said the unsayable and contradicted accepted ideas of 'Form' (Gombrowicz 1988: 157).

Gombrowicz had reacted strongly against the early modernists of Młoda Polska (Young Poland), the literary movement dominant in the years 1890–1918. He looked at the work of a generation of writers – Stanisław Wyspiański (1869–1907), Jan Kasprowicz (1860–1926), Stefan Żeromski (1864–1925), Władysław Stanisław Reymont (1867–1925) and Karol Irzykowski (1873–1944) – but only to question their adherence to petrified rituals, notions of heroism, rural customs, national stereotypes, institutionalised relationships, their outmoded obsession with what was 'proper' and the maturity of their Polish-ness. Of independence he said: 'After our struggles with Russia, with Germany, a struggle with Poland awaited us. It is not surprising therefore, that independence turned out to be more burdensome and humiliating than bondage. As long as we were absorbed with revolt against a foreign power questions such as "Who are we?" "What are we to make of ourselves?" lie dormant, but independence awakened the riddle that was slumbering inside us' (Gombrowicz 1988: 151).

For Gombrowicz, the interwar period had an 'unreal, tawdry, grotesque atmosphere' that limited spiritual and intellectual growth, and the country 'did not grow the stronger for it'. Gombrowicz confessed he was completely bored by the plays of Wyspiański, where the material 'rolled across the heavens of History and Fate' but failed to challenge Polish traditions and assumptions, offered 'nothing enriching from a universal perspective', and proved to be insignificant outside the immediate Polish context. He lamented the influence of the conservative Henryk Sienkiewicz (1846–1916), whom he regarded as a 'first-rate second-rate writer' who had surrendered to 'the service of collective fantasy', and whose idea of God was really a way of being intimate with the nation. He also dismissed Żeromski,

106 Polish writers and tradition

saying he donned the issue of 'the Homeland' as if it were a shirt – 'an unsavoury sight' (Gombrowicz 1988: 23, 154).

He said he found the younger generation of Skamander poets appreciative of the new reality but generally clueless, blocked by complacency and self-obsession. The Kraków avant-garde poets he dismissed as 'indolents, decadents, dreamers, the undereducated, the aborted'. He thought the symbolist and part-time Satanist Stanisław Przybyszewski (1868–1927) was the only writer to attempt a 'revision' of Polish values by introducing writing that 'accommodated nothing, being an unmerciful spiritual unburdening'. Even so, he felt Przybyszewski was overwhelmed by a decadent obsession with himself, 'pretentious, unsavory, twisted, shrill' (Gombrowicz 1988: 155, 161).

Gombrowicz concluded that the writers of the interwar years – both old and young – had failed to challenge the Polish psyche, had not emphasised the damage of the 'inadequate' or 'partial existence' of Poland during the Partitions, and thus had not helped develop a realistic appreciation of the difficulties and responsibilities independence brought with it. Instead, they had allowed Poland to foster a self-congratulatory, anachronistic, retrograde chauvinism. The interwar writers, he said, had failed Poland and certainly offered nothing of use to post-war Poles: 'the period of Polish independence was not a joyous creation, but a painful struggle with the invisible thread of our own inner slavery'. Gombrowicz said he had higher expectations of writers and was happy to have left Poland before he became famous because he felt he would have been ruined by the 'numbing' literary scene (Gombrowicz 1988: 151, 157).

Jewish writers and 1968

While there is no shortage of memoirs and analyses of the Holocaust, comparatively little has been written about post-war anti-Semitism in Poland – particularly the events of 1968 – and its relationship to literary tradition.[23] After 1945, traditional anti-Semitic attitudes were not changed by Jewish involvement in the Communist Party, their role in the communist take-over and their membership of the security services and the army.

For many Jewish writers, the temptation to join the Party had been huge simply because in theory it promised to get rid of anti-Semitism. Jerzy Andrzejewski was one of the very few writers to challenge Polish readers with a story about the fate of the Jews. His novel *Wielki Tydzień* (1945, Holy Week), set in the Easter week of 1943 as ash from the Warsaw Ghetto Uprising fell on the city, is a thoughtful and compelling book, honestly charting opinions – prejudiced, patriotic, intellectual, uncertain, indifferent, even thankful that the Jewish question has finally been 'resolved' – about the destruction of the Jews. Malecki, the main character, and his family act according to their traditional Catholic ideals of civic duty, patriotism and honour, and feel they have done everything good Poles should do up to this point, but faced with the brutal reality of Nazi genocide their best efforts are dwarfed and their traditional values are crushed into

Polish writers and tradition 107

'nothing'. Andrzejewski concentrates on Polish indifference rather than active anti-Semitism, but Polish society does not show up well in this novel. However, for the most part, only two years after the event, still involved in a civil war, Poles were too deeply enmeshed in their own problems to give the fate of the Jews more than passing notice. The behaviour of Poles towards Jews during the war did not attract serious attention until much later, when the gap the Holocaust left in Polish accounts of the war became more obvious. However, the appearance of *Wielki Tydzień* indicated the Party, even if it was not yet considering a direct assault on the Church or traditional Polish values, was considering how to attempt some serious adjustment to the Polish mind-set.[24]

In the period 1952–68, while it became increasingly difficult to repress or censor protest at the way the economy was being handled and the totalitarian style of the government, it also became apparent that a contest was raging within the Party. While many saw communism as a release for the Jews and a chance for social equality, some party members saw anti-Semitism as a useful strategy to hold on to power. As early as 1952 there had been a press campaign to attack 'bourgeois objectivism' in science and 'cosmopolitanism' in literature and the arts: in practice this meant 'outing' prominent Jews – performers, artists, writers, critics, composers, actors, lecturers, Professors – by printing their original Jewish name alongside their current name. As Nina Karsov was to observe, this was 'an anti-Semitism of a type until then unknown, because it was of the Party's own coinage' (Karsov & Szechter 1971: 148).

Hard-line Stalinists in high office either feared the Soviet leadership or, out of ideological belief, felt the system (and their power) needed no revision. The attitude of the hardliners became less tenable and less convincing with Stalin's death. Many of the more intellectually flexible Party members began to feel that Stalinism could be ditched and a more humane and responsive system developed to take its place. These people were often referred to as the revisionists. Many of the revisionists were young, intellectual and Jewish, and many were the offspring of senior Party members. The Party, however, had no mechanisms for listening to criticism and its first response was always to maintain a tight grip on power then to divert aggression elsewhere. In 1964, Karol Modzelewski (1937–2019) and Jacek Kuroń (1934–2004), both Party members, had presented *An Open Letter to the Party* – a supportive but critical manifesto, for which they were expelled from the Party and sentenced to three years in prison.

It was becoming increasingly apparent that in spite of the Party's propaganda, traditional attitudes to the Jews continued to run just beneath the surface. In 1960, for example, Nina Karsov tried to find historian Symon Szechter an assistant. She found a young student who was willing, but once her husband realised Szechter was a Jewish name he vetoed the idea, saying he did not trust Jews (Karsov & Szechter 1971: 115).

In January 1968 the Party banned a production of Mickiewicz's *Dziady*, sparking student demonstrations. Among the youthful protestors at

108 *Polish writers and tradition*

Warsaw University were Jacek Kuroń, Karol Modzelewski, Adam Michnik (b.1946), Irena Lasota (b.1945), Henryk Szlajfer (b.1947) and Barbara Toruńczyk (b.1946) – all of whom went on to play substantial roles in the protest movement and in Solidarność, and all of whom had (to varying degrees) a Jewish background. When students at Warsaw University presented a petition of protest at the banning of the play, 'worker activists' (plainclothes police) and uniformed police attacked them. A protest rally was then brutally attacked by militia from ORMO (volunteer reserve) and ZOMO (mobile riot squad). Within a week student protest had spread to all the major cities.

As the Arab–Israeli war of 1967 got under way it must have seemed to some within the government that critics could be silenced and discontent channelled away from reform by making use of anti-Semitism. An anti-Zionist campaign began in the press, consistently conflating Zionism and Judaism, claiming both were agents of imperialism and enemies of Poland. The Catholic magazine *Znak* was attacked for its revisionist sympathies in the Sejm; First Secretary Władysław Gomułka denounced 'those Zambrowskis, Staszewskis, Słonimskis' and 'company of the Kisielewski and Jasienica kind' and labelled them 'revisionists, Zionists, lackeys of imperialism'.[25] Demonstrations and mass arrests were followed by purges of the army and police. In the universities whole teaching departments were dismissed and prominent professors, including Leszek Kołakowski (1927–2009) and Stefan Żółkiewski (1911–1991) who were revisionist sympathisers, lost their jobs. As the purge developed, Jews were encouraged to leave Poland en masse. An estimated fifty thousand Jews left Poland in the period 1957–9 (including Eva Hoffman b.1945). Some 25–30,000 more left in 1967–8, including Henryk Grynberg (b.1936), who, on an official theatre tour of the USA in 1967, refused to return to Poland. Janina Bauman (1926–2009), a party member who had worked as a top script editor, offered a vivid description of the campaign as she experienced it – demotion, enforced leave, loss of job, threats of violence, spying, denunciations, accusations and intimidation – until she, her husband Zygmunt Bauman (1925–2017) and their children left Poland for Israel (Bauman 1988). In August 1968, international press attention was diverted by the Soviet invasion of Czechoslovakia and suppression of the Prague Spring.

It was during this purge that Nina Karsov (b.1940), who had been raised in a Polish family, first found out she was Jewish. She was told by her interrogators after she had been arrested for collecting materials on political trials. Eventually she was 'allowed' to leave Poland. Later she pondered the complex mechanisms of anti-Semitism and its relation to Polish tradition in a country where Jews effectively no longer lived. As an example, she described her friendship as a young woman with the Klonowski family, whose conversation and manners, and the contents of whose home – paintings, prints and rare books – and whose adherence to the tradition of celebrating Polish Independence Day on 3rd May 'bore witness to their determination to maintain the purity of traditional Polish life'. In their

Polish writers and tradition   109

home Karsov had access to books, ideas and conversation that put her in touch with the 'charm' of a 'bygone era'. It took her a while to realise she was slowly being 'inoculated with a certain myth – the myth of Poland', and being shown a series of altars 'consecrated to the glory of a false notion of Poland'. The fact that these people were anti-Semitic was not immediately apparent because 'their anti-Semitism, like most things about them, was refined and subtle'.

The Klonowskis and Karsov became acquainted with Irena Drzewska-Ruszyc, the muse and lover of the pianist and composer Aleksander Michalowski. Mrs Klonowska befriended her not to celebrate the memory of the musician, but in the hope of becoming 'the priestess of a legend' by acquiring the relics and property of the dead artist when the old lady died. However, Karsov was present and called an ambulance when the old lady had a stroke: Karsov accompanied the old woman to hospital and became her nurse. It was she, rather than Mrs Klonowska, who registered the death, petitioned the Union and National Theatre for money to help bury the old lady. And it was Karsov who hired a lorry to carry the coffin to the grave. Karsov and her granny were the only people at the graveside. When the Chopin Society took over Michalowski's papers, Karsov was tasked with transferring the materials to the archive.

Karsov's visits to the Klonowski home came to an abrupt halt when Karsov was accused of being a cheat. She came to understood that the decision to hand over Michalowski's papers to the Chopin Society was, in Mrs Klonowska's opinion, both theft and sacrilege. The materials should have been handed over to the Klonowskis as 'the only worthy guardians of the Polish tradition'. Years later Karsov was invited to meet with the Klonowskis and reconciliation seemed possible. Karsov commented, 'I was forgiven, since the doors of the guardians of Polish tradition were even then not closed to me'. She chose not to renew the relationship (Karsov & Szechter 1971: 93–98). A little later she commented on Polish tradition and anti-Semitism: 'One's origin in itself is not the deciding factor – it may have little or no effect on the mind. What does affect it is one's upbringing, environment and so on. Theories of blood and heredity and the rest of it are pure racialism' (Karsov & Szechter 1971: 104). Looking back at her experience, Karsov made the point that anti-Semitism in Poland is a tradition all of its own (Karsov & Szechter 1971: 250), even if she later gave herself a reminder: 'Myself: Don't forget that there's an equally strong tradition in Poland of combatting anti-Semitism' (Karsov & Szechter 1971: 255).

More recently, Hanna Krall (b.1937) has attempted to identify the failures and inadequacies of traditional Polish culture, probing in her semi-fictional 'true stories' and journalism why in Poland the values of humanism and the Enlightenment did not produce greater solidarity or fellow-feeling with Poland's Jews. In her shifting and impressionistic novel *Sublokatorka* (1985, *The Subtenant*), she explored the difference between the idea of 'light' and the power of 'darkness', looking at post-war history to test the tradition of the heroic Polish military, the hope of equality held out by

110 Polish writers and tradition

communism and its collapse into anti-Semitism, the revival of hope around Solidarność and the rise of anti-Semitism that followed (Krall 1992).

In her book-length conversation with Marek Edelman – the last surviving leader of the Warsaw Ghetto Uprising – Krall recorded not only his memories of the horrors of the Holocaust and the brutality of decisions forced upon him during the Uprising, but also his puzzlement at being hailed a 'hero'. He felt this description only applied because Poles projected the romantic ideals of heroic resistance and honourable and aesthetically pleasing death onto him in their admiration of his will to fight. He, however, saw only his lack of choice in the matter and felt that to compare his actions with the isolation, humiliation, starvation, death and cremation of millions of Jews who had not had the opportunity to fight was to devalue their deaths. For him in the particular circumstances of the Nazi Occupation, hiding, survival, life at any cost, was also heroic.

Like Karsov, the relationship of anti-Semitism to traditional notions of patriotism, honour and heroism were clearly on Krall's mind since they produced a hierarchy of values in which Poles fought for Poland, but Jews merely fought for their lives. Karsov had to wait until she was outside Poland to express her misgivings. Krall, rather than address these things directly, allowed Edelman's grim narrative to quietly, relentlessly undercut traditional 'bright and beautiful' ideas until very little of honour, heroism or patriotism remained (Krall 1986: 77, 96).

Refuge in tradition

For the communists, Poland, with its strong nationalist traditions, its history of opposition, its Underground civil society and its powerful Catholic identity, was unstable, resistant, unpredictable and largely unyielding. They saw traditional Poland as the root of a serious weakness within the Soviet bloc, something they could not bend to their will and that put them at risk. The irony was that communism, in spite of its claim to be progressive and opposed to the forces of reaction, was massively conservative, poorly educated and nervous of the literary *inteligencja*. Although it did not intend to, it operated to preserve a traditional conspiratorial, oppositional leading role for writers.

Zbigniew Herbert was no old-school romantic conspirator. His attitude to 'national poetry' was not ambiguous, distant or strained: he consistently opposed communism, but he also questioned the nature of patriotism and resistance, felt the nation had suffered 'psychic damage' and now responded only to 'shrill righteousness'. In his poem 'Reflections on the Problem of the Nation' (1961), he wondered whether the idea of 'the nation' was a form of 'indoctrination' and if the Poles were not 'still a barbarian tribe'.

Herbert's faith in Allied military power, the political resolve of 'the West' and the culture of Europe had been severely shaken by the communist takeover. In his poem 'Mona Lisa', he recounted his feelings as he stood in front of the famous painting on a rare trip to the West in 1958–60. He reflected

Polish writers and tradition 111

first on the improbability of his presence: 'so I'm here / they were all going to come'. He also pondered the strange nullity of the experience. What should have been a cultural experience of great resonance proved to be a bitter settling of account: 'between the blackness of her back / and the first tree of my life / lies a sword / a melted precipice' (Herbert 2007: 170–72). Herbert, like many poets in East-Central Europe, was engaged in a rueful adjustment of his attitude to 'the West' and a bitter reflection on poetry and art in Europe. Rather than waiting for the barbarians to arrive (as in Cavafy's poem), Herbert felt the Soviet barbarians had already arrived and that as far as the West was concerned, Poles had been subsumed by them.[26] This made Herbert's insistence on the role of tradition – the one thing he felt he could rely on – all the more pressing.

However, his poetic persona was unwilling to abandon his established (and traditional) political loyalties. His position – Catholic, nationalist and hierarchic – was not far from Conrad's description of himself as 'Polish-Catholic and nobleman', nor from the self-description offered by T.S. Eliot (1888–1965) as 'classicist in literature, royalist in politics and Anglo-Catholic in religion' (Eliot 1928).

Like Eliot, Herbert required an 'active relationship' with tradition and saw this as 'recognition that we are a link in a great chain of generations, which lays a responsibility on us' (Herbert 2010: 614). Herbert insisted that an 'active stance' regarding the past did not signify 'a flight from the now, from disillusionment' (Herbert 2010: 600). He believed tradition was part of any poet's basic intellectual equipment, but he also recognised this was a 'very serious problem' for young Polish poets. He echoed Eliot's idea of literary tradition as a 'great labour' (Herbert 2010: 467).[27]

Herbert's conception of loyalty, patriotism and tradition are often arch, rude and very conservative. When he paraphrased Eliot it was to make elitism explicit: 'No greatness can be separated from its support. The rest are compliant creatures and thoughtless worms' (Herbert 2010: 73).

This attitude comes through in his prose. Herbert, writing about one of his visits to the West, describes his reaction to Dutch art. In the Spanish–Dutch wars he noticed that although Dutch forces gave 'countless proofs of courage, perseverance and determination', the art-work relating to the wars was 'not very patriotic' and there was not a single painting where a defeated adversary was 'dragged behind a victor's chariot in the dust of spite'. Indeed, upon researching further he realised the Dutch armies, except for a helmet, armour plate and a sash, rarely wore uniforms, and this meant they were 'very gray in comparison with the feathered splendor of the French or Italian warriors'. Simply, he concluded 'there was nothing to paint'. And the reason he noted these things was because they contrasted so strongly with his Polish sense of history, experience and tradition.

Herbert's political orientation fuelled disagreements with the inclusiveness of Tadeusz Różewicz (1921–2014) and Jerzy Ficowski (1924–2006), among others, and lay behind a serious clash with Miłosz in 1968. Miłosz had already played a major role in bringing Herbert to Western attention

112 *Polish writers and tradition*

(Miłosz 1965; Herbert 1968). At a dinner party their conversation got onto the subject of the Warsaw Uprising. Herbert became angry with Miłosz, saying he had no right to doubt the correctness of the Uprising as he had not been a member of the Resistance. A long argument followed until, angered by Herbert's aggression, Miłosz departed. After this the two were on very cool terms (www.culture.pl/en/article/the-pen-or-the-pen-a-brief-history-of-polish-literary-beefs). Herbert's poem 'Khodasewich' (collected in *Rovigo*, 1992) is widely understood to be a mealy-mouthed dismissal of Miłosz as a 'half-Russian, half-Pole', 'an émigré by nature', a 'second-rate noblemen' famous for his 'sulks and reveries': 'He himself didn't know quite who Khodasewich was / He floated like seaweed on tempest-tossed waves / Throughout the universe from his birth to his death' (Herbert 2007: 496–7). For Herbert, Miłosz was insufficiently Polish and insufficiently rooted in tradition. After the poem was published, Herbert sent Miłosz a postcard with a picture of an elephant leg hovering over a chicken and the message: 'Don't tread upon', as if Herbert were the one in danger (www.transversal-inflections.wordpress.com/2009/08/14/herbert-vs-milosz).

Herbert wanted recognition for the idea that all writers, but particu-larly poets, are 'a link in a great chain of generations' and felt this imposed certain responsibilities. He listed the poets from whom he took his bear-ings: Jan Kochanowski (1530–84), Franciszek Karpiński (1741–1825), the romantic 'bard' Juliusz Słowacki, and the wartime poets Tadeusz Gajcy and Krzysztof Kamil Baczyński, whose poetry harked back to the romantics and who had both perished fighting with the AK in the Warsaw Uprising. In this brief but significant list we can see the loyalties, hierarchy of values and political obligations that informed Herbert's poetry (Herbert 2010: 664–9). Herbert lamented that 'the Polish tradition' of 'admiration for those writ-ers who have been recognized as the spokesmen for national aspirations' was 'fading away' and spoke explicitly about his own political orientation towards the AK (Poppek & Gelberg 1994).

If we are to believe Herbert, in the clash between the collectivist, didactic and ecstatic ambition of communism and the personal, sceptical and ironic mode of opposition, the simple 'matter of taste' decided the issue. Like his close friend Tyrmand, Herbert identified hypocrisy and boorishness as the defining characteristics of communism. In his poem 'The Power of Taste' Herbert made it clear he thought the communists were uncultured (Her-bert 2007: 409), whereas the Catholic 'soul and 'conscience' are essential elements of his 'taste'.

By the mid 1970s, accumulated social, economic and political stresses were also evident in the literary world and Herbert's reference to 'young poets sticking their tongues out at their predecessors' did not come out of nowhere (Herbert 2010: 614). The political and economic tensions left unresolved after the upheavals of 1956, 1968 and 1970 had begun to build towards the next clash, which would come in 1976. Adam Zagajewski (b.1945) and Julian Kornhauser (b.1946), two young poets from the move-ment known as *Nowa fala* (new wave, the Generation of '68), published a

Polish writers and tradition   113

book entitled *Świat nie przedstawiony* (1974, *The World Un-represented*). This was an impatient attempt to anatomise the failings of contemporary Polish literature in dealing with communism, as well as an ideological and aesthetic manifesto arising from the poets' perception of literature as a tool for building independent thought, self-awareness and self-knowledge in a society which did not encourage such things (Zagajewski & Kornhauser 1974).

The young poets criticised the work of several leading post-war authors, including Stanisław Lem (1921–2006), Wiesław Myśliwski (b.1932), Jan Błoński (1931–2009) and Tadeusz Konwicki, who they said avoided direct description of 'Polish unreality' under communism, preferring to use allusion, allegory, fable, metaphor, Aesopian language and classical mythology. They saw these strategies as weakness and hypocrisy, and demanded that literature provide an accurate description and in-depth analysis of contemporary daily life. Their book was heavily censored and the authors were forced to discuss the problems they wanted to address in precisely the allusive and indirect style they were desperate to avoid and for which they criticised others: by submitting their book for official publication they ran into the very problems that had forced other writers to employ Aesopian strategies.[28]

As a poet who often dealt with fables, classical tropes and mythology to get past the censor, Herbert was one of the young poets' prime targets. However, Zagajewski and Kornhauser were mistaken in believing Herbert was a young poet who had sprung to prominence with the 1956 'thaw', and this led them to misjudge his work (Barańczak 2006: loc 6077–6695). In age, experience, moral tone, political affinity and poetic content Herbert was part of the older wartime 'survival generation'. Herbert saw no point in collaboration, was certain positivism was a waste of time and a deadly compromise that would lead to a 'dead-end of disillusion', and felt the 'paradise of the Positivists' would turn out to be 'empty' (Herbert 2010: 608).

In the years 1950–53, Herbert had published articles, reviews and poetry in *Tygodnik Powszechny* and in *Dzis i Jutro* (*Today and Tomorrow*) under the pen-name Stefan Martha.[29] Only with the 'thaw' of 1956 did he produce his first two collections of poetry, *Struna światła* (*Chord of Light*, 1956) and *Hermes, pies i gwiazda* (*Hermes, Dog and Star*, 1957). After this, as the thaw was slowly reversed, Herbert refused to submit to censorship or work with a state publisher again until the early 1960s. Indeed, in 1994 he boasted: 'I have never visited the editorial offices of any periodical in Soviet-occupied Poland' (Poppek & Gelberg 1994). In 1974–5 Herbert offended the authorities by signing the 'Letter of 15' and the 'Letter of 59' to protest at changes to the Polish Constitution. He also became an editor for the Underground journal *Zapis* (*Record*) and openly supported other clandestine publications. In 1983 he risked serious conflict with the Party by publishing with Instytut Literacki in Paris, but by this time he was well known abroad and his poetry was massively popular with oppositionists.

114 Polish writers and tradition

Herbert's loyalties and wartime survivor mentality are present in his early poems, but particularly clear in 'The Envoy of Mr. Cogito' (1974), the first of his 'Pan Cogito' sequence (Herbert 2007: 333–4).

Herbert, predictably, was irritated and offended by *Świat nie przedstawiony*. He disputed the narrow focus and disagreed with the judgement that to counter censorship it was essential to demolish the aesthetics and strategies of preceding generations. He rejected the demand that the reality of life in Poland be represented in brutal, grotesque or purely aesthetic terms. Herbert discerned that Zagajewski and Kornhauser were responding only to the writing of the post-war generation, rather than the whole literary tradition that lay behind them. Herbert made his irritation clear by pointedly ignoring Zagajewski at a dinner party and, even though Zagajewski later admitted their criticism had been 'naïve gibberish', it was several years before Herbert signalled his forgiveness with the gift of a silk tie (Zagajewski 2004: 115–16).

Ryszard Krynicki (b.1942), who in one of his early poems had said he was compelled to 'do battle with the dead', lined up initially with Kornhauser and Zagajewski but, later in his poem 'And We Really Didn't Know', indicated this might have been an error (Krynicki 2018: 99–100). Although Krynicki was a considerable fan, Herbert's poem 'The Envoy of Mr. Cogito' provoked a response in a poem entitled 'The Tongue, that Wild Meat (for Zbigniew Herbert and Mr Cogito)' in which he writes of 'that inhuman thing which grows in us' (Nyczek 1982: 60).

Despite this, Herbert and Krynicki became close friends. In his 'battle with the dead', Krynicki found ways to accommodate himself to Herbert's sense of tradition and came to acknowledge Herbert as a poetic 'authority'. Krynicki eventually edited a selection of Herbert's work (Herbert 2011). Krynicki's poems 'Crossed-out Opening' (1985), 'I've Known More Good than Evil' (1987) and 'Pigeons' (2002) are all affectionate memories of Herbert. In 2015, Krynicki was awarded the International Zbigniew Herbert Literary Prize for 'outstanding artistic and intellectual achievements referring to the ideas that inspired Zbigniew Herbert's work' (www.fundacjaherberta.com).

Everyone did not feel like Herbert. Miron Białoszewski (1922–83), who had lived in poverty before the war and whose poems and plays had been at the margins of acceptability, surprised the literary world with his *Pamiętnik z Powstania Warszawskiego* (1970, *A Memoir of the Warsaw Uprising*). This was not a conventional memoir, or even a history of the Uprising, but a rambling, fragmented, detailed, digressive monologue about the excruciatingly fearful lives of civilians. Białoszewski was certain this was the greatest experience of his life, and he was unwilling to distort it by forcing his memory of it into a conventional historical narrative or a search for acceptable national 'truths'. Instead, he concentrated on the trivial, the transitional and the uncertain. Nor did he make use of patriotic slogans, extol martial virtue or praise the hierarchical values of the interwar years, but instead showed a world in the process of violent demolition, far from any durable

Polish writers and tradition   115

sense of culture, morality or worth. The suggestion was that the Uprising, wartime heroism and the massive scale of wartime slaughter had all been without ultimate meaning. His unconventional, unheroic, non-patriotic, barely respectful attitude was far from the way the subject was usually treated and its challenge to the traditional norms of patriotism was highly controversial.

By the mid 1970s, writers of all kinds were highlighting the surrealism of Polish daily life and hankering after 'the normal'; they had begun to sense that the Polish literary-political tradition opposed to communism was not leading to anything more than its own recognition. Kornhauser, for example, in a poem called 'Loyalty', referred to a comment by Miłosz that the Polish ethical code was 'based on nothing but loyalty' (Kornhauser 2000: 99).

As the Generation of '68 had done before them, so with considerable arrogance a new generation of 'barbarians' parodied and shouldered aside the older generation, along with the New Wave poets, dismissing them all as 'great dinosaurs from a bygone age' (Dunin-Wąsowic 2000: 366–73). These writers – including Natasza Goerke (b.1960) and Izabela Filipiak (b.1961) – had grown up around the semi-legal journal *bruLion* (*roughDraft*) in the years 1986–99, and they were impatient with the stasis engendered by Martial Law. Their aim was to abolish all taboos, use scandal as a literary strategy, 'confront the extremes of life' and advance their own writing, lives and ambitions as rapidly as possible. Their work included 'feminism, cyber-punk, graffiti and techno culture' and their Polonised version of the diction of New York poets (Dehnal 2008: 11–12).[30]

Looking back

Adam Zagajewski noted that in the twentieth century Polish literary tradition had managed to include figures as diverse as Stempowski, Białoszewski, Szczepański, Gombrowicz, Czapski, Miłosz and Herbert. Each in their own way found a specific 'notion of moral responsibility [...] of seriousness of poetry' that had little to do with 'purely technical considerations' or with the postmodern belief that all meaning was inaccessible. Each writer felt the beneficial impact, the 'muted influence of the Polish nineteenth century anomaly', which still needed 'a constant consultation, a constant conversation' to 'withstand the pressure'. However, the solitude of the writer also needed some 'company, discussion, encouragement' and he noted the correspondence between Schultz and Gombrowicz, Miłosz's connections to Gombrowicz, Andrzejewski, Stempowski, Wat and Rudnicki, links between Mrożek and Błoński, Anna Kamienska's references to contemporary poets, Szczepański's engagement with Conrad and Stryjkowski. He felt someone with a talent for diagrams and drawing should make a map capturing the structure of all that made up Polish literary tradition – the 'exchanges, dialogues and polemics' – but that Miłosz was central (Zagajewski 2007: xii–xiii).

116 *Polish writers and tradition*

Adam Michnik was aware that the impact, currency and legacy of his literary generation was not guaranteed, and he also began to feel that the limitations of traditional Polish culture were a matter of increasing concern. In his essay 'Maggots and Angels' (1979), Michnik examined 'the cult of the heroic sacrifice' in Polish tradition and its creation of 'a beautiful but dangerous ethic'. Adherents to the conspiratorial tradition, he said, 'angelized' themselves, saw the rest of the population as slaves and maggots and felt no restraint in their activities on behalf of the nation. Michnik saw the advantages and disadvantages in this, but despaired of 'maggoty behavior' (Michnik 1987:169–98). Michnik was not alone in his concern. Writing in 1981, Jan Józef Lipski (1926–91) echoed Maria Dąbrowska's interwar concern about 'moral nations' and stressed that the form Polish patriotism took was decisive for the 'moral, cultural and political future' of Poland (Kostrzewa 1990: 54).

This might be characterised as paranoia and cynicism, but Lipski had in mind the anti-Semitic expulsions of 1968 and the re-appearance in March 1981 of Interior Minister Mieczysław Moczar's 'Partisans' in the anti-Semitic, hard-line-nationalist 'Grunwald Patriotic Union'. Shortly after Lipski penned these words, in December 1981, relying on traditional respect for the military and hoping Poles would connect it with Piłsudski's coup, General Jaruzelski declared Martial Law.

What was the attitude of the Party towards Polish tradition? In 1984 Teresa Torańska interviewed Jakub Berman. He had been First Secretary Bierut's right-hand man in the early post-war years and had complete control in shaping official culture, education, propaganda, foreign affairs and security. When Bierut was ousted in 1956, Berman had resigned from the Politburo and shortly afterwards had been blamed for the 'period of errors and distortions' and expelled from the party. In the years 1956–69 he worked as an editor at the influential Książka i Wiedza publishing house. He had been uniquely positioned to observe the Communist Party and the rising tide of protest against it from a cultural perspective. He described Poland as a Pandora's box: easy to release 'evil spirits' from but harder to get back in later (Torańska 1987: 350). He insisted that Czechoslovakia, Romania and Hungary had not suffered as badly as Poland in terms of experience or loss of territory and he spoke directly of the Party's frustration with the problem of the dreams that as a consequence lurked within Polish tradition (Torańska 1987: 353–4).

This was not a position most Polish left-liberals would disagree with, except that it was a communist expressing them. Berman's hope for a change in Polish tradition and the psyche that fuelled it was overtaken by events. The suspension of Martial Law in July 1983 solved nothing: the economy flat-lined, Party membership nose-dived and public indifference to official life, including Round Table talks between the government and Solidarność, was almost total. By the end of 1989 even the hard-line communists realised they could no longer govern and they agreed to almost-free elections. However, for many the chaos that followed the collapse of

Polish writers and tradition 117

communism confirmed the Polish traditions Berman had been trying to re-shape.

In 1993, looking back over the post-war period, Michnik developed a shrewd idea of what lurked within certain strands of tradition. Michnik was aware that traditional conservatism like that of Zbigniew Herbert not only helped sustain opposition to communism but could also support chauvinism. While the collapse of communism opened the way for Polish literature to accommodate itself to the conditions of capitalism, at the same time a vast range of ideas, opinion and ideology (some of them far from 'progressive') could suddenly be expressed without restraint. 'Normalisation' may have begun to edge Polish literature into line with Western conditions, but 'liberty' did not neutralise tradition. For many, the chaos of 'liberty' and the indifference of capitalism meant the certainty offered by tradition became more important, rather than less, and on closer acquaintance the relationship with Europe, which had represented the kind of life to which Poles aspired, once again became troubled and ambiguous. All of which was to aid the rise of illiberal democracy. Understandably, Michnik was reluctant to characterise what came after his generation.

Perhaps the most effective literary summation of Polish experience under communism and what was liberated by its collapse came in 1991, just as the regime finally crumbled away to nothing, when M.S. Huberath (b. 1954) published his short story 'Kara większa' (Greater Punishment) in the journal *Nowa Fantastyka*. The story derives from a tradition of grotesque fantasy, ingenious violence and macabre erotica, based in the judgemental strand of Catholic faith. The modern aspect of the tradition of Polish grotesque dates mainly from the writings of Stefan Grabiński (1877–1936) but has its roots in medieval belief and a vivid perception of the Devil. The story is set in a labour camp that is both punishment centre and hospital, and it follows a character called Rud. The inmates of the camp are tortured, surgically repaired without anaesthetic and then sent either for humiliation or for further torture. Great trouble is taken to ensure the prisoners do not become accustomed to pain, but it gradually emerges that the hideous injuries inflicted on the prisoners during torture and the long operations they endure to repair the damage (all described in detail) are only illusory. An old hand at the camp explains the repetitive punishment regime is that when the pain stops people go back to their old habits – 'wheeling and dealing and skirt-chasing': if they knew they were in fact undamaged they would merely lapse all the sooner (Powaga 1996: 95). Rud, like the other inmates, suffers gruesome torture and surgery. He has a permanent sense of guilt, never questions that he is punished for a good reason, is unsure why he is being punished and surmises vaguely it might have something to do with a girl. Alongside the prisoners in the camp there are also the Un-borns. These are tiny aborted foetuses salvaged from the sewers. They arrive at the camp in sealed buckets and are then stitched together again – with great care taken to ensure that limbs are attached to the correct bodies – and allowed to live for a while.

118 *Polish writers and tradition*

Not only is this an obsessively detailed picture of the technology of Hell – the camp is actually named 'Heaven' – but with its emphasis on punishment, suffering and abortion it is also a grim insight into a resurgent Catholic Church and a culture of blame, judgement and punishment. It vividly displays the obsessions and feverish imagination of the Catholic right wing, which began to emerge as the certainties of communism receded, and as the liberal influence, 'Europe' and ideas of modernity again became a threat to the notion of traditional identity.

Notes

1 Although the bulk of the exiled Poles remained in the west at the end of the war, Modelski returned to Poland, was promoted to general of division and became head of the Special Military Mission to London organising the return of military personnel to Poland. Later he became military attaché to Washington, but when he refused to set up a spy network he was ordered back to Poland. He refused to go, requested asylum in the USA, established contact with Mikołajczyk and other figures of the Polish diaspora and began writing articles about East-bloc intelligence activities. He was sentenced in absentia to fifteen years in prison.

2 SN was made illegal by the postwar Communist Polish government, but survived as part of the sidelined Government-in-Exile. With the fall of communism, SN registered again in Poland in August 1990, but dissolved itself in 2001. Most of its members joined Liga Polskich Rodzin (League of Polish Families).

3 Zygielbojm committed suicide on 11 May 1943 in protest at Allied inaction over the destruction of the Warsaw ghetto. He left a long suicide note addressed to Raczkiewicz and Sikorski (www.archive.is/20121219122815/http://yad-vashem.org.il/about_holocaust/documents/part2/doc154).

4 The novelist Zofia Kossak-Szczucka, although she was an early participant in Żegota, withdrew soon after its inception. She wanted Żegota to be an example of pure Christian charity and argued that the Jews already had their own international charity organisations. She went on to take an active part in *Społeczna Organizacja Samopomocy* (Social Organization for Self-Help, SOS) and acted as liaison between Żegota and Catholic convents and orphanages where Jews were hidden.

5 Wiesław Myśliwski (b.1932), for example, perhaps the least political of Polish writers, in his novel *Pałac* (1970) described the start of World War II as the moment when the landed gentry – the ruling class – ran away in panic, leaving the peasant Jakub alone to wander around marvelling at their woodlands, lake and boats, their peacocks and their palace with its dozens of rooms, artworks and piano. The novel ends in an orgy of vengeful fantasy and apocalyptic visions (Myśliwski 1991).

6 The post-war communist government regarded NSZ as renegades and murderers. In 2012, however, the Sejm passed a bill promoted by President Lech Kaczyński commemorating the 70th anniversary of the foundation of NSZ in 1942.

7 General Paszkiewicz returned to Poland after the war. He joined the Polish People's Army and was appointed a Divisional Commander and Head of Security in Białystok, where he coordinated operations against anti-communist guerrillas. In 1948 he became commander of the Warsaw Military District. After his retirement from active service he worked for the Ministry of Forestry and later became a Sejm deputy. In 1947 he claimed he had been approached by Anders to join a plot to kill Sikorski but had refused. It is possible Paszkiewicz

Polish writers and tradition 119

made the claim as part of the communist government's campaign to discredit Anders (Kochanski 2012: 346).

8 After the war, Klimkowski returned to Poland and wrote *Byłem adiutantem gen. Andersa* (I Was Adjutant of General Anders, 1959). The memoir was widely judged to be without merit, but Klimkowski became a consultant on the film *Katastrofa w Gibraltarz* (Disaster in Gibraltar, 1983, dir. Bohdan Poręba).

9 Although the Polish Parachute Brigade had been formed with the idea of action in Poland, the hope it could be deployed to support the Warsaw Uprising was fanciful at best. Although it was smaller than its British counterparts, the Brigade still required 80 transport planes and 114 gliders and tow-planes (Urquhart 1958: 217–18). To reach Warsaw they would also have needed a substantial long-range fighter escort over German occupied territory. There were no Allied fighter-planes with the necessary range, and the Douglas C-47 Skytrain (a workhorse always in short supply) was the only Allied transport aircraft capable of such a journey. Once on the ground, the Brigade lacked motor transport and resupply would have been impossible.

10 Both Britain and the USA feared his potential as a mischief-maker and refused him a visa until 1949.

11 Yad Vashem has numerous testimonies to anti-Semitism within Anders' army, but 136 of those who remained with Anders were decorated for bravery, including six who received the *Virtuti Militari*, the highest Polish military decoration (Gutman 1977; www.en.wikipedia.org/wiki/Anders%27_Army#cite_note-8).

12 After 1945, Miłosz, along with writers Julian Przyboś (1901–70) and Ksawery Pruszyński (1907–50), became a diplomat for the communists. Shortly after that Miłosz defected to the West, offending both communist and traditionalist sensibilities. His book *The Captive Mind* (1953), an analysis of the contortions writers put themselves through to accommodate communism, written mainly as an explanation for western readers, became a classic, but his reputation was never fully restored.

13 NSZ was said to have connections to the Gestapo and often acted under the pretence that it was the AK. In 1945, NSZ detached itself from the AK (its extreme National-Radical wing had always been outside AK control) and fought the incoming communists (Kertsten 1991: 126–7). NSZ armed resistance to communism continued until 1947, but some units were still thought to be active as late as the 1950s. The communists claimed to distinguish between the various factions of the AK, and said it fought hardest against the NSZ as 'the most fascist', not quite so hard against 'the Piłsudski-Sanacja core of the AK', and claimed to be moderate in its treatment of the peasant battalions (Coutouvidis & Reynolds, 1986: 148).

14 Although Britain had gone to war over Poland in 1939, the balance of power had shifted massively by 1945, when the USA and USSR became the main players. The victory parade through London in June 1946 did not include the Poles, the **fourth largest** contingent in the Allied military. Poles finally held their victory march through London on **10 July 2005.**

15 *Tygodnik Powszechny* had refused to print Stalin's obituary. As a punishment it was transferred to pro-government editors at PAX, a Catholic 'front' organisation set up by ex-ONR Falangist Bolesław Piasecki in a deal with the communists, but financed in part by the Catholic Church. PAX employed ex-members of the AK and had links to the Catholic Charity, Veritas. After the 'thaw' of 1956, the former editors of *Tygodnik Powszechny* were allowed to resume control.

16 The film *Krajobraz po bitwie* (1970, Landscape After Battle, dir. Andrzej Wajda) was based on Borowski's experiences in a Displaced Persons camp after the war.

120 Polish writers and tradition

17 *Volksdeutsche* – a Nazi term meaning an ethnic German living outside the Reich in the Baltic states, Poland, Hungary, Czechoslovakia or Romania.

18 There is a similar inter-play between Maria Dąbrowska's story 'The Village Wedding' (1957) and Mrożek's story 'Wedding at Atomics' (Mrożek 1959). Maria Dąbrowska was probably the last of the positivists. Both stories can be found in Kuncewicz 1962.

19 Mrożek was fortunate in his illustrator, Daniel Mróz (b.1917–93), who had a similar interest in the encounter between the ambiguities of modernity and the constraints of conservative tradition. His satirical drawing 'Z narodowych tradicji tępenia nowatorstwa w sztuce' (From the National Tradition of Eradicating the New in Art, 1957) shows a statue of Tradition with a snail's head surrounded by figures wielding traditional symbols of Polishness (Górka-Czarnecka 2017: 20). Mróz also illustrated the very untraditional works of the aphorist Stanisław Jerzy Lec (1909–66) and the science fiction writer Stanisław Lem.

20 Brandys' diaries were first published by Institut Litteraire in Paris in 1981–2.

21 The influence of these tales can be seen in the writings of Stanisław Lem and Ryszard Kapuściński (1932–2007).

22 Since the collapse of communism, Polish writers have begun to remedy this deficit. Marek Krajewski (b.1966), Joanna Jodełka (b.1973) and Zygmunt Miłoszewski (b.1976) have produced very efficient, fast-paced crime-thrillers.

23 A debate has begun to open up (see Michnik & Marczyk 2018).

24 The book has been reprinted several times, but Andrzej Wajda's film *Wielki Tydzień* (1995), while it won a Silver Bear Award as an Outstanding Artistic Contribution at the 46th Berlin International Film Festival, was a box-office flop.

25 Gomułka was referring to: Roman Zambrowski a leading figure in the Politburo; Stefan Staszewski, head of PAP (Polish Press Agency); Antoni Słonimski, poet, artist, journalist, playwright and president of the Union of Polish Writers; Stefan Kisielewski ('Kisiel', 1911–91), a member of the *Znak* team, who at a Writers' Union meeting in 1968 labelled the government a *dyktatura ciemniaków* (dictatorship of dunces), a name that stung and stuck, but for which he was beaten-up by so-called 'unknown perpetrators' – a euphemism for criminal acts of political violence by members of the *milicja*; Paweł Jasienica (1909–70), a journalist and historian, was smeared by Gomulka, who claimed he had been released from prison after agreeing to cooperate with the communists, causing huge damage to his reputation.

26 Hence the ironic title of his essays on Western art – *Barbaryńca w Ogrodzie* (1962, the Barbarian in The Garden).

27 Eliot said no artist had their complete meaning alone and that writers could not be appreciated except in relation to the writers who went before them, the writers around them, their historical circumstances and what they did with the language and culture they inherited. But he warned that tradition was not merely a matter of 'handing down' unchanged what had been done in the past, nor was it something writers could expect to simply inherit. His point was that for writers, tradition is interactive and dialogic. He believed that a living literary tradition was absorbed from 'active' contact with the writing of the past: engagement, reading, interpretation and discussion. He felt this relationship was a creative and informing power operating on the development of the writer's sense of craft, where each individual drew on the past in order to argue with the present. This was not the same for the general reader or cultured person, who acquired a 'passive' sense of tradition through class background, social position and education (Eliot 1986: 209). In a key passage, Eliot said of tradition: 'If you want it you must obtain it with great labour. It involves in the first place the historical sense of the, which we may call nearly indispensable to anyone who would continue to be a poet beyond his twenty-fifth year; and the historical sense involves

Polish writers and tradition 121

a perception not only of the pastness of the past, but of its presence; the historical sense compels a man to write not merely with his own generation in his
bones, but with a feeling that the whole of literature of the literature of Europe
from Homer and within it the whole of the literature of his own country has a
simultaneous existence and composes a simultaneous order. This historical
sense, which is a sense of timelessness as well as of the temporal and of the time-
less and of the temporal together, is what makes a writer traditional. And it is
what makes a writer most acutely conscious of his place in time, of his contem-
poraneity' (Eliot 1952: 23).

28 The 'charges' levelled by Zagajewski and Kornhauser may have helped the
growth of Underground publishing by focusing the ideas of older novelists in
works like Kazimierz Brandys' novel *Nierzeczywistość* (*Unreality*), published by
NOWA in 1977, and Tadeusz Konwicki's novel *Mała Apokalipsa* (*A Minor
Apocalypse*), published by Zapis in May 1979.

29 *Dzis I Jutro* was a PAX publication. Herbert ceased publication with them in
1953 when *Tygodnik Powszechny* was transferred to PAX control. He decided
further cooperation with PAX was impossible in these circumstances.

30 Although initially reluctant, the editors of *bruLion* did eventually offer a manifesto. They aimed to 'Close the gap between public and private language: partici-
pate in the attempt to create a new model of intellectual culture, a model based
on principles of free association, free expression and on the freedom to set one's
own goals: counteract the ontological degradation of and all elements in the
structure of reality: support and promote different cultural disciplines: and to
promote the young generation at home and abroad' (Dunin-Wąsowic 2000: 368).

5 Hungary – Writers in Transition
Budapest Diary December 1990

The first half of 2009 was dominated by news of economic recession, the Israeli attack on Gaza, the wars in Iraq and Afghanistann the war on the Taliban in Pakistan, financial scandal in the British parliament and a growing crisis over nuclear weapons capacity in Iran and North Korea. Although these months saw the European elections, there was very little coverage in the British press of the election results outside the UK. In Hungary, for example, in the run-up to the European elections and in the election itself, a great deal happened that was little reported. In June 2009 the Federation of Hungarian Police – the police union – signed an agreement of co-operation with the radical nationalist party Jobbik (Magyarországért Mozgalom, Movement for a Better Hungary). The General Secretary of the Federation, in an article in the union newsletter, proclaimed: 'Anti-Semitism is not just our right, it is the duty of every Hungarian homeland lover, and we must prepare for armed battle against the Jews' (Lehaw 2009).

After an anti-Semitic incident, a Molotov cocktail was thrown at a ticket office in Budapest's traditionally Jewish 13th district. This was followed by a demonstration and a counter-demonstration controlled only by a very large police presence. Shortly afterwards, right-wingers put pigs' trotters into the statues of shoes at a monument commemorating the death of 300 Jews who had been forced by the Arrow Cross (Hungarian Nazis) to take off their shoes and attempt to swim the Danube in the closing days of World War II. A demonstration in support of the right-wingers' action was met by a counter-demonstration, a 'flash mob' organised by a group calling itself 'Hungarians Against the Nazis'. They brought flowers. The police struggled to keep the two groups apart. In parliament Gordon Bajnaj, the Hungarian Prime Minister, appealed to all forces of democracy to stand firm against extremism.

Two days before the European elections, Jobbik candidate Krisztina Morvai, a professor of law married to, but separated from, a Jew, responded to a blogger who dared to refer to himself as 'a proud Hungarian Jew' by writing on a conservative Civic Forum website that those who refer to themselves in this way should play with 'their tiny little circumcised tails' and that 'we' were in the process of 'taking back' the country.

Hungary – Writers in Transition   123

At about the same time, the Federation of Gay, Lesbian, Bisexual and Transgender Hungarians petitioned the Hungarian president for support and protection after a gay rights march had been pelted with eggs, stones and petrol bombs. The Hungarian parliament also banned the Hungarian Guard, the uniformed arm of the Jobbik Party: they had been acting in much the same way as the Brownshirts did in 'protecting' party meetings.

At the 2009 European elections, Hungarian politics took a rather large step to the right: the increasingly nationalist and reactionary Fidesz (Fiatal Demokraták Szövetsége, Alliance of Young Democrats) still dominated, but Jobbik won fifteen percent of the Hungarian vote, gained three MEPs, and promptly announced an alliance with the British National Party and the followers of Jean Marie Le Pen, who had both achieved similar success in the elections. Clearly Hungary is now dealing with its failure to tackle the emergence of these themes and its failure to develop another language of politics at the very start of its democracy in 1989–90.

Given that the Hungarian communist regime was much more liberal than the rest of the Eastern bloc and the transition to democracy much less turbulent than elsewhere in Eastern and East-Central Europe, this failure is difficult to explain. But the signs that there was a strong, clearly visible and dangerous element to Hungarian politics – not just conservative or even reactionary but openly racist, openly anti-gay, anti-intellectual, anti-foreigner and anti-romani – were there from the start. Quite by accident I saw some of this for myself just as it began to emerge.

In the spring of 1989, just before the communist regimes of Eastern Europe began their terminal wobble, I made an application to the British Council Specialist Tours Department for a bursary to visit Hungary. I wanted to speak with writers about their role under communism. Arthur Alvarez had said: 'In literary matters, Hungary is a kind of Oxford of Europe, a home of lost causes' (Alvarez 1965). By this he meant that in the nineteenth century it had not been easy to separate art and morals in Hungarian cultural life and that this legacy persisted; that Hungary had largely been resistant to new literary forms, that older forms were still the norm, and that even where new forms of the novel or poetry had developed, romantic and nationalist tendencies still predominated.

Alvarez had been writing in 1961. I wondered what changes more than forty years of communist rule had made. Were the cultural achievements of the Communist Party merely improvements in quantity rather than quality? Did the Communist Party challenge petit bourgeois tastes, or merely pickle them in opposition? Did a sort of nineteenth-century morality still inhabit even the technically sophisticated writing of someone like Péter Esterházy? I wondered if Alvarez's observation was necessarily still true. However, these questions were to remain un-answered and largely un-asked because by the time the visit had been processed, approved and arranged nearly a year had passed, and by then the collapse of the communist regimes, which had not even been a vague possibility when I first made the application, was well under way.

124 *Hungary – Writers in Transition*

Enormous changes were sweeping over East-Central Europe and events were unfolding so rapidly it was difficult to keep up. By the time I arrived in Budapest, my original project was already a part of history and irrelevant to the people with whom I would be in contact. Nevertheless, rather than waste the opportunity of speaking with writers from another culture about their work, I felt I should try to take a snapshot of what they thought of the transition in that particular fortnight, 3–16 December 1990.

After the collapse of communism, Hungary had moved very quickly to establish its democracy and the first national elections had just taken place. The SZDSZ (Szabad Demoktraták Szővetsége, Alliance of Free Democrats), a liberal party that had its roots in opposition to the communist Kadar regime, had just suffered a heavy (and predictable) electoral defeat. Fidesz, a new libertarian anti-communist party, had just emerged and was growing rapidly. The ruling party was now the MDF (Magyar Demokrata Fórum, Hungarian Democratic Forum), a centre-right Christian democrat party. I stayed in a Ministry of Art and Culture hostel called the Hotel Maros, a short underground ride from the city centre. And waiting at the hostel on my first morning was an official translator called Judit. What follows here are my diary notes from that visit.

*

Tuesday: 17.00 Miklós Vajda (1931–2017), editor of the *New Hungarian Quarterly*, has arranged a programme of visits and meetings for me. A tall courteous man, he is busy translating into Hungarian, with evident distaste, a play by Agatha Christie. He hands me copies of the *New Hungarian Quarterly*. I used to read it in Poland in the 1970s. It has a new slimmed-down look and design, as does, so Vajda tells me, the magazine's entire operation. The sudden withdrawal of government subsidy means that they have lost their offices and storage space and now operate with a staff of five sharing a single office: 'When I entertain someone my fellow workers cannot stay in the same room and continue with their work – so that's why we meet here in a bar.' The bar where we met was dimly lit with red lamps. The waitresses were friendly. Rock and roll thumped away on the juke box.

'There is no good writing at the moment. Everyone is involved with politics, I think. I don't know what writers are doing, but they are not writing. That is all I can say.' My visit, he goes on to explain, almost came to grief right at the very start. The trip had been agreed with the British Council over a year ago. At that time I had suggested meeting György Spiro, Péter Esterházy, Péter Nádas, Péter Lengyel, Istvan Csurka, Sandor Csóori and Otto Orban. However, the Hungarian authorities had only been notified of my visit just before my arrival, and many of the writers I had named were unable to help at such short notice. He has, he explains, done the best he can to set up a different series of meetings.

Hungary – Writers in Transition 125

'Tomorrow you will meet the poet Eva Tóth at the Writers Union. The Union,' he assures me, 'has no future, no function whatsoever, in the new system. But you see, she will tell you different.'

We made arrangements to meet again the following week, after I had delivered my talk about British theatre to Hungarian PEN.[1] On the way home I encounter three long-haired young men wearing the coat, hat and badges of the Soviet Red Army over jeans and trainers. Such is the speed of fashion. Or is it liberty? Or perhaps parody? Or just plain cheek?

*

Wednesday: 09.00 Rita Obodi, Hotel Astoria. This meeting seems to have dropped by the wayside. I was also to have met Luca Haraszti, but he was not available. The day starts instead at 10.30 with Eva Tóth, writer and editor, head of the Foreign Section of the Hungarian Writers Union. We are served coffee in her office. A couple of other officials sit in with us, including a visiting journalist. Eva Tóth says she thinks the Union has a future, but not in the old Stalinist style. She asks me which Hungarian writers I have read. I name Konrád and Haraszti, intending to mention other favourites (Magda Szabo, Ferenc and Frigyes Karinthy, Gyla Krudy, Sandor Weores), but before I could continue she jumped in to ask: 'Why these two?' And before I could answer she continued:

'In considering Hungarian literature it is important to remember that Hungarian is spoken inside and outside Hungary. It is particularly true that Hungarian literature and writers are very important at the moment to the Hungarian minority in Transylvania, for example, where, along with the Catholic Church, the names of Laszlo Tökes and Andras Sütó are important. You mention these particular two writers, Konrád and Haraszti; however… most people would be puzzled that you know these two when there are so many others. Some would say that you know only a half-writer and a non-writer.

> You have to ask yourself why do I know of the work of so few Hungarian writers? And why am I familiar only with particular writers? Why these writers? Why did the West pick on them? You have to ask, and what I want to know is: Why did the West make such a fuss of Konrád and Haraszti. Not because the West was interested in the best of Hungarian literature – that is for sure – because there were better and more interesting and more representative Hungarian writers available. The question is left hanging in the air – not exactly un-asked, not exactly un-answered. The doubt is there, about the reality of their worth, their talent, their reputation, their thinking, their loyalty. Is this the paranoia of living in a literary ghetto, of not quite knowing the worth of your own work outside your immediate circle? Is it frustration, envy, fear?

126 *Hungary – Writers in Transition*

This tutorial is interrupted by a phone call. The Bulgarian Writers' Union think that a proposed visit by Hungarian writers should be called off because in Sofia they have no heat or light after the fall of the government last week. Our conversation and my visit are cut short while Eva deals with this emergency. On the way out, a local journalist stops me:

Tell me about samizdat publications in Britain.

Is she being serious or ironical? I can't tell. Just stupid maybe. Everybody shouts at her in Hungarian and she backs off rapidly. Then comes running back and hands me her card. On my way home I saw a massive bank of TVs, like a wall, in the underground station at Deak ter, with people crowded round, five or six deep, to watch pop videos. On the platform Hungarian women from Romania, dressed in embroidered sheepskins, scarves and long skirts, dodge the police patrols around the station to sell their hand-made embroideries, cheeses, home-brew and sheepskins.

*

Thursday: 10.00 Bari Károlyi (b.1952), a romani poet. A small, dark man. Very delicate frame, a quiet and gentle manner, very likeable. I know almost nothing about him and have only read a few of his poems in translation, but he is clearly a very talented poet. Judit tells me his poetry has caused quite a stir recently as he has begun to reveal the still strong anti-romani prejudice in Hungary by talking about his own very rough time in the army when he was called up for military service. He is curious to know why he has been invited to talk to me. He quizzes me about who sent me and why. He fears my visit has been financed and set up as a provocation by the new MDF – who it appears are not new, not very democratic and not much of a forum either. But they are very Hungarian. Very. He is cautious and slightly worried by who I might be. Judit tells me he is reassured when I say I know nothing at all about him. He asks who had suggested his name and is relieved to hear that it was Eva Tóth.

Judit tells me that if I had met the playwright Istvan Csurka, Károlyi would have refused to meet me. Apparently Csurka recently appeared on TV and used this to stir up anti-Romanian, anti-Jewish and anti-romani feeling among a rather battered working class as they cast around for someone to blame for their misfortunes. He says he finds Csurka and his ideas very worrying and difficult to explain. He is very twitchy about what is about to happen here. He says Csurka's TV appearance has been condemned in a letter of protest by ninety-nine members of the Writers' Union, but this will still not affect 'the primitive man'. He is disturbed and cannot understand why Miklós Vajda had suggested I might meet with Csurka and says there could be no such thing as balanced, honest and objective reporting where an open and avowed fascist was concerned. 'This is not yet a democracy, you know.' I agree, but say I would prefer to let Csurka condemn himself out of his own mouth.

Károlyi says: 'There should be no platform for those who deny basic freedoms to others. Why do you need to hear this man for yourself?' It seems that the price of further conversation with Károlyi is that I agree not to meet with Csurka. I know that Csurka has not agreed to meet me, so I agree to this condition.[2] He has his victory, and we talk for about two and a half hours. Károlyi tells me he wrote a poem about the Russian army when he was nineteen years old, for which he was sent to a correction camp and then to a prison where he shared a cell with murderers. He seems OK now, but he says he still cannot speak about everything he experienced then. He's one of seven children, he says, all of whom accept as normal that he is an artist. He was interested to hear I had lived in Poland and in Wales. He wanted to hear more about the languages in these places. He asked very pointed questions about who speaks what language in Wales, when and why.

Károlyi is a collector and sifter of romani lore and culture and tells me he has identified dozens of different surviving dialects and several quite distinct languages within the romani community of Hungary. He is also collecting stories of the romani Holocaust – an event in which Hungarians are implicated. I imagine this does not make him popular. Sitting in the coffee bar he tells me one of the stories he has collected about a romani man whose family of seven children had all been killed as part of a Nazi experiment during the war, with the connivance of the Hungarian government. As a result of this loss his mother went mad and set fire to his home, badly burning him.

Asked if he still loved this country he answered yes, he did, and then died. His point, Károlyi said, was that love of country is never simple and definitely not one-to-one. On the way home that night a romani band was playing in the underground station. There was a small crowd gathered around them, at once fascinated and slightly afraid, enjoying the music but not too sure they should. People here are afraid of romanies and also nervous about questions of identity. The question of someone's ethnicity – Jewish in particular, but romani too – is important. On TV I watched the Benny Hill show dubbed into Hungarian, followed by the Soviet News and Sesame Street, both in Russian, and then the Polish film Man of Iron, with Ukrainian sub-titles.

*

Next day I met Péter Esterházy (1950–2016) in the Gelert Espresso Bar. He was wearing an old black duffle coat, complete with wonderful Hussar frogging on the front and sleeves. He later admitted the coat had belonged to Count Esterházy (his grandfather). Esterházy is a Catholic, father of four and Hungary's best-known experimental novelist and story writer. Technically he is a count – heir, if the communists had not deemed otherwise, to a

128   *Hungary – Writers in Transition*

vast series of lands, estates, castles and a massive fortune. He recently made quite a splash by announcing that he had no intention of seeking to reclaim any of these privileges and that he is not in favour of making religious education in schools compulsory. For about an hour or so Judit faithfully and accurately translated our conversation. Esterházy listened very carefully to my questions in English and it seemed to me that he understood perfectly and was using the time it took Judit to translate in order to compose his answer. Perhaps he was uncertain of his English or just needed time to 'get his ear in'. Maybe he was checking us out, working out what the sub-text of my visit might be. When he finally spoke in English it was worth waiting for.

'The secret is in the language. Party language from the mid-1970s showed an increased use of the passive voice. This is a rather awkward phenomenon, but an effective way of avoiding saying who did things, who was responsible, since in the passive no active agent need be named. One of the results of the Party's use of language is pressure on words like "we". We are changing society – no you are changing it. We are building socialism – no you are building it. This put an even greater distance between the party and the public, between political language and the language of the streets. Now there are new pressures on the same words. Once when a poet said "we" we knew who "we" was. Now that community of interest has been broken: the basic relationship between writer and writer, writer and reader, reader and reader, and their relationship to politicians – who occupied an entirely different territory – have all been broken up. Now we are fragmented. We always knew what we were against, but not exactly what we were for. Now when a politician – or a writer, for many writers have become politicians – says "we" we don't know to whom he is referring.

> Here it is an accident that we work and we receive money. We certainly don't appear to earn money. Work and money are two separate notions. We look at the West and we cannot imagine the incredible hard work that goes on there – not just to make money and stay alive, but also to build and maintain democracy. It took hundreds of years to build this system, but we expect to have it in a few minutes. This learned behaviour is very deep, almost a reflex. Now we have a situation where the forces that caused those reflexes have gone, but the reflexes – primitive, xenophobic, anti-Jewish, anti-romani even – remain. It is not part of the New, it is part of the Old. It is a scandal and a tragedy that someone of Michnik's sensibility and intellect and experience should be treated as Wałęsa has treated him. Now I must take each and every word into my hands as if for the first time, and I must study these words to see what they contain now and what they might contain in the future. I need to make a whole new dictionary.

*

At lunchtime next day I went to the Múzeum Kávéház, next to the Nemzeti Múzeum, to meet Miklós Haraszti (b.1947). He is best known as

Hungary – Writers in Transition   129

the author of *Worker in a Workers' State*, a book about his experiences of working in a socialist tractor factory and revelations of increasingly harsh (capitalist, even) shop-floor practice. He is also the author of *The Velvet Prison*, a book highlighting the ambiguous position of writers and artists within socialism. With schnitzels before us so large they hang over the edges of the plates, he started to talk: he needed no translator.

'I'm not one of those people who believe we should call this part of the world Central Europe. I mean – East or Central or East-Central, it's not the West. That's all. And anyway Central Europe is not a geographical concept. I mean it has to include Moscow, parts of Poland, the Czech lands, western Hungary, Transylvania, parts of Yugoslavia, but it's more an attitude rather than a place. The whole social democratic experiment has failed here – anything that sounds or looks at all like 'socialism' is extremely unpopular just now. What we will probably develop here is a rather liberal democratic, rather than a social democratic, system. We can't have a parliamentary system like Britain because that idea is embedded in British history and culture and we don't have either that history or that sort of culture. Our democracy needs to be seen as more direct and personal. We will probably develop a presidential democracy like the USA – or more exactly we – all the countries of this region – will become like Canada.

'Lech Wałęsa will certainly win the next elections in Poland, but very soon after that it will become clear to the electorate that he cannot deliver any solution simply because he has none. That is when the intellectuals, the liberal democratic elements, will win elections and voters will see their success in forming an effective government and in creating effective policies. Now is a very troubled time when there are all sorts of problems to do with unsatisfiable desires and frustrations, but very soon I think you will see all these countries – from the Baltic states right down to the Adriatic – becoming a solid bloc of liberal democratic states. Only then will it be possible for us all to make sensible, ecologically sensitive policies for the whole region. But the West must realise that if it does not make a big effort to put money into the area, to make it part of the West both politically and economically, then we will become just nothing – dangerous, backward-looking, hateful – just like the East, locked into pointless, senseless squabbles about borders and minorities. Like us with Romania now. Of course Romania will eventually have to give minority rights, but it would do so much quicker as part of an advanced European economic society where borders and boundaries mean next to nothing – which was why we opened up our borders a year ago. We realised this, even if the Romanians don't quite grasp it yet. But perhaps there they already need a second revolution.

'*The Velvet Prison* is an absolutely out-of-date book – completely useless to us now. At the moment I am not writing anything. I'm too involved with the politics of the SZDSZ – and politics is as dirty a business as you can imagine. It has nothing to do with ideology or anything like that, and a great deal more to do with personal, primitive urges, with individual desires. I hope I don't have to do this for too long. It is not that I feel good about politics, or even that I feel superior, a leader or anything like that. No,

130 Hungary – Writers in Transition

it's simply that I feel I can do something perhaps a little better than a few others. Maybe it is ego, my split personality, but I think I see things differently and I want to act. I have a point of view, some ideas, some knowledge of society that might be useful.

'I would describe the main political parties thus: SZDSZ is a progressive, even a revolutionary-democratic party trying to present itself as a party of conservative and cautious change. Its members are trying to appear to be yuppies. The MDF is a conservative and rather nationalist party of extreme caution, masquerading as a party of revolutionary democratic vigour. Fidesz is a party of yuppies and would-be businessmen masquerading as politicians. The Smallholders Party is a joke that will be annihilated at the next election. They want to re-privatise the land currently held by cooperatives, along with all the land redistributed under the communist land reforms. But they do not take into account the difficulty of legally depriving those who now work the land of their livelihood in order to reimburse those who have not worked that land for nearly forty years. It is a party that makes promises it cannot keep in order to get votes. It will be the first casualty in any election.

'The silent majority – confused that in all this change nothing has really changed at all, that no party actually seeks to represent the workers, the ordinary people – nobody asks what they want. Because of this, ordinary workers look at the current parties and don't see themselves taken care of, don't see themselves cherished or considered. They don't vote because there is no one to vote for. They don't care if a party is right-wing or left-wing just so long as it cares for the workers – which itself is a mark of confusion since no right-wing party ever took care of the workers, except in so far as they were useful to the leadership in extending their control even further.

'I don't think things will go badly for us here – not as badly as for Romania and Poland. But it is certain that in time all these countries will settle down into very ordinary, very boring little places. That's how it should be. The fact is that this revolution means the end of working-class solidarity because it means not only the birth of democracy, but the birth of post-industrial society. It brings with it the whole possibility, the atomisation and self-interest of post-modernism. The workers may not know or care about the name for this, but they know that it means simultaneously the beginning and the end of worker power, or working-class politics. They sense this. They feel it. They had class solidarity, now they want to be citizens.' Lunch was over, a waiter cleared away our plates and we paid the bill. Haraszti admired my notebook: 'You have such beautiful things in the West.' It was a plain, ordinary journalist's notebook. 'But tell me,' he said, 'do you make a lot of money writing?' 'Writing? In the West? No, that is almost impossible. I am very resourceful, but can't make a living as a writer and I don't know anyone who can. I do other things to make a living. Mainly I teach.' Without another word, without even goodbye, Haraszti got up and walked out of the restaurant. I followed him into the street, but he was walking away at great speed.

*

Hungary – Writers in Transition 131

On Sunday I meet with the poet Sandor Csóori (1930–2016) for after-lunch coffee in the Agelik Espresso Coffee Bar. Apparently, it is an established habit of his to meet friends at this time. When we arrive there is something of an atmosphere. Nothing you can put your finger on, but definitely something in the air. Csóori is holding court to a group of about fifteen people. He is speaking loudly, with expansive hand and arm gestures. He notices us, but makes no attempt to acknowledge us and carries on with his speech. Judit bristles: she has taken an immediate dislike to the man. She says nothing, but I can sense that she is uncomfortable. She sits next to me, translating in a whisper.

'Since the old regime collapsed we are inundated by waves of kitsch, in writing, in TV, in films. We are like tourists who buy all kinds of rubbish simply because they don't know what is good and what is true. It is as if the whole of Hungary has been reduced to the role of a tourist who is just passing through, quickly snapping up trifles and rubbish, not knowing good from bad. We see this perhaps worst of all in our journalists, many of whom were responsible for telling us how to be good communists, and who now tell us how to be good democrats. We need to know from our politicians and from our journalists what is real and what is true. They tell us only what is real, but not what is true, whereas writers told us what was true but not what was real. Now we have a need to know both what is real and what is true. It's not like it was under the communists – the withdrawal of publishing subsidies has meant that we don't know where we are or where we are going.

'And what are we doing to protect our rural writers, our peasant artists? Nothing. At. All. And yet they have such a purity about them in their style, their vocabulary, in the verse forms and themes. They are craftsmen. When you read them it is like watching someone work a design in wood. They are the essence of Hungarian-ness. Our peasants, they are pure. They are our only hope.

'I belonged to the opposition for many years – perhaps nearly 30 years – and now, even though my party is in power I cannot rid myself of this habit. I have to be in the opposition. I don't want power. That's just too difficult. It's not a writer's business – power. But opposing, criticising, observing, pointing out? Yes. A writer is always opposing something and the first thing he opposes is himself. It's a kind of ongoing crisis, an argument with myself. At the moment journalists say that the ruling party has three sections: the populist, the nationalist and the Christian conservative. What can I say? That isn't true, these three groupings. I feel I have all these things in me, but I still feel I am an oppositionist.

> Something happened to writers, to my friends, as soon as they became politicians. My friend Antal – we had known each other for years – I swear within five minutes of him becoming a minister he was different, treated me differently, as if he was a superior, within five minutes we had an argument. I thought we had won. In fact we did win. But now

132   Hungary – Writers in Transition

I ask: who is we? What did we win? Who won what? Stalin said: whoever is not with us is against us. Kadar said: whoever is not against us is with us. I say: whoever is with us is surely against us.

A couple of days later I found out that Csóori felt himself to be in disgrace when we met him and that the gathering was of his loyal supporters. He had written an article in the Democratic Forum weekly paper *Hitel*, in which he said that there were clear limits to the understanding and sympathy that the Hungarian Jews might feel with the state of Hungary and with Hungarians. His point was that Jews were not fellow Hungarians, and to put a distance between Hungarians and Jews.

*

Monday. The day starts with me meeting Judit at the Kossuth Metro 3rd Square, ground level, under the shelter. We have an appointment at 10.00 with Gy. Horvath Laszlo (b.1950) of the Europa publishing house, which specialises in foreign language and translation publishing. He gets straight down to business.

Five years ago there were twenty-five state-owned publishing houses. Now there are 470 privately owned companies, mostly producing poor quality best sellers. The public are only buying escape literature – best sellers. Our distributors now refuse to handle certain books and some kinds of books, so we have been forced to cancel production of serious books, books about recent events, about political history. We simply cannot sell plays at all. Our problem is now the distribution network, which is, of course, state-owned, but due for privatisation. Next year, when the privatisation will get under way, when the economy will be in serious trouble, we will almost certainly see a collapse in publishing – a collapse that can only be cured by a new distribution system and by a more stable economy, one that restores purchasing power to the reader.

We talk for a little while about this situation. I say that this is very similar to what has happened in Poland, where the state publishing houses died on their feet, where the distributors simply pulped most of the editions they had in storage, and where privatisation did not solve the problem of the lust for best sellers, escape literature and pornography, but rather made it even more difficult for serious books to find readers.

*

Monday: 15.00 I met Iván Mándy (1918–95), a short story writer, in a busy café he frequents every afternoon at this time. He is a tiny old man, rather impish, slightly dandified and 'olde worlde' in a Viennese sort of way. He starts to talk about a book he wrote a few years ago about the secret life of

Hungary – Writers in Transition   133

furniture. Judit dutifully, and with a straight face, translates a trite stream of fanciful drivel. I ask a question but his answer is evasive. He refuses to talk about other writers, publishing, politics or recent events. When I ask him a direct question about how he understands the present situation and how it affects his work and how it might develop he shrugs, makes a face and carries on chattering about the inner life of a wardrobe and the ambitions of a chair. What am I to do with this man? I wait until he goes over to speak to the waitress and ask Judit what the hell is going on. She says: 'I think he is an old fool. Either that or he wants you to think he is a fool because he thinks you are a spy of some kind. Drink your coffee and let's go. He has no intention of talking sense and I don't know why he agreed to meet you.'

*

At 18.00 I met György Konrád (b.1933) at his home. Konrád is the author of several novels but is probably best known in the West for his book *Antipolitics* (1984) and for his trouble-making study (with Iván Szelényi) *The Intellectuals on the Road to Class Power* (1979). His wife answered the door and quickly ushered us into his writing room in the basement. He apologised at once for not being able to prepare anything for me, but invited me to ask any questions I wanted. Unfortunately, however, he could hardly make good on this offer since everything I wanted to know fell within a remit of strict confidentiality imposed by his role as president of International PEN. 'So, are you at least enjoying your role as president?' I asked. 'No,' he said, 'not in the least. You know things in Yugoslavia are going very, very badly. Really they are all behaving abominably; even the writers are accusing each other of atrocious behaviour and splitting along ethnic lines. It puts PEN in a very difficult position when they propose resolutions... well, let's just say it is very trying.'

It soon emerged that he did not really want to be interviewed. Instead, he wanted to ask me about a recent trip I had made to Poland: whom I had met, what they had said, what I had seen on the streets. 'You know, Poland is the most populous state in this part of the world and we keep an eye on it because what happens there, if it does not eventually happen here too, at least it affects us. So please excuse my nosiness.'

He was president of PEN, an organisation to which I also belonged; he was asking me for information that he clearly needed, so what else could I do? This conversation and his subsequent questions took up most of our visit. Judit saw that she was not needed and closed her eyes for a well-earned nap. At the end of my 'report' he said: 'Poland and Romania are a long way behind in their development of a liberal and democratic understanding of "post-socialist" political life. It seems that in Bohemia and in Hungary the greatest distance has been travelled and the greatest tolerance shown, the intellectuals lead while the demagogues follow. However, in Slovakia and Moravia, Poland and Romania, the demagogues have a much higher profile and as a result these societies are much less accepting, tolerant and much

134 *Hungary – Writers in Transition*

less stable. There the intellectuals are not accepted as leaders – indeed in Poland they are often thought of as crypto-communists, Jews in disguise.

> The confusion we see now among intellectuals here was absolutely predictable. It is very ironic – a cruel Central European joke. Those who historically were always the opposition, who did not want power, are now the leaders. They have power, but what to do with it? How to redistribute, in a just way, properties that were confiscated and nationalised by the previous regime? Who could possibly want such a task? The Smallholders Party, for example, just today, broke its ruling alliance with the Hungarian Democratic Forum. But they have no idea how to proceed. The East-Central European intellectuals knew what they were against, but not what they were for. They fall out with each other as soon as they have power. They were very comfortable within the old regime – and it was possible for them to be both comfortable and opposed. Now they have rather lost control. It is not possible to limit a revolution, to say: "No, this isn't exactly what we had in mind." But they realise now they have rather demolished their own very comfortable position and this makes them nervous, depressed, irritable, not altogether happy. They are the winners, the people who led, the people who rule (well some of them), but they are also the losers. They got class power in a way they never expected. That is, through the collapse of this comfortable system, which they criticised from within, never expecting it to collapse and still less expecting to be given power.

On the way home the street corners seemed to be filled with people selling everything and nothing. Not only a few things you can't get in the shops, but mainly the things you could get in the shops, but at higher prices. Capitalism or what? Also there were dark-faced Transylvanian Hungarian women in black scarves and smoke-darkened embroidered sheepskins, embroidered shirts, long red dresses and boots. They were selling goat cheeses and fantastically embroidered tablecloths. Parts of Budapest look like a mini oriental bazaar – just like Sarajevo used to look.

*

On Tuesday Judit and I catch the train to the shores of Lake Balaton, to the writers' retreat at Szigliget. Before our arrival in the early afternoon some of the writers appear to have been having a heavy drinking session. We are greeted at the door by an unsteady writer with dark rings under his eyes who explains that he wants to go to the bar in the village but is too scared because on one side of the road there is a big dog and on the other side there is a wheel. This makes sense to him, but not to me. Judit says nothing, but I can see she already has one eyebrow raised. Almost immediately darkness descends and it begins to snow hard: within a couple of hours it is clear that we will not be taking long walks along the shores of the lake or even to the village.

Hungary – Writers in Transition   135

In the evening, with snow deepening outdoors, we gather in the dining room. After dinner people sit around chatting. One of the writers is drunk and a little agitated. Judit says my presence has upset him, though so far I have spoken to no one. Judit translates rapidly and quietly:

> 'I pity English Literature. I pity it. You go along in it and then you smell this thing, this shit-stink, this Ezra Pound. You just smell him.' He turns to me. 'So you have been reading Konrád and Haraszti... A Jew and a crazy communist. It's a Zionist conspiracy that these two are so well known abroad. But I can't speak of [he gave a long list of names] and if they are not Zionists, they are bourgeois.' Several people immediately got up and left the room. I was not sure where this was going, but I felt uncomfortable. I tugged Judit's sleeve. She nodded, and without a word we also left.

I spent the remainder of my time at Szigliget in my room writing.

*

My talk on British theatre at the PEN Club coincided with the prime minister opening an exhibition of Hungarian samizdat publications. I was no competition. Most of the members of PEN voted with their feet and only a handful of writers were present. My theme was the devastation of the arts – but particularly theatre – under the free market strategies imposed by Margaret Thatcher. In particular I talked about the pressures on writers and also about the attempts to censor Howard Brenton's play *The Romans in Britain*. This was something of which I had first-hand experience. I had covered the story of the banning of the play in Swansea for *The Stage*.

My talk went down like a cup of cold sick. I had not realised how much naïve admiration there was for Margaret Thatcher. 'Why,' said one ageing writer, 'would you seek to defend what is clearly a very poor and tasteless play, a play by a communist, if I am not mistaken? Surely they were right not to want this thing on the stage.'

'Well,' I replied, 'Brenton is drawing parallels between past events and the present situation – it is always embarrassing for the British when you talk about anything to do with Ireland. And just because Brenton is a communist doesn't mean he is wrong, does it? And when you say he is a communist you should recall that in the West we have more than one kind of leftist – not just Stalinists. Besides, we all belong to PEN, don't we? An organisation opposed to censorship of any kind. My feeling is that, even if the play is bad (and I don't think it is), it should not be censored. If it is a bad play it will not need a censor to finish it. But to censor the play before it is performed is to censor the ideas it contains – but perhaps I am teaching granny to suck eggs: you are all experts in the distortions wrought by censorship.'

The ageing writer sighed loudly, looked very, very uncomfortable and rather unhappy with my reply. I persisted:

'In the West we don't have the same experience as you in dealing with censorship or with communism, and I am sure you find me quite naïve...

136   *Hungary – Writers in Transition*

But just because you are in the process of getting out from under communism, that does not mean you are free from the problem of censorship or free to ignore it. The journal *Nagyvilág* recently published some long extracts from Brenton and Hare's play *Pravda*. When the editors there first saw the script they said it was irrelevant to the Hungarian situation. Now though, things have changed. Maxwell, Murdoch and the Springer press are all here in Hungary and suddenly the problems outlined in Pravda are Hungary's problems and the play is suddenly massively relevant. So far Maxwell, Murdoch and Springer have left the literary publishing houses alone, but they have made huge purchases in the Hungarian newspaper industry.

> It is not for me to tell you about the dangers and difficulties of censorship, but I can tell you there is more than one way to shape ideas in society. And one of them is through monopoly – by shaping taste and opinion. Let's talk again in ten years; by then whether Brenton is a communist will be a non-issue. Who knows, by then you might even be in agreement with him... In years to come you may find you actually need "communists" like Brenton.

The after-talk drink was brief and frosty. It was as if I had handed them a penknife from my pocket and asked them each to perform their own appendectomy.

*

Thursday: 11.45. I meet Miklós Vajda again at the Espresso Déryné. He says: 'Well, did you meet everyone? What did they say?' I give him a brief summary of the last few days. I mention the comments made about Hungarian writers and the West at the Writers' Union on my first day, tell him about Csóori and about my visit to Szigliget. Instead of attempting an explanation, he asks me: 'So, what do you make of all that?' I say: 'There is all the normal jealousy and envy that marks out any community of artists. But on top of that I sense fear and a terrible confusion... I picked up a very clear anger that Konrád and Haraszti were writers known to me, while other writers considered more worthy were not; and intense frustration that these two had a wide audience in the West and are known as "Hungarian writers". This was not only because they were not considered to be good writers – one of them is not considered to be a writer at all, but that it is – and this was quite clear – because they are seen as Jews or communists, promoted by foreign Jews over and above other deserving writers who were "more representative" or "more typical". Which I take to mean "more Hungarian", in some way.' Vajda looked pained, shrugged, glanced around the room. 'Well, I'd say you read the situation very well.'

*

Hungary – Writers in Transition 137

Friday: 10.00 Professor László Kéry (b.1951), editor of the journal *Nagvilag*. Professor Kéry has heard on the grapevine that I mentioned his magazine at my PEN lecture. He is delighted. On my question about anti-Semitism he says slowly: 'You must remember that over 600,000 Hungarian Jews died during the war. And the Hungarian government cooperated in this. At the end of the war it was impossible to speak or think or deal rationally, either with the co-operation or with the continued existence of Jews in Hungary. Even now, it seems, it is impossible to be rational about this.'

On Soviet TV I watch thirty girls in swimsuits parade around in front of very low-angle cameras while a Cossack band play 'Ave Maria' on pan pipes and an accordion. To me the band looks like Freddie and the Dreamers on speed. The programme is called 'The New Model Today 1990' and it is sponsored by the Why Not? Model Agency. What kind of style is this?

*

Writing as a professional occupation has been a tremendously ambiguous project in this part of the world. It was not only a way of limiting the power of the government, but also of licensing certain parts of the opposition and certain timely ideas. The East-Central European writers have lost their constituency to the politicians. No one, they say, is reading and no one is writing. Publishing is reeling from the withdrawal of state subsidy and a sudden flood of kitsch, popular novels and pornography.

It is clear from the way that the democratic opposition has been led by writers, and by the speed with which the writing fraternity has transformed itself into an active political stratum, that without the advent of 'socialism' this class would not necessarily have become writers at all. Indeed, it seems probable that a great number of them would rather have become professional politicians.

The intellectuals were on the road to class power here, and now they have that power. But the effect is as dignified as a dog chasing a motorcycle: even if the dog catches the bike, the dog won't know what to do with it. Writing and reading in post-war East-Central Europe have been a way of raising the level of culture and at the same time of levelling the various degrees of culture. It was a way of excluding certain ideas and promoting others – and you did not have to be for the regime to enjoy a decent, comfortable life. It was enough to avoid problem areas and to write about other things.

Literature, here as elsewhere, was a way of absorbing 'marginal elements' – people whose ideas had put them in prison, or prevented them from getting a university education or becoming professionally qualified: the outsiders, the loners. One short story, a few poems and there, they had a career, they could join the Writers' Union, their first volume was on the way. And of course in those days the publishing houses told the distributors what to sell, and the subsidies for all concerned were fat.

138 *Hungary – Writers in Transition*

The unusually powerful role of writers in East-Central Europe – as in South America, Israel and emerging African states – is a result of the under-development of those states in economics.

For historical reasons the slow emergence of urban consciousness, reflected in the failure to develop democracy or capitalism, also resulted in a failure to find or generate sufficient political and economic outlets for the intelligentsia. Scandinavia and Finland experienced something like this but found a way out of the situation.

Is it possible to imagine Poland and Hungary as social democratic Scandinavian-style states? Given their geographical and historical situation, with so many invasions and hostile neighbours, the answer must be no. Plus, of course, their position as transitional societies (on a spectrum of feudal → industrial; despotic → democratic; tribal → nation states) makes it even more unlikely. The impact of industrial organisation on these societies – sandwiched between the Soviet Union / Russia and Germany / the West – made the nation-state a fetish with no release in empire or in self-government. Further, each of these states feels threatened internally by 'alien' minorities.

As it worked its way through these societies, capitalism served only to make economic differences seem like ethnic differences. These societies may have aspired to Scandinavian-style democracy, but before now, in this part of the world, they never had the remotest chance of developing it.

What are the main modes of government and opposition at present? It seems to me that both the MDF and the SZDSZ benefit from the publicity of the debate about Hungarian identity. Democratic Forum benefits because it can portray the rival SZDSZ as a 'Jewish Party', while SZDSZ benefits by accusing the government, or at least some of its ministers and supporters, of being 'communist'. Fidesz is able to condemn the government and the other opposition parties as being communist. However, to say that someone is a communist is often to imply that somehow they are also a Jew or a Jewish sympathiser. Or vice versa.

Another way that Jews are identified is with the label 'urbanist' – as opposed to the populist/nationalist label 'ruralist'. These labels also clearly distinguish between the rural power base of the Democratic Forum and the urban Budapest power base of SZDSZ. I kept waiting for someone to use the word 'cosmopolitan': in Poland this was a codeword indicating 'Jewish influence', but it has not happened.

*

Outside my hotel, Judit, clad in an orange skirt, a sheepskin jacket, a brown fur hat and a stylish purple shawl, gave me a goodbye hug.

'Usually I have to go on tours of factories and farms to translate for foreign economists and such like. In all my years as a translator I never met such people as I have in the last few days. For years I read their books and I was in awe of them – our intellectuals, our writers, our thinkers and leaders.

Hungary – Writers in Transition   139

But then you come along and start asking them questions – nice questions, good questions – and what do I find? They are all idiots. They don't know any more than me. It has been wonderful working with you; I never had such a good time. Don't feel obliged to write, but a postcard would be nice.' And off she went into the sleet, her purple shawl flapping in the wind.

One week after my visit and I think that, just as in the new creeping democracy of Poland, I could feel the approaching, encroaching power of the minds of the opposition parties and the new government struggling to shape a language from their imaginations; their fearful and fevered images continually poke through the 'new rationality', and hardly disguise what really drives them – and on this I find a passage at the end of my Budapest notebook which reads: 'Destruction of the ability to assess worth; personal combination of pragmatic elements and rituals; Increasingly threatening role of magical elements – status, power of slogans, Jews, foreigners – as a basic and unquestioned part of life; increasingly arbitrary decision-making by the government because it cannot spell out why it is making certain decisions – it dare not; and this encourages the same at a personal level. Either a language of democratic politics and negotiation is struggling to get born, or, if historical precedent is resumed, this is the language of politics in Hungary'.

Some economic problems and political difficulties are so complex and intractable that it is almost impossible to form an opinion on them – indeed it is this impossibility that makes the questions of identity, loyalty and trust-worthiness issues on which everyone can and does have an opinion and that provide a useful diversion from the main problem: these things appear to be a solution. And of course the prime targets are the Jews, the romanies, intellectuals, communists and 'anti-Hungarian elements' who are thought to be plotting somewhere. The only doubt that remains in this is whether the awareness of Jewish identity, which shades over into anti-Semitism, is a newly inflated political concept, useful for the moment, or whether this harks back as a steadily constant historical presence in Hungarian society, no less present for being largely ignored by the communists. It seems to be the latter, rather than the former.

The big question now is clearly that of national identity. They are asking not only about individuals – who is like me and who is not – but also, what is Hungary? Alvarez, who was here in 1961, seemed to think that somehow there was no Hungary, that a Hungarian identity still had to be formed and that the nation really only existed in the language and in the imagination. That may be so. But Hungary is such a mixture of peoples it would be possible to cause real havoc here simply by insisting on an ethnic idea of Hungarian-ness.

There is a great deal of confusion, and along with the other traditional scapegoats, in particular the Jews – called Zionists, Urbanites, bourgeois or, in the code of Central European Stalinism, 'cosmopolitans' – are being blamed for communism and for opposition to communism, for repression and for struggle against repression, for loss of freedom and for the confusions

140 Hungary – Writers in Transition

of 'freedom'. The speed with which this phenomenon has revealed itself and the suddenness of the debate over the last few months indicate a current of thought, a deep-seated problem, an element of paranoia that has been present, if unexpressed, for a very long time. I didn't hear the sound of marching columns mobilising to support the idea of an expansionist, racially purified Greater Hungary, but I did hear them shuffling their feet.

Notes

1 Hungarian PEN is part of International PEN (Poets, Essayists and Novelists), an international writers' organisation whose website states: 'Originally founded in 1921 to promote literature, today International PEN has 145 Centres in 104 countries across the globe. It recognizes that literature is essential to understanding and engaging with other worlds; if you can't hear the voice of another culture how can you understand it?' (www.internationalpen.org.uk). Because it was both independent of the Communist Party and opposed to censorship, PEN was a constant irritation to the governments of the Eastern bloc.

2 In 1993 Csurka left the MDF to form the MIEP, the Hungarian Justice and Life Party. In the 1998 elections he led them to victory and they became the first openly anti-Semitic party to enter the Hungarian parliament since the end of World War II. At that election the coalition of the MSzP (Hungarian Socialist Party) and the SZDSZ was defeated and a new centre-right alliance dominated by Fidesz was formed.

6 Poland translated
Post-Communist writing

It is now nearly thirty years since, exhausted by the long struggle, Poland emerged from the grey, half-lit austerity of communism to the glitzy neon 'bling' of West European capitalism and the rapidly developing global economy. At the collapse of communism, Polish intellectuals sought a 'return to Europe' and found talk of a 'common European home' very seductive. However, that excited idealism passed quickly into a more pragmatic and resigned relationship. In May 1990, as Poland conducted its first 'genuinely free' local elections, Ryszard Kapuściński, always an acute observer, warned that Poland's well developed culture of resistance and opposition now sat uneasily with the actuality of independence and the responsibilities of democracy (Tighe 1991: 106–7).

Poland soon discovered that it was not a unified social entity working towards a common national goal, as tradition and the popular imagination had it, still less a coherent democratic entity making rational political choices. It was a *miazga* (mush). While private farmers, the Church, the universities and small scale businesses still existed, the civil society developed by the opposition in the 1970s and 1980s had been forced into a deceptively influential underground existence that, with the collapse of communism, was immediately contested, pushed aside or ignored. Most other elements of civil society – property rights, individual human rights, legal structures and independent institutions – had been destroyed, demolished, dismantled or deformed by communism (Keane 1988).

The Polish *inteligencja*, whose life and role had been inadvertently prolonged by communism, were brought to an abrupt halt not by a political campaign but by the power of the market. The *inteligencja* was no longer fundamental to the transformation of cultural or political life: consumer choice, the increasing influence of international culture, the Americanisation of popular culture, the power of international capital, the impact of a liberal-democratic political culture on a political scene that had more than its fair share of moralists, teachers and utopian critics, the increasing influence of 'experts' and the ambitious rise of would-be professional politicians all helped to render the *inteligencja* marginal and substantially altered the role of writers (Kurczewska 1995).

142 *Poland translated*

It also became clear that class was not to be the political force it was elsewhere: Poland's class structure had been attacked by Nazism, then levelled by fifty years of communism: there is now no significant property-owning middle class and 'the workers' are fragmented in their ambitions and opinions. There is a small 'red bourgeoisie' made up of former communists and state functionaries, well placed to make good with its contacts and inside knowledge in politics and the market; and there is a small 'petit bourgeoisie' that emerged from the flourishing communist black market and moved straight into the new market economy. Private farmers and rural cooperatives of the emerging 'green bourgeoisie' seem to be the only clearly defined and effective political interest group to have emerged so far.

Political battle-lines now intersect rather unpredictably, not over ideas of left and right, but more often over whether Poland should define itself as a narrow ethnic nationalism or as a broad civic patriotism. But they also intersect on attitudes to communism – on the one hand those prepared to work with reformed ex-communists and those who feel communists should be permanently barred (or worse) from all public life. There are also those who want all industry and enterprise nationalised and those who want some other arrangement. There are those who want to see the traditional values of the Catholic Church legislated into all areas of Polish life and who assert that this is part of the very definition of Polish-ness; they are opposed by those who regard them as retrograde and a block to Poland joining the modern European nations, and those who believe the Church should have a purely supporting, spiritual role rather than a leading political role. There are some who 'put their trust' in the ordinary Pole under a strong leader, opposed by those who feel this borders on fascism and that solutions should be negotiated democratically. There are those who see Poland's future as a part of Europe, and those who prefer a more 'natio-centric' Poland (Michnik 1990).

The concept of ethnic Polish-ness and the idea of the staunchly Catholic Pole as the basis for the state are under pressure as Poland starts to disentangle aspirations for independent political life from the tendency towards an obscurantist and perverse nationalism (Gomułka & Polonsky 1990). Adam Michnik has repeatedly said in essays and in editorials for *Gazeta Wyborcza* that development of democracy in Poland is largely a question of whether Poles remain 'slaves to gesture, producing a nationalist-populist political culture richly decorated with religious symbols' (Michnik 1987), or whether they take 'responsibility for themselves by doing some serious thinking about their place in the world' (Michnik 1998).

Under communism, literature had often been an *inteligencja* domain, the continuation of politics by other means. If communism did not succeed in turning Poland into a version of the Soviet Union, it did succeed in wasting talent, spoiling innovation and forcing ugly mutations and long delays on Polish culture. Its conservatism inadvertently pickled literary traditions, forcing writers to maintain an engagement with older forms and to persist in concern with 'the matter of Poland'. It blocked writers, forced them to

Poland translated   143

play games with the censor, to embed their comment and criticism in cunning allegories. While the collapse of communism made the older writers pause, and where possible to take stock, adapt and rake through the past, it did not produce any stunning revelations about the communist era or a flood of previously censored or suppressed books. Most of what needed to be said, had, in fact, got past the censors one way or another. Nor did the collapse produce a flood of new writers eager to take up the opportunities offered by the free market. Instead, bookshops, fuelled by Poland's massive cottage-translation industry, were filled with slick popular literary products: US criminal fiction, bonk-busters, romance and thrillers. The changes forced younger writers to ask difficult questions: What is Poland now? Who are the Poles now? What do Poles think and feel about themselves, the world, their neighbours, their past, their future? What do writers want to write and what do readers want to read? Poland is struggling to drag itself out of the tail-end of the eighteenth century, deal with the consequences of the twentieth century and simultaneously encounter the twenty-first century. It is against this background that the writing of the last twenty years has appeared.

*

A review of Polish–Jewish relations was inevitable – and with it the realisation that Poland is essentially Post-Jewish. Jewish life in Poland was not a closed world, and several accounts of the Holocaust experience have been published in Poland.[1] However, the chances of these books reaching a wide readership were always small: there was little interest in Jewish experience or culture, there was no longer any sizeable Jewish readership and many Poles felt they had enough wartime horror stories of their own. The Jews were gone, and for many years that was as all there was to say. Where their property had not been stolen by the Nazis, the current owners were not particularly curious to hear about survivors. An anti-Semitic pogrom in Kielce in 1947 and anti-Semitic campaigns led by factions within the Communist Party in 1956, 1968 and 1976, undercurrents of anti-Semitism in relations between the Party and Solidarity, and in Solidarity's relations with its own intellectual advisers, even the accusation that communism and the declaration of Martial Law were Jewish plots, all showed that the annihilation of the Jewish community during World War II had done nothing to ease or resolve Polish–Jewish relations in the post-war years. Indeed, the whole complex of issues had simply been driven underground to be brought out by the Party, whenever it was convenient, as a way of resolving political problems 'in favour of Poland' by smearing opposition through an appeal to fear, ignorance, prejudice and paranoia (Gross 2004).

Even so, by the late 1970s an appetite was developing for a version of Polish-Jewish history that had not been processed by nationalist-chauvinists. The first printing of journalist Hanna Krall's *Shielding the Flame*, a long interview with cardiologist Marek Edelman, the last surviving leader

144   *Poland translated*

of the Warsaw ghetto uprising, sold 10,000 copies; the second printing sold 30,000 copies (Krall 1986). However, the reception given to Claude Lanzmann's film *Shoah* (1987), with its revelation of crude stereotypical anti-Semitism among Polish peasants, and the claim by its detractors that the film was simply an anti-Polish provocation, were a sure indicator that public debate was still poorly informed, and operated on a level that was often simply divisive and destructive.

On the other hand, that same year the publication, to great international critical acclaim, of *Annihilation*, the first novel by Piotr Szewc (b.1961), proved that, slowly, change and understanding were possible. The novel is an imaginative recreation of a day in the life of the Jews, Poles, Ukrainians and Gypsies of Zamość in the year 1934. Inevitably it is an ambiguous exercise: Szewc, aware that the life obliterated by the Holocaust cannot be restored, is torn between trying to offer a series of photographs of an ordinary day, one that is like every other, a day when nothing unusual happens, a day when the newspapers carry stories of only 'minor events', and the feeling that even the most trivial image of this lost world and destroyed community has some intrinsic value (Szewc 1999).

By 1988, some writers were beginning to sense what had been lost to Polish culture in the Holocaust. They were also beginning to establish a new perspective on Polish–Jewish relations. Jaroslaw Rymkiewicz (b.1935), in *Umschlagplatz* (1988), his memoir of the search for the architectural details of the railway depot from which the Warsaw Jewish community was despatched to destruction, remembered the anti-Semitic content of the March 1968 issue of *Zycie Warszawy* (Rymkiewicz 1994: 159). He found it utterly baffling that, considering the importance of the place in the history of the Holocaust, there were no photographs of Umschlagplatz and very little in the way of an architectural record of the place. Understandably, however, his challenge to the established pattern of thinking was not easily absorbed or understood, and Rymkiewicz's book first appeared in Polish in France. But this was a foretaste of the challenge to traditional thinking and received opinion that was to come.

In 1988, Jan Gross' *Neighbours*, with its revelation that the massacre of Jews in the village of Jedwabne had been conducted not by Nazis but by Poles, sparked off a controversy that has remained painful, revealing and cathartic in equal measure, and which inevitably brought the subject of Polish-Jewish history into the open in a way it had never been before (Gross 1988; Polonsky 1990; Polonsky & Michlic 2004).

However, Hanna Krall (b.1937) moved the debate in a different direction – away from revelation and recrimination and into an assessment of the long-term effects of the Holocaust. Krall began her career in 1955 as a journalist on *Życie Warszawy*. In 1966 she began writing for *Polityka*, travelling widely in the USSR, Western Europe, America and provincial Poland. However, with the declaration of Martial Law in 1981 she resigned and published only in underground journals. In 1985 her fictional autobiography *The Subtenant* appeared, for which she was awarded the Solidarity

Poland translated   145

Cultural Prize (Krall 1992). Between 1994 and 2001, several of her 'True Stories' appeared in *Gazeta Wyborcza*. Twelve of these stories have been gathered under the title *The Woman from Hamburg* (Krall 2006). The stories are all based in fact, but around them Krall has constructed multi-layered narratives told in deceptively simple neutral prose. Her themes are the search for personal identity and the vagaries of destiny. Taken together, the stories are challenging and provocative in their association and questioning.

In the story 'Salvation', Krall writes of the search for the grave of the *tzaddik* of Lelów. He had been buried in the Jewish cemetery, but after the war a warehouse for agricultural implements had been built over the cemetery. The searchers get permission to take up a section of the floor of the warehouse and dig for the body. In a corner of the warehouse they erect a monument and once a year they meet to remember their *tzaddik*. They remember that he taught: 'Whosoever, whether man or nation, has not achieved awareness of his own errors, will not achieve salvation. We can be saved to the extent that we are aware of our own selves'. Upon being reminded of this, Josef, the son of the dead village glazier, remembering the eight hundred Lelów Jews who did not survive the Holocaust, replies: 'Here, there is no salvation, rabbi. Here there was no room for God' (Krall 2006: 185, 193). Krall's point is that for many Jewish survivors the Holocaust left them in the midst of an ongoing crisis and a loss of faith that undermined their identity and changed the way the way they saw themselves and the world. Clearly, the *tzaddik*'s teaching has application for the conduct and awareness not only of individuals but also of Germany and Poland, but the very powerful suggestion is that this also helps us to understand the state of Israel.

In 'Hamlet' Krall writes of the pianist Andrzej Czajkowski (better known perhaps as Andre Tchaikowski), the sometime pupil of Artur Rubinstein, who willed his skull to the Royal Shakespeare Company. She writes of his homosexuality, of the difficulties of his relationships and friendships, and of his impossible personality. But she also writes of his positive qualities. And this is linked to his childhood in wartime Warsaw. In the ghetto his mother gave him to his grandmother, who had managed to get Aryan papers. His grandmother dyed Andrzej's hair, disguised him as a girl, got him out of the ghetto and hid him in a wardrobe at a friend's apartment. Czajkowski's mother stayed and died in the ghetto with her lover. Czajkowski survived but grew up to hate his grandmother. Later, as a brilliant young pianist, he changed his name from Andrzej Czajkowski to Andre Tchaikowski. He also discovered that he was homosexual, but this did not prevent him trying several times to prove he was 'a real man', always with the same woman and always with disastrous consequences. In later life he underwent psychoanalysis and wrote a document that was a conversation with his dead mother.

In 'The Decision' Krall tells the story of Peter Schok of Amsterdam, an ex-hotel-receptionist working as a masseur. In the first line of the story she says: 'I did not like him'. He is the partner of her friend Benjamin. Peter takes her out for the day to a Portuguese synagogue and the Jewish

146 *Poland translated*

Museum. It is in the museum, in presenting the artefacts to her and showing her around, that he comes alive. This is around the time when deaths from AIDS were increasing and the homosexual community felt itself to be under siege. A short while later Peter and Benjamin's relationship breaks up; Peter has already found a new lover and Benjamin explains this as Peter's fear of true love, which might, he thinks, be a consequence of Peter's Jewish ancestry, even though, as Krall points out, his mother had spent the war in Britain and Peter was born ten years after the war. Peter falls ill with AIDS. He arranges permission for an assisted death. The death passes off quietly and a funeral is held – Peter has already produced his own colourful obituary notice. At the funeral, where most of those attending are suffering with AIDS, synagogue music is played, along with the sound track of Bette Midler songs from the film *The Rose*. Next morning they place flowers at the monument to homosexuals killed in the Nazi camps – three pink triangles descending into the canal: 'To the question: What connection is there between AIDS and the camps and the war? they reply that it is discrimination and hatred' (Krall 2006: 258).

Eva Hoffman, whose family survived the Holocaust but left Poland in 1959, is also concerned to see the debate from a different angle (Hoffman 2004: 138). While Polish-Jewish history has not been a major theme in recent Polish literature, in an odd way the ghost of a Jewish past and the absence of Jews in contemporary Polish life often figure on the margins of what is said and thought, and it is clear from the reaction to a film like Spielberg's *Schindler's List* (1993) and the difference it has made to the revival of the Kraków ghetto district of Kazimierz that, if nothing else, there is a growing consciousness of an absence, even if opinion is divided as to what the meaning of that absence might be and that consciousness is sometimes kitschy, opportunistic and aimed at promoting tourism. After more than fifty years of misunderstanding, separation and competing Polish and Jewish martyrologies, there has been a brief period of what Eva Hoffman has called 'symbolic action'. The question facing writers now is how exactly to understand, represent and pass on the trauma of their joint Polish–Jewish history, and how to overcome the memories and misunderstandings of the past for the inheritors of the second and third generations of post-Holocaust Poles and Jews. As Hoffman put it, it is a question of what we do with what we know.

*

The review of Poland's literary past is often abrasive. Antoni Libera's *Madame* bears comparison with James Joyce's *Portrait of an Artist as a Young Man* and with Charles Webb's *The Graduate*. It purports to have been written in an attic in Gdańsk during the early months of Martial Law, while the author, who is on his own admission 'corrupted by literature', was hiding from the authorities. The tale is set in Warsaw a few years earlier, not a 'time

Poland translated   147

of real terror', 'just grey and bleak and miserable', the period of 'our little stabilization'.

The plot is concerned with a self-absorbed but academically gifted high school student who falls in love with his beautiful, mysterious, thirty-two-year-old French teacher, Madame. As the student becomes more desperate to 'know' his teacher, he stalks her. He finds out where she lives and where she studied, he finds out who she studied with and then begins to shadow her through her social circle. He discovers that her father had gone to Spain to fight for the Republican cause; after the intervention of the Comintern and the victory of the nationalists he had fled to France and stayed on to fight in the Resistance. After the war, in the early 1950s, fearing the French right wing had killed his wife, he had returned to Poland with his daughter. Poland at that time was still in the grip of Stalinist paranoia. Although her father may have felt safer in Poland, it was not long before the communists, suspicious of anyone who had not fought in a communist organisation in the Spanish civil war, arrested him. He died in prison, leaving his daughter, who had been born and brought up in France and whose French was perfect, trapped in a country where she felt a stranger.

As the student finds out more about his teacher, he also begins to understand Polish communist attitudes to the study of foreign languages and pushes at the boundaries of the kind of education allowed under the communist regime. Although he does succeed in befriending her, it is on her terms rather than his. What is revealed through his interest in French and in his French teacher is Poland's recent history.

In another section, by emphasising the birthplace of the philosopher Schopenhauer 'in the supposedly pure-Polish city of Gdańsk!', Libera undermines a substantial strand of post-war communist propaganda effort.

Beneath the struggle with his predatory and yet romantic feelings for his teacher and his discoveries about the reality of her life and past, his efforts to get his show on stage, to run a jazz band, his despair at certain kinds of literature and his cynicism about the achievements of communism, the novel is an extended meditation on Polish identity.

Throughout the novel, literature is a touchstone for character models and moral examples. The student appears to have read everything. But it is to Joseph Conrad's novel *Victory* that he returns again and again. Libera chose his target carefully. Żeromski's novel *Ashes* (1904) was a Polish literary classic and standard high school set-text. It dealt with the subject of Polish soldiers in Napoleon's armies who went to Spain thinking they were fighting for Poland's freedom, but who, after taking part in the siege of Saragossa and a vicious anti-guerrilla campaign, return to Poland 'broken men with ashes in their hearts', having failed to bring about Poland's independence. However, Libera's classroom discussion is a little unfair to Żeromski. He was in fact a socialist sympathiser who was worried by the rise of neo-romanticism that accompanied Polish independence. He was also a friend of Conrad in the 1920s: Conrad supported his candidacy for the Nobel Prize.

148   *Poland translated*

Żeromski's book *Przedwiośnie* (1924) dealt very effectively with the political, intellectual and economic chaos of the post-Partition years and might have been a rather fairer summary of his contribution to the emerging cultural life of Poland, but would not have made Libera's point so clearly.[2]

At the same time the student begins to attend university, Madame qualifies to run a new kind of school where everything is to be taught in French and she leaves Poland on a training course, clearly planning never to return. Gradually the student comes to see his teacher not as simply a rare beauty and a challenge, but as someone trapped by circumstance, and in doing so he comes to understand something more of the nature of the world that he inhabits. By seeing her as 'born of mysterious, exceptional parents... handsome, quick-witted, and strong-willed' he comes to see her as 'sorely tried by Fate's adversities; caught and imprisoned by the Bolshevik pygmies occupying Poland and now exerting all her cunning to find a way out of the trap' (Libera 1998, 2001: 309). He begins to understand that she has been playing a very long game and developing a strategy that will, indeed, enable her to leave Poland. His triumph is that, rather in the manner of Joseph Conrad, he does not see this as running away, 'jumping ship', desertion or treachery (Libera 2001: 309).

With its constant questioning of the nature of Polish-ness and the reality of Poland's achievements in the arts and politics, the book opened up difficult territory for Poles who clutched at nationalism as a source of certainty in a rapidly changing and uncertain world. And Libera did this at a time when it was not only just possible to voice these things for the first time, but at a time when such questioning was both inevitable and deeply unpopular.

Andrzej Stasiuk (b.1960) is one of the most interesting and challenging of the new generation of post-communist writers. While the collapse of communism allowed a much freer approach to literary experimentation, Stasiuk's refusal to be lured into the new morality embodied in the 'freedoms' of capitalism clearly reflects the disillusion of many of his generation. Born into a working-class Warsaw family, Stasiuk was expelled from vocational school and then conscripted into the army at the time of Martial Law. He deserted (some say he broke out in stolen tank), was caught and spent eighteen months in jail. Although his first book, an account of his imprisonment, was a literary success, in the late 1980s he abandoned Warsaw, moved to a remote district on the Ukrainian border, continued his writing far away from the literary world, and supported himself and his family by breeding llamas and running his own small press.

Stasiuk's *White Raven* concerns a group of friends who decide to spend a short vacation in the mountains, where one of them commits a gratuitous murder. This act destroys their friendship and sense of group solidarity and forces them to adopt an attitude of 'every man for himself' as they flee through the mountains in a blizzard. The blizzard and the mountain scenery provide a sharp romantic contrast to the developing mood of the group. The novel reflected the desperate confusion and loss felt by many Poles in the years between the imposition of Martial Law and the collapse of communism. The novel won him the Kultura Prize and the Koscielski Prize (Stasiuk 2000). *Tales of Galicia* was a novel told in linked short stories and concerned the way in which a small Galician community faced the traumatic economic changes of the 1990s (Stasiuk 2003). In *Nine* he looked at the life of Pawel, a young businessman, as he falls victim to loan sharks, drug dealers and small-time gangsters amid the hostile Warsaw cityscape. It is a tale in which the post-communist younger generation find themselves adrift in a world where the moral strictures of the Church and the stricter social codes of opposition no longer apply, but where the new freedoms bring no satisfaction, just a sense of amoral disconnection (Stasiuk 2007).

Though at odds with the communist system, Stasiuk clearly found the pace and the nature of change distasteful and problematic: his rejection of city life – particularly that of Warsaw – and his determined interest in, ease with and celebration of provincial life and the natural world is part of a clear centrifugal tendency among the younger generation of Polish writers.

*

The post-communist poetry scene in Poland has changed so rapidly it has hardly been possible to get to grips with the ideas of one movement before it has blurred into the next. In spite of the arguments and differences, a broad pattern is discernible. For the poets of the 1980s, Poland's situation seemed endlessly dreary and all hope for public life permanently mired. From the imposition of Martial Law in 1981, a trend emerged for fragmentation and privatisation in poetry and in society; in part this was a reaction of general mistrust as Martial Law divided opinion and loyalties. In many ways, for poetry the move from the final days of communism into the post-communist experience was not a clean break, or even a series of breaks, but rather a steady transition, and for the poets of the new democracy, capitalism and freedom – their new condition – brought new frustrations.

The New York School that emerged in the late 1980s and early 1990s was led by a group calling themselves the O'Harists. They turned their back on the work of Miłosz, Barańczak, Herbert and Szymborska, and their quarrelsome punkishness, sensationalist brutalism and graffiti-anarchism, while it reflected an ambition towards novelty-capitalism, provoked some to label them 'the Barbarians'. In their turn, the O'Harists predictably accused the younger poets who reacted against them of recycling the better poetry of the past into a meaningless mish-mash in the name of New Classicism. And while this poetic tiff was still in process, the Banalists began to emerge. Poetic journals too have been through great changes, and probably *bruLion* (meaning foul papers or rough draft) will come to be seen as the publication most representative of the changing face of these years.

While the grand narrative of the communist era and the criticism it provoked have now gone, the new poets often felt denied the muse of censorship, the dignity of exile, the strength of community solidarity and the fuel of opposition. In 1991 Zbigniew Machej (b.1958), in his poem 'An Old

150 *Poland translated*

Prophecy', was aware of what had been lost and cynical about what was to come. His conclusion was that in the new context fairy stories would prevail as 'the wolf shall lie down with the black sheep and the ugly duckling' (Pirie 1993: 150). Marzanna Kielar (b.1963) lamented that 'nothing separates us from the other side anymore' (Mengham et al. 2003: 85). For this generation, communism may have gone, but the world it created is depressingly still the one that Poles must inhabit: the promise of ease, wealth and freedom promised in advertisements remains elusive.

In general, the younger poets question whatever it is they are told they belong to – Poland, a community, a market, a housing estate or a village. The poetry of Dariusz Sośnicki (b.1969) is full of stinking fish tanks, cabbage smells, blocked drains, boilers, steam, body odours, drying washing, plodding trams and tight clothes. It is not as a patriotic flag that he sees himself, but rather as a flapping towel: 'Wet, we fold ourselves in four and lie down to sleep' (Mengham et al. 2003: 185). Krzysztof Jaworski (b.1966) celebrates Paris not for its beauty, culture, food or galleries, but simply because, unlike Poland, 'no-one talks about dollars' (Mengham et al. 2003: 79–81).

Marcin Swietlicki (b.1961) insists in his poem '...ska' (the title suggests Polska – Poland) that the new freedoms have only installed a new, unspecific unease revolving around words like 'independence, liberty, equality, fraternity, Poland from sea to shining sea, unemployment, taxes, *Gazeta Wyborcza*'. He sees post-communist Poland as a 'concentration garden' rather than a concentration camp (Mengham et al. 2003: 209–213).

*

George Steiner said 'Totalitarianism makes provincial' (Steiner 1979: 159). He was thinking of the way that Nazism managed to cut off the arts in Germany from 'all that was alive and radical in modern art'. Milan Kundera was to express the same idea with a different emphasis when he complained that with communism writers often felt themselves cut off from the culture, innovation and the style of the West (Kundera 1984a: 96). Polish communism was authoritarian rather than totalitarian and it is possible to see that the contest between the Party, the Church and the opposition through the post-war years was really about moral authority, over who had the right to rule and the right to criticise, about who occupied the moral high ground. Polish communists were happy as long as they were seen to hold power, but they never knew quite what to do with it.

Communist authoritarianism in Poland operated to install a narrow, boorish provincial mentality as the political and cultural norm: through censorship and propaganda it attempted to neuter the *inteligencja*; it cut off Poles from their own history, did not allow them to come to terms with the new Poland while forcing them to accept it. Since the apparatus of the Party was so intimately connected to the move from the country to the city, from the East to the West, from the old Poland into the new post-German Poland, and from the defeat of 1939 to the ambiguous 'victory' of 1945,

Poland translated   151

as well as with an ongoing and overarching concern for Poland's security, it was often hard for Poles to separate the fact of their continued existence from the less popular aspects of communist rule: the communists seemed to make their presence and their rule the price the country had to pay for its existence. This authoritarian provincialism also manifested itself in opposition to communism. Wałęsa's war 'against the intellectuals' saw Polish workers as provincial, but saw intellectuals as the untrustworthy product of Warsaw. In Wałęsa's mind this was a clear division.

The Communist Party's habit of using the 'recovered territories' as a dumping ground for discomforted settlers from the east and for all manner of political discontents and misfits was just storing up trouble for itself. However, post-war Polish provincialism had an additional element: the Polish provinces of the west and north are not the old rural Polish *kresy* (eastern borderlands) moved westwards, but well developed ex-German territories. 'New Poland' (post-war, urban, industrial, with numerous universities and a substantial population of young people) is often thought of as somehow inferior, not quite genuine. In the popular imagination, 'Old Poland' (pre-war, traditional, rural, agrarian) is the 'real Poland'.

Young Polish writers barely remember communism and see it as something of interest only to their parents. For them the most important and substantial realisations have been that they inhabit a post-German place and that in their family lore there is another culture at work – that of the old Polish east. Leszek Szaruga, editor of the underground *Puls*, spelled out some of the complications that the Party's mission to settle the 'eternally Polish lands' sought to eradicate, suppress or ignore, pointing out that his own father was born in Odessa but was of Lithuanian and Greek lineage (Szaruga 1997: 172).

Understandably, the loss of the east and the discovery of the German-ness of 'the recovered territories' has been most significant for young Polish writers brought up in those areas. Marek Krajewski's *Death in Breslau* (the first of a quartet of thrillers) is set in 1933, just after the Nazis were elected to power. It shows the swift descent into corruption as the police force is Nazified and political policing becomes the order of the day. Decadent violence is at the heart of the book – the bodies of a young woman and her maid are found in a train, naked and with scorpions writhing in their slashed stomachs. The plot is complex and we are presented with a gallery of supporting characters: aristocrats, prostitutes, Gestapo, Jews, Freemasons, corrupt ministers, merchants. However, it must be said that one of the major attractions, and perhaps even one of the thrills, of the book is the city itself, which is unmistakably German Breslau, a sprawling, vibrant, decadent crossroads, a major a railway town, an artistic and business centre, rather than the more familiar war-damaged Polish city of Wrocław. In a manner reminiscent of Günter Grass' recreation of Danzig's buildings and streets, in this novel everything is referred to by its pre-war German name rather than the post-war Polish equivalent. This is a bold departure from communist practice: in its own way it indicates something of the fascination young

152 *Poland translated*

Poles have for the ghosts of another time and another culture that inhabit their streets and towns, and it restores something of the history of the place; at the same it time lays claim to the place in a new way (Krajewski 2008).

Paweł Huelle (b.1957) has taken up the German-ness of the past in novels and stories set in Gdańsk – *Who was David Weisser?* (Huelle 1991), *Mercedes Benz* (Huelle 2005), *Castorp* (Huelle 2007a), and *The Last Supper* (Huelle 2008). Huelle is a remarkable talent and one of the few writers to have established a reputation outside Poland. In his novels – and particularly in his best-known work, the part-mythological, part-satirical, part-tall story, *Who was David Weisser?* – he is concerned with exploring the secret topography of the German heritage, the hidden ethnic make-up of the city, and to lay bare the complexity of its historical identity, but he does this in a way that challenges the cut-and-dried answers offered by the Party (Huelle 1987, 1991).[3]

In 'The Table' the narrator's parents argue about a table left to them by Mr Polaske, a German resident expelled to the West. His father attempts to cure a wobbly leg, but this does not work and he ends up by destroying the table. The young narrator and his father set about searching for a new table only to find that the shops, fulfilling the national plan for furniture, have only triangular tables. They decide to find a carpenter who will accept a 'private commission'. Their search takes them out of the ruined city of Gdańsk, eastwards into the fens of the Wisła delta. There they find a Mr Kaspar and his Mennonite wife, share in his illegal butchery business, drink homebrewed juniper beer, and learn something of the not-quite-hidden history of the delta and its occupation by the Poles. They get their table. Domestic squabbles fade away. Then they are visited by Mr Polaske, the German who had given them the original table. He brings them gifts from the West but fails to notice they have a new table and the young narrator notes enigmatically: 'From then on time went by differently, and only I knew why' (Huelle 1991, 1994).[4]

Much is hinted at in the story, but little is explained. The idea that a German could be on friendly terms with a Polish family undercuts a great deal of post-war propaganda. The figure of the Mennonite wife, for example, though she hardly speaks, and has only a broad brimmed black hat to remind her of her Mennonite past, is an important figure because as pacifists the German Mennonite communities of the delta were among the first victims of the Nazis. She is the last Mennonite and it is important for the young narrator to realise that in German Danzig, Germans too were victims of Nazism. The theme of the table is Biblical: 'Thou preparest a table before me in the presence of mine enemies: thou anointest my head with oil; my cup runneth over' (Psalm 23). What has been revealed to the young narrator is hard to put precisely into words but, as is often the case with short stories, is powerfully suggested: it is a view of another way of thinking about the world; a connection to the past, to people and to feelings that contradict politics; but nevertheless to the reasons why things are the way they are.

Poland translated 153

Huelle, like Günter Grass, finds his imagination stirred by the half hidden, half secret, little discussed German-ness of Gdańsk, by the fact that everything he can see in his home town – the roads, streets, factories, ship-yards, public buildings and districts – once had different names. It is clear that for most of the post-war period the Party was terrified that a re-united Germany would come looking for its lost lands, not seeking sentimental tourist souvenirs, but re-possession. The Party's attitude to the 'recovered territories' slowed down any real appreciation of the history and any under-standing that might have led to easier relations with Germans over their lost homes. Perhaps because it was forbidden to acknowledge the German-ness of the past, Huelle, like his protagonist David Weisser, has taken 'particular pleasure in hunting the traces of the German presence' (Huelle 1991: 53).

Huelle also found that in order to make his way around the woods and valleys of Polish Gdańsk suburbs he had to seek out a map of Danzig from the Nazi era.[5]

Stefan Chwin's *Death in Danzig* also takes up the complex mixed parent-age of the city of Gdańsk. He also takes up Poland's literary heritage: the suicides of the Polish writer and artist Witkiewicz and the German author Kleist form part of the backdrop to a description of Danzig as it became Gdańsk, and of the Poles who came to colonise the ruins after 1945. There is a quiet emotional intensity in this long, loving description of the city. The novel follows the fortunes of several of the new citizens: Hanemann, a sur-geon from the Danzig medical academy, who is struggling to come to terms with the loss of a female friend in a sailing accident; Adam, a mute boy found in the ruins; Hanka, a young Ukrainian woman who has some murky episode with the partisans in her past and is now hunted by the authorities. The novel raises the question of whether Witkiewicz was morally right to commit suicide in 1939 rather than live under the Russians, or whether, as one of Hanemann's young pupils puts it, 'he should have put away his razor and gone on living the way we do? Here in this new Poland?' The novel also gives voice to the thought that haunted Poles in the city from the end of the war up to the collapse of communism: 'Right now they (the Germans) hate the Russians and the Russians hate them, but as soon as they get friendly again, Russia is going to give Gdańsk back to them. And let them do what-ever they want with us' (Chwin 2005: 219–20).

As the strength of German claims to western Poland died away and the threat of revanchism receded, so its usefulness in Polish politics declined. As a consequence, openness to, and willingness to engage with, the Ger-man past of the new Poland has developed. This can be seen very clearly in post-communist poetry. Marzanna Kielar was born and brought up in Gołdap, in what until 1945 had been German East Prussia, but which now forms part of Polish Mazuria. Her poetry is a long love affair with a land-scape with which she has established a strong emotional bond. This is a dark place, but it is not a haunted landscape: the houses and lakes have no ghosts. Nevertheless, it is a strangely monochrome world where the occa-sional colour – a rose, a patch of blue sky, rust – comes as a shock. Her

154 *Poland translated*

relationship to the place is one where, as her syntax judders and the ambiguities pile up, out of a profound mistrust of words she refuses to name things but nevertheless finds a sacred conversation (Kielar 2006: 16).

The theme of living in post-German Poland emerges very strongly in several other poets, but particularly in the work of Tomasz Różycki (b.1970), from the Silesian town of Opole. Unlike many of his contemporaries, Różycki looks to the poets of the recent past for his historical and poetic bearings. His first volume of poems was called *Vaterland* (1997), and it set out to explore the nature of the Polish Fatherland built in the ruins of the Nazi Fatherland. However, lurking behind this challenging conundrum was his own family history and the loss of a different Fatherland: like millions of other Poles, his family had been uprooted from their home in Lwów at the end of the war and expelled westwards into the new People's Republic of Poland. He presents us with a series of overlapping fatherlands, each with its own time, place and emotional life (Różycki, 2007: 21).

In 'Anima, There and Not There' he describes the need to put down a claim on specific territory and shows a wandering mud-spirit trying to take possession of a soul that has been loitering in a room for three days, trying to find new clothing for itself. The title is a pun in Polish, and its presence alerts us to a tension. Anima sounds like the words 'a nie ma' – meaning 'but it isn't'. So the title might be read/sound something like: 'But it isn't, but it is'. It is rare that Polish writers make use of puns: the language does not seem to lend itself to wordplay as easily as English. Clearly this is a reference to Poles inhabiting the new territories and trying to make them their own: 'it isn't Poland, but it is'. Perhaps this is a suitable comment on the nature and permanence of borders, states, citizenship and identity. This undercutting tension and edgy unease continue in Różycki's more recent work *Kolonia* (2006), where he looks at modern Polish Opole and historical Polish Lwów and sees them both as kinds of colony. His interrogation of the word 'colony', particularly in the poem 'Electric Eels', reduces the significance of previous colonisation and occupation to a flag on a pole, traces buried in the earth – bottle caps, glass, a fish spine, charcoal, random cardboard boxes, bobby pins, hair – and to the fears these traces arouse. These ideas are a serious challenge to much that goes to make up the nationalist identity in Poland.

*

Perhaps the biggest change since the collapse of communism has been the rise to prominence of women writers. Although there were women writers in the late nineteenth century, several distinguished women writers in interwar Poland and women writers under communism (including 1996 Nobel Prize winner Wysława Szymborska), the Polish canon is dominated by male writers. The 'emancipatory promise' of communism did little to aid women since, in spite of its propaganda of liberation, the development of full

Poland translated   155

employment, free day care for children, support for single parents simply swapped abortion for effective contraception and added the difficulties of managing a career to the many other responsibilities Polish women already had. Where women were involved in literature, it was almost always rather hesitantly, as editors, anthologists, translators and teachers of literature. If they actually wrote, it was usually poetry (Forum Polek 1988).

The collapse of communism set off an echo to the conservative attitudes of the Catholic Church. It set in motion a general call for women to 'return to the kitchen', saw pressure to reverse abortion laws and left male power structures unchallenged: as before the collapse of communism, there was still very little interest in feminism, which was widely regarded as a Western fad, and women were slow to see themselves in explicitly feminist activities and organisations. The 1990s saw the start of a massive wave of unemployment and economic migration to England, Eire, France and Germany – an estimated five million Poles sought work in the UK and Eire in the period 2004–8 – with consequent pressure on family life. Against this background women were increasingly drawn into pornography, drugs, prostitution and people-trafficking (Schwartz & Von Flotow 2007: 7–32). In spite of this, right across the former Soviet bloc, several women have begun to establish considerable reputations as prose writers.

It is difficult to grasp the extent to which, for many people, the collapse of communism and the arrival of capitalism not only undermined old established certainties but corroded all sense of political perspective. In Dorota Masłowska's novel *White and Red*, this is a major theme. Against the background of a trade war against the Russian-dominated black market, the local government have decided to paint the roads and houses half white half red as a gesture of patriotism and a test of citizen loyalty ('either you're a person or a prick') and to run a pageant to crown one of the local girls as 'Miss No Ruskies'. Meanwhile, a tracksuited young man known as Nails pretends to be an expert in sand (he thinks sand is 'ferrous') and snorts illegal substances at any and every opportunity. While trying to dump his junkie girlfriend Magda he finds out that she has, in fact, dumped him. He meets and is attracted to Natasha who, in her relentless drive for chemical stimulation, searches his apartment and almost destroys it in the process. He then meets Angela, a vegetarian goth who refuses to eat sugar because she believes it is made from the ground up bones of animals. Later he meets the extremely 'straight' Ala, who is currently dating the man who stole Nail's girlfriend Magda.

In its atmosphere, in the less-than-smart charmlessness of its characters and its relentless observation of the Polish drug sub-culture, the novel is very close in spirit to Irvine Welsh's novel *Trainspotting*. It portrays a generation who do not have communism to fight, who do not see any solace or strength in the Catholic Church and who have no ideological or spiritual resistance to the seductive power of capitalism as represented by the drug trade. What the novel shows is an exhausted, aimless, de-politicised generation lacking

156 *Poland translated*

in the moral certainty of communism or resistance and desperately lacking in any kind of political perspective[6] (Masłowska 2005: 15–16).[7]

Masłowska was twenty-one years old when she wrote this, her first novel, and she had already won the *Polityka* Prize. It was a most assured debut. However, the changes made to the title between the Polish, US and British editions clearly reflect an uncertainty about the novel, its relationship to the Cold War, to current political realities and, of course, as to its possible readership.

Natasza Goerke (b.1960) was born of 'assimilated Jewish family' in Poznań. She left Poland in 1984 and now lives in Hamburg, but she continues to publish in Polish magazines and journals. She won the *Czas Kultury* Prize in 1993. Her first publications were greeted with immediate acclaim, but while her short prose pieces often baffled readers with their unexplained turns and dry humour, her later books have evinced confusion and frustration in her readers as she has refused to shoulder any of the traditional responsibilities of the writer and refused to make her stories conform to the conventional notion of narrative or meaning. Her third book *Farewells to Plasma*, for example, contains a series of prose pieces that are playful, bizarre, shifty, absurd, satirical and strategic by turns. She has an ironic attitude to the Polish literature of the past and says Mickiewicz's patriotic poem *Konrad Wallenrod* (1828) 'can make the delight in reading poetry disappear for years, leaving in return only sadness, glasses, and a yearning for a lost paradise'.

Another impressive debut has been that of Olga Tokarczuk (b.1962). Her first novel, *House of Day, House of Night*, is a set in her home town of Nowa Ruda (formerly German Neuerode), south of Wrocław, next to the Czech border. The book lacks a conventional plot, but is rather a kind of dream catcher, gathering up the memories, sleeping dreams and waking reveries of this tiny town. With the help of the elderly and rather erratic Marta, the narrator collects the history of the place in the stories of the people who now live there, in the memories of the Germans who come back to photograph the vacant plots where their childhood homes used to stand, in the local secrets, internet fantasies, lore of the land, mushroom gathering tales and in the endless search for buried German treasure.

These are ambiguous tales of ambiguity. The place, as the title indicates, is neither one thing nor the other, not day nor night, not entirely Polish nor exactly ex-German. The German-ness of the place has not entirely surrendered to Polish-ness. The theme is announced in a dream at the very start of the book: 'I could see a valley with a house standing in the middle of it, but it wasn't my house, or my valley, because nothing belonged to me. I didn't even belong to myself' (Tokarczuk 2002: 1). Variations on this theme appear throughout the book. Nowa Ruda is located in a valley so deep and the surrounding mountains so high that in the months October to March the sun cannot shine there – even daylight is gloomy. The local saint Kummernis, who was obsessed by the gradations of light and dark, is said to have been crucified by her father for her Catholic devotion and refusal to marry: she appears in carvings with naked breasts but also with Christ's head and beard. Paschalis, the monk who writes her story, is tormented by his own ambiguous and uncertain sexuality: even though he is a monk he wants to be regarded as a woman and in his one sexual encounter can make love only when he is dressed as a woman (Tokarczuk 2002: 138).

Even a traditional recipe for the poisonous Lurid Boletus mushroom is ambiguous. The mushrooms are said to attack the kidneys, killing by accumulative damage: 'by eating these mushrooms you will end up both alive and dead simultaneously, a certain percentage alive and a certain percentage dead. It is hard to say at what point one passes into the other' (Tokarczuk 2002: 174–5).

This feels very different from the writing of the communist years: it is post-modern, post-communist, post-oppositional, post-German, perhaps even post-national. There is an almost Zen quality to the vision of identity, time and location. Tokarczuk was awarded the prestigious Nike Award and the Günter Grass Prize before going on to win the Nobel Prize for Literature itself in 2018. She is unusual in that her work, while classified as serious literature, is also regarded as in the 'bestseller' category.

*

For all its continuities and engagement with the past, parts of the Polish literary scene are changing towards a more westernised pattern. The 'Best Seller', for example, is not typically a Polish creation. Most Polish readers complain that their national literary product is 'all head and no legs' – intellectual and packed with deep thoughts but lacking a well told plot. This may be why foreign thrillers have been so popular in translation.

The development of a home-grown popular literature is something new and the works of Andrzej Sapkowski (b.1948) have rather upset the traditional literary scene. The first two of his novels, *The Last Wish* and *Blood of Elves*, were translated into English (Sapkowski 2007, 2008). They are loosely constructed, episodic fantasies of the sword and sorcery variety – part of a much larger dungeons and dragons gaming phenomenon – about Geralt, the 'witcher' of Rivia. Geralt's pseudo-medieval world is a continuation of the long tradition of fantasy in Polish literature, blending romanticism with Catholicism. Geralt struggles with ghouls, ghosts, elves, vampires, *strzygi* (vampire-demons, usually female), demons and hundreds of other evil beings, all of which he vanquishes through his supernatural strength, moral superiority, fighting skill and intelligent use of magic. The appeal of the solitary man fighting his way through a world populated by tricky demons and blood sucking temptresses is understandable, and it is not hard to read into them Catholic parables about the developing battle between good and evil or, equally, parables about the demons and denizens of capitalism, which have of late much troubled the realm. Sapkowski's books have taken Polish readers by storm, received good reviews from *Polytika*, *Playboy* and *Gazeta Wyborca* (among others) and have been translated into

158 *Poland translated*

several other languages. Sapkowski has also received literary prizes including the prestigious Paszport Award and the national Nike Award. For a fantasy writer, this is substantial recognition.

The internet has also opened up new ways of writing and thinking about writing. One development in this area has been to connect readers inside and outside Poland, allowing readers to shape their own definitions of who and what they are, and what they want to read, through blogging. It is here that the stricter nationalist and linguistic definitions of what might be considered 'Polish' have begun to come under pressure from younger 'media-savvy' readers and bloggers. Visitors to the Culture Vulture website might be surprised to find that younger Polish readers join with other readers from around the world and, writing in English, praise the 'exquisite tradition of Polish poetry' but question the definition of a Polish writer as one who writes in Polish, lives in Poland or adheres in some way to the 'thousand year traditions of Polish-ness' through their ethnic identity. The Polish economic diaspora and the community of political exiles is huge, but fractured by age, issues of regional, dialectal and religious identity, and political orientation. However, where Poles of second, third or fourth generation born abroad may no longer speak the language, the question of who is or is not Polish is no small issue. Understandably, many young Poles of the diaspora want to assert their Polish-ness and their right to belong, but their instinct is for wider, more inclusive definitions of themselves and their identity. On Culture Vulture several readers cite Joseph Conrad, Isaac Bashevis Singer and even Günter Grass as kinds of Polish writer (Culture Vulture 2006).[8]

*

During the Cold War the Polish government did little to promote Polish culture abroad, including failing to support the translation of Polish literature. However, since the collapse of communism, the Polish Ministry of Culture's Instytut Książki, the National Heritage of the Republic of Poland and the Polish Literary Fund have cooperated to set up the © Poland Translation Programme. Also, Central European Classics, originally conceived and financed by an Oxford-based charity, has presented several key classical texts. However, since there is no political advantage to be gained from supporting translations through major publishing houses, interested readers now have to search through the output of the smaller independent publishers on both sides of the Atlantic. And the question of the market remains: can we be sure that publishers are concerned about bringing us the best that has been thought and said in Polish letters, or simply what is exotic and, above all, what will sell?

How well does what has been translated into English represent post-communist Poland? Apart from the inevitable problem of the time-lag and the difficulties of translating one culture and set of politico-literary paradigms for a different readership, the publication of Polish translations has become

Poland translated   159

slightly more complex with the end of the Cold War. Why are particular books chosen for translation? The kind of answer we might expect has changed. The choice of Polish books for translation was dictated during the Cold War by the major US and UK publishing houses, dominated by questions of what would discomfort communism as much as what was well written and original. There is the strong possibility that some titles were supported by funding from the CIA (Stonor Saunders 1999).

*

As a consequence of its history, tradition in Poland is almost always assumed to be positive. The writer in the Partition years (and with slight variations throughout East-Central Europe) functioned as oppositionist and repository of national identity. This function might have been expected to lapse with independence, as notions of tradition came under intense pressure from modernist writers and artists of all kinds. However, war and the Nazi occupation halted literary development and tradition again became a sustaining element of national life. With the communist take-over, the powerful traditions of the Partition era and the wartime years were re-deployed to help counter *socrealizm* (socialist realism), quietly undermine Party propaganda and support those who dared to read between the lines.

There is a generational aspect to this. With the collapse of communism, the 'barbarian' writers of the late 1970s and 1980s were shortly superseded by a younger generation of writers who believed there was nothing for them in *bruLion*, that the journal was hopelessly stuck in the past. They also felt that battles with communism were now simply a non-issue, part of history, something their parents had worried about. However, they soon found they were now deprived of the 'great cause' that had driven previous generations of writers and given them a readership. Instead, young writers had to find their own themes. And they had to do this while dealing with the vagaries of capitalism, where good writing did not necessarily result in literary recognition or the establishment of a reputation, and where sales were often the result of successful marketing rather than literary talent. For example, Karpowicz, who was familiar with the classic works of Mickiewicz, Sienkiewicz and Prus, said he would not want to live through his childhood, youth and teenage years again, and he was clear his problems had not so much been communism but rather the history that created the traditional Polish mind-set (Karpowicz 2008: 126).

The new generation did not issue manifestos and did not give itself a group-name; it's writers operated independently rather than as a movement; they did not cluster around a particular magazine, but haunted chat-rooms, posted material on their websites and felt themselves to be European.

While older writers were still published and found a readership, younger writers with no experience of war or communism felt themselves to be free to write as they please but still slightly disadvantaged. For them tradition proved to be a something of a straightjacket. When writers tried to break

160 Poland translated

with tradition, they found it nevertheless dominated. While tradition did not necessarily determine what could be written, it determined what could be said safely in public, what was acceptable, how new work was understood and received. In reference to hypertext novels the term *liberatura* (liberation+literature) has begun to emerge, indicating that the escape is from tradition, traditional literary forms and traditional identity. But while new writing is often relentlessly avant-garde – disjointed, miniature, hybrid – the content, however challenging, unorthodox and questioning of traditional values, is often judged by notions of acceptability shaped and determined not by the market but by tradition. With 'freedom', tradition ceased to be the guide it had once been and quickly acquired a restrictive political ambition: what for some was normal questioning, literary innovation and progress, for others proved to be a break with national tradition, a challenge to established identity and perhaps even a kind of treachery.

If politics is now the arena where Poland will decide what it wants to become, literature is the place where Poles discuss who and what they are. It has not been possible to include here all the new writers worthy of note, but enough of their work has been translated into English for us to glimpse some of the debates and transitions taking place deep within Polish culture. Clearly, post-communist writers are moving into the realms of self-reflection and entertainment, but they are also taking an audit of their political past and their literary and cultural heritage. Poland is still discovering itself: looking long and hard at what it has gained, grieving for that which has been lost. And that which has been lost – the millions dead, the entire Jewish population, the lands of the old East – is enormous. That which has been gained – the new territories, a connection to the West, capitalism and the market economy, a renewed awareness of multi-culturalism – though it connects on some levels to the interrupted life of the old Polish commonwealth, is unfamiliar, slightly awkward and still vaguely unsatisfactory.

Polish literary culture cannot help but reflect on itself and its experience, but the post-communist writers have been slow to emerge. Perhaps, as the subsidy and prestige once offered to writers and publishers is no longer available, everyone has simply been trying to earn a living. Perhaps readers were looking for something different: certainly the 'matter of Poland' is no longer urgent or necessary: it is optional. And perhaps the difficulties of bridging the gap between the old and the new realities have simply been so huge that it has taken time to process and shape into literature.[9] The new writers are the products not of the new freedoms, but without doubt products of the homogenised workers' world of communism, but in a way that communism never achieved in its lifetime: rather than that of a standard-setting oppositional *inteligencja*, their view is that of the worm's eye: their work is provincial and personal rather than national.

It is clear that, marked so deeply by the dire experience of the twentieth century, Poland's interest in, and arguments with, itself are still by far the strongest element in contemporary writing. Given that these arguments are to do with the extremes of human experience, with challenging tradition

Poland translated 161

and with recognising and absorbing a changing identity, contemporary Polish writing is not an 'easy read'. Precisely for this reason it is not a readily marketable international commodity. 'Politics' tells us about the observable surface of events in Poland. If we want to know about the inner life of this, the most populous of the East-Central European states, about the continuing impact of the worst the twentieth century had to offer, about the subterranean passages by which the past percolates through to shape the present and the future in the long, slow drip of consequence, transition and re-definition, it is to Polish literature we must turn.

Notes

1 Many of these are available in English, for example: Edelman (1990); Szpilman (2000); Grynberg (1993); Fink (1989); Wojdowski (1997); Ficowski (2000).
2 A discussion of Żeromski's life and work can be found in Miłosz (1983: 365–9). Extracts from *Ashes* can be found in: Mikoś (2006). Żeromski's reputation did not fare well with the post-communist generation. Jacek Dehnel's ageing character Lala, recalling her life in inter-war Poland, says of him: 'Żeromski meant the world to our generation. The fact that privately he behaved like a rat was quite another matter, but for most Poles he was an unquestioned authority on moral, social and political issues' (Dehnel 2019: 163).
3 Another example of the way that earlier German inhabitants haunt the imagination and memory of Polish towns can be found in Springer (2017).
4 This story can also be found in Halikowska and Hyde (1996).
5 For details of censorship surrounding the 'Recovered Territories' see Tighe (1990) and Leftwich-Curry (1984).
6 For example, Ignacy Karpowicz (b.1976) has the narrator of the novel *Gesty* (2008, *Gestures*) recalling his mother weeping while on TV General Jaruzelski announced not Martial Law, but that there would be no bed-time story that night (Karpowicz 2008: 82).
7 Originally published in Poland as *Wojna polsko-ruska, pod flag biało-czerwona* (*War Polish-Russian, Under the White-Red Flag*) it was published in the US under the title *Snow White and Russian Red* (Atlantic Monthly: NY, 2005). *White and Red* is the title of the edition released for sale in the UK.
8 Other useful sites dealing with Polish recent literature are www.polishwriting. net and www.CESLIT (Central European and Slavic Literature in Translation).
9 Two early attempts to chart possible new directions were March (1990) and March (1994).

7 Lustration
The Polish experience

Over the last forty years, debates about the nature and legality of transitional justice have featured as part of regime-change in South Africa, Rwanda, Bosnia, Northern Ireland, Sierra Leone, Cambodia and in all the post-communist states of Eastern and East Central Europe. From place to place, transitional justice has taken many forms: criminal prosecutions, truth commissions, reparations programmes, memorialisation of victims and various kinds of institutional reform, particularly in justice, policing and the security services (What is Transitional Justice? 2011). Sometimes a simple declaration of involvement or a straightforward statement of professional work for the regime would suffice; in other cases nothing short of a full-scale inquiry or a legal investigation of criminal activity was necessary. Although for many the driving force behind the quest for transitional justice was a desire to avenge the wrongs and crimes of the past, for those with an eye to the future the main aim was to repair public trust by addressing human rights violations, reforming institutions and restoring confidence in the justice system.

Lustration often figures in transitional justice. The term is derived from Latin and from the Roman practice of *lustrare* or *lustratio*, meaning ritual public cleansing, or purification by the rite of expiatory sacrifice. The word was loaned into Polish as *lustracja*. Polish usage includes the Roman sense of public ritual, but more generally means inspection, audit and scrutiny; for example, in Polish idiomatic speech it is possible to *lustrować kogoś z góry na dół* – 'look somebody up and down' (Stanisławski 1970: 467). However, since the collapse of communism, there is another sense to the word. In Polish the word *lustracja* is very close to the word *lustro*, 'a mirror', which suggests a process of self-examination, and the verb *lustrować* is understood now as 'to look at someone very carefully in order to see what was hidden at first'. This is the way the word is now used in public debate. The assumption is that something is hidden (Grzyzło 2007).

For intellectuals, lawyers and academics the fear was that if there was no reckoning with the past, communism would haunt Poland just as Nazism haunted Germany and Vichy collaboration haunted France. Lustration was at first the most popular technique of transitional justice, a way of 'outing' communists and police informers, but while it proved to be most revealing of the political past, what it revealed was not always easily digestible, and it very quickly proved to be the most problematic and least controllable choice. Calls for lustration emanated from those describing themselves as democrats and from self-confessed authoritarians, from academics seeking to understand the past through documentation, from those with a genuine sense of justice and a desire for truth, from journalists with a nose for scandal and from victims of the communist regime. For some – mainly ambitious politicians seeking an advantage – this became a necessity, a process on which political careers depended. While lustration was revealing of the whole of emerging Polish political culture, to a very great extent it is the story of the post-communist right-wing.

Even so, the end of lustration in Poland cannot be presented as a defeat for the Right and a victory for the liberal-Left. Nor was it simply a case of Europeanists triumphing over nationalists, urbanites over populists, pluralists over authoritarians, or intelligentsia over workers.[1] In practice lustration undermined all parties, fed paranoia and generated opposition, which made its own use of lustration. The collapse of lustration came with the realisation that over more than forty years communism had manufactured a reality, undermined normality and corrupted morality to such an extent that it simply was not safe to undertake lustration with any hope of 'justice' or 'truth': there was no certainty about what lustration would reveal, when the revelations would stop or which revelations were true.

Zbigniew Herbert on the need for judgement

After 1989 the push for lustration grew out of the pent-up frustrations and bitterness of forty-five years of communism, but also out of a very strong judgemental strand in Polish culture, particularly in conservative Catholic and nationalist traditions. The poet Zbigniew Herbert (1924–98), for example, had distanced himself from communism while he was still a young man after observing Soviet behaviour in wartime Lwów, and his main problem with his literary contemporaries was the ease with which the Soviets had 'enslaved' Poland's intellectual elite in the first decade after the war. Herbert's first volume of poems appeared with the thaw of 1956, and while he continued to write and publish in Poland, he remained opposed to communism.

In an interview given in 1985, Herbert said he regarded communism as 'the heir of ONR', 'Polish Fascism', 'a crime against culture', 'a crime against the young generation' and 'a crime against the Holy Spirit'.[2] He said all those responsible should 'go to the desert and do penitence'. Herbert could not imagine an end to the communist system and hoped to die 'unreconciled' to the world of communism (Trznadel 1987: 557–75). Although Herbert sensed a purging of guilt was inevitable eventually, he felt the conversation about communist crimes should have taken place 'in 1955 or 1956' and he lamented (Trznadel 1987: 569).

Herbert insisted on remembering the victims. He called for 'precision' and scrupulous accounting, and there was a sense that this included a settling of

164   Lustration

debts. He anticipated the dilemmas of the post-communist politicians, but there is no sense that drawing a line under the experience of communism would be acceptable.

It is important to remember that when Herbert wrote *Report from a Besieged City*, the end of communism was still unimaginable. Also, while Herbert gave voice to a feeling many experienced, he was a poet, not a politician, and even after the collapse of communism the difficulties of transitional justice were not for him to solve. With its insistence on conscience, his attitude appealed to staunch and unyielding opponents of communism – particularly those on the Right but also to Polonia, the huge Polish émigré community, which mainly took its bearings from the conservative Polish Catholic Church, the pre-war nationalist politics of Endecja (National Democracy), the Sanacja (Cleansing) regime, the ethos of the wartime AK (London-backed Home Army) and the surviving members of the Polish government in exile, none of whom were in the least bit sympathetic to communism. Herbert's poetry spoke to the injured, the victims of communism, and it fed into a desire for accounts to be rendered one way or another. However, while as a moral stance this was impressive and offered sustenance to oppositionists under communism, after the collapse of communism it left much to be desired in terms of finding a way forward in practical politics and effective justice.

Among the dissident, left-liberal and artistic communities grouped around the newspaper *Gazeta Wyborcza*, many of whom were familiar with Herbert's work and would become involved with issues of justice in the transitional period, a different attitude prevailed. For most of this circle, and notably Wisława Szymborska, attitudes were often less judgemental, more nuanced, flexible and pragmatic (Szymborska 1995: 178).

Lustration 1989–2006

The Round Table talks, which began in February 1989, marked the reluctant acceptance by PZPR (*Polska Zjednoczona Partia Robotnicza*, Polish United Workers Party – the Communist Party) of the fact that after more than forty-four years they still had no mandate to rule. The talks ended with an agreement that the communists would share power with the opposition but also with the tacit understanding that there would be no prosecutions, no revenge and no lustration. Instead both sides would, as Tadeusz Mazowiecki put it, draw a *gruba kreska* (a thick line) under the whole communist era. In the circumstances – the fall of the Berlin Wall and the collapse of the USSR still lay in the future and could barely have been imagined – this was the best the leadership of Solidarność could have hoped to achieve. However, after the elections agreed at the Round Table had taken place, Solidarność woke up on 5 June 1989 to find it had trounced the communists to win 160 of the available 161 Sejm (Polish Parliament) seats. The communists, even with seats reserved for them in the Sejm, had to admit they could not form a government. This was an overwhelming and totally

Lustration 165

unexpected victory for Solidarność and, while what remained of the PZPR went into recrimination-mode, Solidarność panicked about suddenly inheriting responsibility for Poland's massive ongoing economic crisis.

In August 1989 Tadeusz Mazowiecki was sworn in as prime minister, with General Jaruzelski as president: 'Your president, our premier', as Adam Michnik put it. This was an effective compromise and worked well for both sides in this first transitional phase. At the same time, the unity that had enabled Solidarność to proceed, a social agreement as to what the union was opposed to, began to fragment over the issue of what its members wanted to achieve. This was inevitable: even at its zenith, Solidarność – generally tolerant, pluralistic and democratic – was the only unofficial conduit for all kinds of opinion. Electoral victory now gave Solidarność problems as the sense of national unity immediately evaporated and its support base became increasingly fragmented. Solidarność was united only in its opposition to communism; beyond that there was no agreement or common vision of what the future Poland should be. In an atmosphere where everything that had been suppressed for years was now possible, it was not unusual to see gangs of skin-heads, sometimes carrying Nazi flags, roaming the streets of Warsaw and Kraków chanting 'Polska dla polaków' (Poland for Poles), to see anti-Semitic graffiti and for people to wear 'Chrobry' sword-pins in their lapel, a symbol of the pre-war right-wing Endejca (National Democracy) Party. This reactive and very substantial move to the right affected the conduct of the whole political spectrum.

In 1990 Jaruzelski was replaced by Lech Wałęsa as president. In order to boost his presidency, Wałęsa moved towards a more populist position and 'declared war' on the Mazowiecki government, whom he described as 'egg-head intellectuals' who were taking too long over the reforms necessary to turn Poland into a free market economy. Wałęsa also distanced himself from the intellectuals of KOR (Komitet Obrony Robotników, Committee Defending Workers) who had advised Solidarność through the 1980s. He claimed that his former allies Bronisław Geremek[3] and Adam Michnik were communist sympathisers, and that former dissident Jacek Kuroń, who had recently become Minister of Labour, was simply a communist in disguise. Wałęsa also made much of the fact that Kuroń, Michnik, Geremek and Mazowiecki were of Jewish ethnic origin, whereas, Wałęsa repeatedly pointed out, the Polish public need not fear him because he and his family were 'pure, real Poles, one hundred percent, of at least three generations', and he called on Jews to 'stop concealing themselves and reveal their identity'. In opening up a 'war at the top', Wałęsa irreparably damaged relations with his former allies. In this environment the right-wing developed very rapidly, and as it engaged with the elections of 1990–1993 the various parties very quickly became increasingly reactionary, vociferous and vengeful, and together they began to form 'a stubborn, closed front' (Pyzik 2014: 188).

Wałęsa was not alone in making use of anti-Semitism. The mysterious maverick Canadian businessman Stanisław Tymiński's fascistic Party X

166 Lustration

opened its presidential electoral campaign in September 1991 with the claim that ex-Prime Minister Tadeusz Mazowiecki, Prime Minister Jan Krzysztof Bielecki, Finance Minister Leszek Balcerowicz, a large number of ministers, senators and deputies including Antoni Macierewicz and Jan Olszewski, and the actor Daniel Olbrychski were all Jews and involved in a plot to import Soviet Jews and American-Jewish finance to destroy Polish industry and agriculture. However, Tymiński, who was widely rumoured to have connections to the communist secret police, lost the election to Wałęsa at a second ballot, but he nevertheless polled a substantial 25.75 percent of the vote (Merkl and Weinberg 2013).

Seeing the leadership squabbling and behaving in an undignified manner, the electorate became increasingly 'stubborn, unstable and apathetic' (Jasiewicz 1995: 156). Because communism had not been defeated but had negotiated its own demise, Poles did not experience any real sense of victory; and without victory there was no sense of judgment, only a lingering sense of grievance. For a while this was held in check, but immediately after the 1992 general election Antoni Macierewicz, the new minister of the interior, an ex-communist, dissident activist in KOR, now turned born-again Rightist, who had been given the task of cleaning up the Ministry of Interior Affairs and the Security Service, suddenly produced a list of sixty-four members of the Sejm, most of whom were members of the opposition, who he claimed had been informers for the communist secret police – either TW (*tajny współpracownik*, secret collaborators) or KO (*kontakt operacyjny*, operational contacts). The Sejm was furious and, while it voted Olszewski's government out of office within 24 hours, it was nevertheless compelled to act on Macierewicz's claim. Immediately, the Sejm set up a committee to investigate the list and soon concluded that in fact only ten names could be considered as serious suspects and only six of these had actually signed compromising documents (Rosenberg 1995: 234–51). The list was not made public, but it emerged that Cardinal Glemp had encouraged Olszewski and Macierewicz to release it, even though the list was said to contain the names of several members of the Church hierarchy. It also emerged that Lech Wałęsa was one of those named as an informer. This was the first example of 'wild lustration'. The Sejm passed its first lustration bill shortly afterwards, but even as queues began to form to view the secret files, the Constitutional Tribunal declared the law unconstitutional. It was clear Mazowiecki's 'thick line', which had allowed all ex-communists to take part in politics as long as they agreed to abide by democratic principles, had been abandoned.

In 1993 a new, entirely post-communist government was elected, and as a result a number of communist *nomenklatura* officials[4] were fired from the Council of Ministers, many of them to enter good jobs in banking. Polish slang referred contemptuously to these people as *spadachoniarzy* (parachutists) because they jumped from Party-protected positions into good jobs in the private sector using their *znajomości* (contacts, connections). In the months following the elections prosecutions were scheduled to investigate

Lustration 167

the shootings in Gdańsk in 1970, the murder of Father Popiełuszko, the destruction of Politburo files in 1989 and the legality of the declaration of Martial Law in 1981. For a while it began to look as if the idea of lustration might just fade away.

Wisława Szymborska, although she was not to live to see the end of the lustration debate, had a very clear sense that the end of communism should have brought clarity, knowledge and understanding of Poland's past experience. She was very uneasy about where the lustration process was headed and what it would mean for the development of democracy, for political culture and for Polish culture as a whole.

Szymborska's intuition was not much mistaken. In 1996 a new lustration law was proposed and passed the following year, and this was followed by changes to the status and role of the Rzecznik Interesu Publicznego (Spokesperson of the Public Interest), who now handled lustration issues. This official was responsible for reviewing lustration declarations and initiating legal proceedings. At this stage the declarations required were a simple form of public confession which, once enacted, enabled officials to hold on to public office in spite of a communist past provided they had broken no laws. In many ways this was as progressive as the post-apartheid South African system and in general it worked very well (Czarnota 2008). Under the new law presidential candidates were required to declare all connections to the communist regime, and almost immediately Lech Wałęsa was again accused of being a police informer. It was only in August 2000 that he was officially cleared to run again for president.

However, the new law was not severe enough for many of its critics. In December 1996 several newspapers covered a survey by Ośrodek Badania Opinii Publicznej (OBOP, Centre for Public Opinion Research) that showed that seventy-two percent of respondents were convinced that many high-ranking officials had been informants and collaborators for the secret police, seventy-seven percent believed that these officials should be removed from office and fifty-seven percent supported lustration. By December 1997 that number had risen to seventy-six percent (Czarnota 2008: 243).

In 2001, in an attempt to prevent abuse of the files, it was decided to open up the Security Service archive to the public. However, there were controls on the release of information: after a request was made it would take six months before an individual's file would be made available and in each case the names of all agents and informers would be blacked out. In addition, individual files would only be opened when IPN (Instytut Pamięci Narodowej, Institute of National Remembrance) judged that the person concerned had been a 'victim of repression'. IPN was concerned not to make the same mistakes the Germans had made in opening up the Stasi files, where complete openness had proved to be massively socially demoralising (Ash 1997; Funder 2003). In 2003 IPN was obliged to cooperate with the newly created Agencja Bezpieczeństwa Wewnętrznego (ABW, Agency of Internal Security), and the newly created Agencja Wywiadu (AW, Agency of Intelligence). In 2002 Tadeusz Kwiatkowski, head of Wałęsa's presidential office,

168   Lustration

was found guilty of failing to disclose that in 1969–70 he had voluntarily delivered information to the Security Service even though he had only been officially registered as an informer in in the years 1974–5. At the same time Sławomir Wiatr, Poland's Commissioner for European Integration, admitted he had secretly informed for the police. However, it gradually emerged that some agents and informers were still cooperating with the security services and these people were not subject to lustration arrangements.

Even though the lustration process was slow and far from thorough or perfect in its judgement, the IPN files were subject to abuse and political manoeuvre. In 2004 the journalist Bronisław Waldstein, unhappy at the failings of the lustration process, took matters into his own hands when, without permission, he made a list of names from the IPN files. This case has an interesting backstory that says much about the complications of Poland's political life. In the mid-1970s, while he was studying in Kraków, Waldstein had fallen in with Lesław Maleszka and Stanisław Pyjas. They were part of a group of student activists who were critical of the regime and who read and circulated banned literature. After a while the trio began to receive anonymous letters claiming that Pyjas was a police informer and containing personal information that only someone close to the trio could have known. In 1977 Pyjas died, it was claimed, after a drunken fall down the stairs of his student dorm. It was widely suspected he had been thrown to his death by the Security Service and serious student protest followed. After the collapse of communism and the opening of the secret police archives it emerged that Pyjas had realised Maleszka was the police informer and Pyjas had probably been killed to prevent him revealing this. Maleszka's code name was 'Ketman', a revealing choice derived from one of the very conflicted characters in Czesław Miłosz's *The Captive Mind* (1953), the classic study of intellectual compromise under communism.

Twenty-five years later Waldstein released his list of informers as a kind of revenge, little imagining the social damage it would cause and without realising his list contained both actual informers and also members of the opposition whom the SB (Służba Bezpieczęstwa, Security Service) hoped to coerce into acting as informers. He posted his list on the internet in 2005 and several of the victims initiated court cases for slander. The film *Trzech Kumpli* (Three Pals, directed by Anna Ferens and Ewa Stankiewicz, 2008) tells the story in some detail. Indeed, it was only with the release of this film that it became known Maleszka was working as an editor for the anti-lustration newspaper *Gazeta Wyborcza*. Adam Michnik, though severely discomforted, did not change his attitude to lustration, and his failure to dismiss Maleszka caused several of the newspaper's journalists to resign.

While most of those identified as collaborators and informers were vulnerable because they were now outside the protection of the PZPR, some collaborators were very well placed after the collapse of communism, though their proximity to power often seems to have corrupted them. In 1989, for example, in the closing days of the communist regime, Lew Rywin, a film producer associated with Steven Spielberg's *Schindler's List*

Lustration 169

and Roman Polański's *The Pianist*, had become deputy head of the Polish Radio and TV. In July 2002, as new media laws were being prepared by Leszek Miller's post-communist government, Rywin offered Adam Michnik the chance to help shape these laws in a way that would be favourable to *Gazeta Wyborcza*: all he asked in return was a huge bribe. After five months of cogitation, Michnik published their recorded conversation. The scandal that followed forced the Sejm to set up a special investigatory committee and the publication of its proceedings contributed to the collapse of the first post-communist government in 2005. Clearly Rywin felt his proximity to power and some *wysoki protekcja* (high protection) made him a serious power-broker in the post-communist world. It later emerged that Rywin had been an informer for the Ministry of the Interior in the years 1982–6.

Lustration and the Fourth Republic

After elections in 2005 and 2006, Poland was ruled by the identical twins Jarosław and Lech Kaczyński, prime minister and president, representatives and leaders of their own right-wing party PiS (Prawo i Sprawiedliwość, Law and Justice).[5] They were in coalition with LPR (Liga Polskich Rodzin, League of Polish Families), led by virulently homophobic creationist Roman Giertych, who campaigned against the EU on the grounds that it is a 'centralised socialist super-state'.[6] They were also in coalition with the ultra-nationalist party Samoobrona (Self-Defence), led by Andrzej Lepper. The coalition parties agreed that membership of the EU would undermine the Polish national character by unleashing a tidal wave of contraception, abortion, homosexuality, godlessness, cosmopolitanism (the communist code-word for Jewish influence) and liberalism (the new code-word for Jewish influence). They stressed 'national identity' and 'Catholic values', promised to fight corruption, and called for a radical change to the lustration laws to take revenge on former communists and finally cleanse the country's public life of 'red poison'. PiS had very rapidly become a coalition of all those hostile to Poland's post-communist economic, cultural and constitutional development and the liberals and leftists who had created them from the wreckage of communism: this they condemned as a corrupt 'power-system'.

The coalition was supported by the highly influential Redemptorist priest and media personality Fr. Tadeusz Rydzyk, who believed that Poland was not ruled by Poles but by 'hidden Jews'; it was also supported by the independent Catholic Radio Maryja, run by Rydzyk. From its start this station appealed to, and rapidly became the voice of, the economically unprepared, poorly educated, fearful and discontented; amongst other things it opposed abortion, campaigned for the death penalty, spoke of the EU as a 'gay conspiracy', and referred to 'homosexual terror' and 'sodomitical unions'. Radio Maryja and PiS were actively hostile towards anything that resembled the 'revisionism' of the 1950s and 1960s, and to anyone who had contested communism from a liberal-Catholic, dissident-left or centrist position.[7]

170   Lustration

One of coalition's first acts was to abolish the *Wojskowe Służby Informacyjne* (WSI, Military Information Service). The employees of this service had strong links to organised crime in Poland and abroad. They 'cooperated' with Soviet intelligence, and had been involved in several commercial, economic and political scandals in the 1990s, including attempts by high-ranking Moscow officials to take over Polish media and the Polish petrol monopoly. They had also microfilmed information to pass to the Russians while destroying other sensitive files. They were accused of embezzling public funds, influencing privatisation for their own benefit and investing operational funds in private enterprises. WSI was clearly a good place to start any 'housecleaning' operation. In the following months two lieutenant-colonels received prison sentences and a new military security service was established. Although anti-lustrators feared the abolition of WSI would compromise national security, it seems to have been a successful operation and this success persuaded the brothers to develop lustration further as a political strategy (Kaj & Metzger 2007).

The WSI had such a strong influence in Poland in the 1990s that it coloured the brothers' understanding of how the rest of Polish society operated in the transition to democracy. The Kaczyński brothers believed that the communist collapse of 1989 had in fact been a kind of communist coup. They believed that, instead of a transition to democracy, a secret network of former communists had managed to adapt, steal and retain power. The negotiated, bloodless transfer of power, they said, disguised the manoeuvres by which the communists had regrouped and, with the help of the communist secret police, placed their agents and favourites in key national economic and political positions, enabling them to keep for themselves enormous wealth that rightly belonged to the Polish people and to secretly dominate the Third Republic.

While he was editing *Tygodnik Solidarność* (1989–90) Jarosław had begun to refer to the *konspiracja* (conspiracy), and he now stoked paranoia by referring to a secret *pakt* (pact) or *układ* (arrangement) between the communists and the left-liberal opposition. Along with Generals Jaruzelski and Kiszczak, the twins had in their sights ex-communists, post-communists, *nomenklatura*, leading Solidarność activists, former dissidents such as Bronisław Geremek and the liberal intellectuals around Adam Michnik. Jarosław referred to them as 'pseudo-elites and eggheads' and labelled them 'the Warsaw-Kraków salon'. He claimed that Michnik's *Gazeta Wyborcza*, by opposing lustration, was trying to gloss over 'reality'. The Kaczyński twins planned to 'out' this communist Mafia and called for a 'Fourth Republic' to promote 'purification' and a permanent 'moral revolution'.[8]

The brothers had only to hint at conspiracy to conjure up the *Żydokomuna* (Judeo-Communism), a pejorative term for an anti-Semitic stereotype popular in the inter-war period particularly after General Piłsudski's death, alleging a Jewish–communist conspiracy to seize power and generally 'bring Poland down'. In inter-war Poland the idea of the *Żydokomuna* assumed an almost mystical connection between Jews and communism, but this had

Lustration   171

little to do with the reality of Jewish life and conflated anti-Semitism with fears of Russia and with Catholic terror at 'God-less' communism (Schatz 2004: 20). In the post-war years the term *Żydokomuna* was shorthand for the belief that 'Jews had *en masse* supported Communism in Poland [...] made up the vast majority of its adherents [...] enjoyed privileged positions in the regime and benefited from it while imposing it on everyone else' (Gross 2006: 192). It would have been more accurate to say that while Jews had played a very important role in the Polish Communist movement, the Jewish population in general was far from sympathetic to communism (Schatz 2004: 21). However, after the Holocaust Poland had no active Jewish community: most of the survivors, numbering perhaps 200,000, left Poland in 1947; a further 20,000 Jews were expelled from Poland in a Party faction fight in 1968. Anti-Semitism in post-war Poland seems to have been a deeply embedded political strategy rather than a reflection of public opinion. The Kaczyński brothers had a reputation for being 'clever' and this hint was astute – it appealed to Poland's 'subcutaneous' anti-Semites, but at the same time it was anti-Semitism without Jews, a smear without actually smearing.

What kind of threat did communism pose at this point? The PZPR had reached its largest membership of about three million in the summer of 1980, just as the shipyard strikes broke out in Gdańsk. However, this should be seen as a measure of cynicism rather than popularity. After the declaration of Martial Law in December 1981 the membership became demoralised and numbers declined rapidly as the PZPR became increasingly and irrelevant, even to its own membership. PZPR documents show that by May 1987 only about twenty-five percent of the surviving membership was politically active; more than sixty percent paid dues but were inactive; and fifteen percent of the membership did not renew their membership that year (Szczerbiak 2001: 130–49). As Soviet power began to disintegrate, the PZPR suffered a catastrophic defeat in the semi-free elections of 1989 and dissolved itself in January 1990. Many of the active membership went on to form SdRP (Socjaldemokracja Rzeczpospolita Polski, Social Democracy of the Republic of Poland), a new Western-style social-democratic party that polled nearly nine percent of the vote in the 1990 presidential elections, and in the national elections of 1991 gained sixty deputies and forty senators; though it was the second largest party in the Sejm it was not invited to join a coalition government and dissolved itself in 1997. The Left Alliance as a whole, on which the SdRP depended to form a government, was not popular with the electorate. There was inevitably a fraternity among the ex-members of the PZPR and *nomenklatura*, and there may have been a few unrepentant communist hard-liners who dreamed of a return to power, but with the collapse of the Soviet Union they lost their guarantor and with the demise of WSI they lost the last vestige of a power base. By 2006 the old Left was too fragmented and demoralised to pose a threat to emerging democracy or the adoption of capitalism; the new left-liberals were interested only in democracy and the transition to a capitalist economy. The *pakt*

172   *Lustration*

as imagined by the Kaczyński brothers was nothing more than a chimera, but it represented an easy route to power.

In December 2006 the Kaczyński brothers, claiming that the whole political system had fallen under the influence of hidden communists, and now routinely branding all political opponents as 'gangsters', 'cronies' and 'reds', set about revising the lustration laws. From March 2007 the Rzecznik Interesu Publicznego was placed under the control of IPN, while IPN was restructured and given a new role. IPN had initially been set up in 1998 to supervise the massive State Security apparatus archive and to investigate Nazi and communist crimes. Now its title was changed: Instytut Pamięci Narodowej – Komisji Ścigania Zbrodni Przeciwko Narodowi Polskiemu (IPN – Commission for Prosecution of Crimes against the Polish Nation). This commission prepared lustration procedures and was given powers to maintain a register of lustration statements, to analyse lustration statements and collect information necessary for prosecution; it also prepared and published catalogues of documents containing personal data indicating whether an individual was regarded by the security services as a secret informer or had assisted in collecting information for the police. There was massive public support for such a move. In a poll conducted by Centrum Badania Opinii Społecznej (CBOS, Center for Research into the Opinion of Society), sixty-two percent of those polled believed anyone in a public position who had collaborated with the secret police should be fired (*O Lustracji* 2007).

The old law had defined collaboration as: 'a conscious and secret cooperation with operational or investigating units or organs of the state security as a secret informer or as an assistant of operational gathering of information' (Kaj & Metzger 2007). The Constitutional Tribunal had declared there were five conditions necessary to the definition of a collaborator: first, there had to be contact with the secret police during which a transmission of information took place; second, that collaboration had to have been conscious and the collaborator must have been aware they were in contact with the secret police; third, collaboration must have been secret; fourth, there must have been an operational gathering of information by the secret police; fifth, it was not enough for there to have been a declaration of collaboration, there must have been material, conscious and specific actions of collaboration (Kaj & Metzger 2007).

Definitions were confusing and so wide that they included not only actual collaborators but also those who had agreed to collaborate but then done nothing. Also the Lustration Bureau of IPN was now tasked with compiling and publishing catalogues and personal data on public figures who had been connected in any way with the secret police – informers, collaborators, agents, employees, senior functionaries of the Communist Party and those who had been placed under surveillance. The release of these catalogues was immediately declared an infringement of civil liberties and blocked by the Constitutional Tribunal.

Lustration 173

The new law proposed three years' imprisonment for anyone found guilty of imputing that Poles had taken part in Nazi or communist crimes 'against the Polish nation'. The phrase 'against the Polish nation' was deeply problematic because it seemed to deny citizenship to Polish Jews, denied the actuality of Polish experience in the twentieth century by implying there had been no Polish collusion with Nazism, and suggested the crimes of communism had no Polish element – that the crimes of these periods had all been committed by foreigners, outsiders, or perhaps even, as wits suggested, by visitors from outer space.

Lustration by IPN's commission now became obligatory for fifty-three categories of people born before 1st August 1972 and holding positions of significant state employment and public responsibility: lawyers, public notaries, attorneys, journalists, civil servants, police, journalists, teachers and academics. This law required about 700,000 people to submit declarations on their relationship with the security services and to face prosecution and a ten year ban on working in their profession if they lied. Several leading journalists – including Ewa Milewicz, Jacek Żakowski, Wojciech Mazowiecki, Piotr Najsztub and Tomasz Lis – immediately issued statements refusing to comply. Professor Jan Turulske of the University of Bialystok Institute of Chemistry submitted his affidavit with the words 'kiss my ass clowns' written across it (Kaj & Metzger 2007). However, under threat of the new law, two highly placed media personalities – Milan Subotić, the deputy programme director of TVN, the largest private TV channel, and Bogusław Wołoszański, a very well respected and popular director of historical documentaries – confessed they had collaborated with the security services.

As the new law came into effect, protest and opposition began in the universities. In several places resolutions were passed and boards of management produced open letters voted through unanimously, even when it was known that senior university figures had been informers. Several academics who had signed agreements with the police claimed this had only been to enable foreign travel. Many university boards decided unanimously not to submit lustration declarations until the Constitutional Tribunal had made a final decision on the legislation. Without a doubt, the senior members of the legal, artistic, academic and media communities were all inclined to just let the matter of lustration drop (Roszkowski 2009).

In April 2007 the historian and MEP Professor Bronisław Geremek declared at the European Parliament that he would refuse to comply with the new law (technically it had not in fact passed into law yet) saying, as a matter of principle, it violated moral principles, threatened freedom of expression, media independence and the autonomy of the universities. The Kaczyński brothers immediately moved to have him dismissed as an MEP. However, in May 2007 key articles of this law were challenged by the Constitutional Tribunal, which proceeded to 'gut' the brothers' bill, rendering it inoperative (Shore 2013: 335–6). The tribunal ruled that 'lustration cannot

174 Lustration

be used to punish people as a form of revenge', and that 'an elected official cannot lose his mandate for refusing to fill in the declaration' (Michnik 2007). The Kaczyński brothers did not accept this and publicly insulted the members of the Constitutional Tribunal. Even so, what remained of the bill provoked a renewed interest in lustration.

One of the first to be accused under the new law was Lech Wałęsa. In June 2007 Sławomir Cenckiewicz and Piotr Gontarczyk, historians working at the IPN, produced 780 pages of documentary evidence identifying Wałęsa as 'Bolek', a police informant active in the years 1970–76. They published a book the following year claiming that the verdict of the Lustration Court in 2000 that had cleared presidential candidate Wałęsa of cooperation with the SB was profoundly mistaken. The documentation was plentiful, but given that Wałęsa was interviewed frequently in these years it was not surprising. While they could claim that Wałęsa had 'contributed to the evidence of the security apparatus' in interviews, they could not show any evidence of active collaboration. Wałęsa had always said he signed several police documents without paying too much attention to the content just to secure his release. In this sense the 'evidence' was meaningless. However, his first term as president (1990–95) had been marked by his often poor and unpredictable judgements: possibly this was because the outgoing communists exerted pressure on him, threatening to release this documentation in order to ensure a smooth transition for themselves. They also showed that in his first term as president, Wałęsa had done his best to destroy compromising archive materials (Cenckiewicz and Gontarczyk 2008). However, even before most people had a chance to read the book, Władysław Bartoszewski, Bronisław Geremek, Tadeusz Mazowiecki, Adam Michnik, Wisława Szymborska, Andrzej Wajda and many other artists and media celebrities sprang to his defence with an open letter of protest.[9]

The Catholic Church, which up to this point had supported lustration, now found itself in difficulties. Although the Church as a 'private enterprise' had not been subject to lustration, it now fell within the power of the new law. To a certain extent an element of cooperation with communism had been inevitable after Cardinal Wyszynski's historic compromise with communism, and had been encouraged by nominally Catholic 'front' organisations like Caritas and Bolesław Piasecki's PAX organisation, and by the Catholic Znak deputies to the Sejm, all approved by the PZPR. However, the Kaczyński brothers believed certain members of the hierarchy had compromised their calling by cooperating far too closely. In 2006 the nomination for Bishop Stanislaw Wielgus to the post of Archbishop of Warsaw showed the extent of the institutional compromise. Even though several journalists had hinted there were files on Wielgus in IPN showing he had collaborated with the intelligence service, Wielgus claimed he had only endured standard interviews before he was allowed to leave the country on a research scholarship. His nomination was supported by Radio Maryja and by Rydzyk and his followers and, because it opposed lustration, by *Gazeta Wyborcza*. However, in a public statement made in

Lustration 175

Warsaw Cathedral in front of President Lech Kaczyński at what should have been his inauguration ceremony, Wielgus resigned. Later statements from the Vatican indicated the Pope had instructed him to step down when details of his activities became known. Although Wielgus claimed he had signed documents under duress in 1978 and that these related only to his own academic research, journalists working for *Rzeczpospolita* discovered files in the IPN archive that revealed he had knowingly collaborated with the SB by informing on students in 1967, while he was a theology student at the Catholic University of Lublin.

The Church immediately set up its own investigatory commission and in June 2007 it came to the conclusion that during the communist years twelve other bishops and possibly as many as fifteen percent of the clergy had also been police informers. Even Father Popiełuszko, who had later been tortured and murdered by the SB, had been spied on by members of the clergy. Several resignations from the Church hierarchy followed – including Father Janusz Bielański, rector of Kraków's Wawel Cathedral. Michnik again criticised the process of lustration and defended the bishop. Rydzyk also defended the bishop but also claimed the coalition government, and the Kaczyński brothers in particular, had fallen under the influence of the Jews. By this stage a great many organisations, including the Catholic Church and Warsaw University, were beginning to talk of civil disobedience and a national boycott of the legislation. Taken together, these events made the parties of the Right very uncertain about how to proceed, made the role of lustration and the future of IPN unclear, made any alliance with the Church unstable and brought the whole of the Kaczyński brothers' plans into question.

In practice, the new law threatened a wide range of political discussion and opinion. It also threatened academic research and work in the historical archive. In particular, Jan Gross' book *Neighbours*, about the wartime Polish massacre of Jews in the village of Jedwabne, now faced a possible prosecution. The threat of prosecution also delayed publication in Poland of Gross' follow-up book *Fear*. Lustration was also a real problem for the Polish academic community since they were obliged to declare their connection to the Security Service. As many of the top university posts and promotion often came about as much through Party connections as through merit, lustration was bound to compromise the idea of professional academic integrity. According to Wojciech Roszkowski's survey of materials, in 1982 Warsaw Polytechnic University had forty-nine informers; in 1981 at Kraków University there were eighteen informers, twenty-five 'operational contacts' and eleven 'service contacts'; and in 1983 the Catholic University of Lublin had thirty-nine informers.

Without doubt, by the time the Kaczyński brothers came to power the processes of the new democracy were proving slow and cumbersome. Poland's politicians were not yet used to the routines of ritualised parliamentary confrontation and still had difficulties shifting from the language of power to the language of compromise and manoeuvre. The economic

176   *Lustration*

reforms undertaken by Balcerowicz were proving unpopular. In spite of the presence of hordes of Western economic advisers, the privatisation and marketisation of the Polish economy had still hardly begun and yet some sectors of the population were experiencing real hardship. Acceleration of the process was thought to be a form of political suicide. In the absence of effective politics, new jobs, Western standards of material comfort and a fully convertible currency, the brothers were consistent in offering someone to blame. However, having started to 'out' those they held responsible, the brothers quickly discovered lustration was a sword that cut both ways: not only was it difficult to confine lustration solely to the members of the *pakt*, but it provoked a reaction from those who felt threated. The brothers did not seem to realise how vulnerable they were.

Lustrators lustrated

Up to this point the Kaczyński brothers had used strong anti-homosexual rhetoric and attempted to pass laws preventing homosexuals from working as teachers. Lech Kaczyński, while he was Mayor of Warsaw, had banned the Warsaw Gay Pride march in 2004 and again in 2005. However, in 2006, when it became apparent the gay community was ignoring the ban, the president had ordered the Warsaw City Council to suppress the event. Police in riot gear stormed Le Madame – Warsaw's 'queer' club, hub of the cultural life of the gay community – and hundreds of supporters barricaded themselves inside the building. The siege lasted five days.

In June 2006 the brothers sacked Mirosław Sielatycki, Director of the Polish National Teacher Training Centre, for distributing a school manual on how to teach tolerance. The manual had been prepared by the Council of Europe (of which Poland is a member) and included material on non-discrimination against homosexuals and the rights of same-sex couples. When asked about this incident, the newly appointed Director of the National Teacher Training Centre, Teresa Lecka, said the offending manuals had been locked up, and would not be distributed further (Ireland 2006).

Up to this point the public had accepted that Jarosław Kaczyński was a little unusual – media profiles portrayed a fifty-year-old bachelor still living with his ailing mother and Alik, his cat. However, in October 2006, in an atmosphere of increasingly hysterical homophobia, commercial TV network TVN24, alongside *Gazeta Wyborcza*, the country's most important daily newspaper, and *Rzeczpospolita*, Poland's second-most important newspaper, all carried documents from the files of the communist SB. Some of these documents were only recently declassified, and some had been leaked. The documents discussed Prime Minister Jarosław Kaczyński's homosexuality and worried that Jarosław Kaczyński's homosexuality 'could threaten democracy'. The documents were part of an investigation into right-wing political parties begun in 1992 by the Urząd Ochrony Państwa (UOP, State Protection Office, founded in 1990 to replace the communist SB) and revealed that SB Colonel Jan Lesiak, had instructed: 'It is advisable

Lustration   177

to establish if Jarosław Kaczyński remains in a long-term homosexual relationship and, if so, who his partner is'. From the documents it was clear the SB had been instructed to spread rumours about him.

Rumours about Jarosław's homosexuality had been around for a long time. Many remembered that thirteen years earlier President Lech Wałęsa, in an interview on TVP1, had joked that when the Kaczyński brothers attended his birthday party 'Lech came with his wife and Jarosław came with his husband'. On 14 October 2006 Lech Wałęsa appeared on Polish commercial TVN's programme 'Teraz My' (Now Us), and he was asked by the programme's anchors about the earlier broadcast. Wałęsa was pleased to recall his comment and repeat it (Ireland 2006). Journalist Michał Rolecki, of the website *GayPoland.pl*, who had recently had a TV programme suppressed in which Jarosław Kaczyński's sexual preference was openly assumed, said Jarosław's homosexuality had been 'quite obvious to the general public ever since Wałęsa's original televised comment' (Ireland 2006).

Indeed, it was widely suspected that Lech Wałęsa, who served as president from 1990 to 1995, had initiated the UOP investigation when he wanted to get rid of the Kaczyński brothers: they had been his advisers in underground Solidarność, but as counsellors at the presidential palace they continually briefed against him and plotted tirelessly to set his other advisers against one another. Although the SB documents were released in 2006, they dated from a time when the UOP was still the direct heir of the old communist SB: UOP personnel consisted largely of people employed before the collapse of the communist regime who had worked for the SB and who were politically opposed to the Kaczyński brothers. If this was so, then it was an alliance between ex-dissidents, Solidarność leadership and the remnants of the old communist regime, very much in line with the *pakt* the Kaczyński brothers imagined. But, in so far as such an unlikely alliance existed even on a temporary basis, it was the creation of the Kaczyński brothers' lustration policy. Whoever ordered the investigation into the private life of Jarosław Kaczyński, the release of security materials indicated a campaign to undermine the coalition government by driving a wedge between coalition partners and their supporters – primarily the Catholic Church.

However, the Kaczyński brothers could not turn back. In March 2007 Roman Giertych, Education Minister and leader of the League of Polish Families, announced that the government planned to fast-track legislation banning all discussion of homosexuality, including information about HIV/ AIDS, in schools and educational institutions, and threatening teachers and lecturers with fines and imprisonment. In May 2007, after EU commissioners warned the Polish government that this legislation contravened European law on human rights, the bill came before the Sejm and several Polish MPs walked out in protest (www.news.bbc.co.uk/1/hi/world/europe/6596829). On 28 May 2007 Ewa Sowińska, the Kaczyński brothers' Ombudsman for Children, joined the drive to curb what she called 'gay propaganda' by announcing she was banning BBC's popular TV series *Teletubbies* because Tinky-Winky (the purple one) carried a handbag and was therefore

178   *Lustration*

promoting homosexuality to children. 'I learned that there could be some hidden homosexual undertones' ('Tinky-Winky controversy').

By the spring of 2007, the brothers' coalition was mired in corruption and engulfed by scandal; their prime minister had been 'outed', their relations with the Church were strained to breaking and their lustration laws were in tatters. The popularity of the Kaczyński brothers fell to an all-time low in the polls and threatened to bring down the coalition.[10] The brothers hit back by leaking carefully chosen secret files about communist informers and police spies to the press. This counterstrike was intended to re-direct the attention of the electorate and damage the opposition in the run-up to the October 2007 elections. It was designed to show that all those who opposed the Kaczyński brothers were tarred by the brush of communism and could not be trusted.

One of the Kaczyński brothers' first victims was the recently deceased writer and journalist Ryszard Kapuściński (1932–2007).[11] In May 2007, just after the Constitutional Tribunal had intervened in the lustration laws and four months after Kapuściński's death, rumours began to circulate suggesting he was some kind of 'agent' or informer for the SB. The rumours were even discussed in the foreign press. In the week 21–28 May, the Polish edition of *Newsweek*, followed by a large number of American, German and British newspapers including *The International Herald Tribune*, *The Independent* and *The Guardian*, reported that in the years 1967–72 Kapuściński had written reports for the Polish intelligence service under the code name 'Poet' and later 'Vera Cruz'. Polish *Newsweek* said Poland's intelligence agencies had tasked Kapuściński with collecting information on American companies and citizens, as well as the intelligence agencies of the US, Israel and West Germany. As examples, it mentioned that in 1970 Kapuściński wrote a five-page report on the general situation in Latin America, focusing on Cuban foreign policy; a three-page report on the political situation of Mexico; and three character profiles on influential people he had met abroad. The journal went on to say that when Kapuściński returned to Poland in 1972 his file had become inactive and quoted a 1981 secret police document saying that Kapuściński 'did not pass on any essential material the secret police were interested in'. Polish *Newsweek* claimed it had based its report on documents found in the former SB archives, held by the state-run IPN. However, Polish *Newsweek* soon admitted that the journal had done no archive research: the file had been leaked to it by IPN spokesman Andrzej Arseniuk.

Kapuściński's membership of the PZPR was public knowledge. As a journalist and employee of the communist state – and even as a Party member – Kapuściński had little say in the terms of his work: if the police granted him a visa to leave the country on condition that he report to them on his return, that was what he had to do. This was common knowledge and applied to every citizen who applied for a passport. It quickly became clear that Kapuściński had damaged no-one and revealed nothing of value to the police about friends, colleagues or acquaintances. Indeed, if the police had read his newspaper articles they would have learned little about Polish politics, but would have been well informed about foreign affairs: the reports he gave them were often simply drafts of his newspaper articles. However, this was not a genuine intelligence gathering operation, nor was it simply a question of revealing a police 'informer'. It was an exercise of power, a form of control. It is highly unlikely the police read his reports or his newspaper articles. So why 'leak' such inconsequential information about a man who had only recently died? The attempt to turn Ryszard Kapuściński's pragmatic professional decisions into something else was a smear that did not in fact amount to very much, but the content was not the main point. The smear was a demonstration of power and a warning to others (Traynor 2007).[12]

Adam Michnik and the idea of lustration

Adam Michnik, a long-time dissident, advisor to Solidarność, close friend of Zbigniew Herbert and editor of *Gazeta Wyborcza*, Poland's first independent and most popular national daily newspaper, wrote with concern about post-communist Poland and its expectations. He and his paper, along with SLD (Sojusz Lewicy Demokratycznej, Democratic Left Alliance) and PSL (Polskie Stronictwo Ludowe, Polish People's Party), were staunch but thoughtful opponents of lustration. In October 2007 Adam Michnik published an article in *Gazeta Wyborcza* about the Kaczyński brothers' political plans for the Fourth Republic, describing it as being founded on suspicion and fear (Michnik 2011: 141).

Michnik experienced the fear engendered by lustration but saw where the need for judgement felt by his close friend Zbigniew Herbert led (Michnik 2011: 141–2). For him, the Kaczyński brothers were a peculiar parody of the diligent Stalinist apparatchik, working to squash all opposition by smears and crafted convictions. The figure of the avenging post-communist 'lustrator' was one Michnik returned to (Michnik 2011: 153).

Michnik was clear that the annihilation of one's enemies in time of social peace (however fragile) and democracy (however imperfect) could only lead to the destruction of both social peace and democracy (Michnik 2011: 168). For Michnik, lustration was a kind of moral evil on a par with the Spanish Inquisition, Stalin's show trials and the McCarthy witch-hunts, feeding paranoia and anti-Semitism (Michnik 2011: 166).

After 1993 Michnik often appeared isolated. Some of his readers resented that he seemed to blur the distinction between right and wrong, between good and evil. Also, Michnik's generosity towards his erstwhile opponents often made him look less than reliable as a political figure. Revelations that he drank whiskey with General Jaruzelski and on several occasions had dinner with Jerzy Urban, Jaruzelski's reviled henchman, did not impress the general public and, whatever the merits of his testimony, Michnik did himself little good by appearing for the defence in the case against General Kiszczak. His liberal stance was sorely tested on several occasions,

180 *Lustration*

particularly in the case of Lesław Maleszka. His dealings with Lew Rywin were also seen as devious and less than straightforward. The case of Cardinal Wielgus, however, embarrassed him most of all because there he found himself more or less on the same side as Radio Maryja. However, Michnik, well in advance of most observers, had seen past the desire for judgement to the paranoia lustration would create. Nevertheless, by 2011 Michnik, who had previously opposed all attempts at lustration, felt the only way forward was to release all the secret files – fake and real – for public scrutiny simply so they could not be leaked selectively by politicians seeking to gain advantage.

Politics, it is often said, is a dirty business. Writers, lawyers and academics like to think of their occupations as its opposite – somehow clean and pure, connected with art, research and the intellectual search for truth, self-knowledge and wisdom. But these professions (and particularly writers) do not operate in a void: they work and write out of their own identity, sympathy and understanding. In many ways literature, law and the study of history imaginatively recover and rehearse the existential questions humans ask themselves about how to live their life, square their actions with the demands of conscience and deal with the consequences of decisions. However, while these professions all think of themselves as a kind of social barometer, commenting independently on political life and the morality of their time, this does not mean they all agree on basic issues or come up with similar answers to existential questions. What Michnik and others learned was that, while the way forward was never easily apparent, lustration made for unpredictable revelations, strange reversals and unlikely alliances.

Leszek Moczulski and the experience of lustration

The unpredictable nature of lustration for communists and oppositionists alike can be seen in the case of Leszek Moczulski (b.1930), a man of impeccable right-wing credentials, a vigorously anti-communist politician, journalist and military historian, and leader of KPN (Konfederacja Polski Niepodległej, Confederation for an Independent Poland). Although Solidarność had felt compelled to defend KPN against police brutality in 1980–81, the union and the intellectual advisers of KOR had never been at ease with the anti-Semitic *prawdziwy polacy* (true Poles) of KPN (Ash 1983: 216–17).[13] Moczulski had criticised Mazowiecki's 'thick line', calling repeatedly for 'radical' lustration and vigorous de-communisation. Elected to the Sejm in 1992, KPN joined the coalition government, but then left as Moczulski claimed they were lackeys of (as the occasion demanded) Western bankers, German revanchists or Russian imperialists (Czarnota 2008: 229). Moczulski took a leading role in several Sejm commissions, including work on the new constitution, and planned to run for president, but Antoni Macierewicz (who now claimed to have a list of over 100 journalists recruited as informers) accused him of being 'Lech', an informant for the Security Service, and obliged him to withdraw from the election. In 1997 Moczulski asked the

Lustration 181

lustration commission of IPN to investigate the charges against him and in 1999 took part in *autolustracja* (self-lustration), where he made a declaration of his involvement with the security services. However, the court quashed his declaration, saying he had 'lied methodically' by attempting to hide 'secret paid collaboration' in the years 1969–77, when he reported on colleagues at the weekly newspaper *Stolica*.[14]

As a result of the accusations against Moczulski, KPN's fortunes languished and electoral support declined. KPN eventually split into two factions, with the rival leaders expelling each other. In 2004 Moczulski dissolved KPN only to have the rival faction re-register as KPN–OP (KPN – Obóz Patriotyczny, KPN – Patriotic Camp). In 2005 Moczulski, who was about to complete his PhD and resume an academic career, again petitioned the lustration tribunal of IPN to investigate, claiming the documents had been falsified. The appeal failed, but in 2008 the Supreme Court over-ruled this decision, saying that although he had been a paid informer, the information Moczulski provided had not been important. The court hinted that it was not convinced by the documentary evidence and pointed out the discrepancy of Moczulski being both a paid informer and an active and frequently imprisoned oppositionist. In 2009 Moczulski completed his *habilitacja* (higher doctorate), and in 2011 his case came before the Strasbourg Court of Human Rights, which ruled the lustration process had been a violation of his right to a fair trial and referred the case back to the Warsaw District Court. In Warsaw the re-examination of the evidence against Moczulski began in 2013. In 2015 Polish President Bronisław Komorowski decorated Moczulski with the Grand Cross of the Order of the Rebirth of Poland, indicating he had been forgiven for any indiscretions he might have committed. However, the initial charge had effectively lost Moczulski control of his party and ended his political career.

The end of lustration

Plans for a Fourth Republic unravelled very quickly, partly because they relied on an unstable coalition, partly because lustration generated a self-defeating paranoia, and partly because the Fourth Republic demanded impeccable moral standards from the government seeking to create it. Hard on the heels of Jarosław's embarrassing 'outing', the activities of Andrzej Lepper, deputy prime minister and minister for agriculture in the Kaczyński coalition, brought matters to an unexpected conclusion. Lepper had always been a dubious asset for the coalition. In 2001 he had been sentenced to sixteen months in jail, and in 2002 had faced criminal charges for slander after levelling corruption accusations against ministers and members of parliament; later he was charged with assault, blocking roads and dumping grain on railroad tracks. At about the same time it emerged that Lepper, who had favoured economic connections with Eastern Europe rather than the EU and USA, had accepted an honorary doctorate from MAUP (Міжрегіональна Академія Управління Персоналом, Mizregionalna Akademia Upravlinya

182 *Lustration*

Personalom, Interregional Academy of Personnel Management), a private educational establishment in Ukraine that openly disseminated anti-Semitic courses and materials.[15]

While the Kaczyński brothers were prepared to use indirect anti-Semitism, they were not prepared for an open connection of this kind. In December 2006 Lepper was accused of demanding sexual favours in return for an appointment to a senior regional Samoobrona Party post, in the course of which, it was said, he had fathered an illegitimate child. Lepper claimed this was a 'sting' and a smear by the Kaczyński brothers. The charge of sexual harassment was eventually dismissed and the paternity case quashed after a DNA test, but in July 2007 Prime Minister Kaczyński accused Lepper of corruption and asked President Kaczyński to remove Lepper from the cabinet and coalition, only to find this damaged the coalition's majority in the Sejm. Almost immediately Prime Minister Kaczyński was forced to invite Lepper to re-join the coalition and cabinet. This manoeuvre convinced the Sejm it was being brought into disrepute and the members called for its dissolution and for new national elections.[16]

The announcement of new elections coincided with a moment of pent-up national grief and an emotional outpouring at the release of Andrzej Wajda's long-awaited film *Katyń* (2007) about the NKVD (Naródnyy Komissariát Vnútrennikh Del, People's Commissariat for Internal Affairs) massacre of 17,000 Polish officers in 1940. The film had been made under the patronage of President Lech Kaczyński, who then controversially tried to make use of the film for his own propaganda purposes in the election campaign: the electorate noticed this but instead of generating support, it was condemned as a manipulation. Also, while the electorate tolerated Jarosław's homosexuality, it did not approve of the hypocrisy of his attempt to suppress homosexuals. Further, it associated the Kaczyński brother's smears and 'sting' tactics not with an improved sense of morality but with the old communist trick of *prowokacja* (provocation), and did not approve of that either. The Sejm elections in October 2007 saw an increased turnout and a protest vote that routed the coalition and elected the centre-right Civic Platform Party and Prime Minister Donald Tusk.[17]

Lustration and the push for the Fourth Republic were finished, but the revelations about lustration were not quite over. Prime Minister Donald Tusk's assistant, Michał Boni, just before accepting a ministerial post in the new government, confessed that in 1985 he had signed a declaration of cooperation with the Security Service. In fact, he had been named as a collaborator in Macierewicz's 1992 list. His confession and apology on live TV were presented as his own personal tragedy: the SB, he said, had blackmailed him into cooperation after finding him in bed with a woman who was not his wife.

In 2012 General Gromosław Czempiński, former head of Urząd Ochrony Państwa (UOP, State Protection Office), publicly admitted to manufacturing fake police reports during the communist years, when he served in the SB. His purpose had been to undermine the credibility of prominent opponents

Lustration   183

of the regime and to discredit dissidents by destroying their good name in private life, 'revealing' secrets about their friendships, contacts or sexuality, or by claiming they worked as police spies or informants. These reports were known as *fałszywki* (falsies, fakes). They were usually signed by invented police officers, or the signatures of the alleged collaborators were Xeroxed from other documents (even copies of copies were used) and pasted into *fałszywki* to make them appear authentic (*Gazeta Wyborcza*, 2012). This problem had in fact been highlighted in a court case as early as 2000: The court case made use of a document written by Major Adam Styliński in 1985 during an internal investigation at the Ministry of Interior Affairs that described in detail the production and wide-spread use of *fałszywki* during the Martial Law period (www.en.wikipedia.org/wiki/Lustration_ in_Poland). On the back of Czempiński's admission it was possible to see that as the various post-communist political factions jostled for power, the release of SB files containing *fałszywki* had led to a number of high profile accusations – most notably against Lech Wałęsa, Władysław Bartoszewski, Professor Jerzy Kłoczowski and the photo-journalist Małgorzata Niezabi- towska – often followed by equally high profile law suits for slander.[18]

In December 2014, on Polskie Radio (Polish Radio), General Kiszczak, after serving a spell in prison for his part in the death of miners at the Wujek colliery during the imposition of Martial Law in 1981 – the first and one of the very few cases where a high functionary of the communist state was found guilty and sentenced to jail – added to the doubts and confusions when he admitted that not only were the IPN files corrupted by the presence of *fałszywki*, but the files of actual informers had for the most part already been destroyed by the Security Service: 'After 1989, whoever approached me about destroying their records, I always destroyed them – everybody's'. He stressed these records applied to 'numerous people who were by no means small fish. These were serious people – writers, great actors, politicians'. He refused to name anyone in particular but went on: 'I often see them on TV as they spit venom on me' (Radio Poland: www. thenews.pl/1/9/Artykul/191250,Polish-Communist-police-chief-admits-de- stroying-informers-records#sthash.0t3ZoXKi.dpuf).[19]

In fact the SB had long been involved in disinformation and the man- ufacture of documents. As early as 1966 Marek Hłasko (1934–69), who been blackmailed into becoming a police informer before leaving Poland in 1958, wrote of his and Czesław Miłosz's experiences. Even though they had abandoned communist Poland and 'chosen freedom', the USA would not grant a visa because it suspected them of being communist 'plants' (Hłasko 2013: 94–5).

The exact extent of the secret police files is still unknown, but it has been estimated that by 1987 the SB files contained 3.1 million cards, ninety lin- ear kilometres of documents, and files on some 98,000 informers. In 1999 eighty linear meters of 'lost' documents, including signed declarations and payment details, were discovered in the basement of the security police headquarters in Warsaw. However, what survives is only a fraction of the

184 *Lustration*

documentation that once existed. Between August 1989 and February 1990 the police and SB worked hard to destroy their secret files. They destroyed their records on senior Party politicians and those identified as likely to become leading post-communist politicians; they also destroyed 1,200 files on prominent informers and all the materials on the infiltration of the Catholic Church. The police and SB were not the only ones destroying evidence at that time: when students stormed PZPR headquarters in Warsaw in the autumn of 1989 they found shredding machines and dozens of sacks of shredded documents (Stan 2010: 88–9).

Of the 23,000 people who submitted to *autolustracja* up to 2010, only a handful were ever proved to be 'lustration liars' and even fewer were forced to leave their jobs or face punishment as informers (Stan 2010: 97).

*

The drive for lustration and the Fourth Republic arose at a time when, after years of being the communist government's largely silent (and consequently prosperous) partner, the Catholic Church was manoeuvring to embed itself in post-communist Poland as an official state religion: militant traditional Catholicism (sometimes referred to as *czarnokracja*, literally blackocracy, after the black garb worn by priests and nuns) was resurgent and Radio Maryja had begun to push a line so virulently fundamentalist it was even a matter of concern to the Polish Episcopate and the Vatican (Watt 2006). It also came as Catholic-nationalist assumptions were placed under great stress with the rehabilitation of the Polish Government in Exile and consequent review of its attitudes to the Warsaw Uprising and the civil war that followed, and also from the challenge to Poland's well developed sense of victimhood arising from the revelation of the wartime Polish massacre of Jews at Jedwabne.

The drive for lustration also came at a time when the material wealth promised by capitalism and 'the West' consistently failed to arrive, and while poverty and hardship in Poland actually increased.[20] For many of the older generation, the communist era, though it was massively inefficient and lacked civic freedoms, increasingly came to represent a semi-mythical, lost, easy time of free medical care, equality, security and stability. Polish pensioners in particular feel excluded from 'normal' life in the post-communist era. In contrast, democracy, with its multitude of decisions and responsibilities, seemed disappointingly tricky.[21] Although the struggle for democracy had been long and hard in Poland, now there was very little interest in actually voting: participation in elections – because they did not produce strong leadership or decisive action – was very poor.[22]

Age was also a significant factor in the debate since lustration only really concerned those who had been adults during the lifetime of communism. In general, although the journals *Trybuna* (which ceased publication in December 2009), *Polityka*, *Nie*, *Przegląd*, *Rzeczpospolita* and *Gazeta Wyborcza* all ran lustration scoops at one time or another, writers, artists,

Lustration 185

media personalities, lawyers and journalists tried to avoid getting dragged into the lustration fight. A few of the older generation of writers, film-makers and artists came forward for auto-lustration, but for the most part those who had been compromised under communism were at the end of their energy and patience, at the end of their careers and in many cases in the final days of their life, and so tended to keep quiet. Nevertheless, the lustration drama was played out in a very public and sensational fashion in the newspapers and on TV, often involving reporters, media personalities and public figures who were themselves likely to be subject to lustration. But for the younger generation of writers, journalists, lawyers and artists, born in the mid-1970s and started their careers after 1989, it was for the most part a non-issue and did not concern them.

However, the collapse of communism was the absence of structure, of guiding principle and of political framework, and this was keenly felt both by the opponents of communism and by the opponents of capitalism. Capitalism brought a relentless churning and a new kind of indifference, though it did not necessarily provide a satisfactory substitute for what had been. For many what remained was a hunger for engagement, an increasingly desperate need for certainty and stability, and a nagging need to feel this all made some sort of sense. If during the communist years life for many had been 'elsewhere', after the collapse of communism, for many the feeling was that in spite of their best efforts life had still somehow managed to pass them by.

Political life was seen as almost exclusively the domain of the *inteligencja* (intelligentsia), and the battles of lustration were fought almost entirely within the political class of a particular age-group. However, in ever more difficult economic circumstances, professionals of all kinds were too preoccupied earning a living for lustration and the issues of the past to become a serious and consistent electoral issue. This was far from the traditional 'leading role' the Catholic Church and the *inteligencja* claimed for themselves during the Partitions or in competition with communism. In re-focusing the energy of the *inteligencja*, turning it into an adjunct of the economy, capitalism had done a more thorough job in a decade than communism had managed in forty-five years. The bulk of the electorate invested little hope in politics, fluctuated from 'apathy to aggression and back' (Jasiewicz 1995: 152), and had little interest in political life beyond, perhaps, the fleeting promise of 'bread and circuses' offered by lustration.

The experience of communism burned a deep scar in the psyche of the older generation, but lustration was nothing like the healing required. Leszek Moczulski, Zbigniew Herbert, Marek Nowakowski, Wisława Szymborska and Adam Michnik all came to their own conclusions about how to relate to communism, how to apply transitional justice, how to live with their conscience and how to move beyond communism. While some of those involved in the lustration debate tried to develop a line of thought that would enable Poland to proceed in 'normality', the Kaczyński brothers attempted to make short-term political capital out of the everyday

186 *Lustration*

difficulties, deformities, ambiguities, accommodations and compromises required of Poles under communism – the ordinary, the extraordinary, the talented, the misguided and people of principle alike – few of whom ever had any choice but to make the best of their situation. Even though it must have been clear that the moment for legal action with some hope of justice had passed, the Kaczyński coalition scrapped Mazowiecki's 'thick line' to pursue the paranoid fabrication of the *pakt*. Theirs was a dirty war in which they tried to settle scores and 'out' their opposition rather than reckon with the past. They made a humiliating farce out of Poland's attempt to come to terms with the 'red ghosts' of its communist past (Ash 2007). Virtually the only writer to voice support for PiS was Andrzej Sapkowski (b.1948), author of the 'Witcher' series of fantasy novels.

In practice, while the lustration debate provides a window on the development of post-communist political culture in Poland, the long hand-over period meant that the quest for justice of any kind was compromised right from the start. The pursuit of 'traitors', 'criminals' and those with a 'suspicious' past merely fuelled paranoia and encouraged the well-established Polish sense of victimhood. It also provided a whole range of those who were 'in' on the plot against Poland. The believer could take their pick at any given moment: Germany, Russia, the European Union, multi-culturalism, homosexuality, Western consumerism, Western cosmopolitanism, Jews, hidden Reds, secularists, humanists and liberals. What mattered to PiS, Radio Maryja and those members of the electorate who believed in the *konspiracja* was simply that without being able to say exactly how or why, Poland's liberals were somehow traitors.

The poet Wisława Szymborska was one of the first to see that the desire for lustration arose out of frustration, but also that it fed a kind of hatred. *Gazeta Wyborcza*, which opposed lustration, published 'Nienawiść' (Hatred), her protest poem about the kind of Poland and the kind of politics she saw emerging from the ruins of communism (Szymborska *1995*, 181–3).

In the squalid chaos of the Polish lustration debate, the desire for revenge that obsessed so many of the country's rulers detracted from finding a solution to the problems of the economy and wide-spread hardship. Paranoia and chauvinism ran rampant; careers were not often made but frequently damaged or broken; there was no great improvement in access to justice and the very little truth revealed was often unintentional, compromised and unpalatable.

Notes

1 Lustration could be inserted into many other key Polish binary intersections of the time: government / nation; authority / society; city / countryside; new authorities / old authorities; communists / others; rich / poor; parties / other parties; parts of government / other parts of government; parts of Solidarność / other parts of Solidarność; Wałęsa / Mazowiecki.

2 ONR (*Obóz Narodowo-Radikalny*, National Radical Camp), also known as RNR (*Ruch Narodowo-Radikalny*, National Radical Movement) or ONR-

Lustration 187

Falanga. A pre-war party that openly copied the Italian Fascists in blending Catholicism and nationalism; it was mainly active in the universities and was responsible for a series of attacks on Jewish students. Its leader, Bolesław Piasecki, was arrested after the war, made a deal with the communists and became leader of the pro-regime Catholic PAX organisation.

3 Bronisław Geremek (1932–2008) was born in Warsaw. He graduated in 1954 from the Faculty of History at Warsaw University, and after study at the École Pratique des Hautes Études in Paris completed his PhD in 1960 and his *habilitacja* (higher doctorate) in 1972 at the Polish Academy of Sciences (PAN). He was a lecturer at the Sorbonne in Paris and the manager of the Polish Culture Centre in Paris 1960–65. From 1980 to 1981 he was an advisor to Solidarność and was interned with the declaration of Martial Law. He continued in the role of advisor to the Underground union and was re-arrested. In 1989 he was appointed associate professor at PAN (Polish Academy of Science). He had honorary degrees from numerous universities, was a member of Academia Europea, the PEN Club, the Société Européenne de Culture, fellow of Collegium Invisibile and Chair of European Civilisation at the College of Europe.

4 *Nomenklatura* from Latin *nomenclatura*: a list of names. In common usage, a list of approved 'loyal' individuals drawn up by the PZPR from which all key positions in the state, party apparatus, administration, justice, diplomacy, police, military, press, publishing, film, education, sport and banking were appointed: a list of those granted privileges by the PZPR. In Poland, of the 1,200,000 'management and responsibility' posts, perhaps 200,000 were *nomenklatura* posts reserved for PZPR members, and a further 900,000 were controlled appointments for those deemed suitable by the PZPR. It is thought that when families were taken into account, over two million Poles (ten percent of the population) owed their jobs, incomes and place in society to *nomenklatura* protection ('Apparatus Power', 1981: 55–6).

5 Jarosław and Lech Kaczyński (b.1949) were the sons of Rajmund (an engineer, veteran in the London-backed Armia Krajowa and survivor of the Warsaw Uprising) and Jadwiga (a philologist at the Polish Academy of Sciences). As children the brothers starred in the film O *dwóch takich, co ukradli księżyc (The Two Who Stole the Moon*, 1962), based on a popular children's story. In the 1970s both brothers were active in the Free Trades Union movement KOR (Komitet Obrony Robotników, Committee Defending Workers), and as middle-ranking advisors to Solidarność both were arrested and Lech was jailed during Martial Law. Wałęsa appointed Jarosław executive editor of *Tygodnik Solidarność*, the union weekly, 1989–90. In 1990 the brothers created the Christian-Democratic party Porozumienie Centrum (Centre Understanding), but abandoned it to found the PiS in 2001. Widely regarded as Poland's most influential politician, Jarosław was a frontbench MP 1991–3 and 1997–2005, leader of PiS, and prime ministerial candidate in the Sejm elections of September 2005.

6 Roman Giertych (b.1971) was descended from a long family line of military, Catholic, right-wing nationalists. He campaigned to remove Kafka, Dostoevsky and Gombrowicz from school reading lists and to replace them with ultra-nationalist Catholic authors. He believed in a literal interpretation of the Book of Genesis and wanted Darwin outlawed.

7 In the late 1980s, Rydzyk's Radio Maryja International in Balderschwang, West Germany (a forerunner of the Polish Radio Maryja) was closed down by the local authorities, accused of purveying violent racism, xenophobia, primitive and paranoid homophobia, and anti-Semitic and anti-abortion opinion. The German government now blocks access to the Polish Radio Maryja website. In 1991 Rydzyk moved his operation back to Poland and started Radio Maryja in the northern Polish city of Toruń. It was so successful that three years later it

188 *Lustration*

went nation-wide. This was followed by the launch of the daily newspaper *Nasz Dziennik* (*Our Daily*), with a circulation of 200,000, and in 2003 by the launch of the TV station *Trwam* (I Abide). Together these organisations are known as the Radio Maryja Family. Rydzyk had been instrumental in helping to found and support LPR, but when PiS became the leading party in the coalition he switched his support. Jarosław Kaczyński and other right-wing politicians were frequent guests on Radio Maryja. The Redemptorist Order is by vocation a zealous missionary society preaching to the poor, mainly in the Third World. They take a vow of poverty, chastity and obedience, along with a vow of 'perseverance', specifically to live as part of their congregation until death, and consequently they refuse all ecclesiastical appointments. Rydzyk's media empire is independent of the Catholic Church and the episcopate's efforts to control him have never been more than half-hearted.

8 The First Republic (1573–1795) was brought to an end with the partition of Poland by Russia, Prussia and Austria; the Second Republic (1918–1939) was brought to an end by the Soviet and Nazi invasions; the era of the People's Republic of Poland is generally ignored in this schema; the Third Republic is said to have begun with the collapse of communism in 1989.

9 In Wajda's film *Wałęsa: człowiek z nadziei* (Wałęsa: Man of Hope, 2013), Wałęsa's wife Danuta upbraids him for signing police documents so casually. Wajda explained he did not want to make this film but felt he had to, not for Western consumption, but to put a younger Polish audience that was already showing a lack of interest in recent history in touch with the figure of Wałęsa and the experiences and achievements of his generation. www.en.wikipedia.org/wiki/Walesa._Man_of_Hope. The financing of this film offers an interesting insight into the underbelly of Polish political and artistic life, which lustration did little to affect. Originally the film was to have been funded by Amber Gold, as one of several backers, but this company was found to be trading as a bullion store and acting as a bank without a licence and with an empty bank account. However, when Agencja Bezpieczeństwa Wewnętrznego (ABW, Agency of Internal Security) raided Amber Gold's offices in Gdańsk in August 2012 they seized an undisclosed quantity of gold. The company, which owed 50,000 clients 80,000,000 zł. (20,000,000 euros), was liquidated by the Prosecutor's Office the following month (Polskie Radio, 17 August 2012: Radio Poland: www.thenews.pl/1/12/Artykul/109461,Gold-seized-during-inspection-of-collapsed-lender-Amber-Gold). The case forced a delay to the launch of the film as producers sought other backers and tried to distance themselves from Amber Gold. When asked to comment on this at a press conference, Michał Kwieciński of Akson Studios said: 'Film is an art. It cannot be created amid a climate of suspicion, witch hunts and political games' (Radio Poland: www.thenews.pl/1/9/Artykul/109516,Walesa-biopic-will-not-have-Amber-Gold-as-investor). The suspicion is that Amber Gold's investment in film was to launder 'dirty money', possibly from WSI: Kwieciński's comment implies a political motive behind the prosecution and perhaps an attempt by Wałęsa's opponents to sabotage the film.

10 Around the same time rumours circulated to the effect that Jarosław Kaczyński held some affection for Polish MP Jolanta Szczypińska. While they enjoyed the publicity, both denied allegations of an impending marriage and the general conclusion was that the rumour was a 'beard' – a disguise – put out to mislead the gullible as to Jarosław's sexual preference and protect his political connection to the Catholic Church.

11 Kapuściński had begun work on the weekly journal *Polityka* in 1957 and joined PAP (Polish Press Agency) in 1964 to become Poland's first foreign correspondent. For nearly twenty years he was quite literally Poland's eyes and ears in the

Lustration 189

world. By the time he returned to Poland in 1980, Kapuściński had covered wars in Honduras and El Salvador, a revolution in Zanzibar, a coup in Tanganyika, the South African invasion of Angola, a revolution in Burundi, civil war in Nigeria, the end of Haile Selassie's reign in Ethiopia and the collapse of the Shah's regime in Iran. Kapuściński was the best known of a generation of respected Polish journalists who came up through the communist youth movement, developed a hard-hitting, wry, subtle and allusive style in response to censorship, were increasingly worried by what they saw of contemporary Polish life and increasingly disillusioned by the PZPR.

12 At about the same time that the charges against Kapuściński were made, Wojciech Giełżyński (1930–2015), award winning journalist and foreign correspondent, member of the PZPR 1960–81, confessed to very similar 'cooperation' with the security service in the years 1958–64. In spite of this he was awarded the Knight's Cross of the Order of the Rebirth of Poland and Gold Cross of Merit.

13 KPN was the East Block's first independent political party, but because it refused to accept the leadership of the communist party, it remained officially un-registered. It was based on the nationalist policies of Józef Piłsudski and the pre-war *Sanacja* regime, supported by the ideas of the anti-Semitic, nationalist *Endecja* party led by Roman Dmowski. KPN called for the transformation of the communist planned economy into a free market economy, and it used thinly veiled anti-Semitic comment – 'Poland for the Poles' and 'Poland for Real Poles' – as its most favoured slogans. In the years 1979–81 KPN provided the bulk of Poland's political prisoners. In 1989 neither the PZPR nor Solidarność had felt obliged to invite KPN to the Round Table Talks, but in the first elections KPN enjoyed some electoral success.

14 In 1946 Moczulski was a member of the anti-communist resistance in Sopot, but in 1947 changed sides and became a member of the communist youth movement. He joined the PZPR in 1950 and went on to graduate in law, after which he became a journalist for *Trybuna Ludu* and *Życie Warszawy*. He was expelled from the PZPR in the 1950s for 'national deviationism', but seems to have been re-instated. He was expelled again in the 1970s, and this started a period of political re-orientation for Moczulski. He began work with the Civil and Human Rights Movement, but soon parted with them and in 1979 formed KPN. In 1985 Moczulski issued a memorandum calling on the governments of the UK and USA to fulfil the promises of the 1945 Yalta Conference and organise free elections in Poland. For this and other provocations Moczulski was frequently arrested and imprisoned – he spent a total of about six years in jail. In 1991 Moczulski put himself forward as a presidential candidate but polled only 2.5 percent of the vote. In 1992, after moderating its extremist image but campaigning vociferously for the departure of the 60,000 Soviet troops still in Poland, KPN won forty-six seats in the Sejm to join the four main parties in a 'moderate' coalition government. However, when Prime Minister Olszewski refused to appoint Moczulski as Minister for National Defence (a role he said he had been promised), he withdrew KPN from the coalition. Moczulski's secret police file can be viewed at www.lustracja.net/index.php/tajni-wspolpracownicy/183-leszek-moczulski-tw-sb.

15 The Simon Wiesenthal Center had accused MAUP of disseminating anti-Semitic propaganda and urged the Ukrainian authorities to revoke its accreditation.

16 In 2011 Lepper was found dead in his Warsaw office, hanging from a ceiling hook for a boxing punch-bag. A coroner's inquiry determined the cause of suicide was probably 'crushing depression' brought on by the sex scandal, spectacular political defeat and the enormous financial debt resulting from the collapse of Samoobrona, followed by the failure of Lepper's business ventures.

190　*Lustration*

17 President Lech Kaczyński, his wife, 94 military leaders and members of the Polish government died in an air-crash while attempting to land in dense fog at Smolensk, Russia, in April 2010. They had been on their way to commemorate the Katyń massacre. After the crash Jarosław Kaczyński claimed it was no accident but the 'assassination' of the Polish government by the KGB. He benefited politically from sympathy over his brother's death and moved rapidly to reinvent PiS as a party promoting Polish victimhood and anti-German and anti-Russian attitudes, a party of grassroots national unity and 'ethno-confessionalism' (Polish Catholicism), which resembled Piasecki's ONR-Falanga of the interwar years. He also decided to run for president. In the run-up to the 2015 Sejm elections he claimed migrants from the Middle East were bringing cholera and dysentery to Europe and spreading 'various parasites and protozoa'. He also claimed that Donald Tusk was in league with President Putin and that Angela Merkel owed her position to the Stasi. In October 2015 PiS was elected as the ruling party – post-communist Poland's first non-coalition government. In February 2016 Christian Davies wrote of PiS: 'Commonly labelled conservative or nationalist, Law and Justice blends the religious and patriotic rituals of Poland's long history of resistance to foreign oppression with hostility to free-market capitalism and a heavy dose of conspiracy regarding the machinations of Poland's enemies. It is the vanguard of a movement that goes far beyond the party itself, supported by sympathetic smaller parties, ultra-Catholic media, nationalist youth organisations and an assortment of cranks and cynics who share hostility to liberalism in all its guises. As PiS foreign minister Witold Waszczykowski told the German tabloid *Bild*, the government "only wants to cure our country of a few illnesses", such as: "a new mixture of cultures and races, a world made up of cyclists and vegetarians, who only use renewable energy and who battle all signs of religion [...] What moves most Poles is tradition, historical awareness, love of country, faith in God and normal family life between a woman and a man"' (Davies 2016).

18 Władysław Bartoszewski's (1922–2015) career is too varied to be easily summarised. He was born in Warsaw, studied at Warsaw University, was imprisoned in Auschwitz and was released in 1941. He was a member of the AK (Home Army) as liaison to the Warsaw ghetto leaders and co-founder of Żegota, a wartime organisation to aid Jews. Arrested by the communists in 1946, he was then released 1954. He gained his PhD in Cambridge and taught modern history at the Catholic University of Lublin. He protested at the 1976 constitution changes and was dismissed from his post in 1977. He was imprisoned during Martial Law for his work with Solidarność. In the years 1990–95 he was Polish Ambassador to Austria. He had been a leading member of the Catholic Znak group in the Sejm, a TKN (Flying University) lecturer, and General Secretary of Polish PEN. Antoni Macierewicz alleged that Bartoszewski had been an agent of Soviet special services.

Jerzy Kłoczowski (b.1924) was an AK (Home Army) survivor of the Warsaw Uprising, where he lost his right arm. He gained his PhD at Toruń University. He was professor of history at the Catholic University of Lublin, a member of Solidarność, a Senator, member of the Senate Committee for Foreign Affairs, Polish representative on the executive board of UNESCO, the first President of the Joint Committee of UNESCO and International Committee of Historical Sciences, and Polish representative at the Council of Europe. At various times he was awarded the Order of the White Eagle, Virtuti Militari, the Cross of Merit with Swords, and the Cross of Valour. In 2004 Stanisław Michalkiewicz, writing in *Najwyższy Czas!* (*Highest Time*), claimed Kłoczowski was SB agent 'Historyk', active from 1961.

Lustration 191

In December 2004 the photo-journalist Małgorzata Niezabitowska (b.1948), who had been spokesperson for Tadeusz Mazowiecki's government, was accused in the newspaper *Rzeczpospolita* of secret collaboration with the SB. She claimed the documents in IPN had been rigged to identify her as agent 'Nowak'. Initially IPN refused her the status of 'victim', implying that it trusted the archive; however, after a lengthy investigation, in June 2006 they declared she had not in fact been an agent. In January 2007 the Warsaw Court of Appeal found she had been registered without her knowledge as an SB informer and, although she had been interrogated, had refused to become an informer. Her SB 'handler' nevertheless wrote reports of meetings that never took place and included information taken from a secret wiretap of her apartment. However, IPN then appealed against this judgement and the case went back to court. In 2010 the Warsaw District Court discontinued proceedings as Niezabitowska decided to make an *autolustracja* statement.

19 General Czesław Kiszczak (b.1925) was initially a member of the PPR (Polish Workers Party), then of the PZPR (Polish United Workers Party), Minister of Interior Affairs 1981–1990, the architect of Martial Law, a close associate of General Wojciech Jaruzelski, and (briefly) Poland's last communist Prime Minster.

20 It is difficult to establish precise figures, but using the World Bank's definition of *Absolute Poverty* (the percentage of population living on less than \$4.30 per day) it has been estimated that by the late 1980s 5–10 precent of the Polish population was living in poverty. In the years 1994–2001, *Subjective Poverty* (where households judged themselves poor / very poor) remained stable around thirty-three percent, but *Relative Poverty* (those living on the poverty threshold) rose from 13.5 percent to seventeen percent. *Absolute poverty* in the period 1997–99 affected 8.4 percent of the Polish population and rose to about 13.3 percent in 2005; it fell to around 5.6 percent by 2008, but rose again to 6.5 percent by 2011 (Emigh et al. 2001: 86–7; GUS 2012). Since then poverty in Poland has been described as *stable and shallow*, meaning few live significantly below the poverty line as defined by World Bank, but poverty in Poland remains a continuing concern.

21 Ostalgia, a sentimental, good humoured, generally un-political nostalgia for daily life in the 'old east' of Soviet times, is a widespread feature of post-communist life for the older generation (Koczanowicz 2008). In its East German variety, it is best illustrated by Wolfgang Becker's film *Good Bye, Lenin!* (2003). Several East German cities have retained the *Ampelmännchen*, a traffic light showing a green man in a jaunty hat at pedestrian crossings, sometimes referred to as 'Ossie' by West Germans: the same sign figures on numerous postcards and souvenirs. In Poland writers were among the first to notice the chill wind of capitalism and lament the withdrawal of subsidy for publishing, but artists were not shy of expressing their dismay and lamenting some aspects of the change (Husarka 1994): repeats of communist-era TV shows are massively popular and there are several Polska Rzeczpospolita Ludowa (PRL, Polish People's Republic) style discos and bars in Warsaw and Kraków. In 2009 the Polish National Gallery in Warsaw organised a 'PRL' exhibition including a canteen with appropriate menu (and smells), a milk bar and an *inteligencja* apartment full of books, which proved to be massively popular (Esche et al. 2009). In 2011 the New Museum, opened in New York with an exhibition devoted to Ostalgia. In November 2015 a Soviet themed four-storey shopping mall opened in the Belarus capital of Minsk (on Lenin Street, by the Proletarian Metro station) complete with posters, uniformed attendants, a 'Stalin Bowling Alley' and an actor dressed as Lenin ('Belarus opens Soviet-themed mall' BBC News, 9 November 2015: www.bbc.co.uk/news/blogs-news-from-elsewhere-34768381).

192 *Lustration*

22 Turnout at the elections to the Sejm was as follows: 1989: 62.7 percent; 1991: 43.2 percent; 1993: 52.1 percent; 1997: 47.9 percent; 2001: 46.29 percent; 2005: 40.57 percent; 2007: 53.88 percent; 2011: 48.92 percent. In the years 1990–2010 turnout was slightly better for Presidential elections, hovering between 49–61 percent, which seems to indicate that Poles were more interested in 'leadership' than in government (www.wikipedia.com, 'Polish_parliamentary_election'). However, in the 'mature' democracies of the West (UK, France and USA) a turnout of forty percent is normal, and a forty percent share of the vote is considered a substantial measure of support.

8 The end of history, return to Europe, and rise of illiberal democracy

After Stalin's death there had been repeated attempts to persuade the Party to liberalise, but the result had been a series of intense conflicts in 1956, 1968, 1970, 1976, 1980 and then the long years of grim stalemate after the declaration of Martial Law. However, at the end of 1989, communism suddenly collapsed. Something longed-for happened at a time when it was thought impossible. Events in Hungary and Czechoslovakia were not much different. The collapse brought capitalism and democracy to people, many of whom understood them simply to be the opposite of communism, and who believed that without communism they would be both rich and free. Poland was as surprised by the collapse of communism in 1989 as it had been by independence in 1918. Just as Partition convinced many Poles they were 'innocent pilgrims', only for independence to contradict them, so communism convinced many Poles they were 'angels' and the Party were a bunch of 'maggots', only for 'freedom' to prove otherwise.

Shock therapy

Polish international debt in 1970 had been almost insignificant at about $100m, but after a very poor harvest the government attempted to remove subsidies on food. The result was a series of massive demonstrations: the milicja and army response left forty-four dead and more than a thousand injured; three thousand were arrested. Władysław Gomułka was replaced by Edward Gierek as first secretary. As the Party had done in 1956, he reversed the price increases, offered wage increases, promised sweeping economic reforms and political change, and took on substantial foreign loans. The plan was to invest 38.5 percent of the loans in fixed industrial assets and fund a real wage-rise of seventeen percent. However, the communist system was not built to accommodate this kind of hard-currency cash-flow and the whole thing was so badly managed that Gierek actually spent 69.5 percent of the loan on investment and wages rose by thirty-six percent. At the same time the Middle East war of 1973 drove up oil prices and the cost of industrial imports on which Polish industrial investments now relied. Poland's foreign debt grew rapidly from about $700m in 1972 to

194 The end of history

$6b by 1975 and thereafter, as Neal Ascherson put it, the graph of debt just climbed vertically (Ascherson 1981: 109; Ash 1983: 15).

By the mid seventies it was obvious to Western banks that their loans – based on the flow of petro-dollars – had been invested in vast, hopelessly outdated, massively inefficient industrial enterprises that would never operate at a profit. And where this was not the case, the money had been spent on subsidising basic commodities. The banks began to suspect that rather than modernising the economy, investing in agriculture, improving living standards or creating new housing, further loans would be used to pay the interest on earlier loans. In 1976, in order to introduce some element of 'market reality' into the economy, the Polish government again attempted to remove subsidies on a wide range of products, including food; this again resulted in violence and the price rise was postponed. The communists tried again in 1980 and the result was Solidarność, followed by a year of stalemate and the declaration of Martial Law.

After joining the IMF in 1986, General Jaruzelski's military government was forced to attempt restructuring the economy. However, as Gierek had found, it was not possible to introduce elements of a free market while retaining a planned economy, and by 1989 Poland had paid off only about 20%–30% of its debt. Jaruzelski was cornered and began to feel the government would lose nothing by talking with dissidents and oppositionists – they might have something interesting to say, could be a useful bargaining chip with Western governments and could always be blamed if things went wrong. He agreed to Round Table talks, but these did not go as anyone predicted. In the USSR glasnost and perestroika were gaining momentum, and the Polish communists, instead of hanging on to power at all costs, agreed to move over quietly, to shift to a market economy and to hold almost-free elections. The communists thought they were playing 'the long-game' and would be able to resume power once the economy improved. But within a few weeks the communist regimes in Hungary, Czechoslovakia, East Germany, Bulgaria and Romania all disappeared. Almost overnight the political and economic climate changed, and while much of the Polish debt was written off, the remainder was rescheduled for repayment by 2024. That Poles felt easy about casting off communism came as a surprise only to a few hard-line communists who had spent their lives within the Party bubble (Rae 2012).

However, the sudden transition to modernity stretched East-Central Europe over two time zones – one based in the late 1940s (but not so very different from fifty years before that where the horse and cart were still common in country districts), the other located at the end of the twentieth century as it nudged towards the millennium. The leap meant moving from the age of the manual typewriter, skipping entirely the intervening period of golf-ball-IBM typewriters and even daisy-wheel printers, to land in the early days of the mobile phone and the Wi-Fi laser printer. This leap was neither joyful nor simple, and the sudden transition to modernity affected

The end of history   195

all aspects of life, but particularly national identity, in ways that very few had foreseen.

In the months after the collapse of communism, a social schism rapidly developed in Poland reminiscent of nineteenth century arguments between the *narodowcy* (nationalists) and the *zachodniofile* (Westernophiles), both intent on their definition of Polishness and their vision of the future. The Polish *inteligencja* wanted to espouse Western liberal values and spoke of a cultural 'return to Europe' (Jedlicki 1999). Most Poles were impatient to join the EEC (as it then was) and to enjoy the products of a market economy. Also, to distance themselves from the USSR and emphasise they were, after all, the easternmost bastion of Western civilisation, the military and politicians were anxious to join NATO.

However, after the initial excitement, the pace of reform was slow and, with the end of communism, it became clear that Poland's economic infrastructure, which had struggled for more than a decade, was in a state of rapid collapse. Signed into law in December 1989 and starting in January 1990, Leszek Balcerowicz (professor of economics, governor of the Central Bank of Poland, deputy prime minister and minister of finance) introduced his policy of 'shock therapy'. There was no time to ease the adjustment or prepare the workforce: state subsidies across a wide range of good and services were simply withdrawn. Almost overnight real incomes fell by forty percent, state pensions (there was no other kind) were reduced to almost nothing and more than three million (roughly eleven percent of the workforce) lost their jobs (Marvin 2011).

Also, just because the law no longer forbade it did not mean that private enterprise immediately and automatically became everywhere apparent. A great many Party functionaries, *nomenklatura* and bureaucrats metamorphosed into eleventh-hour anti-communists, well-connected, smooth-talking pluralists, ambitious politicians and ubiquitous *biznesmen* (businessmen). These people are often referred to as *spadachroniarzy* (parachutists), because when they jumped from the Party, they used 'connections', padded bank balances, access to 'services' and 'protection' to ensure they landed softly in good jobs.

The buzz-words of the new vocabulary (often in English) were 'business', 'dealer', 'market economy', 'joint-venture', 'fax', 'manager', 'democratisation', 'civil society' and 'Europe'. However, after more than forty years of communism, there was no stock exchange, little in the way of international banking and the *złoty* was not an 'exchangeable currency'. Under communism almost everyone had been an employee of the state, so there was no class of 'home-grown' risk-takers, entrepreneurs, investors or experienced businessmen, only officials, clerks, office-managers, bureaucrats and administrators. Although Western economists talked glibly about 'the market', the economies of East-Central Europe were dominated not by the market but by a barely functioning state sector. Apart from the agricultural sector, much of which was still privately owned, and a substantial *czarny*

196   *The end of history*

rynek (black market), there was no private sector and no way to establish a market price for any commodity produced in the state sector.

Balcerowicz's 'shock therapy' was also hampered by problems with the revised Polish constitution, constant conflict between the president and the prime minister, and by the fact that no less than twenty-nine political parties were returned to the first parliament. The centre-left coalition government, tarnished by the connection of its membership to communism, was constrained by the vested interests of the surviving bureaucracy, state-owned industry, the judiciary and the banks: by 1994 only about sixteen percent of state-owned enterprises had been sold off. The slow progress made all politicians figures of suspicion for the public and an easy target for the increasingly vociferous right wing.

At the same time Poland, still burdened by international debt, was encouraged to spend scarce hard currency employing 'advisers' from the Rand Corporation, Thatcher Foundation and the Freedom Foundation, who all pushed for massive privatisation and the sale of public wealth, preferably to Western multi-national enterprises, international franchises, moguls like Rupert Murdoch and Robert Maxwell, and conglomerates like the giant Springer Press. However, foreign entrepreneurs, while they were prepared to set up their own enterprises, were reluctant to buy the decrepit and outdated steel-works, coal mines, shipyards, shoe factories, textile mills and chemical works – all massively over-staffed, relying on huge government subsidy, running at an incredible loss and producing small quantities of goods that either did not sell on the open market or were diverted to the black market.[1] Suddenly companies like Pollena, the state-owned cosmetics giant, began to lose their previously captive domestic market to the slick advertising of foreign competitors like Nivea, Dove, L'Oréal and Estée Lauder ('Polena Ostrzeszów'). Pollena survived, mainly because it came to specialise in natural and ecological products, but many state concerns could not compete in a free market and either went bankrupt or they were forced to sell off the bulk of their facilities to foreign competitors, who promptly closed them down. However, the arrival of foreign firms also operated to stimulate the economy, contribute to employment, increase production and consumption, and provide tax revenues for further start-up enterprises. In what was now an almost totally un-regulated and un-monitored economy, about six thousand foreign firms established themselves in Poland and perhaps a million tiny start-up companies emerged from street-trade, independent agriculture and the black market (Cienski 2018).

Adam Michnik, Lech Wałęsa (b.1943), Leszek Balcerowicz (b.1947), Jacek Kuroń (1943–2004), Karol Modzelewski (b.1937), Tadeusz Mazowiecki (1927–2013), Bronisław Geremek (1932–2008), Zbigniew Bujak (b.1954) and many others who ten years before had been dissidents, Solidarność activists and KOR advisors defending workers' rights, now found themselves in government, or serving as senators and Sejm deputies, imposing unpopular austerity measures – measures similar to those the communists had unsuccessfully tried to impose in 1956, 1970, 1976 and 1980.

The end of history 197

From the moment communism collapsed, Polish society began to experience fear, confusion and a huge and sudden *ciemnota* (darkening) (Jenkins 1991). The public asked: 'have we endured long years of hardship, harassment and Martial Law for this?' They noted that many of the new leadership were intellectuals and dissident former Party members and that some were Jewish, and many concluded that if the people who had once claimed to defend the workers now peddled the same harsh policies the communists had tried to impose, this surely confirmed their suspicion of 'plots against Poland', 'hidden communists', 'hidden Jews', 'treacherous intellectuals' and 'enemies within'. This was good reason for hostility towards all politicians, suspicion of 'others', indifference to democracy and, increasingly, resistance to the modernity peddled by 'Europe'.

Left-liberal thought and intellectual discussion, already compromised by a connection to the Party, appeared increasingly ponderous, idealistic, naive and irrelevant (Michnik 2011: 159). The problems of democratic decision-making, the difficulties of deciding on a political future and the reality of economic reform all fed a pervasive, lingering, reactionary, populist paranoia from which the right wing and the Church gathered strength. Also, after the misery of 'shock therapy', instead of bringing serious re-training, up-skilling and investment for international competition, both the myriad tiny start-up companies and the giant multi-nationals offered mainly unskilled work and insecure, short-term, zero-hours contracts. As far as the multi-nationals were concerned, Poles were cheaper than Western workers, but even as they set up their factories the multi-nationals were already considering Romania, Bulgaria or the Far East, where workers were cheaper still and labour laws much weaker, and beyond that they were contemplating how to replace workers with robots (Meek 2017: 3–15).

By the mid 1990s 'shock therapy' had begun to show some positive results, but success was ambiguous and uneven: in general the larger cities did well; the towns did less well; state-owned industry, where it had not been sold off or collapsed entirely, did very badly; but rural areas and the eastern borderlands remained almost untouched. Peasant farmers were tied to their property and could not be easily retrained or redeployed, nor could their holdings be made more economically viable. Ten years after the fall of communism, agriculture generated only about three percent of GDP, but still involved about twenty percent of the population.

'Shock therapy' introduced the stark prospect of economic failure, soaring interest rates, rapid inflation, foreign competition, bankruptcy, homelessness and unemployment where these things had previously been unknown. For many people, rising prices and plummeting living standards meshed intimately with disappointment at the indecisiveness of democracy and the failure of capitalism to immediately improve daily life. At the same time a residue of cynicism and ideas of entitlement and full employment lingered from the communist years, along with a growing resentment at foreign influence, and these fed Poland's well-established cult of victimhood.[2]

198   *The end of history*

The end of history

In 1992 Frances Fukuyama had assured readers that the collapse of communism and the 'victory' of capitalism had certain meaning: 'What we may be witnessing is not just the end of the Cold War [...] but the end of history as such: that is, the end point of mankind's ideological evolution and the universalization of western liberal democracy as the final form of human government' (Fukuyama 1992: 33). In this reading of the moment, the possibility of 'future as change' was greatly reduced: the teleology of globalisation meant nothing more of any great importance was expected to happen in human history on this planet. History and the sense of chronological 'development' that saw the past unfolding into the future as a perpetual series of opportunities for change was collapsed into a repetition of what already existed: democracy and capitalism. This might offer minor variations but could not radically depart from the 'victory' of the present moment. In economic terms this translated as the entrenchment of an economic order that saw neo-liberal capitalism as the final and highest stage of human history – a kind of global capitalist Utopia.

The 'end of history' took the humanist idea of 'progress' towards a 'higher' form of awareness, and existence was stripped of its disruptive and developmental connotations: 'progress' meant political leadership would now ensure better entrepreneurship and greater economic efficiency. Writers in particular took this to mean everything they considered – politics, culture, literature, history, characters, plots, even the language they worked with – would henceforward be merely a kind of recycling. But not everyone agreed with the end of history idea. Misha Glenny had already produced *The Rebirth of History* (Glenny 1993) and Eva Hoffman (b.1945) was shortly to produce *Exit into History* (Hoffman 1993). Neither of these writers saw the collapse of communism as the end of history, and subsequent developments proved them right. Indeed, as these writers pointed out, for something that came to an end in 1989 there had been an awful lot of history since, most of it – particularly in the Balkans, Ukraine, Crimea, Nagorno-Karabakh, Georgia and Chechnya – extremely unpleasant.

If this really was the end of history, somebody forgot to tell the Poles. In terms of its psyche, its inner life, since the collapse of communism Poland felt obliged to recapitulate several stages of its oft obliterated history simply to find itself and work out what it wanted. For them this was a chance to resume arguments interrupted by Partition in 1772, resumed in 1918, interrupted again in 1939 and continued only *sotto voce* after 1945. At his inauguration, President Lech Wałęsa demonstrated this resumption by receiving his symbols of office not from outgoing communist President General Jaruzelski, but from Ryszard Kaczorowski, President of the Polish Government-in-Exile, which had been based in London since 1939 and had never recognised the communist regime: they had refused to return the symbols of government until a legitimate president was elected.

The end of history   199

That communism had not exactly been defeated but had imploded while attempting long-overdue reform did not figure in the 'end of history' version of events. Lacking legitimacy and ideologically bankrupt, the collapse was no wonder: in retrospect the surprise was that communism lasted so long. Even then it was not much of a victory for capitalism – except in so far as communism disappeared – and most of what followed did not endorse the idea of a victory for democracy either. While people had been united in wanting communism gone, there was no consensus as to what should follow. Given the proximity of Russia, capitalism and democracy seemed logical, even essential, but there was no agreement as to what these things might be or how they might come about. Traditional identity appeared to be under threat, capitalism was not well understood, liberal values were not cherished by all and democracy was far from the agreed aim of all East-Central Europeans. For many, the mythology of the 'golden age' of independence was dominated by the folk memory of inter-war dictators like Marshal Piłsudski and Admiral Horthy. Increasingly, a return to the ethno-centric policies of Endecja seemed to offer some solution and refuge from the storm.

It was in this context that the extensive Polish *nomenklatura*, ex-Party people and redundant state employees discovered a path forwards and the method of their own political transformation. In the 1950s First Secretary Gomułka, harking back to the inter-war strategies of Piłsudski, had shown that in Poland communism and nationalism shared a very similar world-view; now, riding a tidal wave of economic hardship, the displaced *nomenklatura* grasped that modernity, liberalism and democracy were strange, unusual and threatening to traditional Polish life. Now, foreigners, 'others', capitalism and the liberalism of 'Europe' could all be used to refinance the economy, but as the old communist job-security evaporated and millions became unemployed, these things could also be combined by populist politicians into a very convenient 'enemy'.

Perhaps the most clear-sighted response came from Edward Luttwak, who pierced the bland language of Fukuyama's prediction to the brutal impact such changes would work and their probable effect. He observed that 'capitalism unobstructed by public regulations, cartels, monopolies, oligopolies, effective trade unions, cultural inhibitions or kinship obligations is the ultimate engine of economic growth'. He went on to say that 'the capitalist engine' achieves growth 'because its relentless competition destroys old structures and methods, thus allowing more efficient structures and methods to rise in their place'. He warned that 'structural change can inflict more disruption on working lives, firms, entire industries and their localities than individuals can absorb, or the connective tissue of friendships, families, clans, elective groupings, neighbourhoods, villages, towns, cities or even nations can withstand'. He predicted that 'security' would become a key issue and that rapid change would deliver a 'product-improved fascistic party dedicated to the enhancement of personal economic security of

200 The end of history

the broad masses of (mainly) white collar working people'. Luttwak saw a party arising that would be like Mussolini's Fascist Party before its alliance with Nazism, not directly racist, but acting as a corporate restraint on corporate Darwinism, delaying and blocking the effects of globalisation. For Poland and Hungary this was to prove a remarkably accurate prediction (Luttwak 1994).

Writers and the return to Europe

Prior to membership of the EU, Polish writers and intellectuals had played an important part in shaping public opinion. In 1991, writer and editor Wacław Pacłowski, sounding a note of desperation, felt that membership would be the only way Poland could move away from the crumbling USSR and at the same time avoid falling under the power of Germany (Zagajewski 1990: 6).

Now we might read Hartwig's shifting perspectives, the emerging ambiguities, the conflict between tradition and the modern, the mismatch of culture and experience as a warning. In 1994 poet Zbigniew Herbert (1924–98) warned that, contrary to expectation, Poland had not in fact been delivered from communism because the 'old professional elites' were still in place (Poppek & Gelberg 1994).

In summary, although the next step seemed logical, Hartwig and Herbert both suggested Poland was not ready for 'Europe', and also perhaps that liberal Europe was not the development model many supposed.

The literary critic Maria Janion (b.1926) anticipated that release from communism and accession to the EU would create a battlefield for conflicting versions of Polish identity. She predicted the 'Romantic paradigm' of Polish culture – that all Poles always behaved according to the 'God, Honour, Fatherland' formulation of Józef Poniatowski (1763–1813) and the idea that to enter the annals of history and achieve greatness it was probably best to die for Poland – would both be challenged by modernity and by contact with the West. In her view, to become a guardian of future Polish culture it was first essential to break the shroud of silence and denial, to recover a memory and to reach an understanding of what had happened to both Poles and Jews under the Nazis. For her this meant criticising and revising Polish myths and self-deceptions (Janion 2000).[3]

In 2000 the literary critic Piotr Śliwiński (b.1962), in an essay entitled 'Are Things Worse or is this Normal? Polish Poetry in the 1990s', admitted that for Poles 'normality' was proving to be a 'challenge of hellish complexity' (Śliwiński 2000: 340). The poet Ewa Lipska (b.1945), in her poem 'Mr Schmetterling thinks about a United Europe', warned that while many saw joining 'Europe' as a solution, others saw EU membership as a mistake, a surrender, 'a misconceived holiday offer', something like 'a stomach medicine, bitter and acrid *Montana* drops... both good and bad for you' (Lipska 2000: 115). In 2002 populist politician Andrzej Lepper (1954–2011), leader of the right-wing Samoobrona (Self-Defence) Party, warned that joining

The end of history 201

the EU would be to 'sell out' Poland. For this he enjoyed a boost from nationalist supporters in the elections of the following year and became a power broker in the next coalition government.[4]

Even Polish football (*piłka nożna* in Polish, but increasingly referred to as *futbol*), stuck in the style, tactics, kit and haircuts of the 1970s, was still a minority interest. However, it was quickly affected by contact with the West and by the 'new financial situation'. As unemployment grew and political protection evaporated, uncensored TV and press coverage began to show the game as it really was: troubled by match-fixing, corrupt refereeing and increasingly by gangs of violent 'supporters'. In 1998–9 FIFA intervened in a long-running dispute between Marian Dziurowicz, president of PZPN (Polski Związek Piłki Nożnej, Polish Football Union), and Jacek Dębski, head of UKFiT (Urząd Kultury Fizycznej i Turystyki, Department of Physical Culture and Tourism), and for a while FIFA threatened to suspend Poland's membership over political interference, before relenting.

In 2000, after Dębski gave an interview in *Gazeta Wyborcza* in which he claimed he had been asked by high-ranking members of RS-AWS (Ruch Społeczny-Akcja Wyborcza Solidarność, Social Movement–Solidarity Election Action, a small right-wing party) to find compromising material on Aleksander Kwaśniewski (Polish president) and Stanisław Paszczyk (President of the Polish Olympic Committee), Dębski was fired from UKFiT and expelled from RS-AWS. Shortly afterwards the press began to expose Dębski's links to organised crime in Austria and it was revealed he had been a secret collaborator with UOP (Urząd Ochrony Państwa, Department of State Protection).[5] In 2001 Dębski was lured out of a restaurant by a call on his mobile phone and killed by a single shot to the head. It is not known if this was a 'hit' by rivals, the mafia or by UOP.[6]

The taint of corruption around Dębski's death was an indicator of changes already in train. Over the following five years there were more stories about players connected to the mafia, the mafia taking a cut of transfer fees, of referees being 'influenced' by the mafia, match-fixing, nepotism and financial shenanigans. The collapse of Klub Pogoń Szczecin in 2003, the rumours of corruption around Poland's bid to host the Euro 2012 competition, the illegal sale of players' picture-rights, and illegal sponsorship deals with the Polish army, ITI (International Trading and Investments, Poland's largest media company) and Tele-fonika (a large mobile phone company) all indicated that while Balcerowicz's 'shock therapy' had reduced government funding for sport from 0.7 percent of the government budget in 1994 to 0.055 percent in 2004, the influx of foreign capital was exerting a new kind of pressure. In the first ten years after 2004 something like €79bn of EU money flowed into infrastructure projects, making capital available for the development of road, rail and air connections, but also for the construction of new stadiums, clubs and training facilities. EU money changed what had been a minority-interest sport into a popular, not always legal, money-making business (Hubbard 2019: 264–75; Wilson 2006: 42–67).

202 *The end of history*

The EU, focused on speeding up the entry process for ex-communist states and then on the introduction and expansion of the euro, failed to notice that while membership was intended to overcome nationalism, it had begun to provoke a nationalist reaction. In 2004, just as Poland joined the EU, Polish theatre sounded a warning note with director Jan Klata's adaptation of Witkiewicz's play *Janulka, córka Fizdejki* (Janulka, Daughter of Fidejk, 1923). There, instead of the Teutonic knights invading Lithuania, the new version of the play offered German EU politicians colonising Poland: in one scene two men in concentration camp uniforms ate from a bag of crisps, indicating that Poland's hunger was to be satisfied only by German-style consumerism. Polish victimhood was pre-figured and confirmed in this image of *resentyment* (resentiment).[7] However, in spite of Poland's fear of German power, their fear of Russia was even greater: to stay unaligned and outside NATO and the EU seemed impossible: to turn westwards was the only possibility.

The price of victory

In the past it had often been the case that the vanquished were forced to emigrate with defeat, but now the sons and daughters of the victorious anti-communists found they had to leave Poland if they were to prosper. With EU membership accomplished in 2004 about two million young Poles left for work in Western Europe. Free movement of people meant that numbers were not monitored closely, but in the UK alone it has been estimated that 125,000 Poles arrived in the first year, rising to between 800,000 and one million by the end of the decade (Fleming 2018: 139). Not only was this exodus very costly in human terms, it was destructive of family life, drained youth, skills and talent out of the Polish economy, and emptied the villages.[8]

For young women in particular, the offer of a well-paid job in the West often turned out to be a lure for people-trafficking, ending in slavery, exotic dancing or prostitution. Even then, in Poland the remittances from this exodus did not raise living standards to Western levels. For those who had been interested in the literary culture of the West, close contact proved to be a disappointment. They quickly discovered that the version of culture established by mass-produced, cheaply priced translations of Western books once offered by the communists was not the reality of Western culture. If anything, Paris, London and Berlin were mostly indifferent and on occasion hostile. The young Poles who went west for work did not necessarily like what they saw: they did not like the harsh capitalism of the black economy, poor accommodation, long hours, low wages, lack of spirituality, absence of family, competition with dark-skinned foreigners and the generally 'hostile environment'. They did not become more secular, multi-cultural or liberal as a result of this encounter: on the contrary, for the most part, traditional conservative, Catholic identity norms were reinforced along with perhaps a deeper appreciation of Poland.

The end of history   203

In the years 2007–15, under a government led by Donald Tusk and PO (Platforma Obywatelskie, Civic Platform), there was a brief economic boom, but this was brought about by EU subsidies and by exporting unemployment rather than by any real improvement in the economy as a whole. The Polish automotive industry, constituting about eleven percent of Polish GDP, was perhaps one of the more successful areas of the economy and a good example of EU investment. The Polski Fiat assembly plant had been established in Poland in the 1920s, and apart from a break during wartime had been a strong presence since the early 1960s, but in the main the Central Plan dictated that Poland bought cars and buses from East Germany and Hungary during the communist period. With the collapse of communism the Polish firm Solaris began to grow, Fiat undertook to expand its operations and several foreign car manufacturers (Opel, Toyota, Volkswagen, MAN, Volvo and Scania) set up factories in the south and west of the country. After 1989 car production increased – there had been a ten-year waiting list for cars throughout the communist period – peaked with 650,000 vehicles in 1999, then declined rapidly. In the period 2000–2003 Poland produced only about 300,000 light vehicles a year. However, after Poland joined the EU the car-market expanded rapidly: subsidy and EU employment laws stabilised production, stimulated sales and persuaded the manufacturers to stay in Poland. Production doubled by 2005–6 and almost tripled by 2009 (GUS 2018).

The shift to the right under Thatcher, Kohl, Mitterrand and Reagan in the 1980s had not encouraged the West to think ahead or consider how a transition might be managed or what might happen in East-Central Europe as a result. Indeed, the decades since the end of the Cold War demonstrated only that, in East-Central Europe, without an existential enemy, global capitalism operated to concentrate wealth into the hands of a tiny minority while it deflected public unease into distrust, paranoia and the search for 'hidden enemies'. In doing so it undermined the trust, compassion and empathy upon which open society, democracy and (ultimately) capitalism depend (Smith 2010). This had not been foreseen in the triumphalism of the end of history, where the important thing was not the installation of effective democratic processes, the development of an effective economy or the growth of a liberal civil society, but simply the 'fact' of 'victory'.

The EU, complacent about its new members and distracted by plans for the euro – a European Monetary Union that, operating without a central treasury, nevertheless attempted to unify EU currency, yoking economies as disparate as the German and Greek – did not register that the political parties rising to prominence in East-Central Europe, though they were happy to accept EU finance and sported the trappings of democracy, were part of a rising 'brown tide' of nationalists and populists who had no interest in 'liberal values', were suspicious of 'foreign influence' and convinced that 'enemies' were plotting.

The idea that they might be morally compromised, in an abusive, inferior, ambiguous, neo-colonial relationship with the EU, with NATO and with

204 *The end of history*

'the West' was confirmed for many Poles in 2007, when it was revealed that President Aleksander Kwaśniewski had agreed to a CIA 'black site', a 'rendition facility' for 'enhanced interrogation', in the Soviet-era military compound at Stare Kjekuty, conveniently near Szmany airport in north-eastern Poland (Grey 2007). That same year, in her poem 'Freedom', Ewa Lipska questioned Poland's sense of its place in Europe, Poland's attitude to 'freedom' and the resurgence of the pietistic Catholic Church (Kovacik 2015: 51).

There was a growing feeling that not only was the Soviet option – communism – utterly and forever tainted, but Poland had tried to improve its economy and repair its political life by importing Western fixes and the solution – capitalism – also appeared to be unacceptable.[9] Indeed, the conflation of capitalism with the idea of 'the West' made it seem the new set-up was indifferent and perhaps even hostile to Polish national identity, while for many Poles national identity seemed one of the few things offering certainty in a rapidly changing world.

The start of the culture war

After communism, Solidarity, Martial Law, economic collapse and reform, the conservative Polish electorate wanted 'certainty and stability' (Millard 2012: 198). That is, they wanted the government to focus on the problem of global economic integration and the reduction of the social hazards of 'financialisation' – in particular the priority of capital over labour, creditor over debtor, boss over worker. However, left and right interpreted these tasks in completely different ways.

For the left, 'certainty and stability' meant espousing liberal-humanist 'European values', grappling with the problematic nature of democracy, cautiously engaging with privatisation and edging softly towards multi-culturalism. In practice, dissidents and liberals had four main aims for Poland: democratic government, a free-market economy, integration into NATO and membership of the EU. It took more than two decades, but by about 2016 all these things had been achieved. However, the exhausted and outnumbered liberal-left had been in difficulties from the start. Firstly, they did not notice when the coalition of oppositionists that had gone to war against communism disbanded upon achieving its main aim. Then, they assumed that after communism the centrality and desirability of liberal-left 'humanist' values was simply self-evident. Thirdly, they underestimated the extent to which they were compromised by their previous connection to communism. Finally, their uncertainty, fear, inexperience and complacency resulted in tactical errors. Adam Michnik admitted: 'We thought regaining our freedom and our sovereignty, our entry into the EU and NATO, should be a fundamental value for everyone. But that did not turn out to be the case' (Sierakowski & Michnik 2017).

For the right, although for the most part they shared an interest in democratic government, a free-market economy, integration into NATO and

The end of history   205

membership of the EU, the relationship to modernity was altogether more uncertain, angular and uncomfortable. Poland's economy had improved considerably since Balcerowicz's reforms – indeed, Poland was the only EU country not to enter recession in the Banking Crisis of 2008–10. This was mainly because Poland's senior bankers – many of them still in position from communist times – had refused to buy into US debt, particularly the toxic 'sub-prime' mortgage market. However, Poland was still one of the poorest countries in the EU and as the number of gated communities – an indicator of insecurity among those with money – rose rapidly to become the highest in Europe, it was increasingly clear that there could be no 'quick fix' for the Polish economy (Johnsson 2013). By 2016, in terms of Purchasing Power Parity, Poland was roughly on a par with Greece, which had lost roughly one third of its economy and was still reeling from its own internal financial crisis and the massive international financial crisis of 2008–10 (World Economic Outlook 2016: Report for Selected Countries and Subjects). According to the best predictions available, it would be 2053 before Poland could match the Eurozone average wage, until 2059 to match the UK, and 2077 to catch up with German wage-levels (Partington 2019).

What complicated matters and brought the feelings of the electorate to light was the Syrian refugee crisis of 2015. The sudden influx of refugees travelling up though the Balkans into Hungary and Austria prompted a massive reaction against the supra-nationalism of the EU and licenced chauvinism on a scale not witnessed in Europe since the 1930s. The 'shock' and shame of reform still lingered and the Polish electorate, menaced by uncertainty, certain only of its victimhood, had increasingly taken refuge in unreconstructed national tradition. In the pursuit of elusive wealth, security and ease, the right wing placed an unfathomable trust in a homogeneous and undiluted national identity by favouring a 'strong', retrograde authoritarian government ruling through moral pressure (blame and shame), and by offering to repair disorder, restore stability and resist the dilution of Christianity and traditional national identity by refusing EU refugee quotas (Cienski 2018).

Dissidents, who had often been sheltered by the Church, compromised and disarmed by loyalty to their former ally, were unprepared for the speed of the Catholic Church's resurgent ambition. The Church had supported Solidarność, but as an institution it had also been the main partner of communism. It had benefited enormously from the deal made by Cardinal Wyszyński in the mid 1950s when it agreed not to stoke opposition and disciplined priests who did. Its loyalty was rewarded, and under communism the Church grew enormously (Brumberg 1983: 317; Piekarski 1979: 44–54; Szajkowski 1983: 19). One of the last acts of the dying Communist Party in May 1989, even as the Round Table talks were taking place, had been to confirm the Church's ownership of Protestant and Orthodox churches given to it by the communists, to return 65,000 hectares of confiscated land and 490 confiscated buildings, and to pay 140,000,000 złoties (roughly €33.5m) for Church property that had not been returned (Cienski 2010).

206 The end of history

The following year, before the first post-communist government had even taken office, the Church resumed teaching religion in schools. A short while later the government agreed to pay the salary of chaplains to the army, police and hospitals, along with 14,000 teachers of religion. In 1991 several Catholic radio stations were licenced, including Radio Maryja, which soon started to pump out dogmatic, anti-Semitic, homophobic, anti-abortion messages and 'séances of hate' directed at former members of the *nomenklatura* (Hoffman 1993: 101). In 1993 the Church campaigned vigorously for legislation to reverse Poland's liberal abortion laws. They wanted a total ban on all forms of abortion with prison sentences for women who had illegal abortions, criminal investigations into 'suspicious' miscarriages and in case doctors unintentionally induced a miscarriage they planned to restrict antenatal testing. In 1997 the Catholic channel TV-Niepokalanów was licenced.[10] The creation of Catholic media outlets was to be a key factor in the rise of PiS (Prawo i Sprawiedliwość, Law and Justice),[11] which rapidly became the unofficial mouthpiece of the Church.

PiS first achieved electoral success as part of a coalition government with the ultra-Catholic LPR (Liga Polskich Rodzin, League of Polish Families), appealing particularly to the private farmers and rural cooperatives of the emerging 'green bourgeoisie' in 'old', rural eastern Poland. Roman Giertych, LPR Minister for Education, in addition to wanting to make all abortion illegal and ban *Teletubbies* as part of a drive to outlaw 'homosexual culture' in schools, made a significant attack on Polish literature by planning to re-write the national school curriculum to reduce obstacles to 'patriotic thought'. He proposed to retain the works of Henryk Sienkiewicz, Cyprian Norwid and Juliusz Słowacki, and to add Jan Dobraczyński (1910–94, best known for his eulogy to Pope Jan Paweł II), but in addition to deleting Kafka and Goethe he planned to drop Witold Gombrowicz.

In his diaries Gombrowicz had been highly critical of the communists, but also of the behaviour of 'true Polish patriots'. In his novel *Ferdydurke* (1937) he told the story of a young man kidnapped by a professor and forcibly indoctrinated into a patriotic version of Polish identity through the 'greats' of Polish literature. Gombrowicz was top of Giertych's 'hit list', which also included 'unpatriotic' writers like Joseph Conrad and S.I. Witkiewicz. The attempted change, which was immediately likened to the behaviour of the Nazis and the communists, provoked a furious reaction from the Polish PEN club. The descendants of Sienkiewicz wrote to Giertych asking that the author's name be removed from the new syllabus and added to the list of the banned. Booksellers made window displays of the books Giertych sought to ban. Contemporary writers also made their feelings known. Novelist Andrzej Stasiuk suggested Giertych should 'go and raise chickens'. Poet Wisława Szymborska accused Giertych of having an 'enormous sense of humour'. The writer Marcin Swietlicki (b.1961) noted that Giertych had mistakenly attributed Plato's *Defence of Socrates* to Aristotle and added: 'I think he has forgotten Plato was a faggot'. Eventually Prime Minister Jarosław Kaczyński intervened to calm public protest and

The end of history   207

over-rule Giertych's proposal. Giertych accused Kaczyński of 'lacking the slightest loyalty' (*The Times*, 9 June 2017).

After several coalition governments stalled, in 2015 PiS was elected as Poland's first non-coalition government. Their electoral success came about for a variety of reasons, but basically the centre-left PO (Platform Obywatelska, Citizens' Platform), though the economy was by this time performing well, lacked dynamism. Many older Poles felt there had been too much change but too little effect, while many younger Poles felt there had insufficient change to radically improve their prospects. PO failed to realise that not only did many voters no longer take an interest in politics, they were so alienated by the antics of politicians and so cynical about what 'freedom' had delivered that they felt could do without 'politics' altogether.[12] For them the reactionary nature of PiS seemed 'natural'. Significantly, PiS was most successful in appealing to miners, farmers, shopkeepers, unskilled workers, the unemployed and pensioners in the more traditional farming areas of Galicia and Congress Poland, much of which had hardly been touched by Balcerowicz's 'shock therapy', and much less successful in the industrialised western and northern territories settled by Poles after 1945.

Although PiS received only nineteen percent of the total possible vote it took this as a popular mandate and began to act as the semi-official mouthpiece of the Catholic Church. In spite of massive opposition, in March 2018 PiS passed legislation so that in effect there was no such thing as a legal abortion in Poland. The very reactionary Polish episcopate, which had been a source of concern at the Vatican since the time of Pope Jan Paweł, seemed to be moving further to the right and senior clerics began to mutter darkly that the new Pope Francis (elected Pope in 2013) was perhaps the most subtle and dangerous communist they had ever encountered. It was around this time that the liberal-left, harking back to pre-war practice, began to refer to the Church as *czarnokracja* (blackocracy). Even so, the Church – which believes the separation of Church and state is a 'communist-inspired idea' – struggled to get itself written into the constitution as *the* state religion, failed to get compulsory religious education back into schools and failed to get crucifixes on school walls.

The leadership of PiS is profoundly suspicious of any success in business – 'the money must have come from somewhere' – and offers a popular blend of ethno-nationalism, socialist inclination and Catholic social thinking: it includes protectionist economic policies, limitations on short-term contracts, a minimum wage, tax breaks for individuals (but not for state-owned enterprises), universal health care, a lower retirement age, a substantial child benefit scheme called 'Family 500+' providing 500zł (approx. 125 euros) per month, an increase in the minimum wage and free medication for over 75s. It was these 'social measures', rather than investment, that caused a surge in consumption and general economic activity in 2015–17. Poland's GDP grew from 2.7% in 2016 to 4.0% in 2017, but the surge was predicted to slow considerably in 2018 ('Poland's GDP Growth to Reach 4% in 2017 Before Slowing Down 2018 says World Bank' 2017).

208 *The end of history*

As part of a promised purge of Polish society and restoration of 'truly national culture', PiS nourished anger with Germany, thinly veiled contempt for the Ukraine, Belarus and Lithuania, and outright suspicion of Russia. It was frustrated that the 'good life' continued to elude it, claimed that 'foreign influence' (shorthand for international Jewry) undermined traditional Polish identity and felt the conservative Polish episcopate was still much too liberal. PiS made use of classic Polish romantic patriotism but projected an image more akin to the muscular positivism of the late nineteenth century. However, in many ways PiS harked back to the political style and policy solutions once favoured by Endecja and by the often-banned ONR-Falanga (Obóz Narodowo Radykalny-Falanga, National Camp Radical-Falange, the Polish Fascist Party), and their idea of 'reform' smacked of the 'cleansing' offered by the inter-war Sanacja regime.

As early as 1984 the Czech writer Milan Kundera (b.1929) had warned that in mythology the smaller nations of East-Central Europe were not only a powerful intellectual and cultural element within Europe, but a 'community of fate' which in the Arcadian version of the myth was a Utopia, but which in reality was a squabbling, suspicious nightmare of conservative attitudes, traditional platitudes, competing national interests and jealous identities. Kundera was aware that East-Central Europe had once been *k. und k.* (Kaiserliche und königliche, **Imperial and Royal**), but had been renamed *kakania* (punning on *kaka*) by the Austrian novelist Robert Musil (1880–1942).[13] Kundera, while accusing the West of 'bowing out' of the fate of 'the East', had also revealed his own deeply ambivalent attitude to the idea of 'Europe' (Kundera 1984a, 1984b). But his warning was not misplaced.

In what since 1945 had been mono-cultural, mono-lingual societies, latent fears, national paranoia and xenophobia were easily ratcheted up by the Syrian refugee crisis of 2015 to emerge as anti-German, anti-EU sentiment. The PiS response to the refugee crisis was indignant, surly and selfish: it claimed the EU was a tame organisation designed to disguise German domination of Europe, and that refugees were a problem created by Germany as part of a plot to dilute Polish culture and compromise Polish national identity. In what was clearly a response to humiliation, marginalisation and powerlessness, the V4 states united in refusing to host any refugees, defining them instead as 'illegal immigrants'. Indeed, PiS Chairman Jarosław Kaczyński said he regarded this refusal as his way of 'showing the sick Europe of today the path back to health, fundamental values, true freedom and a stronger civilization based on Christianity' (Observer View 2018). His comment reveals the assumption that Poland is somehow outside 'Europe' but at the same time represents something more 'healthy' and 'true', more Christian, more civilised, more European than 'Europe'. What Poles had learned was that everything the Communist Party told them about communism was a lie, but everything they had warned of about capitalism was true. But what PiS electoral success revealed was that East-Central Europe was no better prepared for membership of the EU than it had been for the collapse of communism.

Poland and illiberal democracy

The EU allocated Poland a staggering €82.5bn (£74bn) for the years 2014–20. After joining in 2004 it received more than any other member state from the EU Cohesion Fund for infrastructure, development and investment and has profited massively from EU membership. At present about 60% of Poland's public investment comes from the EU and, although PiS supporters are unwilling to recognise this, the economy has improved rapidly as a result.

However, more than a decade after joining the EU, Poland feels ambushed by the small print of their membership and PiS has shown it nothing but contempt (Majchrowicz-Bączyk 2020). In spite of an international outcry, PiS encouraged commercial logging in the primeval 15,000-year-old Puszcza Białowieska (Białowieża Forest) – a Polish National Park, a designated UNESCO World Heritage Site and an 'EU Natura 2000' Special Area of Conservation. PiS ignored EU heritage and environmental concerns, dismissing criticism as 'unacceptable meddling in Polish domestic affairs'. In December 2015 Jarosław Kaczyński, angry with the parliamentary opposition, described them as traitors: 'In Poland, there is a horrible tradition of national treason, a habit of informing on Poland to foreign bodies. And that's what it is, as if it's in their genes, in the genes of Poles of the worst sort' (Lyman & Berendt 2015). Kaczyński's illiberal democracy has several times brought hundreds of thousands onto the streets to protest at budget manoeuvres, police raids on women's organisations, changes to abortion laws, interference in national media, changes to the structure and appointment of the judiciary, and control of the Constitutional Tribunal (Sierakowski 2017).[14]

The speed with which Poland was expected to catch up and digest its own history after the suppressions and distortions of communism proved to be a massive problem, and with anything shameful or unpleasant the default populist position was always 'us and our version of history over you and yours'. Indeed, the end of history ushered in a period when memory itself came under siege – what could be remembered, what should be remembered, what it was appropriate to remember, how it should be remembered and how commemorated – all became contentious and massively politicised (Harper 2018). The publication of Jan T. Gross' *Neighbours* exposed the 1941 massacre of Jews by Poles in the village of Jedwabne. This book confirmed in some detail Maria Janion's prediction of conflict over Polish identity and contradicted Poland's image of itself as heroic. By questioning Poland's traditional monopoly of victimhood, the book highlighted the theme of anti-Semitism in Poland and provoked a bitter debate about Polish–Jewish relations (Gross 1988; Bikont 2004; Polonsky & Michlic 2004). However, instead of addressing the issues raised by Gross's research, PiS first threatened to arrest Gross, then, when they could find no adequate law to do so, threatened to take away his award of the Order of Merit and framed the new crime of 'insult to the Polish nation', which passed into law in February 2018.

210 *The end of history*

Ostensibly this 'defamation law' was aimed at preventing foreign journalists and politicians from referring to 'Polish death camps' when they meant concentration camps, work camps or death camps built by the Nazis during the occupation on Polish territory.[15] However, the effect of the law was also to make it dangerous to attempt any discussion of *szmalcowniki* ('lardies', Poles who blackmailed Jews or betrayed them to the Nazis for payment), the Granatowa Policja (Navy-Blue Police) who functioned under Nazi command, the rash of post-war pogroms, murders and attacks on Jews in Kraków, Łódź, Nowy Targ, Kielce and several other towns, or collaboration with the communists and NKVD during the civil war.[16] Attributing blame to Poles for complicity in Nazi crimes was initially punishable by three years in prison.[17]

In practice the new law reduced the responsibility of perpetrators and made it an offence to argue for any kind of Polish responsibility in relation to crimes against peace, crimes against humanity, war-crimes and the Holocaust. Although the new 'defamation law' specifically excluded scholarly research and insisted on documentary evidence for any accusation, it nevertheless stifled research: in effect it insisted all Poles had always behaved impeccably and made it perilous to assert otherwise. By suppressing discussion and investigation the new law also contradicted PiS efforts to 'out' hidden communists and operated to legitimise a steady growth in anti-Semitism. Effectively, it encouraged a competitive attitude towards wartime suffering – who suffered more, Poles or Jews? Surveys found that the proportion of those who thought Poles suffered as badly as Jews during the war increased from thirty-nine percent in 1992 to sixty-two percent in 2012, while those who thought that Jews suffered more fell from forty-six percent to thirty-two percent. Eighty percent of believed Poles did the 'best they could' to help Jews and more than sixty percent thought Poles had 'no reasons to feel guilty about Jews' (Tilles & Richardson 2018).

Previous Polish governments had tried to balance competing narratives (both self-questioning and self-serving) with calls for documentary historical evidence. Former president Bronisław Komorowski had declared that the Polish 'nation of victims must recognise the difficult truth that it was also a perpetrator'. But PiS wanted to emphasise only the popular narrative of Polish suffering and heroism. By claiming that all those who opposed PiS were unpatriotic agents of foreign interests, enemies within, it fostered the idea that Poland needed to defend itself against enemies without and traitors within. By appealing to a sense of victimhood in Poland's experience of invasion, occupation and subjugation at foreign hands, it promoted a siege mentality while boosting the party's image as the champion of 'true Poles'. It used this mind-set to justify its overhaul of the Polish legal system and the constitution, to control the media and to justify an abrasive foreign policy towards Germany, Russia and the EU.

Whatever its patriotic intention, the 'defamation law' inaugurated a bizarre form of state-sponsored Holocaust denial. In 2017, as the law was being debated in the Sejm, Poland's Minister of Culture publicly questioned

The end of history 211

the authority of the director of the Museum of the History of Polish Jews in Warsaw, whose post was due for renewal (Davies 2018). At the same time, after a lengthy and bitter legal battle, the director of a new World War II museum in Gdańsk was removed from his post for 'failing to give sufficient emphasis to the Polish elements of WWII'.[18] After this a number of museum directors came under attack on right-wing websites and by PiS politicians.

The new law was also credited with launching a campaign of disinformation and abuse by Polish nationalists. For example, fabricated accusations against the museum at Auschwitz included the claim that guides refused to admit that wartime guards at the camp were German, that the Polish flag could not be raised at the camp and that the number of Polish prisoners who died at the camp had never been officially acknowledged.

In February 2019 a conference on the Holocaust at the Paris School of Advanced Studies in the Social Sciences (EHESS) was disrupted by 'extreme right-wing' demonstrators who had travelled from Poland and the UK. Historians, including Jan Grabowski and Jan T. Gross, were interrupted, called 'stinking dirty Jews', 'traitors' and 'communists', and chased by demonstrators. Film of the event was later shown on Polish official media and the Pilecki Institute, a Warsaw-based research centre focusing on totalitarianism, criticised the conference on Twitter (Matthews 2019).

Liberal news and media outlets were early targets for PiS, and the government did not shrink from using economic means to achieve political ends. The PiS government banned state agencies, government-owned companies and government departments from subscribing to, or advertising in, the newspapers that had dared to criticise PiS – *Polityka*, *Newsweek* and *Gazeta Wyborcza* (Election Gazette, edited by ex-dissident Adam Michnik). As advertisements and income transferred to government-controlled and pro-government media outlets, these newspapers saw a huge drop in circulation and revenue. If PiS had not entirely silenced opposition, they certainly muted it (MacDowall & van der Zee 2017).

The Church- and state-controlled media outlets, on the other hand, promoted the PiS line that 'freedom' had been botched. Poland, they claimed, was still run by hidden communists and Jews (though for many these terms were identical): 'outing' them would allow privatisation to flourish and bring wealth to Poland. PiS leader Jarosław Kaczyński (a great admirer of inter-war leader Marshal Józef Piłsudski) made it clear that any 'hand raised against the Church is a hand raised against Poland'. He has spoken of 'Impossibilism' – his theory that no serious reform has been possible in Poland because democratic checks and balances on the government are in fact manifestations of the hidden interests of liberal elites, disguised communists, 'forces abroad' (code for Jewish interests) and foreign powers – basically anyone who disagrees with him – all of whom are joined in a massive conspiracy against Poland.

Kaczyński has fed populist paranoia about plots against Poland with claims that the supreme court is 'the stronghold of post-communists in Poland', that it is 'protecting people who had served the old communist

212   *The end of history*

regime' and that 'the country's judicial system is controlled by lefties and subordinated to foreign forces'. In reality, only about ten percent of judges currently holding office survive from the communist period (Davies 2018). Kaczyński has also suggested that the Smolensk plane crash in April 2010 that killed his twin brother, President Lech Kaczyński, and a large number of government representatives was a Russian plot to aid his rival Donald Tusk, who, he said, was a Russian agent. He referred to those who died in the crash as *poległy* (fallen), and as *bohaterowie* (heroes), as if they had died in battle, linking them with the traditional figures of Polish history. He has said getting to the truth about the crash would signify *zwycięstwo* (victory).

This is not to suggest that all Poles agree with PiS. There have been numerous protests and opposition marches. In July 2017 a demonstration to oppose direct government control of the judiciary was described by the government-controlled channel TVP as a 'street revolt to bring Islamic immigrants to Poland'. TVP characterised the opposition as 'defenders of paedophiles and alimony-dodgers'. On 19 October 2017, outside Warsaw's Palace of Culture, a fifty-four-year-old man distributed several dozen copies of a letter addressed to the Polish people. The letter accused PiS of attacking the Rule of Law, liberal democracy, civil liberties and of undermining the judiciary; it condemned PiS for discrimination against immigrants, women, the LGBTQ+ community and Muslims, and for destroying the environment by supporting coal-based energy and allowing commercial logging in the Białowieża Forest. He then set himself alight. Demonstrations against PiS resulted in a proposed new law making anti-government demonstrations illegal.

But most demonstrations were not anti-government. On 11 November 2017 – in Western Europe marked as Armistice Day – 60,000 Poles marched through Warsaw to celebrate independence from Russia, Austria and Germany at the end of World War I. The march had taken place annually on that date for about a decade, organised by ONR (the revived pre-war Polish Fascist Party), Młodzież Wszechpolska (All-Polish Youth, a far-right youth movement best known for coordinating racist social media campaigns), and Ruch Narodowy (National Movement, ultra-nationalist). Krzysztof Bosak of Ruch Narodowy spoke of Islamisation as 'the process of exchange of population, by which people of European origin are replaced by people from Africa and Asia'. The march attracted members of several other far-right, nationalist and white supremacist groups, including Szturmowcy (Stormers, after the Nazi SA). The march also attracted members of the European 'black block': Tommy Robinson, founder of the English Defence League, and Roberto Fiore, leader of the Italian far-right Forza Nuova (New Force). There were a great many family groups on the march and many attended simply as a demonstration of patriotism. However, marchers carried banners reading: 'Refugees out!', 'Islamic Holocaust', 'White Europe of Brotherly Nations', 'Pure Blood, Clear Mind', 'Europe will be White or Uninhabited', 'We Want God', and written in Gothic script *Deus Vult* (Latin: 'God wills it', the battle cry of the eleventh-century crusaders).

A substantial minority of demonstrators marched under the Celtic cross (a cross with a nimbus or ring around the junction), which has been co-opted as the pan-European symbol of the ultra-right (Davies 2017b; Mason 2017). There was a brief whiff of reality when a TV reporter for TVP Info (now part of the PiS propaganda machine rather than a genuine news outlet) asked a demonstrator what it meant to be on the march. He replied: 'It means to remove from power… the Jews'.

PiS Interior Minister Mariusz Błaszczak described the march as a 'beautiful sight', and tightly controlled TV news reported it simply as 'a great march of patriots'.

PFN (Polska Fundacja Narodowa, Polish National Foundation, set up by PiS in 2016 to 'promote Poland abroad') criticised coverage of the march, claiming the international press slandered the good name of Poland and insulted the Polish people. Polish President Andrzej Duda, a member of PiS, said: '"There is no place in Poland" for xenophobia, pathological nationalism and antisemitism and that the country must remain a land open to all who want to come together and work for the good of the nation', as if he was unaware of the feelings and opinions his party had legitimised (www.theguardian.com/world/2017/nov/13/polish-president-condemns-far-right-scenes-at-independence-day-march).

On 17 July 2017, nearly thirty years after the collapse of communism, a new De-Communisation Bill was signed into law. With this, PiS aimed to prevent the 'propagation of fascism or another totalitarian system' in schools, universities and the press, and set in motion a state-sponsored scheme to remove from public places all statues, monuments and memorials commemorating Red Army war dead, the Soviet contribution to the war against fascism, Soviet–Polish Friendship and the Soviet Liberation of Poland. The law also sanctioned the change of street names commemorating communist heroes and also seemed likely to make the publication of standard texts from the left a questionable act. Violations of this law could be punishable with a maximum two-year jail sentence. The new law is supported by the RN (Ruch Narodowy, National Movement), a political umbrella organisation uniting ONR, MW (Młodzież Wszechpolska, All-Polish Youth, a revived inter-war Catholic-nationalist organisation) and several smaller far-right organisations with roots in inter-war Poland's Endecja movement. Opponents and critics of the new law were labelled 'Russian agents of influence' by TV Channel 1. Within weeks of its appearance, police in Szczecin used the new law to break up an academic conference exploring the legacy of Karl Marx. Shortly after this Marek Jędraszewski, the archbishop of Kraków, endorsed the PiS anti-gay line by warning voters a 'rainbow plague' had replaced the 'red plague' that had once blighted the country.

Polish writers and the right

After 1989 Poland changed rapidly. Writers across the whole of East-Central Europe became increasingly aware that their traditions and experience

214 The end of history

were very different from those of 'the West' and that 'national significance' and their established social role had perhaps blocked them from exploring less easily defined, more personal subjects (Poppek & Gelberg 1994).[19]

Although he had resisted the Party all his adult life, the collapse of communism brought Zbigniew Herbert no great satisfaction. By 1994 he had dismissed most of his contemporaries (Andrzejewski, Iwaszkiewicz, Konwicki, Brandys) as collaborators of one kind or another. He had also broken off his long friendship with Michnik, saying that as the difficulties of freedom became clear Michnik's refusal to adopt an authoritative pose as an intellectual and as a politician indicated a loss of moral direction. By this stage left-liberal opinion (though it had been useful in opposing communism) had become distasteful to him (Poppek & Gelberg 1994).

Women writers in Poland have often stood at an angle to the mainstream male-dominated literary tradition and to the political world. While the novelist Zofia Kossak (1890–1968) might be said to have continued the romantic tradition by exploring male experience of war, resistance and insurrection, Maria Dąbrowska and Zofia Nałkowska situated themselves in the practical, explorative, positivist mode and measured social progress in terms of the opportunities available to women. Women writers had good reason to be critical of traditional attitudes.

Challenges to tradition have come from other directions too, and some of the most serious have come from voices previously excluded from traditional mainstream discourse. And in this it is important to remember that a challenge to the traditional sexual norms of the Church – either from feminism or from the LGBTQ+ community – is by definition a serious transgression of the national code. In conservative, Catholic, post-communist Poland the word *kobieta* (woman) carries traditionalist overtones, while the words *feminizm* and *feminista* (feminism and feminist) are pejorative, signifying to traditionalists something questionable, dubious, unacceptable. *Gender* (usually written in English) is another problematic word, particularly for schools, colleges and universities offering gender studies. The concept of gender is poorly understood but the word, often meaning 'women' but hinting at 'modern women' or LGBTQ+ issues, is often used in reference to any discussion of sex, sexuality or sexual preference and usually signifies a challenge to tradition. 'Gender' has become a political target for the Church and PiS, both of whom have campaigned to 'remove gender from the classroom'. President Kaczyński refers to 'gender' as a hostile ideology and considers 'genderists' as enemies of the nation.

Women writers are aware that they do not live in a post-masculine world, but also that they are probably less hindered now than at any time in Polish history: though their rights to abortion have been severely curtailed by PiS, they are relieved of the responsibility to produce, nourish and protect the nation's youth and if they want to can now write much as they please. Given that travel in the EU is much easier, they have become increasingly aware that the 'inner life' of Poland and the possibilities open to women are

The end of history 215

not like those of Western Europe and this has been both exhilarating and frustrating.

While older, rural Poland is still generally uncomfortable with modernity, young writers do not hanker after the lost *kresy* territories and do not fear a German attempt to regain the 'Recovered Territories': they are haunted by German and Jewish ghosts and conscious that gender roles, sexuality and sexual preference are negotiable in ways that Polish tradition does not easily accommodate (Phillips 2013). Katarzyna Borun-Jagodzińska (b.1956), in her poem 'The Literary Life', supposed that in Poland women might only aspire to be a writer's muse rather than to actually write. Krystyna Lars (b.1950), in 'Soiree at the Czar's Plenipotentiary', wondered what would have become of Polish literature if Adam Mickiewicz had shredded his insurrectionary manuscripts and, instead of going into exile in Paris, had stayed with his Russian friends in Moscow. Anna Piwowska (b.1963), in 'What do Men Bring?', concluded simply 'we always survive them' (Kovacik 2015: 83–97). The potential for apartness from male-dominated tradition is clear in the open appeal to lesbians in the poetry of Izabella Filipiak (b.1961). In her volume *Pani Intuita* (*Ms. Intuition*, 2002), she offered a direct response to Herbert's *Pan Cogito* (*Mr. Thinker*, 1974), rejecting the 'phallocentric order' of his insistence on a male sense of judgement, indomitable male heroism and his male indifference to exile or death (Filipiak 2002).

Writers like Magdalena Tulli (b.1955), Ewa Kuryluk (b.1946), Natasza Goerke (b.1960), Agnieszka Taborska (b.1961), Marzanna Kielar (b.1963), Dorota Masłowska (b.1963), Grażyna Plebanek (b.1967), Wioleta Greg (b.1974) and A.M. Bakalar (b.1975) have all found unsettling ways to 'disrupt ingrained assumptions about aesthetics and literature', to 'undermine qualities considered as the norm in a phallocentric order of things' and to offer instead writing that extols qualities that were 'traditionally considered weaknesses – such as lack of coherence, rationality, and logic' (Schwartz & Von Flotow 2007: 9). But this is ironic and deceptive: the challenge of these writers does not promote weakness, accepts difference, is coherent, rational and strategic.

The transgressive urge of feminist and LGBTQ+ writers in Poland has become increasingly open. For example, Michał Witkowski (b.1975), in the novel *Lubiewo* (*Love Town*, 2005), contradicted the homophobic taboos of the resurgent Church by writing openly of *gey* (gay) life in communist Wrocław against the background of AIDS in Poland. His publisher claims it as 'Poland's first queer novel' (Witkowski 2009: 341). Witkowski gives voice to the marginalised 'doomed old queens', 'drag artists', 'aunties' and 'retired gays' who populate his novel. He openly explores the idea of a 'queer sensibility' and subverts the 'straight' world with characters who rejoice in having both male and female names, who refer to their pick-up place in the public toilets in Park Szczytnicki as 'the front-line' and dwell on the problems of 'coming out', 'cruising', 'cottaging', picking up Russian soldiers and robbing drunks. Witkowski explicitly 'queers' the language

216   *The end of history*

with gay slang, code-words and catch-phrases, double-entendres and arch campiness. The title of the novel refers to Lubiewo in north-western Poland, a town whose name is suggestive because it derives from *lubić* (to love), and where each summer large numbers of gay men camp among the dunes. Witkowski alludes to Gombrowicz, Iwaszkiewicz and Miron Białoszewski (1922–83), who, even if homosexuality shaped their thinking, did not produce overtly 'queer literature'. With its challenge to traditional opinion and its puns on Mickiewicz's sacrosanct romantic text *Dziady* (Forefather's Eve), this novel is part of an interactive exchange, dialogue and challenge to the writing of the past.

The openly gay poet Jacek Dehnel (b.1980) and his husband Piotr Tarczyński live in Gdańsk, where in 2019 the liberal mayor Paweł Adamowicz was assassinated. Together they have written *Tajemnica domu helcelów* (*The Secret of the House of Helcel*, 2015; *Mrs Mohr Goes Missing*, 2019) under the female pseudonym Maryla Szymiczkowa. This popular and successful thriller is set in Kraków in 1893, full of sly digs at tradition and the nature of national identity, and is stuffed with examples of snobbery and the decayed *szlachta* culture that still dominated Polish society at the end of the nineteenth century. The main character is Zofia Turbotyńska, whose husband (she hastens to tell everybody) has recently become Professor of Anatomy at the Jagiellonian University: as a career snob and busybody his elevation is a much-needed boost to her social status. The story is her investigation into a series of deaths at a high-class old people's home – and the solution lies in the complexities of genealogy and intermarriage between the *szlachta* families. At the conclusion of the novel one of the characters whose national identity has been the subject of much debate, speculation and confusion is asked if she is 'Austrian, Polish, Hungarian or Ruthenian?' She replies: 'What does it matter? There's no such thing as a nation, there are only kingdoms and empires. Under one power, under one crown… you'll see that in twenty, at most fifty years from now there won't be any nations. I am myself. Now here, now there' (Szymiczkowa 2019: 292–3). With its echo of Joseph Heller's *Catch 22*, this attitude not only undermines the idea of empire but also the idea of fixed and unalterable national identity. An attitude like this could hardly endear 'Szymiczkowa' to nationalist opinion.

But it is in Dehnel's poetic novel *Lala* (2007) that we find a direct challenge to traditional gender-perception. The novel is a lament for Lala, his grandmother, and concentrates on her stories about life, her marriages, affairs and adventures in inter-war Poland, under Nazi occupation and under communism, but also as part of her struggle with dementia and memory-loss. Lala is very much a representative of her class and her generation in that she is independent, well-read, liberal, generous, and politically and socially savvy. However, the novel identifies with female experience and the real challenge is in the grammar. The past tense in Polish conjugates 'not just by person and number, but also gender'. Thus, the past tense, first-person singular indicative of the verb *być* (to be, I was), is: *byłem* (masc.), *byłam* (fem.). Dehnel uses the feminine form when he refers to himself. This

The end of history   217

causes his father's hackles to rise, but is the occasion of great delight among his 'herd' of female relatives (Dehnel 2019: 319). Obliquely, the novel has a lot to say about the connections between memory, identity and tradition, but also about Polish culture and the idea of Europe. Dehnel believes that 'culture relies on intelligent repetition' (Dehnel 2019: 313), but he asks: 'Europe – what exactly is Europe?' Slowly a picture emerges, but rather than a living culture it is a fantasy derived from his grandmother's stories and it is already in the past tense (Dehnel 2019: 323–5).

In his poetry the idea of tradition is fluid. He acknowledges the influence of Herbert and Miłosz and harnesses terza rima and the traditional Polish thirteen-syllable line with personal rather than national concerns and with satirical comment on the post-communist world. But in *Lala* ideas of tradition, identity, history and Europe collide as something experienced but not yet fully processed. In the end, as Dehnel surveys the 'broad vista of successive generations' and the traditions and memories his family transmitted to him, he acknowledges the idea of transience means 'ancient tradition' and derives from 'the land of my forbears, a non-existent land, that land known as the past'. He experiences tradition, with 'the doors of each generation in turn silently closing behind me', as a process where 'we just keep endlessly laying out a series of self-generating elements. And that is all we need' (Dehnel 2019: 332, 340).

After nearly more than three decades of post-communist 'freedom', Polish writers know they are no longer obliged to consider 'the national question', to declare their credentials, prove their loyalty or enlist support with everything they write – or at last they are not obliged to do these things in the way they were done in the past. They also know that Poles are not obliged to read them. Polish writers and intellectuals are aware that in the 'free market' writing does not necessarily 'do' anything, and even when it does, it takes effect at glacial speeds. Now, lacking the guarantee of quality bestowed by censorship, writers explore, develop and console the post-communist, post-German, post-Jewish 'inner life' and mine the complications of identity. Since 1989 there has been an active reassessment of the standing and reputation of Szymborska, Miłosz, Herbert, the Generation of '68 and the *bruLion* poets (Wilczek 2000: 375–7). There are signs too that younger writers – those who grew up in democratic Poland – have begun to question the political opinions 'about communism handed down by tradition, wondering how things might have gone a differently.

Literary tradition is not only a connection to the writers of the past, it is a prism through which writers view other writers and carries with it an authenticating and legitimising personal power. A living literary tradition looks in three directions: writers look to the past to see how things were done, they look at contemporary writers to see how they are responding to the world around them, and they look to the future to see how their writing might develop. But when writers engage with foreign literature they are forced to consider how 'normal' their assumptions about tradition might be, and to what extent they can transcend their own norms to speak outside

218 *The end of history*

their own culture. Zagajewski, for example, is fascinated by C.P. Cavafy (1863–1933), but he marvels that the Greek poet never mentioned the fall of Constantinople (1453), after which Christian Byzantium crumbled and Islamic Turkish rule expanded into the Balkans. That Zagajewski finds no trace of an event that was possibly even more significant than the Partition of Poland is noteworthy, but leaves Zagajewski bewildered. Translated into Polish terms, the idea that a Polish poet might not be intimately concerned with 'the nation' – even in 2017 – was barely thinkable. And this was the case even for Zagajewski, a poet who spent the years 1982–2002 in Paris (Zagajewski 2017: 86).

But tradition may be regarded ironically by those who stand slightly to one side of the main Catholic tradition. Jerzy Pilch (b.1952), for example, a Lutheran, in his novel *Tysiąc spokojnych miast* (*A Thousand Peaceful Cities*), set in 1963, has Mr Trąba, a verbose Lutheran pastor, consider the nature of tradition. He laments the 'shameful renunciation of the tradition of uprising that has reigned in our land for years' (Pilch 2009: 58). He condemns Polish romantic poets, with the exception of Mickiewicz, as 'for the most part, a gang of hundred-eyed peacocks, which is to say unpunished graphomaniacs endowed with the useless art of rhyme', and then pleads 'but let's not go too deeply into literature, it always condemns one to sterility' (Pilch 2009: 119). He laments that it is no longer possible to join the classical 'Asiatic and European' tradition of terrorism, which consisted mainly of robbing banks, and feels this leaves him no choice but to assassinate First Secretary Gomułka (Pilch 2009: 84).

The argument conveys not only a jibe about the invisible nature of Protestant tradition in Poland and a dig at Polish political tradition, but also confusion about the nature of citizenship and its relation to religion and ethnicity.

It is possible to distinguish several lines, fashions and trends in Polish literary tradition, and while the romantic and the positivist strands together make up the mainstream – surrealism, futurism, modernism, gothic, romance, science fiction, fantasy, personal themes, crime novels, thrillers, criticism of the Church and questioning of identity by the younger generation of writers, many of them women – there is also a substantial avant-garde strand: the tradition of breaking with tradition.

Adam Zagajewski has said that to write in Polish means 'accepting the complex legacy of Polish history' and he has described writing as a struggle to see into the future while feeling 'inspired and impeded by tradition', which he thinks of as 'that great tumult of dead voices' (Zagajewski 2004: 192–8). Writers of the post-communist years are likely to be seen by traditional readers as un-Polish – naive liberals or communist stooges – rather than as patriotic keepers of the national flame. Their struggle is private, personal and usually financially unrewarding: as novelist Andrzej Stasiuk (b.1960) put it, frankly, the act of writing is 'nothing but a form of loneliness' (Burkot 1996: 147).

The end of history   219

Protesting at the way Polish perceptions have been side-tracked, Agata Pyzik (b.1983) wrote: 'we should be addressing the contemporary history of the former East countries, and speaking about its notorious past, but in a dialectical way, where the reshaping of the past by the present and the present by the past can become visible' (Pyzik 2014: 286). However, much to their surprise, the social group of writers and intellectuals who once led the opposition to communism now found themselves increasingly described as dangerous 'hidden enemies'. Any liberal challenge to the 'popular will', Polish victimhood, traditional identity or the authority of the Church risks being labelled 'un-Polish' and any feminist challenge to tradition – particularly to heterosexuality and the 'phallocentric order' – risks being labelled 'unpatriotic'.

When Olga Tokarczuk (b.1962), in a television interview about her recently published novel *The Book of Jacob* (2014), spoke of Poland not as a plucky survivor of oppression but referred to the inter-war 'pacification' of the Ukraine and the Polonisation of minorities, and described Poland as the perpetrator of 'horrendous acts of colonisation', including the imposition of serfdom and various pogroms, right-wingers and patriots branded her a *targowiczanin;* she received death threats and her publisher had to hire bodyguards for her.[20] Her reputation was attacked by right-wing historians from Reduta (Redoubt), an organisation that supports laws aiming to supress the 'defamation of Poland'. A group in Nowa Ruda, where Tokarczuk has a house, posted death threats on Facebook. One message said: 'You'll never be safe now in this country, you'll always be treated as a liar'. Another read: 'Get out of our country since you seem to have such a problem with it'. Another said: 'Hitler's conspirators were Ms Tokarczuk's compatriots'. This last was a reference to the Ukrainians – the surname Tokarczuk is Ukrainian. She confessed: 'I was very naive. I thought we'd be able to discuss the dark areas in our history'. The paradigm had shifted much further than Tokarczuk had appreciated: the definition of who might speak of, and for, the nation, and the opinions they might safely hold, had changed. (www.economist.com/prospero/2016/03/10/olga-tokarczuks-polish-narrative; Armistead 2018).

In October 2019 it was announced that Olga Tokarczuk had been awarded the Nobel Prize for Literature. She was the fifth Polish writer to receive the award. This news was greeted with muted congratulations from PiS-controlled media.

Rather than 'time honoured' mutual respect, the relationship between the various elements of Polish literary tradition have often been a grudging, judgemental hand-shake down the years – full of blame, mistrust, disappointment, unhealed wounds, personal envy, professional rivalry, political animosity, ideological conflict and inter-generational friction. But taken as a whole, Polish literary tradition is a form of engagement, a democracy of the literate: contradiction and confrontation are forms of development, an acknowledgement of what went before, an uneasy accommodation

220   *The end of history*

with a complex cultural inheritance, a re-negotiation of experience and re-interpretation of identity. But because its national identity evolved under great stress, Poland has a combative culture: as a social entity it knows best how to fight. It tends to be unsatisfied with the humdrum, suspicious of the 'normal', judges democracy insufficiently decisive and finds it difficult to shift its perspective on tradition: when challenged, the default position is to refine the definition of who is 'us'. As a reflex this culture tends to identify those outside tradition as foreigners, and those who disagree with tradition as 'not real Poles', even as hidden traitors plotting against Poland.

With the re-emergence of Poland in 1918, and again with the collapse of communism, writers wondered how literary tradition might develop in a democratic Poland. Now, over thirty years since the collapse of communism, in a country dominated by the ultra-conservative Catholic Church and the illiberal PiS, writers wonder how to produce (and sell) something other than recycled national myths and the worship of 'straight', dead, male heroes. Although it is not the prevailing political trend, writers cling to the idea that literature is a key cultural site where the content of words, political ideas, the shifting contours of national tradition, ideas of equality and inclusiveness, and a constantly uneasy sense of identity are all tested. Writing is a focal point where the liberal-left defines its values and gathers its allies to face an increasingly intolerant right.

The Polish Right and 'Europe'

In December 2017 Prime Minister Matuesz Morawiecki, who had just taken office, was tasked with improving Poland's relationship with the EU. He engaged in a massive cabinet 'reshuffle'. Antoni Macierewicz, the defence minister whose radical restructuring of the armed forces was said to have put Poland's security (particularly with regard to Russia) at risk, and who, possibly more significantly, had failed to find any evidence of a Russian plot in the 2010 Smolensk plane crash, was sacked. The environment minister who had tripled logging in the Białowieża Forest, bringing about an EU fine of €100,000 (£88,000) per day, was sacked. Foreign Minister Witold Waszczykowski, widely scapegoated for bungling the relationship with the EU, was also sacked.[21] At first glance the PiS government appeared to be sending a conciliatory signal to the EU. This was confirmed when, in December 2018, President Andrzej Duda, in what was a clear concession to the EU, reversed the PiS decision to force judges appointed by the communists to retire, reinstating two dozen supreme court justices. In November 2019 the ECJ, again attempting to bolster the judiciary against political interference, ruled that PiS could not force female judges to retire five years before male judges and could not allow some judges to stay on after reaching the age of retirement. However, while this was designed to reassure the EU that Poland had no intention of either defying or leaving the EU, it did not defuse the wider confrontation.

Poland continued illegal logging in Białowieża until April 2018 (by which time 190,000 cubic metres of forest – about 10,000 trees – had been felled);

The end of history 221

changes to the constitution were not reversed and Justice Minister Zbigniew Ziobro, author of those changes, retained his post. Poland also continued to refuse a quota of refugees from the Middle East.[22] At the end of 2018 the 74-year-old Lech Wałęsa came out of retirement to campaign against PiS. In retaliation PiS denounced him as a communist stooge. Poland's chances of becoming a 'normal' place receded again ('Poland Judiciary Reforms' 2017; 'Poland's ruling party reinstates supreme court judges' 18 December 2018).

Populism breeds corruption. The big surprise in a country dominated by the moral judgement of an ultra-conservative Catholic hierarchy is that a government mired in corruption should continue to be popular.

In Poland the 'speed and ferocity' of the anti-liberal assault reveals not only the underlying paranoia of Polish society and the weakness of democratic institutions, but the inexperience and 'generally poor quality' of the opposition politicians (Ash 2017a).

In many ways the ambition of the PiS lies somewhere between the nationalism of the inter-war Endecja Party (Narodowa Demokracja, National Democracy) and the racist 'Catholic-totalitarian' ONR-Falanga. However, in its nationalism, its social policies, search for social cohesion, insistence on ethnic and cultural homogeneity, one-party democracy and dislike of pluralism, it also resembles the style of the Communist Party under First Secretary Władysław Gomułka (1905–1982) – a kind of national communism without Marxism. That a contemporary party should resemble the inter-war right wing *and* Polish communism may at first seem odd, but these regimes had much in common: an intimate accommodation with Catholicism; a fear of traitors within and enemies without; the certainty of their own victimhood; the fear of 'foreign influence' and the belief they must act to protect an embattled national identity – which in reality was just about the only thing the rulers and the ruled could agree on. These notions intersect with the belief that somebody – Jews, hidden communists, *geys*, 'genderists', foreigners – must be plotting against Poland and that 'strong' (authoritarian) leadership is needed to create new heroes, extend the national tradition of *żałoba* (mourning) and restore a mythical, mystical national unity.

The ease with which the ideas of the far right now intersect across the whole landscape of Polish conservatism, victimhood, Catholicism and ethno-nationalism to animate ideas of a massive anti-Polish conspiracy indicates how far the language and ideas of the far right have become normative, now bind even those who do not consider themselves to be on the far right and do so in ways PiS seems unwilling to recognise and incapable of controlling. In Poland and Hungary the greatest ally of the illiberal, nationalist right has been the weakness of the centrist and liberal opposition parties.

Illiberal democracy in Hungary

After the uprising of 1956, Hungary had been quiet and (compared to Poland at least) relatively prosperous: censorship and press control had been very relaxed so by the end of the 1980s the lines of control, what it was possible for writers and critics to say, had become very blurry. When

222 The end of history

the time had come, Hungary's transition to democracy had been very low key and undramatic. With the departure of General Secretary János Kádár in 1988, the Hungarian Parliament adopted a 'democracy package' that included trade union pluralism, freedom of association, freedom of assembly, freedom of the press, a new electoral law and a radical revision of the constitution. The changes to the constitution transformed Hungary from a People's Republic to the Republic of Hungary, guaranteed human and civil rights, and ensured separation of powers between the judicial, legislative and executive branches of government. Soviet troops began leaving the country in 1990. Inevitably the first democratic governments formed were coalitions, which, for more or less the same reasons as in Poland, proved to be less than satisfactory.

Since 2014, when it achieved a majority in parliament and could rule without coalition partners, Fidesz (Fidesz–Magyar Polgári Szövetség, Fidesz–Hungarian Civic Alliance) has formed the Hungarian government. Prime Minister Viktor Orbán revels in being labelled an 'illiberal democrat' and in an election speech in 2014 even promised to build an 'illiberal state'. Orbán claims he is engaged in a defence of 'Christian culture' against a 'Muslim invasion' and has often said that forty years ago Europe was Hungary's ambition, but now Hungary is the future of Europe. After his re-election in 2016, Orbán used his 'popular mandate' to fill the constitutional court with allies in order to re-write the constitution, promoted a political colleague to Chief Public Prosecutor, and placed thousands of supporters at the heads of previously independent bodies, including the national bank, election committees, cultural institutes and sporting federations. 'Orbanisation', which fed from a rich stream of national paranoia, was the main agent for a steady rightward shift in Hungarian politics, opening up a space for the growth of the extreme right wing Jobbik Party (Magyarországért Mozgalom, Movement for a Better Hungary).[23]

Orbán made news and media outlets an early target. In October 2016 he engineered the closure of the privately owned, left-leaning, highly critical newspaper *Népszabadság* (*Liberty of the People*). Journalists arrived at work to find they had been suspended and were not allowed into the building. Publication ceased, the website was disconnected and the departure of CEO Balázs Rónai was announced. Acting CEO Viktor Katona announced the liquidation of *Népszabadság* and resigned immediately claiming health problems. Although *Népszabadság* had made a profit of HUF 130 million ($480,000) in 2015, Mediaworks Hungary Zrt (the owners) said closure was a simple business decision. However, meetings between Orbán and Mediaworks had been reported as early as June of that year. Ownership was transferred to a holding company linked to Lőrinc Mészáros, a childhood footballing friend and oligarch ally, who under Orbán tripled his wealth to HF106bn (€327m) and, in a single day, acquired 192 regional newspapers. He is also mayor of Felcsút (Orbán's home village) and chairman of the local Puskás FC, who courtesy of Orbán have a four-thousand-seat stadium – twice the capacity of the entire village population. It has been estimated

The end of history 223

that eighty-three percent of Mészáros' earnings derive from EU funding. This is one of several corruption cases involving Orbán, his family and friends – including EU attempts to recover €283m 'misspent' in building a new Budapest metro line – currently under investigation by OLAF (the EU's anti-fraud office) (Goldblatt & Nolan 2018; 'Mediaworks Hungary suspends publication of *Népszabadság* and nol.hu' 2016).[24]

Andras Schweitzer, vice-chairman of Magyarországi Európa Társaság (Hungarian Europe Society), described how Fidesz, with no significant challenge from the parliamentary opposition, attacked newspapers, university teachers, foreign-owned banks, multi-national utility companies, NGOs and the Central European University. But, Schweitzer said, immigration has received the most attention, with the European Commission, Hungarian-born American billionaire philanthropist and businessman George Soros (b.1930), human rights NGOs and liberal organisations all seemingly implicated in a vast conspiracy (Schweitzer 2017). Orbán, an admirer of Admiral Miklós Horthy, the Hungarian leader who collaborated with the Nazis in deporting the country's Jews, has been particularly active in pursuing Soros, who, he believes, has a masterplan to force the EU to accept millions of Muslim refugees and has accused Germany of 'moral imperialism'. Orbán believes the answer to Hungary's labour shortage is not to be solved by immigration but by 'encouraging' Hungarian women to stay home and produce more babies, and has changed the law so that families with four or more children enjoy a tax reduction.[25]

In 1989 Soros financed Orbán to study in Britain and in 2010 Soros donated 127bn Hungarian Forints ($1m) to Orbán's government to help clean up an environmental disaster when caustic red sludge from an aluminium plant flooded the town of Devecser. Soros also spent hundreds of millions of dollars financing education and civil society projects in Hungary through his OSF (Open Society Foundations). The Central European University, which opened in Budapest in 1991, was probably the most important of Soros' initiatives: it was intended to be the basis of a new, liberal, democratic, transnational, European political and business class – a class dedicated to saving capitalism from itself. However, soon after his election Orbán began to question the status of the university and then began to interfere with the curriculum, first by suspending educational programmes for registered refugees and asylum seekers, and then banning the teaching of gender studies. In August 2017 the CEU reluctantly announced it would no longer recruit students to Budapest and in future would only recruit students to its Vienna campus.

In the spring of 2017 Orbán targeted Soros with a poster campaign drawing on traditional anti-Semitic propaganda images from the 1930s. The demonisation of Soros has legitimised anti-Semitism, which has grown enormously and become far more open since Orbán assumed the Hungarian leadership.

Orbán, who had promised to cut income taxes, offered pro-growth economic policies and whose main platform was anti-immigration, anti-EU

224   *The end of history*

integration and the threat to seek 'moral, political and legal amends' from his enemies, won a third term in office in April 2018. His resounding electoral victory delivered to Fidesz 133 seats in parliament out of a total of 199. The opposition did well only in Budapest; outside the capital the opposition parties were almost wiped out. The leaders of Jobbik and the Socialist Party both resigned immediately, leaving Orbán with no effective opposition ('Hungary's Viktor Orbán Secures another Term with Resounding Win' 2018).

The Organization for Security and Cooperation in Europe (OSCE) described Orbán's 2018 electoral campaign as particularly dirty: Rhetoric was 'hostile, intimidating and, at times, xenophobic' and there was 'limited space for substantive debate', which 'diminished voters' ability to make an informed choice'. They said that public television 'clearly favoured the ruling coalition' and frequently repeated stock film of migrants and invented news items about immigrants. OSCE also said that public funds had been used for so-called government information campaigns and that the electoral process as a whole was characterised by 'a pervasive overlap between state and ruling party resources, undermining contestants' ability to compete on an equal basis'.

Immediately after the electoral victory had been announced, government-controlled Hungarian newspapers began publishing lists of 'Soros agents'. One of the first bills Orbán placed before parliament was aimed at Soros, imposing a twenty-five percent tax on all foreign donations to NGOs backing immigration or supporting immigrants.

Orbán also began a systematic attack on the media empire built up by his childhood friend Lajos Simicska, who in 2015 had been so incensed by Orbán's behaviour he referred to him as *geci* (an obscenity often translated as 'sperm' but more accurately rendered in English as 'cum' or jizm). Less than a week after the 2018 election, in circumstances that are far from clear, after eighty years of publication *Magyar Nemzet* (*Hungarian Nation*), one of the few remaining independent newspapers critical of Orbán, closed. The Lánchíd (Chain or Link) radio station also closed, along with the conservative but independent magazine *Heti Válasz* (*Weekly Reply*). At about the same time Hír TV (News TV), one of the few stations still critical of Orbán, was simply taken over by the government. These moves gave Orbán a virtual monopoly of the Hungarian mass media. Although the state-run media conglomerate has an annual state budget of about 80bn HF (£223m), Orbán denies the government has any control over it and claims its critics are 'agents of Soros' (Walker 2018b; Walker & Boffey 2018).

Orbán's government also began a systematic attack on academic thought about the origins of the Hungarian people. Scholarly opinion is that modern-day Hungarians trace their roots back to non-Indo-European people of the Finno-Ugric language group (including Finns, Estonians and some groups in Russia). Orbán, however, promotes the idea that Hungarians are descended from Turkic nomadic mounted warriors, and he has sent observers to political summits in Turkic countries, set up the Magyar Külügyi

Intézet – MKI (Hungarian Institute of International Affairs – HIIA) to prove the point, and even planned a monument to Attila the Hun. The shift towards Turkish and Central Asian origin is called 'Turanism', was very popular with the far-right Jobbik Party and has now been taken up by Fidesz; it is linked to anti-Western and anti-liberal thought. The idea is not taken seriously by academics outside MKI, and *Oktatói Hálózat* (Academic Network) have criticised this and other developments in a lengthy report (Bajomi et al. 2020).

All the V4 countries still function as notional democracies: the 'brown tendency' of their leaderships does not extend to outright fascism, but rather tends more towards mafia-ism, where the innocent are not exactly persecuted but the guilty are definitely protected. And there are gradations in their authoritarianism. Hungary – where Orbán has re-defined his illiberalism as 'Christian liberty', the constitution has been rewritten to suit the ruling party, the media are controlled by the state, Orbán's cronies are important beneficiaries of government protection and opposition has become difficult and dangerous – is probably the closest to outright mafia-ism.[26] Poland, though less obviously corrupt, is not so very far behind in its authoritarianism. The Czech and Slovak republics, however, are slightly less illiberal and they have begun to distance themselves from Orbán's version of the V4 by asking him not to speak in their name.[27]

The West

The collapse of communism changed the West as well as the East. The West was no longer what it once was, certainly not the Cold War entity that Poles, Czechs and Hungarians had once so admired.

After the 9/11 attack on the US, the disastrous invasion of Iraq, a costly and ineffective invasion of Afghanistan, an equally disastrous intervention in Libya, failure to intervene in Syria, and Trump's admission that the 'reality' of the Middle East was that the Israeli right wing was not interested in a 'peace process', the 'American century' and the 'leadership of the free world' seem to be winding to a conclusion in populism, isolationism, corruption, self-aggrandisement and logorrhoea. The Enlightenment values and aspirations that had driven Western democratic politics were under siege, as were post-war national, economic and security arrangements. Although it was not clear at the time, while the US was engaged in the 'war on terror', the absorption of East-Central Europe changed both NATO and the EU, eroding US leadership and exposing the moral, political and economic position of Germany and the judgement of Chancellor Angela Merkel. The fall of the Berlin Wall not only eliminated the EU's main competitor, it seriously affected the EU's moral compass.

Firstly, in general German policy had been self-centred rather than Europhilic and had given its neighbours increasing cause for concern. While acknowledging that EU banking reform was essential and that currency misalignment was a growing problem, Germany's response to the euro-crisis

226 *The end of history*

of 2008–9 was to delay any attempt to reform either the euro or the banks (Stiglitz 2018). Poor EU controls allowed the Greek government to hide its massive debts, but when the debt was revealed and a bailout became necessary, Germany, in a bizarre combination of rigidity and fecklessness, insisted the Greeks had to repay their debt in full and on schedule. The debt crisis cost Greece 25% of its GDP – an unprecedented sum for any European state in peacetime. By 2018 the Greek economy had flat-lined: debt levels had reached €323bn or €30,000 per person; unemployment stood at about twenty percent and hundreds of thousands of young people had migrated for work. Cuts in wages and pensions of up to forty percent and an aggressive approach to tax collection led to the pauperisation of most pensioners and the collapse of many middle-class enterprises.

The imposition of stringent austerity measures and the rise of the far-right Χρυσή Αυγή (Golden Dawn Party), a Greek General Election, a humiliating rebuff to the newly elected Greek government of ΣΥΡΙΖΑ (Syriza, a radical left coalition) and the failure of their attempts to reschedule Greek debt all made it clear that Germany, operating through the European Central Bank, was prepared to bankrupt a member state and hazard Greek political stability in order to recover its funds. In what Pierre Moscovici (European Commissioner for Economic Affairs) admitted was a scandalous abuse of democratic process, the EU took decisions on the terms of the Greek bail-out behind closed doors. The Greek National Debt is currently estimated at 180% of GDP and repayments, which rely on steady economic growth rather than the flat-line economy they have created, are set to continue at least until 2060 (Prentoulis 2018).

The lack of transparency and the imposition of austerity while Germany prospered put Greeks in mind of the Nazi occupation and may in the long-term have seriously weakened the EU project. Germany's behaviour alienated Italy, Spain, Portugal and Ireland, all of whom, since joining the Eurozone, had begun to experience financial difficulties. Since 2008 seven million EU citizens have amassed the same wealth as the 662 million poorest EU citizens while 123 million EU citizens live on or below the poverty line. After the creation of the Eurozone poverty, inequality, insecurity and feelings of powerlessness – Euroscepticism – became a major contributory factor behind Brexit and in the rapid growth of nationalistic, xenophobic, far-right parties throughout the EU (O'Toole 2018: 131).

Secondly, Merkel's decision in 2015 to accept over one million mainly Syrian refugees alienated Turkey, Hungary, Austria, Poland and the Balkan states, put the EU 'front-line' Mediterranean states under massive stress, hazarded Merkel's leadership, put her government at risk and aided the rise of the neo-fascist AfD (Alternative für Deutschland, Alternative for Germany), which became the third largest party in the Bundestag. By 2018, as voters moved to the right, the twin pillars of post-war German politics, the CDU/CSU alliance and the SPD, suffered a massive drop in support. Right-wing electoral success in Germany bolstered the right wing in Holland, France, Serbia, Italy and Austria, which in turn boosted the standing of the illiberal

The end of history   227

democracies of East-Central Europe, allowing them all to make common cause with the US Alt-Right and Steve Bannon's 'Movement'. Although in November 2016 the EU pledged $450 million for 'building peace', developing infrastructure and as humanitarian aid to the Central African Republic, Germany failed to lead the European Central Bank in using its enormous reserves to solve the refugee crisis at source by investing in a new 'Marshal Plan' for the Middle East and Africa.

Thirdly, constrained by the legacy of Nazism, German politicians were reluctant to admit that with the end of the Cold War, the EU could take greater responsibility for its own defence and security. Of the twenty-seven EU member states, twenty-one have now suspended or abolished military service. Of NATO's twenty-nine members only five – the US (which spends 3.5%), Greece, Estonia, UK and Latvia – met their defence target of 2% of GDP in 2018. Poland and France are close to the target, but Germany has shirked much of its financial contribution to NATO since the fall of the Wall. After absorbing the East German army, the Bundeswehr's strength was reduced, disbanded or redeployed: Germany cut its mechanised force of 500,000 to 62,000 and defence spending slumped to just over 1.24% of GDP. Admittedly, lower national spending on NATO is partly because European defence spending is moving over to PESCO (Permanent Structured Cooperation, established 2017), but the dereliction seems to be fundamental and in June 2018 it was revealed that Germany had only four operational warplanes from a fleet of 128 (Tooze & Vallée 2018; Woody 2018).

Fourthly, under Merkel's leadership, Germany appeared to feel that European unity and continued dominance on the right are more important than the Rule of Law and the moral high ground. The conservative, Christian-Democrat, centre-right EPP (European Peoples' Party, the largest bloc in the European Parliament, which includes Merkel's CDU/CSU alliance) has refused to tell Orbán that Fidesz has crossed several 'red lines' regarding the Rule of Law, judicial independence, press freedom, refugees and immigration. Indeed, Orbán felt sufficiently confident about retaining membership of EPP to aim at a role for Fidesz outside Hungary: he claimed leadership of the European Parliamentary right, saying he is the true heir of Helmut Kohl, represents the core of the EPP and that it is his task to take the EPP back to its Christian roots. He has also made it very clear to EPP that his priorities are Hungary first, the V4 second and the EU a very distant third (Heath 2018).

Lastly, Germany's new 'ostpolitik' has failed to criticise the xenophobic, homophobic, nationalist kleptocracy that is Putin's Russia: bribery, espionage, murder of Russian journalists, email leaks, subversion, direct electronic interference in EU democratic processes and in the Brexit vote, cyber-attacks, the invasion of Crimea, war in eastern Ukraine, attempts to undermine an understanding between Greece and the Republic of Northern Macedonia, a murder using Polonium and a chemical warfare attack in the UK have all been set aside in favour of continuing and developing trade links. Even though Russia refused to ratify the Energy Charter Treaty,

228 *The end of history*

which would have limited Russian political influence on the back of trade, Gazprom's massive Nord Stream project to increase Germany's supply of Russian gas has continued without interruption.[28] The deal was signed in March 2018, only a few days after the chemical attack in the UK. Clearly the gas pipeline is part of a wider political strategy that brings with it an accommodation between Germany and Russia. It has been presented as an effort to stabilise European fuel supplies, one where Germany also avoids paying for high-priced US shale gas, but it is a strategy that promotes fear.

In the Ukraine, the Baltics and East-Central Europe, but particularly in Poland, Germany's policy is seen as playing into the hands of Putin by destabilising and possibly splitting the EU. These states were all offended that they were by-passed by the gas pipeline, and fear that, along with Trump's US, Germany is now in thrall to Russia. They fear US and German (and therefore EU) passivity in the face of Russian resurgence – and see this as an updated version of the Partitions, the Polish–Soviet War of 1921, the Molotov–Ribbentrop pact and the betrayal of Yalta. They also fear a further euro-crisis, an ongoing Syrian refugee influx, increased migration from Africa, rising fuel prices and restricted energy supplies – in all of which Germany (particularly after Brexit) will have a key role.

However, while Merkel and Orbán clashed at a press conference on the subject of European unity in June 2018 – Merkel argued for better asylum procedures while Orbán argued for better fences – there has been little real opposition to Fidesz from Germany. Instead, on the back of the new Hungarian 'slave law', Mercedes, BMW, Daimler and Audi announced expansion plans in Hungary ('BMW to build 1 billion euro car factory in Hungary' 2018).[29]

Liberal crisis

In East-Central Europe the dividing lines are clear: on the one side urban cosmopolitans fear they will be cut off from the liberal, democratic, humanist Western world; at the same time the idea of accepting 'the other' has provoked pious, rural fear that Christianity is being diluted and that national identity is under threat, and has resulted in support for 'strong government'. In the run-up to the 2019 elections a study conducted by the Council for the Protection of the Polish Language (an affiliate of the Polish Academy of Sciences) found that TVP systematically portrayed the PiS with positive words like 'reform', 'sovereign', 'strong', 'hero' and 'patriotic', while the vocabulary devoted to the opposition used words like 'shocking', 'scandalous', 'provocation' and 'putsch' (Davies 2019b). Sadly, but perhaps inevitably, in Poland and Hungary this clash is seen not as an issue of civic responsibility but one of national pride.

The writer Agata Pyzik has said that in post-communist Poland 'what passes for left or liberal' would now be deemed 'conservative or right wing in Britain' (Pyzik 2019: 9). For the most part, the creative inteligencja, Platforma Obywatelska, Sojusz Lewicy Demokratycznej (Democratic Left

The end of history 229

Alliance), Adam Michnik's *Gazeta Wyborcza* and the privately owned TVN cling to the ideas, ideals, standards and culture of the democratic West. Opposed to them and drawing strongly on romantic literary tradition are PiS, the Catholic Church, traditionalists, nationalists and Pan-Slavs. They see themselves as holding back an 'invasion of gays', as representing 'real Poles', promoting 'Christian values' and 'authentic' Polish identity. They claim the centre-left is a 'cosmopolitan liberal elite', love-struck with the idea of the West, misguided, irresponsible, untrustworthy, unpatriotic, un-Polish, crypto-communist, a slave to foreign ideas, disdainful of native institutions, traditions and culture, and lacking practical ideas and solutions. PiS sees the EU as a German-inspired business-form of pseudo-communism (but still a useful source of finance) and does not feel it needs to take 'foreign' opinion too seriously. Indeed, foreigners, multi-nationals, NGOs, Jews, refugees, the EU, liberals, intellectuals, communists and critics of the current regimes are now often spoken of as a vast anti-Polish conspiracy, and increasingly referred to as *oni* ('they'), a word once reserved for the octopus of communism. In 2019, although seventy percent of Poles were favourably disposed towards EU membership, fifty-one percent of Poles would leave the EU rather than accept its ruling on refugees. Opinion is not much different in the other V4 countries (Gromada 2017).

The right-wing leaderships in East-Central Europe can hardly be accused of sustaining deeply held ideological beliefs. Kaczyński and Orbán were both 1980s oppositionists aiming for the end of communism, became trailblazers for the transition to capitalism and democracy in the 1990s, and then became national-populist leaders. The kindest thing we can say of them is that they sniff the wind to scent the public mood, and they are very good at it. But as a result the illiberal democracies of East-Central Europe currently resemble revolutionary Iran, Nazarbayev's Kazakhstan, Mugabe's Zimbabwe, Erdogan's Turkey and Putin's Russia rather than modern European states. And the hate-speech against minorities and opposition parties in both Poland and Hungary now resembles that of the Rwandan genocide in 1994. After the murder of Paweł Adamowicz (1965–2019), the liberal mayor of Gdańsk and founder of PO, by a right-winger with a history of crime and mental illness, ten other Poles were arrested for calling for more murders and acts of aggression. In 2017, after issuing a statement saying refugees and asylum seekers would be welcome in his city, Adamowicz and ten other liberal mayors had been targeted with fake death certificates issued by Młodzież Wszechpolska (All-Polish Youth – a fascistic, homophobic, Catholic Youth organisation allied to right-wing Catholic LPR and the ultra-nationalist RN).[30] Adamowicz's death was widely seen as an echo of the assassination of Poland's first President Gabriel Narutowicz in 1922 (Buras 2019). These are sure indicators of the extent to which the electorate has polarised since 1989, and of how far East-Central Europe has reverted to inter-war habits of mind.[31]

Fidesz and PiS are massively unhappy at the secular life, political processes and Enlightenment values 'Europe' brought with it. They are menaced

230 *The end of history*

by the shadows, spooks, rumours and the unfinished business of history. In East-Central Europe we are witnessing a kind of historical revivalism where the politicians of the right respond to global economic problems by attempting a return to ethno-national purity, to a cleaner, more wholesome time, before errors occurred, before mistaken paths were chosen, before they were cheated out of their history and then cheated of their future. The right wing offers to build a bridge to a 'pure' future identity from an elusive, ever receding past. Zygmunt Bauman (1925–2017) dubbed this phenomenon 'Retrotopia' (Bauman 2017). But, as Heraclitus (535–475BC) pointed out, it is not possible to step into the same river twice: it is not possible to find, still less inhabit, a past identity. And finding victims to blame – new or traditional – does not work either.[32] For the right wing, inconvenient reality constantly disrupts the shimmering hologram of the harmonious future/past, forcing them to search again for the conspiracy that frustrates them.

In January 2018 the EU took Hungary to the European Court of Justice over its assault on political freedoms, media control and its attack on the emblematic CEU. Orbán was already under investigation for (among other things) misspending EU sports funds. At about the same time, after warning the Polish government that placing the judiciary under political control would be an unacceptable constitutional change contradicting 'fundamental European values', the European Parliament's Civil Rights Committee called for the suspension of Polish voting rights. This move is unlikely to succeed simply because Hungary (which faces a similar charge) can veto any move against Poland, and Poland would almost certainly veto any move against Hungary. By this time both Hungary and Poland had already been referred to the ECJ for refusing to accept a mandatory quota of refugees. However, the ECJ works very slowly and the EU prefers 'dialogue' to discipline and so has been reluctant, or perhaps unable, to enforce its version of 'democracy'.[33]

European Commissioners discussing funding allocations for the period 2021–8 and desperate to avoid a Polish/Hungarian veto decided to explore tying future development funding to compliance with measured democratic standards – namely, separation of powers, freedom of the press, human rights and shelter for a refugee quota. In June 2019 the ECJ, having learned the lesson of its failure to prevent Hungary rigging its courts, made a landmark ruling that enforced early retirement of Poland's Supreme Court judges would be unlawful. Mindful that future finance might be in jeopardy, the Polish President indicated he would accept the decision.[34]

However, any serious move to discipline these governments would not only confirm them as the patriotic defenders of embattled national identity beset on all sides by plotters and traitors, but run the risk of pushing the V4 into leaving the EU – an event that would dwarf Brexit. Still defiant, Poland and Hungary, the two largest net beneficiaries of EU funding, face Germany and France, the two main financial contributors to the EU budget: further conflict seems certain. In private and off the record EU leaders have admitted that the rush to expand into East-Central Europe was a mistake. But,

The end of history 231

while its development-finance is still essential in East-Central Europe, the EU is a rallying point for populists: what the V4 politicians have achieved is a bad reputation, their exclusion from lead-work in important committees and working parties, and their restriction to insignificant dossiers.

Clearly right-wing success in East-Central Europe is partly a result of the weakness of centre-left politicians and partly also that we are deep within a liberal crisis, a multi-layered clash between popular will and democratic process. On one level this is a clash between different experiences and competing versions of history, and over the legitimacy, place and standing of East-Central European traditional culture within Europe. However, the argument has spread from economics into the issues of hybridisation, purity, tradition, modernity, 'real national culture' and 'fake national culture'. In this palimpsest, inflexibility and fantasy line up on the one hand, pragmatism and adaptability on the other: the Church versus the inteligencja; ethno-nationalism versus liberal-leftism; Poles versus 'others'; the people versus hidden enemies. The result is that these elements are far from being partners in democracy. In Poland and Hungary the atmosphere is now so poisonous there is no middle ground, no negotiation and virtually no communication between differing points of view (Bill 2014).

This is a crisis in which opportunists thrive, but in which the writers and intellectuals who once drove opposition to communism, are now almost invisible. Under communism the Czech writer Václav Havel (1936–2011) had spoken of 'the power of the powerless', meaning the way writers found of 'speaking truth to power' (Vladislav 1987: 36–122). Writers were important in East-Central Europe while the Russian, Prussian and Austrian empires lasted, during World War II, and again after the war because the communists hoped their support and cooperation would help legitimise the regime. With the collapse of communism, the world of writers changed overnight and their hegemony was suddenly much reduced.[35] In changed circumstances writers, editors and publishers learned that their readers now faced urgent basic problems of survival, had no time to read, could no longer afford to purchase books and, as they often viewed the older generation of writers as tainted by a connection to communism, were no longer swayed by writers' opinions. In Poland, for example, the highly respected literary journal *Zeszyty Literackie*, which had been published successfully in Paris since 1982, moved to Warsaw after 1989. Almost immediately it lost funding from Agora publishing due to a reduction in its circulation: a grant from the Ministry of Culture and National Heritage proved too small to cover its expenses and the magazine folded in December 2018 after 144 issues.

Writers have been forced to learn that the ethical attractions of 'civil society' posed in opposition to communism faded rapidly from public perception. Instead, they have been forced to grasp that part of the power of capitalism and populist governments is their ability to generate their own truth and shape their own dominant ethic, including the promotion of a cartoon version of the political opposition. While the West, in spite of

232   *The end of history*

austerity, has become increasingly engaged with 'post-industrial' and post-materialist' issues, East-Central European populism, in reaction to the penetration of modernity and capitalism, has been concerned with summoning up the heroes of the past, reasserting a traditional identity and redefining its sense of community. If truth is the first victim of war, democracy would seem to be the first victim of economic hardship.

Since the collapse of communism, the bulk of the population has felt itself to be on a scrap-heap of the 'economically unprepared': they feel 'left behind', by-passed, untrained, betrayed by the political class, by history, by change, by modernity and by 'the West'. But the idea that 'left-behind' support for a government fuelled by fear and resentment leaves the electorate even further behind still seems counter-intuitive. Instead, voters, accustomed by history to the idea they must struggle, seek to fight with invisible 'enemies'. The arrival of EU investment and the re-shaping of pensions and family benefits by PiS undercut resentment, but too little to affect populist opinion. The bulk of the Polish and Hungarian electorate likes EU money but feels it has moral superiority over the elites and leaders of the recent past, a cultural and religious superiority to the refugees of the present, a safe haven and certainty in their national identity, and a spiritual superiority over the wealthy but unhealthy 'West'.

Ultra-conservative Catholicism, political immaturity, long years of semi-isolation and opposition, the lack of a well-developed commercial middle class, the reaction against everything connected to communism, fear of 'others', a strong sense of marginality, alienation and victimisation, and the poor performance of the centre-left in a country with almost no history of democratic government have all contributed to the rise of ethno-nationalism in Poland. With variations it is the same throughout East-Central Europe.

However, chauvinism, nationalism and illiberalism are symptoms. The underlying problem is the nature of globalisation, the behaviour of multi-nationals, the reality of neo-liberal economics and the fact of capital accumulation into ever fewer hands. For many in East-Central Europe the EU is not a protective response to globalisation, but an intrusive aspect of globalisation. Over time the EU may be able to correct this impression, reassert its authority, disentangle democracy from populism and win back respect, but in East-Central Europe it will be very difficult to put the genie of ethno-nationalism back in the bottle simply because, to many people, it feels like a 'home-grown' solution, a real defence.

It is unlikely the EU will learn from its periphery, and even if it learns it will not do so quickly: in spite of the EU's financial investment in East-Central Europe it is very probable the 'margins' of Europe will remain marginal. The strength of nationalism predicts this and continuing marginality confirms nationalists in the opinion they were right all along.[36] This is likely to be the outcome if the EU fails to halt illiberalism in Poland and Hungary, much more likely if the EU attempts to slow down funding to the V4, and absolutely certain if the V4 leaves the EU to form an East European Union.

Notes

1 Novelist Len Deighton (b.1929) explored the idea of 'victory' by suggesting that communist economies had been successfully undermined by Western manipulation, and as a novelistic device this has been very effective (Deighton 1989). However, Poles point to Colonel Ryszard Kukliński, who from July 1980 to December 1981 passed 42,000 Warsaw Pact documents to the CIA with information about preparations for Martial Law and Soviet plans to use nuclear weapons in an invasion of Western Europe. Some believe he gave President Reagan the military and economic strategies to win the Cold War, but by this time – as the declaration of Martial Law indicated – communism was already headed for collapse. Polish opinion is divided as to whether Kukliński is a hero or a traitor (*Preparing for Martial Law: Through the Eyes of Col. Ryszard Kukliński* 2014; Weiser 2009).

2 'When perceptions of need-satisfaction decrease but expectations continue to rise, a widening gap is created between expectations and reality. That gap eventually becomes intolerable and sets the stage for rebellion against a social system that fails to fulfil its promises' (Bauman 2017: 97).

3 Janion had traced uncertainty over Polish identity back to the year 966AD, when the first Piast king, Mieszko I (c930–992), forestalled Saxon expansion by setting aside the ancient Slav gods and converting to Christianity, orienting himself and his people towards the west and Roman rite rather than east towards Russia and the Orthodox Church. In doing so he not only deprived the Saxons of a pretext for invasion and bolstered his right to rule 'by the grace of God', but, by seeking to orientate his infant state towards Western Europe, cut off his territory from its ancient Slav roots and its founding myths, unsettling, redefining and complicating tribal loyalties in ways that echo through later Polish national crises (Janion 2006, 2014a).

4 In the 2005 Presidential election, Lepper won 15.11 percent of the vote and went on to endorse Lech Kaczyński of PiS in the second round, effectively granting Kaczyński victory.

5 UOP: the state intelligence agency responsible for intelligence, counter-intelligence, electronic security and telephone wiretaps. It replaced the communist SB (Służba Bezpieczęstwa, Security Service). Because of corruption and its connections to organised crime UOP was itself replaced in 2002.

6 The film *Insulator* (2007: also known as *Warsaw Dark*, dir. Christopher Doyle) was based on the story of Dębski's murder.

7 *Resentyment* (borrowed from French *ressentiment*), meaning the willingness to be offended by anything, to revive the sentiment of ancient resentment (Phillips 2013: 225–40).

8 The exodus from East-Central Europe was dwarfed by the catastrophic rise in emigration from Romania and Bulgaria after they joined the EU in 2007. It is estimated that seventeen percent of the Romanian population departed (www.emerging-europe.com/news/new-statistics-confirm-romanias-demographic-catastrophe). The Bulgarian population is predicted to shrink from seven million to 5.4 million by 2050 and 3.9 million by the end of the century (www.irishtimes.com/news/world/europe/welcome-to-bulgaria-the-world-s-fastest-shrinking-nation).

9 This issue had been anticipated by a Polish joke from the communist years. A candidate for Party membership is quizzed: 'What is the essential difference between communism and capitalism?' The candidate answers: 'Under capitalism it is a case of dog-eat-dog, but under communism it is the other way round'.

10 TV-Niepokalanów, named after the Niepokalanów Monastery of the City of the Immaculate Mother of God, founded in Teresin in 1927 by Friar Maximilian Kolbe (1894–1941). Kolbe, killed in Auschwitz, later declared a martyr and canonised, is now the patron saint of the Polish pro-life movement.

234 *The end of history*

11 PiS formed 2001, in coalition government 2005–7, in opposition 2007–15, majority government 2015.

12 From the improbably high participation in general elections (78.6–98.7 percent) claimed by the communists, voter turnout declined with the collapse of communism and only began to revive after the PiS electoral success of 2005. Even so voter turnout indicates a low level of interest: 1989 – 62.11 percent; 1991 – 43.30; 1993 – 52.08; 1997 – 47.93; 2001 – 46.18; 2005 – 40.57; 2007 – 53.88; 2011 – 48.92; 2015 – 50.92 ('Voter Turnout Poland'). For comparison, UK average turnout in the years 1918–2017 was 72.9% (www.researchbriefings. parliament.uk/ResearchBriefing/Summary/CBP-8060).

13 *Kaka*: from the conjectured Indo-European root-word **kak*, meaning dirt, excrement, dung or defecation. From this English derives *cack* and *cack-handed*, and Greek has κακή (bad or dirty) (Ayto 1990: 90; Partridge 1978: 69).

14 The term 'illiberal democracy' was coined by Fareed Zakaria to define regimes that tried to democratise without first having a 'sturdy' economy structured around a free market and without sound political institutions with effective 'checks and balances' on the executive, including an opposition, freedom of speech and an independent media. Populism, he argued, was always illiberal, was opposed to elites, antipathetic to minorities and an enemy to pluralism: he warned the mix of elections and authoritarianism, without protection for civil liberties and minority rights, encouraged the 'rise of the rest' (Zakaria 2003).

15 In May 2012 US President Obama inadvertently gave offence by referring to 'Polish death camps' in a speech posthumously awarding the Presidential Medal of Freedom to Jan Karski. President Obama later wrote to Polish President Komorowski to apologise.

16 The wartime AK (Armia Krajowa, Home Army) judged *szmalcowniki* to be collaborators and sentenced them to death. The communist Polski Komitet Wyzwolenia Narodowego (Polish Committee of National Liberation), in a decree of 31 August 1944, also condemned *szmalcowniki* as Nazi collaborators. That decree is still valid in Polish law and any person convicted of *szmalcownictwo* during the war faces life imprisonment.

17 The 'defamation law' occasioned international outrage and was denounced loudly by Israel. In late June 2018 the Sejm (Polish Parliament) was hurriedly convened to rush through an amendment to the Act, reversing an amendment adopted the previous January. The new amendment, to take effect immediately, said attributing blame to Poland for Nazi crimes in WWII would no longer be punishable by three years in prison. The amendment had been developed in secret by Prime Minister Mateusz Morawiecki, and Israeli–Polish negotiations on this had been conducted by their intelligence agencies, to prevent the main critic of the law, Minister of Justice Zbigniew Ziobro (Morawiecki's rival for the ear of PiS Chairman Jarosław Kaczynski), getting to know about it. Thus Morawiecki, rather than Ziobro, took credit for salvaging Poland's image. He and Israeli Prime Minister Netanyahu signed a joint declaration ending the dispute over the law and the PiS government purchased full-page ads in the three largest Israeli daily newspapers to announce their agreement (Sierakowski 2018).

18 Professors Norman Davies and Timothy Snyder both resigned from the museum management board in protest. Paweł Machcewicz, Janusz Marszalec, Rafał Wnuk and Piotr M Majewski, the founding historians of the museum, are now suing the new director for infringement of copyright after he altered their exhibition content.

19 Václav Havel (1936–2011) wrote: 'Traditionally in our circumstances more is expected of writers than merely writing readable books. The idea that a writer is the conscience of his nation has its own logic and its own tradition here. For years, writers have stood in for politicians: they were the renewers of the national community, maintainers of the national language, awakeners of the

The end of history 235

national conscience and interpreters of the national will. This tradition has continued under totalitarian conditions, where it gains its own special colouring: the written word seems to have acquired a kind of heightened radioactivity – otherwise they wouldn't lock us up for it! Many of our western colleagues might envy us the degree of attention and social resonance that we enjoy. But it's a double-edged thing: it can bind one, tie one down, limit one. It's as though he were suddenly blocked by his social role, as though, out of respect for the role assigned to him and doubts about his worthiness for it, his voice acquired a stammer; as though he were simply no longer as free as he should be' (Havel 1990: 72).

20 *Targowiczanin* – supporters of the Confederation of Targowica, who opposed to the revision of the Polish constitution of 1791 in the hope that they could restore their status and the political set-up from before the first Partition. Their defeat in 1792 precipitated the second Partition of Poland. The leaders were declared traitors and sentenced to death but never caught. A painting by Jan Piotr Norblin (1745–1830) in the Czartoryski Museum in Kraków records 'The Hanging in Effigy of the Leaders of Confederation in the Aftermath of the Warsaw Uprising' (1794).

21 Foreign Minister Waszczykowski is famous for an interview in *Der Spiegel* where he railed against the 'new mixing of cultures and races, a world of bicyclists and vegetarians who fight every form of religion'. However, he is probably best known for a manoeuvre reminiscent of Jaroslav Hašek's good soldier *Švejk*, when he boasted of meeting with representatives of the invented state of San Escobar to garner support for Poland's application for a place on the UN Security Council ('We Want Our Concerns to Be Taken Seriously' 2017; 'San Escobar: Polish foreign minister's slip invents a country' 2017).

22 The PiS government has claimed that accepting a large number of Ukrainians is its argument for refusing refugees from the Middle East. In February 2018, for example, Beata Kempa, PiS Minister for Humanitarian Aid, claimed Poland had taken in more than two million Ukrainians, implying they were refugees. The Ukrainian government has repeatedly said this is 'erroneous', that at most about 400,000 Ukrainians work in Poland and that Ukrainians 'go to Poland for work, not asylum'. Roughly 1.7 million short-term Polish work registrations were issued to Ukrainians in 2017 – an eightfold increase compared to 2013 and roughly equivalent to about twenty-five percent of the Polish workforce. In general, absorbing this influx of Ukrainians has not been a problem since they replace the two million young Poles who left to find work after 2004. Most of the Ukrainian migrant workers come from western Ukraine, bordering Poland: local Poles refer to them contemptuously as *mrówki* (ants). Applications for asylum in Poland rose steeply in the period 2010–18, to reach about two thousand per year, but only 1–2 percent were approved. Most Ukrainian applicants for asylum are not eligible because Ukraine is a sovereign country with a democratic government that is considered to be fully accountable to its citizens. However, there are about six thousand Ukrainian refugees in Poland (the second largest group after the Georgians), mainly from Donbas in eastern Ukraine where there has been fighting with Russian-backed separatists, and the Crimean peninsula, which Russia annexed in 2014 (Buckley & Huber 2017 ; Shotter & Huber 2018; 'Uchodźcy w polsce' www.uchodzcy.info/info/uchodzcy-w-polsce).

23 A recent international survey found Hungary to be top of the paranoia league, with eighty-five percent of respondents believing in all the current major conspiracy theories, in particular a belief in 'replacement theory' – the idea spawned by the French far-right that refugees and migrants from the Middle East were part of a conspiracy to replace the population of Europe (Addley 2018).

24 According to Transparency International, under Orbán **Hungary slipped down seven places in the Corruption Perceptions Index (CPI), to 64/180, achieving its**

236   *The end of history*

lowest score in the last six years and leaving it roughly on a par with Jordan and Romania, and slightly better than Saudi Arabia and Cuba. They also said that its anti-corruption performance had 'strikingly deteriorated' in comparison to the EU and the other countries of East-Central Europe. Poland is ranked 37/180 on the index ('Hungary Still in Decline CPI 2016' 2017; www.transparency.org/country).

25 When Victor Orbán launched his anti-Semitic poster campaign against Soros he provoked the anger of Israel's ambassador to Budapest. However, Israeli Prime Minister Netanyahu, in what *Haaretz* dubbed 'an illiberal bromance', chose to defend Orbán because Soros was a critic of the Israeli occupation (Pfeffer 2018).

26 In June 2019 the human rights organisation Freedom House downgraded Hungary to 'partly free' country. Hungary is the only EU member state to earn that description (www.freedomhouse.org/report/freedom-world/2019/hungary).

27 The victory of Zuzana Čaputová in Slovakia's presidential election in April 2019, with 58.4 percent of the vote, on a pro-EU programme of anti-corruption, 'humanism, solidarity and truth' may challenge the illiberal tendency further.

28 Nord Stream 1 opened in 2011. The pipeline runs from Vyborg in Russia under the Baltic for 1,200km to Lubmin in Germany. Nord Stream 2 was inaugurated in 2012. Together they have an annual capacity of 55 billion cubic metres of gas: there are plans for two additional pipelines, increasing capacity to 110 billion cubic metres by 2019.

29 The 'slave law' (an amendment to the Hungarian Labour Code) was deemed necessary by Fidesz because of the labour shortage caused when 600,000 Hungarians (ten percent of the total Hungarian workforce) left to seek employment in the EU. The law, which came into force in December 2018, allows employers to demand up to 500 hours of overtime per year from every employee and for payment to be deferred for up to three years. The German motor industry, attracted to Hungary by low wages, ineffective unions and massive tax breaks is happy with the 'slave' law, but thousands of Hungarians have demonstrated against it. In December 2018, when Orbán introduced the law, demonstrators wore badges proclaiming O1G (*Orbán egy geci* – Orbán one sperm). O1G also appeared on windscreens, baked into bread and in graffiti across Budapest.

30 By the autumn of 2019, as Poland moved towards national elections, over forty local authorities proclaimed themselves *Strefa wolna od LGBT* (LGBT free zones). *Gazeta Polska*, a popular right-wing magazine, issued stickers with the caption 'LGBT-free zone' for its readers to attach on cars, doors, windows and in public spaces. Trucks with homophobic pictures toured Polish cities with slogans claiming LGBT people were paedophiles. The Pride March in Białsytok was brutally attacked and over thirty people were hurt, and at the Pride event in Lublin two people were arrested after planting a homemade bomb. www.freedomnews. org.uk/poland-as-governments-anti-lgbtq-campaign-intensifies-homophobes-bring-bomb-to-pride-march; www.en.wikipedia.org/wiki/LGBT-free_zone; www. theguardian.com/world/2019/jul/28/lgbt-gay-rights-poland-first-pride-march-bialystok-rage-violence;www.queer.pl/news/203397/homofobiczna-furgonetka-zrownujaca-lgbt-z-pedofilia-parkuje-pod-kosciolem.

31 While the murder and crime rates are lower than in Western Europe, since 1989 political assassinations and 'hits' have become more common in the V4 countries. In Slovakia, for example, investigative journalist Ján Kuciak and his girlfriend Martina Kušnírová, both aged 27, were both shot dead in February 2018. Kuciak had been investigating 'corrupt Slovak businessmen, EU subsidies, VAT fraud and attempts by Italy's notorious 'Ndrangheta mafia to cultivate ties with Slovak politicians' in the ruling party, Smer-SD (Direction) (Slovakia election: Double murder haunts voters 2020). The murders provoked massive protest demonstrations. Police charged five people with murder and accused multi-millionaire Marián Kočner of ordering the killings: Prime Minister Robert Fico

The end of history 237

resigned, but Smer remained in power until OLaNO, a centre-right anti-corruption party, was returned in February 2020.

32 'For "us" to exist, "they", the "not us", must exist or be conjured up, or in the last resort fantasized' (Bauman 2017: 83). 'Social man fears the Other (the tainted, different man) and tries to destroy him; but [...] paradoxically he needs the Other, and, if need be, creates him, so that by invalidating him as evil, he may confirm himself as good' (Szász 1971: 290).

33 For example, in 2014 the ECJ ruled against Viktor Orbán's government after it removed Supreme Court Justice Andras Baka before his term of office ended. The Hungarian government was content to pay a fine of €100,000 ($117,000), but Baka was not reinstated and the statute that removed him was not withdrawn. Dutch Green MEP Judith Sargentini's report on Hungary, which triggered the EU's action against Hungary in September 2018, otherwise languished and was not been presented to EU ministers. Zoltán Kovács, Orbán's spokesman, dismissed the report as part of a 'political plot' by George Soros (Rankin 2019). In March 2019 EPP (European People's Party – a transnational group composed of Christian-democrat, conservative and liberal-conservative parties) debated whether to expel Fidesz. However, EPP, astonished at its own boldness, got cold feet at the last moment and decided instead to suspend Fidesz, allowing Orbán to ignore their criticism and claim he had in fact temporarily withdrawn from the group. For more on the EU's poor record of disciplining its members see Webb 2008: 236–8.

34 Having apparently accepted defeat, PiS began a secret campaign against the judges. In August 2019, Łukasz Piebiak, Deputy Minister of Justice, formerly a regional judge, was fired when it emerged he had been attempting to harass, intimidate and blackmail judges who resisted PiS attempts to control the judiciary. Among other activities he had circulated a four-page dossier of lurid claims about the private life of one particular judge to some two thousand people. It seems likely that Zbigniew Ziobro, Poland's Justice Minister, knew about Piebiak's activities (Davies 2019a).

35 Unlike the communist years, there are now no accurate publishing statistics available for Poland. It is estimated there are over 1700 active publishers: of these in 1996, about one hundred released thirty to one hundred titles, and thirty produced more than one hundred titles. Average print-runs are estimated at 12,500–20,000 copies; more than eighty percent of the book market belongs to just thirty imprints. PWN (Polskie Wydawnictwo Naukowe, Polish Scientific Publishers), which mainly publishes encyclopaedias, along with the school publisher WSiP (Wydawnictwa Szkolne i Pedagogiczne, School and Pedagogical Publishers), together account for forty to fifty percent of annual turnover. The number of bookshops has fallen to around three thousand, and many of these are tiny. A few publishers have begun to tackle this problem by opening their own bookstores or in-house book clubs. Foreign 'bestsellers' translated into Polish still dominate the fiction market (Lottman 1998).

36 At the European elections in May 2019, Fidesz and PiS were again endorsed by the electorate: Fidesz gained thirteen out of twenty-one seats in the European Parliament; PiS gained twenty-four seats out of fifty-one (www.theguardian. com/world/ng-interactive/2019/may/26/eu-election-results-2019-across-europe). However, at the Polish national elections in October 2019, PiS lost control of the Senate and in the lower house won 235 of the 460 seats, giving it a bare majority. This was far from the landslide victory PiS had predicted. Kaczyński was said to be 'very grumpy' about the result (www.theguardian.com/world/2019/oct/14/poland-populist-law-and-justice-party-increases-majority).

Bibliography

Adamczyk-Garbowska, M., Prokop-Janiec, E., Polonsky, A. and Zurek, S.J. (eds.) (2016) *Polin: Jewish Writing in Poland* (Oxford: Littman)

Addley, E. (2018) 'Study shows 60% of Britons believe in conspiracy theories'. www.theguardian.com/society/2018/nov/23

Alvarez, A. (1965) *Under Pressure: The Writer in Society: Eastern Europe and the USA* (Harmondsworth: Penguin)

Anders, J. (2009) *Between Fire and Sleep: Essays on Modern Poetry and Prose* (New Haven: Yale University Press)

Anderson, P. (1984) *Lineages of the Absolutist State* (London: Verso)

Anon (2009) 'Hungarian MEP elections'. *Hungarian Spectrum*. www.esbalogh. typepad.com/hungarianspectrum/2009/06/after-the-hungarian-ep-elections

'Apparatus Power' (Winter 1981) *Labour Focus on Eastern Europe*, no.4/4–6

Arciszewski, F. (1956) 'Some remarks about the strategical significance of the new and old Soviet-Polish Border', in: Kraszewski, S. (ed.) *Fifty Years of Polish Scholarship: The Polish Review 1956-2006* (Kindle Edition, New York: Polish Institute of Arts and Sciences of America), 206–356

Armistead, C. (2018) 'Interview Olga Tokarczuk': www.theguardian.com/books/2018/apr/20/olga-tokarczuk-interview-flights-man-booker-international

Arnold, S. & Żychowski, M. (1965) *Outline History of Poland: From the Beginning of the State to the Present Time* (Warsaw: Polonia)

Ascherson, N. (1981) *The Polish August* (Harmondsworth: Penguin)

Ascherson, N. (1987) *The Struggles for Poland* (London: M. Joseph)

Ascherson, N. (2017) 'Diary'. *The London Review of Books*, 19 October.

Ash, T.G. (1983) *The Polish Revolution: Solidarity 1980-82* (London: Jonathan Cape)

Ash, T.G. (1989) *The Uses of Adversity* (Cambridge: Granta)

Ash, T.G. (1990) 'Eastern Europe: Aprés le Deluge, Nous', in: *Writings on the East: Selected Essays on Eastern Europe from The New York Review of Books* (New York: New York Review of Books)

Ash, T.G. (1997) *The File: A Personal History* (London: HarperCollins)

Ash, T.G. (2007) 'Poland has made a humiliating farce out of dealing with its red ghosts'. www.theguardian.com/commentisfree/2007/may/24/comment.comment

Ash, T.G. (2017a) 'As well as protesting, Poles need to strengthen their state'. *The Guardian*. www.theguardian.com/commentisfree/2017/jan/05/protest-poles-state-law-and-justice-party-polish-democracy

Bibliography 239

Ash, T.G. (2017b) 'Yes, we can halt the rise of the international far right'. www.theguardian.com/commentisfree/2017/nov/17/international-far-right-poland-march-nationalism

Auden, W.H. (1979) *Selected Poems* (New York: Vintage Books)

Ayto, J. (1990) *Dictionary of Word Origins* (London: Bloomsbury)

Bajomi, I., Bozóki, A., Csáki, J., Enyedi, Z., Fábián, I., Gábor, G., Gács, A., Galicza, P., Gyáni, G., Haris, A., Heller, M., Jászay, T., Kenesei, I., Klaniczay, G., Krusovszky, D., Kubínyi, K., Kulcsár, V., Lővei, P., Máté, A., Mélyi, J., Nagy, G., Pásztor, E., Polyák, G., Radó, P., Rényi, A., Rényi, A., Sirató, I., Tőkei, E., Váradi, A., & Vásárhelyi, M. (2020) 'Hungary Turns its Back on Europe: Dismantling Culture, Education, Science and the Media in Hungary 2010–2019'. www.oktatoihalozat.hu/wp-content/uploads/2020/03/angol.pdf

Banville, J. (2019) '"My Ties to England have loosened": John le Carré on Britain, Boris and Brexit'. www.theguardian.com/books/2019/oct/11/john-le-carre-truth-was-what-you-got-away-with

Barańczak, S. (1990) *Breathing Under Water and Other East European Essays* (Harvard: Harvard University Press)

Barańczak, S. (2006) 'Zbigniew Herbert and the Critics', in: Kraszewski, S. (ed.) *Fifty Years of Polish Scholarship: The Polish Review 1956-2006* (Kindle Edition, New York: Polish Institute of Arts and Sciences of America)

Bauman, J. (1988) *A Dream of Belonging: My Years in Postwar Poland* (London: Virago)

Bauman, Z. (2017) *Retrotopia* (London: Polity)

BBC News (2015) 'Belarus opens Soviet-themed mall'. *BBC News.* www.bbc.co.uk/news/blogs-news-from-elsewhere-34768381

Benecke, E.C.M. (ed.) (1915) *Tales by Polish Authors* (London: Marshall & Co)

Bethell, N. (1976) *The War Hitler Won: September 1939* (London: Futura)

Bethell, N. (1980) *The Palestinian Triangle: The Struggle Between the British, the Jews and the Arabs 1935-48* (London: Futura)

Białoszewski, M. (1977) *A Memoir of the Warsaw Uprising* (Evanston: Northwestern University Press)

Bienvenu, H. (2016) 'Newspaper Closes in Hungary, and Hungarians See Government's Hand'. www.nytimes.com/2016/10/12/world/europe/hungary-newspaper-nepszabadsag

Bikont, A. (2004) *My z Jedwabnego* (Warsaw: Prószyński i S-ka)

Bill, S. (2014) 'Seeking the authentic: Polish culture and the nature of postcolonial theory'. www.nonsite.org/article/seeking-the-authenic-polish-culture-and-the-nature-of-postcolonial-theory

Bloom, H. (1973) *The Anxiety of Influence: A Theory of Poetry* (Oxford: OUP)

Bloom, H. (2019) *The American Canon: Literary Genius from Emerson to Pynchon* (New York: Library of America)

BMW to build 1 billion euro car factory in Hungary' (2018). uk.reuters.com/article/us-bmw-production-factory/bmw-to-build-1-billion-euro-car-factory-in-hungary

Bobińska, C. & Pilch, A. eds. (1975) *Employment-Seeking Emigrations of Poles World-Wide XIX and XX c* (Kraków: Państwowe Wydawnictwo Naukowe)

Bobrowski, T. (1900) *Pamiętki*, vol I (Lwów)

Böhler, J. (2018) *Civil War in Central Europe 1918-21: The Reconstruction of Poland* (Oxford: Oxford University Press)

Bold, A. (ed.) (1970) *The Penguin Book of Socialist Verse* (Harmondsworth: Penguin)

240 *Bibliography*

Borowski, T. (1978) *This Way for the Gas, Ladies and Gentlemen* (Harmondsworth: Penguin)

Brandys, K. (1982) *Rondo* (New York: Farrar Straus Giroux)

Brandys, K. (1984) *Warsaw Diary: 1978-81* (London: Chatto & Windus)

Brown, M. (2017, September 8) 'John le Carré on Trump: Something seriously bad is happening'. www.theguardian.com/books/2017/sep/07/john-le-carre-on-trump-something-truly-seriously-bad-is-happening

Brumberg, A. (ed.) (1983) *Poland: Genesis of a Revolution* (New York: Vintage)

Buckley, N. & Huber, E. (2017) 'Poland weighs benefits of surge in migrants from Ukraine'. www.ft.com/content/aeda9ebe-3afa-11e7-ac89-b01cc67cfeec

Buras, P. (2019) 'The killing of Gdańsk's mayor is the tragic result of hate speech'. www.theguardian.com/commentisfree/2019/jan/17/gdansk-mayor-pawel-adamowicz-killing-poland

Burkot, S. (1996) *Literatura polska w latach 1986-95* (Kraków: Wydawnictwo Edukacyjne)

Burnside, J. (2019) 'Landmark poems of the last century': www.theguardian.com/books/2019/oct/03/landmark-poems-of-the-last-century

Canetti, E. (1987) *The Conscience of Words & Earwitness* (Picador: London)

Carlyle, T. (1993) *On Heroes, Hero-Worship and the Heroic in History* (Yale: Yale University Press)

Cenckiewicz, S. & Gontarczyk, P. (2008) *SB a Lech Wałęsa* (Gdańsk-Warszawa-Kraków: IPN)

Charles, G. (ed.) (1925) *Great Short Stories of the World* (London: Heinemann)

Chwin, S. (2005) *Death in Danzig* (London: Secker & Warburg)

CIA (2014) *Preparing for Martial Law: Through The Eyes of Col. Ryszard Kukliński* (Kindle: CIA)

Cienski, J. (2010) '*The Catholic Church's post-communist windfall*'. *GlobalPost*. www.pri.org/stories/2010-10-28/catholic-churchs-post-communist-windfall

Cienski, J. (2018) *Start-Up Poland: The People Who Transformed an Economy* (Chicago: University of Chicago Press)

Cohen, N. (2017) 'The Dirty Tricks that Demonise George Soros': www.theguardian.com/commentisfree/2017/apr/15/dirty-tricks-demonise-george-soros

Conrad, J. (1908) *A Set of Six* (London: Dent)

Conrad, J. (1968) *Lord Jim* (Harmondsworth: Penguin)

Conrad, J. (1970) *Notes on Life and Letters* (London: Dent)

Conrad, J. (1972) *Tales of Hearsay & Last Essays* (London: Dent)

Conradi, P.J. & Martin, S. (eds.) (1999) *Cold War, Common Pursuit: British Council Lecturers in Poland 1938-98* (London: Starhaven)

Coutouvidis, J. & Reynolds, J. (1986) *Poland 1939-47* (Leicester: Leicester University Press)

Culture Vulture (2006) 'Polish Writers' www.blogs.guardian.co.uk/culturevulture/archives/2006/01/30

Czapski, J. (2018a) *Inhuman Land: Searching for the Truth in Russia 1941-42* (New York: New York Review of Books)

Czapski, J. (2018b) *Lost Time: Lectures on Proust in a Soviet Prison Camp* (New York: New York Review of Books)

Czarnota, A. (2008) 'The politics of the lustration law in Poland, 1989–2006': www.is.muni.cz/el/1422/podzim2012/MVV32K/um/Lustration_readings_-_short.pdf

Davies, C. (2016) '*The conspiracy theorists who have taken over Poland*'. *The Guardian*. www.theguardian.com/world/2016/feb/16/conspiracy-theorists-who-have-taken-over-poland

Bibliography 241

Davies, C. (2017a) 'Polish government brings forward plans to assert control over judges'. www.theguardian.com/world/2017/jul/18/polish-government-brings-forward-plans-to-assert-control-over-judges

Davies, C. (2017b) 'More girls, fewer skinheads'. www.theguardian.com/world/2017/nov/18/more-girls-fewer-skinheads-polands-far-right-wrestles-with-changing-image

Davies, C. (2018) 'Poland's Holocaust law triggers tide of abuse against Auschwitz museum'. www.theguardian.com/world/2018/may/07/polands-holocaust-law-triggers-tide-abuse-auschwitz-museum

Davies, C. (2019a) 'Top Polish official resigns over alleged harassment of judges'. www.theguardian.com/world/2019/aug/21/top-polish-official-resigns-over-alleged-harassment-of-judges

Davies, C. (2019b) 'Cruder than the Communists: Polish TV goes all out for right-wing vote': www.theguardian.com/world/2019/oct/11/cruder-than-the-communists-polish-tv-goes-all-out-for-rightwing-vote

Davies, W.J.K. (1973) *The German Army Handbook 1939-45* (New York: Arco)

Dehnel, J. (2008) *Six Polish Poets* (Todmorden: Arc)

Dehnel, J. (2019) *Lala* (London: Oneworld)

Deighton, L. (1989) *Hook, Line and Sinker* (London: Grafton)

Deutscher, I. (1981) *The Non-Jewish Jew and Other Essays* (London: Merlin Press)

Deutscher, I. (1982) 'The Tragedy of the Polish Communist Party', in: Eve, M. & Muson, D. (eds.), *The Socialist Register 1982* (London: Merlin)

Długosz-Kurczabowa, K. (2018) *Wielki Słownik Etymologiczno Historyczny Języka Polskiego* (Warsaw: Polski Wydawnictwo Naukowe)

Döblin, A. (1991) *Journey to Poland* (New York: Tauris)

Drewnowski, T. (ed.) (2007) *Postal Indiscretions: The Correspondence of Tadeusz Borowski* (Evanston: Northwestern University Press)

Dunin-Wąsowic, P. (2000) 'BRULION', *The Chicago Review: New Polish Writing*, 46(3 & 4), 366–373

van der Dussen, J. & Wilson, K. (eds) (1993) *What is Europe?* (Milton Keynes: Open University)

Edelman, M. ([1945] 1990) *The Ghetto Fights* (London: Bookmarks)

Edwards, R. (1998) *Panzer: A Revolution in Warfare 1939-45* (London: Brockhampton)

Eliot, T.S. (1928) *For Lancelot Andrewes* (London: Faber & Faber)

Eliot, T.S. (1952) 'Tradition and the Individual Talent', in: *Selected Prose* (London: Faber & Faber)

Eliot, T.S. (1986) *On Poetry and Poets* (London: Faber & Faber)

Emigh, R.J., Fodor, E., Szelényi, I. & Tarkowska, E. (2001) 'The radicalisation and feminisation of poverty', in: Emigh, R.J. and Szelényi, I. (eds) *Poverty, Ethnicity, and Gender in Eastern Europe during the Market Transition* (Westport: Greenwood Publishing)

Engel, D. (1987) *In the Shadow of Auschwitz: The Polish Government in Exile and the Jews 1939-42* (Chapel Hill: University Press)

Engel, D. (1993) *Facing the Holocaust: The Polish Government in Exile and the Jews 1943-45* Chapel Hill: University Press)

Esche, C., Mossiah, R.K. & Topalska, S. (2009) 'Lost and found: Communism nostalgia and communist chic among Poland's old and young generations'. www.humanityinaction.org/knowledgebase/62-lost-and-found-communism-nostalgia-and-communist-chic-among-poland-s-old-and-young-generations

242 Bibliography

Esslin, M. (1970) *Three East European Plays* (Harmondsworth: Penguin)

Eve, M. & Musson, D. (eds.) (1982) *The Socialist Register 1982* (London: Merlin)

Ficowski, J. (2000) *Regions of the Great Controversy* (London: Newman-Hemisphere)

Filipiak, I. (2002) *Pani Intuita* (Warsaw: Nowy Świat)

Filipowicz, K. (2019) *The Memoir of an Anti-Hero* (London: Penguin)

Fink, I. (1989) *A Scrap of Time* (Harmondsworth: Penguin)

Fleming, M. (ed.), (2018) *Brexit and Polonia: Challenges Facing the Polish Community during the Process of Britain Leaving the European Union* (London: PUNO)

Flood, A. (2014) 'UK publishes more books per capita than any other country, report shows'. www.theguardian.com/books/2014/oct/22/uk-publishes-more-books-per-capita-million-report

Flood, A. (2018) 'John le Carré letter reveals author's contempt for British political class'. www.theguardian.com/books/2018/may/22/john-le-carre-letter-british-politics

Forczyk, R. (2019) *Case White: The Invasion of Poland 1939* (London: Osprey)

Forum, P. (1988) *Forum Polek: Polish Women's Forum: A Women's Anthology in Polish and English* (London: Forum Publication Group)

Fuks, M., Hoffman, Z., Horn, M., & Tomaszewski, J. (1982) *Polish Jewry: History and Culture* (Warsaw: Interpress)

Fukuyama, F. (1992) *The End of History and The Last Man* (Penguin: London)

Funder, A. (2003) *Stasiland: Stories from Behind the Berlin Wall* (London: Granta)

Garliński, J. (1969) *Poland, SOE and the Allies* (London: Allen & Unwin)

Garliński, J. (1985) *Poland in the Second World War* (London: Macmillan)

Gazeta Wyborcza, editorial (2012) 'Czempiński u Olejnik: teczka Lecha Wałęsy to falszywka'

Glenny, M. (1993) *The Rebirth of History: Eastern Europe in the Age of Democracy* (London: Penguin)

Glenny, M. (2009) *McMafia: Seriously Organised Crime* (New York: Vintage)

Głowiński, M. (2005) *The Black Seasons* (Evanston: Northwestern University Press)

Goerke, N. (2001) *Farwells to Plasma* (Prague: Twisted Spoon)

Goldblatt, D. & Nolan, D. (2018) 'Viktor Orbán's reckless football obsession': www.theguardian.com/news/2018/jan/11/viktor-orban-hungary-prime-minister-reckless-football-obsession?

Gombrowicz, W. (1973) *A Kind of Testament* (London: Boyars)

Gombrowicz, W. (1988) *Diary Volume One 1953-56* (Evanston: Northwestern University Press)

Gomułka, S. & Polonsky, A. (eds) (1990) *Polish Paradoxes* (London: Routledge)

Górka-Czarnecka, J. (2017) *Daniel Mróz* (Krakow: Artemis)

Górski, G. (2017) *The Polish Underground State 1939–45* (Saarbrücken: Lambert AP)

Gramsci, A. (1971) *Prison Notebooks* (London: Lawrence & Wishart)

Grey, S. (2007, June 7) 'Secret CIA prisons confirmed by Polish and Romanian officials'. www.theguardian.com/world/2007/jun/07/usa1

Gromada, A. (2017) 'Pride is at stake in Poland's tussle with the EU'. www.theguardian.com/commentisfree/2017/aug/01/poland-tussle-eu-populist-leaders-nationalist-feeling-judicial-reforms

Gross, J.T. (1988) *Neighbours: The Destruction of the Jewish Community in Jedwabne, Poland 1941* (London: Random House)

Gross, J.T. (2004) 'After Auschwitz: The reality and meaning of postwar anti-semitism in Poland', in: Frankel, J. (ed.) *Dark Times, Dire Decisions: Jews and Communism* (Oxford: Oxford University Press)

Bibliography 243

Gross, J.T. (2006) *Fear: Anti-Semitism in Poland after Auschwitz* (New Jersey: Princeton University Press)

Grynberg, H. (1993) *The Victory* (Evanston: Northwestern University Press)

Grzyzło, D. (2007) *Lustration: The case of Poland* (Kraków: Uniwersytet Jagiellonski, Wydział Filozofii, Instytut Filozofii) www.iphils.uj.edu.pl/democracy/htm/papers/Dariusz_Gryzlo

GUS (2012) *Główny Urząd Statystyczny – Ubóstwo w Polsce w 2011r.* Warsaw: GUS – Główny Urząd Statystyczny. www.stat.gov.pl/obszary-tematyczne/warunki-zycia/ubostwo-pomoc-spoleczna/

GUS (2018) Główny Urząd Statystyczny – Polski Związek Przemysłu Motoryzacynego. www.pzpm.org.pl/en/Automotive-market/Motor-Vehicle-Production-in-Poland

Gutman, Y. (1977) 'Jews in General Anders' army in the Soviet Union'. www.yad-vashem.org/odot_pdf/Microsoft%20Word%20-%206217.pdf

Halikowska, T. & Hyde, G. (eds) (1996) *The Eagle and the Crow: Modern Polish Short Stories* (London: Serpent's Tail)

Hamšík, D. (1971) *Writers Against Rulers* (London: Hutchinson)

Harper, J. (2018) *Poland's Memory Wars: Essays on Illiberalism* (Budapest: Central European University Press)

Havel, V. (1990) *Disturbing the Peace* (London: Faber & Faber)

HC Deb (1944) vol. 398 cc2260-303: www.api.parliament.uk/historic-hansard/commons/1944/apr/06/polish-forces-great-britain-anti-semitism

Heath, R. (2018) 'Viktor Orbán cements place in Europe's new center right'. *POLITICO*. www.politico.eu/article/viktor-orban-epp-hungary-reshapes-european-center-right

Herbert, Z. (1968) *Zbigniew Herbert Selected Poems* (Harmondsworth: Penguin)

Herbert, Z. (1985) *Barbarian in the Garden* (Manchester: Carcanet)

Herbert, Z. (2007) *The Collected Poems 1956-1998* (New York: Ecco)

Herbert, Z. (2010) *Collected Prose 1948-1998* (New York: Ecco)

Herbert, Z. (2011) *Wierszy rozproszonych (Rekonesans)* (Krakow: Wydawnictwo a5)

Herbert, Z. (2014) *Notes Herbertowski* (Kraków: Austeria)

Herling, G. (1987) *A World Apart: Imprisonment in a Soviet Labour Camp During World War II* (Oxford: OUP)

Hłasko, M. (2013) *Beautiful Twentysomethings* (DeKalb: Northern Illinois University Press)

Hobsbawm, E. & Ranger, T. (eds) (1983) *The Invention of Tradition* (Cambridge: Cambridge University Press)

Hoffman, E. (1991) *Lost in Translation: Life in a New Language* (London: Minerva)

Hoffman, E. (1993) *Exit into History: A Journey through the New Eastern Europe* (London: Heinemann)

Hoffman, E. (1998) *Shtetl: The History of a Small Town and an Extinguished World* (London: Secker & Warburg)

Hoffman, E. (2004) *After Such Knowledge: A Meditation on the Aftermath of the Holocaust* (London: Secker & Warburg)

Hubbard, R. (2019) *From Partition to Solidarity: The First 100 Years of Polish Football* (Leicester: RAH)

Huelle, P. (1991) *Who was David Weisser?* (London: Bloomsbury)

Huelle, P. (1994) *Moving House* (London: Bloomsbury)

Huelle, P. (2005) *Mercedes Benz* (London: Bloomsbury)

Huelle, P. (2007a) *Castorp* (London: Bloomsbury)

Huelle, P. (2007c) 'The Map', in: Zagajewski A. (ed.) *Polish Writers on Writing* (San Antonio: Trinity University Press)

244 *Bibliography*

Huelle, P. (2007b) *The Last Supper* (London: Bloomsbury)

Hughes, H.S. (1988) *Sophisticated Rebels: The Political Culture of European Dissent, 1968–87* (Cambridge, MA: Harvard University Press)

'Hungary Still in Decline CPI 2016' (2017) Transparency International: transparency. hu/en/news/cpi-2016-magyarorszag-tovabbra-is-lejtmenetben

'Hungary's Viktor Orbán Secures another Term with Resounding Win' (2018) www.theguardian.com/world/2018/apr/08/hungarys-viktor-orban-secures-another-term-with-resounding-win

Husarka, A. (1994) 'Post no bills: Polish artists mourn their good life under communism', *New Yorker*, 69, 62–65

Ireland, D. (2006) 'Direland: Poland's anti-gay prime minister outed as the government continues to spew homo-hate'. *Gay City News*. www.direland.typepad. com/direland/2006/10/polands_antigay

Ionescu, G. (1965) *The Break-Up of the Soviet Empire in Eastern Europe* (Harmondsworth: Penguin)

Iwaszkiewicz, J. (2002) *The Birch Grove and Other Stories* (Budapest: CEU Press)

Janion, M. (2000) *Do Europy tak, ale razem z naszymi umarlymi (Into Europe, yes, but with our dead)* (Warsaw: Sic!)

Janion, M. (2006) *Niesamowita Słowiańczyzna (Weird Slavism)* (Warsaw: Wydawnictwo Literackie)

Janion, M. (2014a) 'Poland between the West and East'. www//rcin.org.pl/ Content/51830/WA248_71041_P-I-2524_janion-poland.pdf

Janion, M. (2014b) *Hero, Conspiracy, and Death: The Jewish Lectures* (Frankfurt am Main: Peter Lang)

Janowski, M., Jedlicki, J. & Micińska, M. (eds) (2014) *A History of the Polish Intelligentsia* (New York: Peter Lang)

Jasieński, B. (2014) *The Legs of Izolda Morgan* (Prague: Twisted Spoon Press)

Jasiewicz, K. (1995) 'The Polish voter', in: Bernhard, M. & Szlajfer, H. (eds) *From the Polish Underground: Selections from Krytyka, 1973-93* (University Park: Penn State Press)

Jedlicki, J. (1999) *A Suburb of Europe: Nineteenth Century Polish Approaches to Western Civilisation* (Budapest: Central European University)

Jenkins, N. (ed.) (1991) *The Works* (Cardiff: Welsh Union of Writers)

Johnsson, P. (2013) 'Gated communities – Poland', *Baltic Worlds*, 3–4, 26–32. www.balticworlds.com/poland-holds-the-european-record-in-housing-for-the-distrustful

Kaj, M. &Metzger, M. (2007) 'Justice or revenge? The human rights implications of lustration in Poland'. *Humanity in Action*. www.humanityinaction.org/ knowledgebase/165-justice-or-revenge-the-human-rights-implications-of-lustration-in-poland

Karol, K.S. (1983) *Solik: Life in the Soviet Union 1938-46* (London: Pluto)

Karpowicz, I. (2008) *Gestures* (Victoria: Dalkey Archive)

Karski, J. (2019) *Story of a Secret State: My Report to the World* (London: Penguin)

Karsov, N. & Szechter, S. (1971) *In the Name of Tomorrow: Life Underground in Poland* (New York: Schocken)

Keane, J. (ed.) (1988) *Civil Society and the State* (London: Verso)

Kemp-Welch, A. (2008) *Poland under Communism: A Cold War History* (Cambridge: Cambridge University Press)

Kersten, K. (1991) *The Establishment of Communist Rule in Poland: 1943-48* (Berkeley: University of California Press)

Kielar, M. (2006) *Salt Monody* (Brookline: Zephyr)

Bibliography 245

Kijowski, A. (1983) 'The Writer and the State', *Tri-Quarterly*, 57 (Spring/Summer)

Kochanski, H. (2012) *The Eagle Unbowed: Poland and the Poles in the Second World War* (London: Penguin)

Koczanowicz, L. (2008) *Politics of Time: Dynamics of Identity in Post-Communist Poland* (New York: Berghahn)

Kołakowski, L. (1981) *Main Currents of Marxism vol 2: The Golden Age* (Oxford: Oxford University Press)

Konrád, G. (1984) *Antipolitics* (London: Quartet)

Konrád, G. & Szelényi, I. (1979) *The Intellectuals on the Road to Class Power: A Sociological Study of the Role of the Intelligentsia in Socialism* (London: Harvester)

Korboński, S. (2004) *Fighting Warsaw: The Story of the Polish Underground State 1939-45* (New York: Hippocrene)

Kornhauser, J. (2000) 'Loyalty', *The Chicago Review: New Polish Writing*, 46(3 & 4), 99

Kostrzewa, R. (1990) *Between East and West: Writings from 'Kultura'* (New York: Hill and Wang)

Kott, J. (ed.) (1990) *Four Decades of Polish Essays* (Evanston: Northwestern University Press)

Kovacik, K. (ed.) (2015) *Scattering in the Dark: An Anthology of Polish Women Poets* (New York: White Pine)

Koziński, B. (2016) *Determinants of the Ethnic Policy of the Polish Government in Exile in the Years 1939-47* (Warsaw: Wydawnictwo Naukowe UKSW)

Krajewski, M. (2008) *Death in Breslau: An Eberhard Mock Investigation* (London: Maclehose)

Krall, H. (1986) *Shielding the Flame: An Intimate Conversation with Dr Marek Edelman, The Last Surviving Leader of the Warsaw Ghetto Uprising* (New York: Henry Holt)

Krall, H. (1992) *The Subtenant ~To Outwit God* (Evanson: Northwestern University Press)

Krall, H. (2006) *The Woman from Hamburg and Other True Stories* (New York: Other Press)

Kraszewski, S. (ed.) (2006) *Fifty Years of Polish Scholarship: The Polish Review 1956-2006* (Kindle Edition, New York: Polish Institute of Arts and Sciences of America)

Krynicki, R. (2017) *Magnetic Point* (New York: New Directions)

Krynicki, R. (2018) *Our Life Grows (Uncensored)* (New York: NYRB)

Kuncewicz, M. (ed.) (1962) *The Modern Polish Mind* (London: Secker & Warburg)

Kundera, M. (1984a) *A Kidnapped West or Culture Bows Out* (Cambridge: Granta)

Kundera, M. (1984b) 'The tragedy of Central Europe', (Edmund White, tr.), *New York Review of Books*, 31(7), 1–14.

Kundera, M. (2007) *The Curtain* (London: Faber)

Kundera, M. (2009) *Encounter* (London: Faber)

Kunicki, M.S. (2012) *Between the Brown and the Red: Nationalism, Catholicism and Communism in 20th Century Poland – The Politics of Bolesław Piasecki* (Athens: Ohio University Press)

Kurczewska, J. (1995) 'The Polish intelligentsia: Departure from the scene', in: Bernhard, M. & Szlajfer, H. (eds) *From the Polish Underground: Selections from Krytyka 1978–93* (Philadelphia: Pennsylvania State University Press)

Lawrence, D.H. (1950) *Selected Essays* (Harmondsworth: Penguin)

246   *Bibliography*

Leavis, F.R. (1948) *The Great Tradition* (London: Chatto & Windus)

Leavis, F.R. & Leavis, Q.D. (1970) *Dickens the Novelist* (London: Chatto & Windus)

Le Carré, J. (2017) *A Legacy of Spies* (London: Viking)

Lechoń, J. (2007) *Karmazynowy Poemat* (Michigan: Michigan University Press)

Leftwich Curry, J. (1984) *The Black Book of Polish Censorship* (New York: Vintage)

Lehaw, J. (2009) 'Proud Hungarians must prepare for war against the Jews'. www. haaretz.com

Lemnis, M. & Vitry, H. (1981) *Old Polish Traditions in the Kitchen and at the Table* (Warsaw: Interpress)

Lesnikowski, W. (1996) *East European Modernism: Architecture in Czechoslovakia, Hungary and Poland Between the Wars* (London: Thames & Hudson)

Libera, A. (2001) *Madame* (Edinburgh: Canongate)

Lipska, E. (2000) 'Mr Schmetterling thinks about a United Europe', *The Chicago Review: New Polish Writing*, 46(3 & 4)

Lottman, H.R. (1998) 'Publishing in Poland'. www.publishersweekly.com/pw/print/19980504/21244-pw-publishing-in-poland

Loughrey, C. (2019) 'Independent bookshops on the rise for the second year running'. www.independent.co.uk/arts-entertainment/books/news/independent-bookshops-rise-2018-data-high-street-uk

Lukas, R.C. (2001) *The Forgotten Holocaust: The Poles under German Occupation 1939-44* (New York: Hippocrene)

Luttwak, E. (1994) 'Why Fascism is the wave of the future'. *London Review of Books*. www.lrb.co.uk/the-paper/v16/n07/edward-luttwak/why-fascism-is-the-wave-of-the-future

Luxemburg, R. (1977) *The Industrial Development of Poland (1898)* (London: Campaign)

Lyman, R. & Berendt, J. (2015) 'As Poland lurches to right, many in Europe look on in alarm'. www.nytimes.com/2015/12/15/world/europe/poland-law-and-justice-party-jaroslaw-kaczynski

Lynskey, D. (2019) 'Is the political novel dead?'. www.theguardian.com/books/2019/aug/24/is-the-political-novel-dead

MacDowall, A & van der Zee, B. (2017) 'Local media are simply disappearing'. www.theguardian.com/media/2017/nov/30/closure-of-nepszabadsag-hungarian-daily-highlights-threat-to-independent-media?

Majchrowicz-Bączyk, A. (2020) 'EU funds in Poland 2014–20': www.roedl.com/pl/en/services/state_aid:advice/eu_funds_in_poland_20142020

March, M. (ed.) (1990) *Child of Europe: A New Anthology of East European Poetry* (Harmondsworth: Penguin)

March, M. (ed.) (1994) *Description of a Struggle: The Picador Book of Contemporary East European Prose* (London: Picador)

Marvin, T. (2011) 'Shock therapy'. *Prospect*. www.prospectjournal.org/2010/11/11/shock-therapy-what-we-can-learn-from-poland

Marx, K. (1967) *The Eighteenth Brumaire of Louis Bonaparte* (Moscow: Progress Publishers)

Masłowska, D. (2005) *White and Red* (New York & London: Grove/Atlantic Monthly)

Mason, P. (2017) 'This weekend's march in Poland proves the far right isn't going away without a fight'. www.theguardian.com/world/2017/nov/13/polish-president-condemns-far-right-scenes-at-independence-day-march

Bibliography 247

Matthews, D. (2019) 'Holocaust historians suffer antis-Semitic abuse at conference'. www.timeshighereducation.com/news/holocaust-historians-suffer-antisemitic-abuse-conference

Mayewski, P. (ed.) (1958) *The Broken Mirror* (New York: Random House)

McEwan, I. (1984) 'An interview with Milan Kundera', *Granta*, 11, 19–38

McGilvray, E. (2013) *A Military Government in Exile: The Polish Government in Exile 1939-1945: A Study of Discontent* (Warwick: Helion Studies in Military History)

'Mediaworks Hungary Suspends Publication of Népszabadság and nol.hu' (2016). www.budapestbeacon.com/mediaworks-hungary-suspends-publication-of-nepszabadsag-and-nol-hu

Meek, J. (2017) 'Somerdale to Skarbimierz'. *London Review of Books*

Mendel, H. (1989) *Memoirs of a Jewish Revolutionary* (London: Pluto)

Mengham, R., Pióro, T. & Szymor, P. (eds.) (2003) *Altered State: The New Polish Poetry* (Todmorden: Ark)

Merkl, P.H. & Weinberg, L. (2013) *The Revival of Right-Wing Extremism in the Nineties* (London: Routledge)

Michalów A. & Pacławski W. (eds) (1991) *Literary Galicia: From Post-War to Post-Modern: A Local Guide to the Global Imagination* (Krakow: Oficyna Literacka)

Michnik, A. (1987) *Letters from Prison: And Other Essays* (Berkeley: California UP)

Michnik, A. (1990) 'The two faces of Europe', in: *Writings on the East* (New York: New York Review of Books)

Michnik, A. (1998) *Letters from Freedom: Post-Cold War Realties and Perspectives* (Berkeley: California University Press)

Michnik, A. (2007) 'The Polish witch-hunt'. *New York Review of Books*. www.nybooks.com/articles/2007/06/28/the-polish-witch-hunt

Michnik, A. (2011) *In Search of Lost Meaning: The New Eastern Europe* (Berkeley: University of California Press)

Michnik, A. & Marczyk, A. (2018) *Against Anti-Semitism: An Anthology of Twentieth-Century Writings* (Oxford: OUP)

Międzyrzecki, A. (1991) 'What does the political scientist know', in: Barańczak S and Cavanagh C (eds.), *Polish Poetry of the Last Two Decades of Communist Rule: Spoiling Cannibals' Fun* (Evanston: Northwestern University Press), 59–60

Mikołajewski, L. (2018) *Disenchanted Europeans: Polish Emigre Writers from 'Kultura' and Postwar Reformulations of the West* (Bern: Peter Lang)

Mikoś, M.J. (2006) *Polish Literature from 1864-1918: Realism and Young Poland. An Anthology* (Bloomington: Slavica)

Millard, F. (2012) *Democratic Elections in Poland 1991-2007* (Oxford: Routledge)

Miłosz, C. (1965) *Postwar Polish Poetry* (New York: Doubleday)

Miłosz, C. (1981) *Native Realm: A Search for Self-Definition* (London: Sidgwick & Jackson)

Miłosz, C. (1983) *The History of Polish Literature* (Berkeley: California University Press)

Miłosz, C. (1988) *The Collected Poems 1931-1987* (London: Viking)

Miłosz, C. (1992) *Beginning with my Streets: Baltic Reflections* (London: Tauris)

Miłosz, C. (1996) *Legends of Modernity: Essays and Letters from Occupied Poland 1942-43* (New York: Farrar, Straus & Giroux)

Miłosz, C. (2003) *New Collected Poems 1931-2001* (New York: ecco)

248   Bibliography

Miłoszewski, Z. (2018) *Priceless* (Seattle: Amazon Crossing)

Mrożek, S. (1959) *Wesele w Atomicach* (Kraków: Wydawnictwo Literackie)

Mrożek, S. (1962) *The Elephant* (New York: Grove Press)

Mulley, C. (2012) *The Spy Who Loved: The Secrets and Lives of Christine Granville: Britain's First Female Special Agent of the Second World War* (London: Macmillan)

Myśliwski, W. (1991) *The Palace* (London: Peter Owen)

Najder, Z. (ed.) (1964) *Conrad's Polish Background: Letters to and from Polish Friends* (Oxford: OUP)

Najder, Z. (1983) *Conrad under Familial Eyes* (Cambridge: Cambridge University Press)

Nałkowska, Z. (1932) 'Organizacja erotyzmu', *Wiadomości Literackie*, 9(25/442)

Nałkowska, Z. (2000) *Medallions* (Evanston: Northwestern University Press)

Nałkowska, Z. (2014a) *The Romance of Teresa Hennert* (De Kalb: Northern Illinois University Press)

Nałkowska, Z. (2014b) *Choucas* (De Kalb: Northern Illinois University Press)

Nałkowska, Z. (2016) *Boundary* (De Kalb: Northern Illinois University Press)

New York Review of Books (1990) *Writings on the East* (New York: New York Review of Books)

Nolan, D. & Walker, S. (2018) 'Hungarian journalists admit role in forging anti-migrant "atmosphere of fear"'. www.theguardian.com/world/2018/apr/13/hungary-journalists-state-tv-network-migrants-viktor-orban-government

Nowak, J. (1982) *Courier from Warsaw* (Detroit: Wayne State Press)

Nowakowski, M. (1983) *The Canary and Other Tales of Martial Law* (London: Harvill)

Nowakowski, M. (2007) 'Szpiegowali mnie przyjaciele' (My Friends Spied on Me) in: *Dziennik O Lustracji: Sposobie Ujawniania Materialw Zgromadzonych w IPN (June 2007) CBOS*. www.cbos.pl/spiskom.pol/2007/k_102_07.pdf

Nyczek, T. (ed.) (1982) *Humps & Wings: Polish Poetry Since 1968* (San Francisco/Los Angeles: Invisible City)

'Observer View on the EU's Eastern Bloc' (2018). www.theguardian.com/world/commentisfree/2018/jan/07/observer-view-european-union-eastern-bloc-hungary-poland

O Lustracji: Sposobie Ujawniania Materialw Zgromadzonych w IPN (2007) CBOS. www.cbos.pl/SPISKOM.POL/2007/K_102_07.PDF

Orwell, G. (1968) *Collected Essays, Journalism and Letters*, vol. 4 (Harmondsworth: Penguin)

OSCE (2018) 'Limited election observation mission Hungary—Parliamentary elections'. www.osce.org/odihr/elections/hungary/377410?download=true

O'Toole, F. (2018) *Heroic Failure: Brexit and the Politics of Pain* (London: Head of Zeus)

Partington, R. (2019) 'Poles will return east to higher wages and jobs, and UK will lose out'. www.theguardian.com/business/2019/feb/24/poles-return-east-higher-wages-job-uk-lose-brexit

Partridge, E. (1978) *Origins: A Short Etymological Dictionary of Modern English* (London: Routledge & Keegan Paul)

Perechodnik, C. (1996) *Am I a Murderer? Testament of a Jewish Ghetto Policeman* (Boulder: Westview)

Peterkiewicz, J. & Singer, B. (eds) (1970) *Five Centuries of Polish Poetry* (Oxford: OUP)

Bibliography 249

Pfeffer, A. (2018) 'Netanyahu and Orban'. www.haaretz.com/israel-news/.premium-the-netanyahu-orban-bromance-that-is-shaking-up-europe-and-d-c-1.6290691

Phillips, U. (ed.) (2013) *Polish Literature in Transformation* (Zürich: LIT Verlag)

Piekarski, A. (1979) *Freedom of Conscience and Religion in Poland* (Warsaw: Interpress)

Pilch, J. (2009) *A Thousand Peaceful Cities* (Rochester: Open Letter)

Piłsudski, J. (1972) www.en.poland.gov.pl/Jozef,Pilsudski.%281867-1935%29, 1972.html

Pirie, D. (ed.) (1993) *Young Poets of a New Poland* (London: Forest/UNESCO)

Plach, E. (2006) *The Clash of Moral Nations: Cultural Politics in Pilsudski's Poland 1926-1935* (Ohio: Ohio University Press)

Plokhy, S. (2019) *Chernobyl: History of a Tragedy* (London: Penguin)

'Poland Judiciary Reforms' (2017). www.bbc.co.uk/news/world-europe-42420150

'Poland's GDP Growth to Reach 4% in 2017 Before Slowing Down 2018 says World Bank' (2017). www.worldbank.org/en/news/press-release: 2017/ECA/019

'Poland's Ruling Party Reinstates Supreme Court judges' (2018) www.ft.com/content/5b2e48f4-ed7a-11e8-8180-9cf212677a57

'Polena Ostrzeszów' (2020). pollena.com.pl/65-zestawy-kosmetykow

Polonsky, A. (ed.) (1990) *My Brother's Keeper: Recent Debates on the Holocaust* (London: Routledge)

Polonsky, A. (ed.) (1993) *Studies from Polin: From Shtetl to Socialism* (London: The Littman Library of Jewish Civilization)

Polonsky, A. & Adamczyk-Garbowska, M. (2001) *Contemporary Jewish Writing in Poland: An Anthology* (Lincoln: University of Nebraska Press)

Polonsky, A. & Michlic, J.B. (eds) (2004) *The Neighbours Respond: The Controversy over the Jedwabne Massacre in Poland* (Princeton: Princeton University Press)

Poppek, A. & Gelberg, A. (1994) 'Mr. Cogito's duels: Zbigniew Herbert: A conversation' (*Tygodnik Solidarność*, no: 46/321). www.ruf.rice.edu/~sarmatia/495/herbert

Powaga, W. (ed.) (1996) *The Dedalus Book of Polish Fantasy* (Sawtry: Dedalus/Hippocrene)

Prentoulis, M. (2018) 'Greece may still be Europe's sick patient, but the EU is at death's door'.www.theguardian.com/commentisfree/2018/aug/21/greece-europe-eu-austerity

Prokop-Janiec, E. (2003) *Polish-Jewish Literature in the Interwar Years* (New York: Syracuse University Press)

Prus, B. (1956) *Kroniki* (Warsaw: Państwowy Instytut Wydawniczy)

Pyzik, A. (2014) *Poor but Sexy: Culture Clashes in Europe East and West* (Winchester, UK: Zero Books)

Pyzik, A. (2019) 'Poland'. *London Review of Book*

Radio Poland (2020a). www.thenews.pl/1/12/Artykul/109461, Gold-seized-during-inspection-of-collapsed-lender-Amber-Gold

Radio Poland (2020b). www.thenews.pl/1/9/Artykul/191250, Polish-Communist-police-chief-admits-destroying-informers-records#sthash.0t3ZoXKi.dpuf

Radio Poland (2020c). www.thenews.pl/1/9/Artykul/109516, Walesa-biopic-will-not-have-Amber-Gold-as-investor

Rae, G. (2012) 'Public debt in Poland: The debt crisis in Poland and its impact on society'. www.cadtm.org/IMG/pdf/public_debt-2.pdf

Rankin, J. (2019) 'EU leaders must do more to save rule of law in Hungary, says MEP'. www.theguardian.com/world/2019/jan/30/eu-leaders-must-do-more-to-save-rule-of-law-in-hungary-says-mep

250 Bibliography

Reiman, D.H. & Powers, S.B. (eds) (1977) *Shelley's Poetry and Prose* (New York: Norton)

Rosen, M., Roberts, D., Mian, E., France, M. & Cummins, A. (eds) (2017) *Writing with Punch: How novelists are Taking on the World* (London: Prospect)

Rosenberg, T. (1995) *The Haunted Land: Facing Europe's Ghosts after Communism* (London: Vintage)

Roszkowski, W. (2009) *Post-communist lustration in Poland: A political and moral dilemma* Warsaw: Congress of the Societas Ethica. www.societasethica.info/past-conferences-papers/2009-warsaw/1.334527/Roszkowski.pdf

Roth, J. (1984) *Flight Without End* (London: Peter Owen)

Roth, P. (2002) *Shop Talk: A Writer and his Colleagues and their Work* (London: Vintage)

Różycki, T. (2007) *The Forgotten Keys* (Brookline: Zephyr)

Rudnicki, S. (1993) 'From "Numerus Clausus" to "Numerus Nullus"', in: Polonsky, A. (ed.) *Studies from Polin: From Shtetl to Socialism* (London: Littman)

Rupnik, J. (1989) *The Other Europe* (London: Channel Four Books)

Rymkiewicz, J. (1994) *The Final Station: Umschlagplatz [Paris: Instytut Literacki]* (New York: Farrar, Straus, Giroux)

Sandauer, A. (2005) *On the Situation of the Polish Writer of Jewish Descent* (Jerusalem: The Hebrew University Magnes Press)

'San Escobar: Polish Foreign Minister's Slip Invents a Country' (2017). www.bbc.com/news/world-us-canada-38582447

Sapkowski, A. (2007) *The Last Wish* (London: Gollancz)

Sapkowski, A. (2008) *Blood of Elves* (London: Gollancz)

Schatz, J. (2004) 'Jews and the communist movement in interwar Poland', in: Frankel, J. (ed.) *Dark Times, Dire Decisions: Jews and Communism* (Oxford: OUP)

Schneider, P. (1992) *The German Comedy: Scenes of Life After the Wall* (New York: Tauris)

Schwartz, A. & Von Flotow, L. (eds) (2007) *The Third Shore: Women's Fiction from East Central Europe* (Dingle: Brandon)

Schweitzer, A. (2017) 'Why Viktor Orbán has a problem turning his country against immigrants'. www.theguardian.com/commentisfree/2017/sep/08/viktor-orban-immigrants-hungary-immigration-fears-pro-eu

Sebestyen, V. (2009) *Revolution 1989: The Fall of the Soviet Empire* (London: Phoenix)

Segal, H.B. (1996) *Stranger in our Midst: Images of the Jew in Polish Literature* (Ithaca: Cornell University Press)

Segev, T. (2000) *One Palestine Complete: Jews and Arabs under the British Mandate* (London: Abacus)

Shore, M. (2006) *Caviar and Ashes: A Warsaw Generation's Life and Death in Marxism 1918-1968* (Yale: Yale University Press)

Shore, M. (2013) *The Taste of Ashes* (London: Heinemann)

Shotter, J. & Huber, E. (2018) 'Polish companies target Ukrainian workers as consumers': *The Financial Times*. www.ft.com/content/f6a2e838-8350-11e8-96dd-fa565ec55929

Siciński, A. (1971) *Literaci polscy: przemiany zawodu na tle przemian kultury współczesnej* (Wrocław – Warsaw – Kraków – Gdańsk: Instytut Filozofii i Socjologii: Zakład Narodowy Imienia Ossolińskich Wydawnictwo Polskiej Academii Nauk)

Bibliography 251

Sierakowski, S. (2017) 'Mourning Poland's burning man'. www.project-syndicate. org/commentary/poland-self-immolation-by-slawomir-sierakowski-2017-10

Sierakowski, S. (2018) 'Poland's dictatorship of myth'. www.project-syndicate.org/ commentary/poland-memory-law-amendment-by-slawomir-sierakowski-2018-08

Sierakowski, S. (2019) 'Teflon Populism'. www.project-syndicate.org/commentary/ poland-law-and-justice-immune-to-scandals-by-slawomir-sierakowski-2019-06

Sierakowski, S. & Michnik, A. (2017) 'Europe's new eastern question'. www. project-syndicate.org/onpoint/europe-s-new-eastern-question-by-slawomir-sierakowski-2017-11

Sienkiewicz, H. (1931) *Tales from Sienkiewicz* (London: Everyman)

Śliwiński, P. (2000) 'Are things worse or is this normal? Polish poetry in the 1990s', *The Chicago Review: New Polish Writing*, 46(3 & 4)

Słonimski, A. (1926) 'Historia Pikadora'. *Wiadomości Literackie*

Slovakia Election: Double Murder Haunts Voters (2020). www.bbc.co.uk/news/ world-europe-51657803

Smith, A. (2010) *The Theory of Moral Sentiments (1759)* (London: Penguin)

Sontag, S. (1982) *A Susan Sontag Reader* (Penguin: Harmondsworth)

Springer, F. (2017) *History of a Disappearance: The Story of a Forgotten Polish Town* (New York: Restless Books)

Staar, R.F. (1962) *Poland: 1944-62: The Sovietization of a Captive People* (New Orleans: Greenwood)

Stan, L. (2010) *Transitional Justice in Eastern Europe and the Former Soviet Union* (Abingdon: Routledge)

Stanisławski, J. (1970) *Wielki Słownik Polsko-Angielski* (Warsaw: Wiedza Powszechna)

Stape, J. (2008) *The Several Lives of Joseph Conrad* (London: Arrow)

Stasiuk, A. (1995a) *White Raven* (London: Serpents Tail)

Stasiuk, A. (1995b) *Tales of Galicia* (Prague: Twisted Spoon)

Stasiuk, A. (2007) *Nine* (London: Harvill-Secker)

Steiner, G. (1979) *Language and Silence* (Harmondsworth: Penguin)

Steiner, G. (1983) *The Portage to San Cristobal* (London: Faber)

Steiner, G. (1998) *After Babel: Aspects of Language & Translation* (Oxford: OUP)

Stiglitz, J. E. (2018) 'Can the euro be saved?. www.project-syndicate.org/commentary/ next-euro-crisis-italy-by-joseph-e--stiglitz-2018-06

Stonor Saunders, F. (1999) *Who Paid the Piper: The CIA and the Cultural Cold War* (London: Granta)

Strugatsky, B. & Strugatsky, A. (1977) *The Roadside Picnic* (New York: Simon & Schuster)

Stryjkowski, J. (1972) *The Inn* (London: Barrie & Jenkins)

Swan, O. (2013) 'The Polish duel and its last apologia', *The Polish Review*, 58(1), 3–14. www.history.lsa.umich.edu/PSA/Article%20Prize%202015/Swan.pdf

Szajkowski, B. (1983) *Next to God...Poland* (London: Pinter)

Szaruga, L. (1997) 'Post German, post Jewish' in: Petrie, R. (ed.) *The Fall of Communism and the Rise of Nationalism* (London: Index on Censorship/Cassell)

Szász, T. (1971) *The Manufacture of Madness* (London: Routledge, Keegan & Paul

Szczerbiak, A. (2001) *Poles Together? The Emergence and Development of Political Parties in Post-Communist Poland* (Budapest: Central European University)

Szewc, P. (1999) *Annihilation* (Normal: Dalkey Archive)

Szpilman, W. (2000) *The Pianist* (London: Phoenix)

Szymborska, W. (1995) *View with a Grain of Sand: Selected Poems* (London: Faber)

252 Bibliography

Szymiczkowa, M. (2019) *Mrs Mohr Goes Missing* (London: Point Blank Press) (*Tajemnica domu helcelów*, 2015)

Taylor, J. (1981) *Five Months with Solidarity* (London: Wildwood)

The Guardian (2001) 'Campaigns of a TV Stuntman'. *The Guardian*

The Times (2017). www.thetimes.co.uk/article/writers-facing-expulsion-from-Poland's-schools

Thompson, E.P. (1979) *The Poverty of Theory and Other Essays* (London: Merlin)

Thompson, E.P. (1985) *The Heavy Dancers* (London: Merlin)

Thompson, E.P. & Smith, D. (eds) (1980) *Protest and Survive* (Harmondsworth: Penguin)

Tighe, C. (1990) *Gdansk: National Identity in the Polish German Borderlands* (London: Pluto)

Tighe, C. (1991) 'Interview with Ryszard Kapuścinski', in: N. Jenkins (ed.) *The Works* (Cardiff: Welsh Union of Writers)

Tighe, C. (2010) 'Poland translated: the post-communist generation of writers', *Studies in East European Thought*, 62, 169–195

Tighe, C (2016) 'Lustration – the Polish experience', *Journal of European Studies*, 46, 338–373

Tilles, D. & Richardson, J. (2018) 'Poland and the Holocaust: A new law exposes the problematic nature of Holocaust remembrance'. *History Today*. www.history-today.com/daniel-tilles-and-john-richardson/poland-and-holocaust?

'Tinky-Winky Controversy' (2020). www.digplanet.com/wiki/Teletubbies#Tinky_Winky_controversy

Tischner, J. (2005) *Etyka Solidarności Oraz Homo Sovieticus* (Kraków: Znak)

Tokarczuk, O. (2002) *House of Day, House of Night* (London: Granta)

Tokarczuk, O. (2019) 'Nobel Lecture'. www.culture.pl/en/article/olga-tokarczuks-nobel-lecture-the-tender-narrator

Tooze, A. & Vallée, S. (2018) 'Germany's great European heist'. www.project-syndicate.org/commentary/germany-european-defense-free-riding-by-adam-tooze-and-shahin-vallee-1-2018-05

Topolski, J. (1986) *An Outline History of Poland* (Warsaw: Interpress)

Torańska, T. (1987) *Oni: Stalin's Polish Puppets* (London: Collins/Harvill)

Traynor, I. (2007) 'Famed Polish writer outed as spy in anti-communist purge'. www.theguardian.com/world/2007/may/21/pressandpublishing.booksnews

Trznadel, J. (1987) 'An interview with Zbigniew Herbert', *Paris Review*, LIV(4), 557–575

Tyrmand, L. (2014) *Diary 1954 (1980)* (Evanston: Northwestern University Press)

Urquhart, R.E. (1958) *Arnhem* (London: Cassel)

Vincze, Z.K. (2017) 'Breaking the silence: being Jewish in Hungary today', *Jewish Renaissance: A Fresh Perspective on Jewish Culture*, 25

Vladislav, J. (ed.) (1987) *Václav Havel, or Living in Truth* (London: Faber & Faber)

'Voter Turnout Poland' (2020). www.idea.int/data-tools/question-countries-view/521/242/ctr

Walker, S (2018a) 'Viktor Orbán Secures Another Term with Resounding Win'. www.theguardian.com/world/2018/apr/08/hungarys-viktor-orban-secures-another-term-with-resounding-win

Walker, S. (2018b) 'Emboldened Viktor Orbán cracks down on friend turned foe'. www.theguardian.com/world/2018/aug/12/orban-tightens-grip-on-hungary-as-oppositions-power-wanes

Bibliography 253

Walker, S. & Boffey, D. (2018) 'Hungary election: OSCE monitors deliver damning verdict'. www.theguardian.com/world/2018/apr/09/hungary-election-osce-monitors-deliver-damning-verdict

Wat, A. (1990) *Lucifer Unemployed* (Evanston: Northwestern University Press)

Wat, A. (1999) *My Century: The Odyssey of a Polish Intellectual* (New York: Norton)

Wat, A. (2018) *Against the Devil in History: Poems, Short Stories, Essays, Fragments* (Slavica: Bloomington)

Watt, N. (2006) 'Anti-Semitism live'. *The Guardian.* www.theguardian.com/world/2006/jun/05/poland

Webb, A. (2008) *The Routledge Companion to Central and Eastern Europe since 1919* (Abingdon: Routledge)

Weissbort, D. (ed.) (1991) *The Poetry of Survival: Post-War Poets of Central and Eastern Europe* (London: Anvil)

Weiser, B. (2009) *A Secret Life: The Polish Officer, his Covert Mission, and the Price he Paid to Save his Country* (New York: Public Affairs)

'We Want Our Concerns to Be Taken Seriously' (2017). www.spiegel.de/international/europe/poland-foreign-minister-waszczykowski-interview-a-1140629

'What is Transitional Justice?' (2011). International Center for Transitional Justice (ICTJ). www.ictj.org/about/transitional-justice

Wilczek, P. (2000) 'Polish Nobel Prize winners in literature: Are they really Polish?', *The Chicago Review: New Polish Writing*, 46(3 & 4), 375–377

Williams, R. (1976) *Keywords* (London: Fontana)

Wilson, J. (2006) *Behind the Curtain: Travels in Eastern European Football* (London: Orion)

Wiskemann, E. (1966) *Europe of the Dictators 1919-45* (London: Fontana)

Witkiewicz, S.I. (1985) *Insatiability* (Quartet: London)

Witkowski, M. (2009) *Love Town* (London: Portobello Books)

Wittlin, J. (2018) *Salt of the Earth* (London: Pushkin Press)

Witts, N. (1985) *Something Broke in Poland*, *BBC Radio* 4

Wojdowski, B. (1997) *Bread for the Departed* (Evanston: Northwestern University Press)

Woody, C. (2018) 'Germany has a "massive problem" that has reportedly knocked almost all of its Eurofighter Typhoon fighter jets out of commission'. www.uk.businessinsider.com/german-military-fighters-jets-not-ready-for-combat

'World Economic Outlook 2016. Report for Selected Countries and Subjects', World Economic Outlook/IMF. www.statisticstimes.com/economy/european-countries-by-gdp-per-capita

www.archive.is/20121219122815/http://yad-vashem.org.il/about_holocaust/documents/part2/doc154

www.culture.pl/en/article/the-pen-or-the-pen-a-brief-history-of-polish-literary-beefs

www.culture.pl/en/artist/slawomir-mrozek

www.economist.com/prospero/2016/03/10/olga-tokarczuks-polish-narrative

www.emerging-europe.com/news/new-statistics-confirm-romanias-demographic-catastrophe

www.en.wikipedia.org/wiki/Anders%27_Army#cite_note-8

www.en.wikipedia.org/wiki/LGBT-free_zone

www.en.wikipedia.org/wiki/Lustration_in_Poland

www.en.wikipedia.org/wiki/Walesa._Man_of_Hope

254   Bibliography

www.freedomhouse.org/report/freedom-world/2019/hungary

www.freedomnews.org.uk/poland-as-governments-anti-lgbtq-campaign-intensifies-homophobes-bring-bomb-to-pride-march

www.fundacjaherberta.com/aktualnosci/item/438-ryszard-krynicki-laureat-nagro-dy-im-zbigniewa-herberta-2015

www.irishtimes.com/news/world/europe/welcome-to-bulgaria-the-world-s-fastest-shrinking-nation

www.lustracja.net/index.php/tajni-wspolpracownicy/183-leszek-moczulski-tw-sb

www.news.bbc.co.uk/1/hi/world/europe/6596829:   'Poland   urged   to   halt   'homophobia'

www.pl.wikipedia.org/wiki/Jerzy_Klimkowski

www.queer.pl/news/203397/homofobiczna-furgonetka-zrownujaca-lgbt-z-pedofil-ia-parkuje-pod-kosciolem

www.researchbriefings.parliament.uk/ResearchBriefing/Summary/CBP-8060

www.statista.com/statistics/261278/number-of-books-sold-in-the-uk

www.theguardian.com/world/ng-interactive/2019/may/26/eu-election-results-2019-across-europe

www.theguardian.com/world/2017/nov/13/polish-president-condemns-far-right-scenes-at-independence-day-march

www.theguardian.com/world/2019/jul/28/lgbt-gay-rights-poland-first-pride-march-bialystok-rage-violence

www.theguardian.com/world/2019/oct/14/poland-populist-law-and-justice-par-ty-increases-majority

www.transparency.org/country/HUN

www.transparency.org/country/POL

www.transversalinflections.wordpress.com/2009/08/14/herbert-vs-milosz

www.uchodzcy.info/info/uchodzcy-w-polsce

www.wikipedia.com, 'Polish_parliamentary_election,_1989', '1991', '1993', '1997', '2001', '2005', '2007', '2011'

www.yivoencyclopedia.org/article.aspx/Banking

www.yivoencyclopedia.org/article.aspx/Polish_Literature

Websites

Zagajewski, A. (1990) *Solidarity, Solitude* (New York: Ecco)

Zagajewski, A. (2004) *A Defense of Ardor* (New York: Farrar, Straus and Giroux)

Zagajewski, A. (2007) *Polish Writers on Writing* (San Antonio: Trinity)

Zagajewski, A. (2017) *Slight Exaggeration* (New York: Farrar, Straus and Giroux)

Zagajewski, A. & Kornhauser, J. (1974) *Świat nie przedstawiony* (Kraków: Wydawnictwo Literackie)

Zajdlerowa, Z. (1989) *The Dark Side of the Moon* (Hemel Hempstead: Harvester)

Zakaria, F. (2003) *The Future of Freedom: Illiberal Democracy at Home and Abroad* (New York: Norton)

Zamoyski, A. (1987) *The Polish Way* (London: John Murray)

Ziegler, P. (1970) *The Black Death* (Harmondsworth: Penguin)

Zimmerman, J.D., (2015) *The Polish Underground and the Jews, 1939–1945* (Cambridge: CUP)

Żeromski, S. (2007) *The Coming Spring* (Budapest: Central European University)

Index

abortion laws 206
Adamowicz, Paweł 229
Aesopian language 113
Afghanistan: Soviet war in 7, 31, 41, 45, 47; US invasion of 225
Agudat Israel Party 78, 79
AIDS 146, 177, 215
Ali, Tariq 18
Allason, Rupert 18
Alternative für Deutschland (AfD) (Alternative for Germany) 226
Alvarez, Arthur 21, 52, 123, 139
American literary tradition 20
Anders, Władysław 91, 92
Andropov, Yuri 7
Andrzejewski, Jerzy 96, 104, 106–107
'And We Really Didn't Know' (Krynicki) 114
Anielka (Prus) 53–54
'Anima, There and Not There' (Różycki) 154
Annihilation (Szewc) 144
Antipolitics (Konrád) 30, 133
anti-Semitism 10, 63–65, 78, 106–110, 116, 143–144, 165–166, 170–171, 181–182; and Austria 39; and Hungary 122, 135, 136, 137, 139, 223; Kundera on 37; and ONR 186n2–187n2; and Polish armed forces 93, 119n11; and Polish 'defamation law' 209–211, 234n17; and Polish Government-in-Exile 88–89
Arab-Israeli war 1967 108
Archer, Jeffrey 18
'Are Things Worse or is this Normal?' (Śliwiński) 200
Armia Krajowa (AK) (Home Army) 90–91, 92–93, 95, 112, 234n16

Arseniuk, Andrzej 178
Arts Council of England 42
Ascherson, Neil 86, 194
Asch, Sholem 73
Ashes (Żeromski) 147, 161n2
Auden, W.H. 17
Auschwitz 98, 211, 233n10
Austen, Jane 20
Austro-Hungarian Empire 33, 39
autolustracja 181, 184, 185
avant-garde literature 74, 76, 106; Gombrowicz 70; post-communist 160; Skamander movement 66; Witkiewicz 36

Baczynski, Krzysztof Kamil 112
Bainbridge, Beryl 18
Bajnaj, Gordon 122
Balcerowicz, Leszek 195, 196
Balfour Declaration 78
Banking Crisis 2008–10 205
'barbarian' writers 115, 149, 159
'Bartek the Conqueror' (Sienkiewicz) 56
Bartoszewski, Władysław 174, 183, 190n18
Bauman, Janina 108
Bauman, Zygmunt 108, 230
BBC World Service 6
Bejtar (Zionist organisation) 75, 83n18
Berger, John 19
Berlin 5, 9
Berlin Wall 22–23, 225
Berman, Jakub 80, 116–117
Bezrobotny Lucyfer (*Lucifer Unemployed*) (Wat) 77
Białoszewski, Miron 114–115
Białowieska Forest 209, 212, 220–221
Bierut, Bolesław 116

258   Index

'Birch Grove, The' (Iwaszkiewicz) 69
Black Death 32
black market 4, 5, 10, 142, 196
Blair, Tony 18, 19
Błoński, Jan 103, 113
Blood of Elves (Sapkowski) 157
Bloom, Harold 20
Bobrowski, Kazimierz 55
Bobrowski, Mikolaj 55
Bobrowski, Stefan 55
Bobrowski, Tadeusz 54
Bocheński, Adolf 80
Boni, Michał 182
Book of Jacob, The (Tokarczuk) 219
Book of Laughter and Forgetting, The (Kundera) 27
Borowski, Tadeusz 98–99, 119n16
Borun-Jagodzińska, Katarzyna 215
Bosak, Krzysztof 212
Boziewicz, Władysław 71, 82n14
Brandstaetter, Roman 74–75
Brandys, Kazimierz 96, 104–105
Brenton, Howard 135–136
British Council in Poland 6
British Jewish Brigade 93
British National Party (BNP) 123
Broniewski, Władysław 80
Brown, Gordon 19
bruLion (*roughDraft*) (journal) 115, 121n30, 149, 159
Brześć affair 64, 65
Brzozowski, Stanisław 58–59
Bujak, Zbigniew 196
Burhardt-Bukacki, Stanisław 88

Campbell, Alastair 18
Canetti, Elias 14
Čapek, Karel 37
capitalism 46, 138, 184, 198–200; and culture 42, 43–44; and economic migration 202; and the end of communism 8–9, 171, 195–196; and European unity 41; and globalisation 203; and *inteligencja* 185; and Polish economy 175–176
Captive Mind, The (Miłosz) 119n12, 168
Čaputová, Zuzana 236n27
Carlyle, Thomas 17
car manufacturing 203, 228, 236n29
Catch 22 (Heller) 216
Catholicism and the Church 118, 187n7–188n7, 205–206; and Herbert 23, 111; and lustration 169, 174–175; and nationalism 184,

186n2–187n2, 187n6; and neo-positivism 101–102; and PiS 207; and Poland 13, 16, 51, 57, 142, 184, 190n17; and right wing politics 208, 221, 229; and women's rights 69, 155
Caudwell, Christopher 17
Cavafy, C.P. 111, 218
Celtic Christianity 33
Celtic fringe literature 19
Cenckiewicz, Sławomir 174
censorship 113–114, 135–136, 142–143, 149, 150, 217, 221
Central European Classics 158
Central European University (CEU) 223
Chernobyl nuclear melt-down 8, 25n6, 40–41, 45
'Chief Culprit, The' (Jasieński) 71
Chopin Society 109
Choucas (Nałkowska) 68
Christianity 33–34, 45, 222, 228; *see also* Catholicism and the Church
Churchill, Winston 18, 91, 93
Chwin, Stefan 153
Clark, Alan 18
Clarke, Kenneth 18
CND/END 30–31
Cohn, Adolf Jakub 72–73
Cold War 2, 41, 45, 233n1; and Central Europe 30; and culture 38, 158–159; and Germany 12; and nuclear arms race 31; Soviet threat to Poland 7
collaboration and lustration 172–173
Comintern 79
commercialism and society 46–47
Commission to Investigate Nazi War Crimes 98
commoditisation of the arts 42, 46, 48
communism 4–5, 6–7, 13, 22–23, 231; and anti-Semitism 143; collapse of 8–9, 45, 46, 117, 141, 155, 185, 193, 194, 198–199; and culture 37–38, 42–43, 150; and Czechoslovakia 26; and European culture 28–29; and Hungary 123–124; and Jewish writers 106, 107; and Jews 76; and neo-positivism 101–106; and Polish literature 15–17, 96–101, 142–143; and post-WWII Poland 95, 147, 163–164; and Russia 34–35; and tradition 110, 116
Conrad, Joseph 20, 24n2, 54–55, 71, 82n8, 147–148, 206
conservatism and literature 18–19

Index 259

Constitutional Tribunal and lustration 172, 173–174
Cook, Robin 18
Corruption Perceptions Index and Hungary 235n24–236n24
'Crossed-out Opening' (Krynicki) 114
Crusades 34
Csóori, Sandor 131–132
Csurka, Istvan 126–127, 140n2
Currie, Edwina 18
Czajkowski, Andrzej 145
Czapski, Józef 61, 66, 70, 80, 115
Czarne skrzydla (Black Wings) (Kaden-Bandrowski) 67
Czarnolas literature 59, 74–75, 82n5, 83n17
Czechoslovakia 41; and inter-war culture 37; and Kundera 26–27; post communist 39, 193; Prague Spring 40, 108
Czempiński, Gromosław and fake police reports 182–183

Dąb-Biernacki, Stefan 87
Dąbrowska, Maria 62, 67, 214
Danzig 151, 152–153
Davies, Christian 190n17
Death in Breslau (Krajewski) 151–152
Death in Danzig (Chwin) 153
Dębski, Jacek 201, 233n6
'Decision, The' (Krall) 145–146
De-Communisation law 213
Dehnel, Jacek 216–217
Deighton, Len 233n1
democracy 17, 129, 138–139, 142, 171, 184, 196, 198–199
Deutscher, Isaac 73, 74, 75
Dickens, Charles 20
Dmowski, Roman 63, 86
Dobbs, Michael 18
Döblin, Alfred 21, 83n19
Drang nach Osten (drive to the east) ١ 11, 32, 34
drugs 5, 36, 155
Drzewska-Ruszyc, Irena 109
Duda, Andrzej 220
duelling 71, 82n14
Dziady (Mickiewicz) 52, 103, 107–108, 216
Dziennik (Diary) (Gombrowicz) 37, 105

economic migration 155, 202, 233n8, 235n22, 236n29
economic reforms in Poland 8–9, 10, 193–194, 195–196, 203–205, 207

Edelman, Marek 110, 143–144
'Electric Eels' (Różycki) 154
Eliot, George 20
Eliot, T.S. 111, 120n27–121n27
'Emigration of Talent, The' (Orzeszkowa) 55
Empson, William 17
Endecja movement 59, 60, 61–62, 63, 64–67, 82n6; and anti-Semitism 78–79, 189n13, 208, 213; and Jewish writers 76; and Żeromski 70
Endelmanowa-Rosenblattowa, Czesława 72
'Envoy of Mr. Cogito, The' (Herbert) 114
eroticism 69, 117
Esterházy, Péter 127–128
euro crisis 225–226
European Court of Justice (ECJ) 220, 230, 237n33
European culture 11–13, 28; death of 27; and East-Central Europe 30, 208, 229–230, 231; Eastern and Western 47; and identity 48; and Poland 65, 77, 99, 101, 104, 141, 195, 202; and unity 38, 41–42
Europeanisation 29
European Peoples' Party (EPP) 227, 237n33
European Union (EU) 12, 41, 46, 225–227, 230–231, 232; and Germany 32; and Hungary 223–224; and Poland 169, 200–205, 208–209, 220, 229
Exit into History (Hoffman) 198

Faraon (Pharoah) (Prus) 54
Farewell Party, The (Kundera) 27
Farewells to Plasma (Goerke) 156
Fear (Gross) 175
Fellowes, Julian 18
feminism 69, 155, 214–215
Ferdydurke (Gombrowicz) 70, 206
Fiat 203
Fidesz (Fiatal Demokraták Szővetsé - Alliance of Young Democrats) 123, 130, 138, 140n2, 237n36
Fidesz-Magyar Polgári Szövetség (Fidesz-Hungarian Civic Alliance) 222, 223, 225, 227, 237n33
Filipiak, Izabela 115, 215
Filipowicz, Kornel 99–100
Fiore, Roberto 212
Fiszbach, Tadeusz 4, 5, 24n4
Fleming, Ian 18

260   *Index*

Flight without End (Roth) 34
food subsidies 8, 193
football, capitalism and crime 201
Forsyth, Frederick 18
Fourth Protocol, The (Forsyth) 18
'Freedom' (Lipska) 204
Fry, Stephen 18
Fukuyama, Francis 198, 199
futurism 67, 77

Gajcy, Tadeusz 112
Gazeta Wyborcza (magazine) 145, 164, 168–169, 179, 229; and Kaczyńskis 170, 176; and lustration 174, 186
Gdańsk 3–4, 152–153
Gdańsk University 3–4, 5
gender issues 67, 69, 214–215
Generał Barcz (Kaden-Bandrowski) 67
Geremek, Bronisław 165, 173, 187n3, 196
German-ness and 'recovered territories' 151–152, 156
Germany 11–12, 46, 48–49; East European resentment of 32, 202, 228; and EU 225–227; invasion of Poland 85; and nuclear weapons 31; and Russia 227–228
Gesty (*Gestures*) (Karpowicz) 161n6
Ghost, The (film) 18
Giełżyński, Wojciech 189n12
Gierek, Edward 193, 194
Giertych, Roman 169, 177, 187n6, 206–207
Glenny, Misha 198
globalisation 47, 198, 199–200, 203, 232
Głowiński, Michał 74
Goerke, Natasza 115, 156
Gojawiczyńska, Pola 67
Gold, Amber 188n9
Gombrowicz, Witold 36–37, 70, 101, 105–106, 115, 206
Gomułka, Władysław 108, 120n25, 199
Gontarczyk, Piotr 174
Good Bye, Lenin! (film) 191n21
Gorbachev, Mikhail 8, 40
Grabiński, Stefan 117
Graduate, The (Webb) 146
Gramsci, Antonio 13, 21
Granica (*Boundary*) (Nałkowska) 68–69
Gran, Maurice 18
Grass, Günter 21, 101, 153
Great Tradition, The (Leavis) 82n3
Greek economic crisis 226

Gross, Jan 144, 175, 209
Grynberg, Henryk 108
Gummer, John Selwyn 18

'Hamlet' (Krall) 145
Hamlet (Shakespeare) 103
Haraszti, Miklós 128–129, 136
Harris, Robert 18
Hartwig, Julia 200
Hašek, Jaroslav 37, 235n21
'Hatred' (Szymborska) 186
Havel, Václav 29, 231, 234n19–235n19
Heraclitus 230
Herbert, Zbigniew 3, 23–24, 71, 110–114, 115, 121n29; and communism 16, 96, 117, 163–164, 200, 214; and tradition 21; and values 14; and World War II 94
Hermes, pies i gwiazda (*Hermes, Dog and Star*) (Herbert) 113
'Herostrates' (Lechoń) 66
Hertz, Paweł 97
Herzl, Theodor 83n21
Heti Válasz (*Weekly Reply*) (magazine) 224
Heydrich, Reinhard 84
history, end of 198
Hitler, Adolf 34, 39
Hłasko, Marek 100, 183
Hoffman, Eva 56, 58, 79–80, 146, 198
Holocaust, the 12, 33, 35, 234n15; and Hungary 137; and Polish anti-Semitism 88–89, 106–107, 210–211; and Polish 'defamation law' 234n17; and Polish Jews 80, 145, 146; and Polish society 84, 143–144; and romani community 127; and writers 98–99
homophobia 169, 176, 177, 182, 206, 213
Horváth László, Gy. 132
House of Cards (TV series) 18
House of Day, House of Night (Tokarczuk) 156–157
Huberath, M.S. 117
Hudd, Roy 18
Huelle, Paweł 152–153
'Human Telegraph, The' (Prus) 102
Hungarian identity 127, 138–140, 224–225
Hungarian literature 125–126
Hungary 221–225; author's diary December 1990 123–140; politics in 122–123, 129–130, 133–134, 138–140, 140n2

Index 261

Hurd, Douglas 18
Hutsul people 78, 83n20

Iłłakowiczówna, Kazimiera 65, 82n12
illiberal democracy 221–225, 234n14
imperialism and separatism 39
Instytut Pamieci Narodowej (IPN)
(Institute of National Remembrance)
167–168, 172–173, 178; and fake
police reports 183, 191n18; and
Wałęsa 174
Insulator (film) 233n6
inteligencja 56–57; and communism 16,
97–98, 100, 150–151; and lustration
185; persecution of 94; and Polish
independence 61; and Polish
partition 51; post-communist 141
*Intellectuals on the Road to Class
Power, The* (Konrád and Szelényi)
133
International Monetary Fund (IMF) 194
International PEN 133, 135, 140n1
internet and writing 158
Ionescu, Ghiță 16
Islamic fundamentalism 47
Islamophobia 212, 222, 223
Israel 37, 225, 234n17, 236n25
'I've Known More Good than Evil'
(Krynicki) 114
Iwaszkiewicz, Jarosław 67, 69
Izrealita (magazine) 73

Jabotinsky, Ze'ev 78
James, Henry 20
James, P.D. 18
Janion, Maria 200, 209, 233n3
*Janulka, córka Fizdejki (Janulka,
Daughter of Fidejk)* (Witkiewicz)
202
Jaruzelski, Wojciech 7, 165, 179,
194
Jasienica, Paweł 120n25
Jasieński, Bruno 67, 71, 77
Jaworski, Krzysztof 150
Jay, Antony 18
Jedlicki, J. 59
Jewish banks 72, 83n15
Jewish culture 37
Jewish emigration 108
Jewish-Polish writers and 1968
106–110
Jews: and Hungary 132; and Poland
53, 54, 62, 65, 72–80, 143–145,
165, 171; and Polish Government-
in-Exile 88

Jobbik (Magyarországért Mozgalom
- Movement for a Better Hungary)
122–123, 222
Jobitinsky, Ze'ev 83n18
Johnson, Boris 18, 19
Johnson, Uwe 101
Joke, The (Kundera) 26
Journal of European Studies, The 1
Joyce, James 146
Jur-Gorczechowski, Jan 67–68

Kaczorowski, Ryszard 198
Kaczyński, Jarosław 169, 187n5,
188n7, 206–207, 208, 234n17;
and Białowieża Forest 209; and
communist conspiracy theories
170–172, 190n17, 211–212; and
homosexuality 176–177; and
lustration 172–175, 178–179,
181–182, 185–186; and Solidarność
177
Kaczyński, Lech 169, 187n5, 233n4;
and communist conspiracy theories
170–172; death of 190n17; and
'genderism' 214; and lustration 172–
175, 178–179, 181–182, 185–186;
and NSZ 118n6; and Solidarność
177
Kádár, János 124, 132
Kaden-Bandrowski, Juliusz 67
Kafka, Franz 37
Kamienny świat (World of Stone)
(Borowski) 98
Kapuściński, Ryszard 141, 178–179,
188n11–189n11
'Kara wieksza' ('Greater Punishment')
(Huberath) 117–118
Karmazynowy Poemat (Crimson Poem)
(Lechoń) 66
Károlyi, Bari 126–127
Karpiński, Franciszek 112
Karpowicz, Ignacy 159, 161n6
Karski, Jan 89–90, 94–95
Karsov, Nina 95, 107, 108–109, 110
Katyń (film) 182
Katyń massacre 94, 102
Kennard, Sir Howard W. 89
Kéry, László 137
'Key and the Hook, The' (Wat) 104
'Khodasewich' (Herbert) 112
*Kidnapped West or Culture Bows
Out, A* (Kundera) 27–30, 33, 34–36,
37–39, 41–42, 43–49, 49n1, 208
Kielar, Marzanna 150, 153–154
Kijówski, Andrzej 15–16

262   Index

Kinnock, Neil 18
Kipling, Rudyard 52
Kis, Danilo 29
Kisielewski, Stefan 120n25
Kiszczak, Czesław 170, 179, 183, 191n19
Klata, Jan 202
Klimkowski, Jerzy 91–92, 119n8
Kłoczowski, Jerzy 183, 190n18
Kochanowski, Jan 82n5, 112
Kołakowski, Leszek 108
Kolbe, Maximilian 233n10
Kolonia (Różycki) 154
Komorowski, Bronisław 181, 210
Komunistyczna Partia Polski (KPP) (Communist Party of Poland) 62, 79
Komunistyczna Partia Robotnicza Polski (KPRP) (Communist Party of Polish Workers) 60, 82n9
Konfederacja Polski Niepodległej (KPN) (Confederation for an Independent Poland) 180, 181, 189n13, 189n14
Konrád, György 29, 30, 133–134, 136
Konrad Wallenrod (Mickiewicz) 51, 156
Konwicki, Tadeusz 104, 113
Korboński, Stefan 90, 95–96
Kornhauser, Julian 112–113, 114, 115, 121n28
Korzeniowski, Apollo 54–55
Korzeniowski, Teodor 54
Kossak-Szczucka, Zofia 67, 118n4, 214
Kotarbiński, Tadeusz 79
Kot, Stanisław 89
Krajewski, Marek 151–152
Krajobraz po bitwie (*Landscape After Battle*) (film) 119n16
Krall, Hanna 109–110, 143–146
Krasiński, Zygmunt 52
kresy region of Poland 2, 62, 66, 82n7; and border wars 60; and Jews 72
Krushchev, Nikita 35
Krynicki, Ryszard 114
Krzyżacy (*Teutonic Knights*) (Sienkiewicz) 54
Księga narodu polskiego i pielgrzymstwa polskiego (*Book of Polish Nation and Polish Pilgrimage*) (Mickiewicz) 51
Kuciak, Ján 236n31–237n31
Kukiel, Marian 88, 89
Kultura (magazine) 99, 101
Kuncewiczowa, Maria 67
Kundera, Milan 26–30, 44, 150, 208

Kuroń, Jacek 29, 107, 165, 196
Kwiatkowski, Tadeusz 167–168
Kwieciński, Michał 188n9

Lala (Dehnel) 216–217
Lalka (*Doll*) (Prus) 54
language: and culture 14–15, 38; Esterházy on use of 128; and Jewish identity 73–76, 79; and tradition 50
Lars, Krystyna 215
Last Wish, The (Sapkowski) 157
'*Latarnik*' ('Lighthouse Keeper') (Sienkiewicz) 54
Laughable Loves (Kundera) 26
Lawrence, D.H. 11, 20
Leavis, F.R. 20
le Carré, John 19, 23
Lechoń, Jan 66
Lecka, Teresa 176
Le Pen, Jean Marie 123
Legenda Młodej Polski: Studia o strukturze duszy kulturalnej (*The Legend of Young Poland*) (Brzozowski) 59
Lem, Stanisław 113
Lepper, Andrzej 169, 181–182, 189n16, 200–201
Lesmian, Bolesław 66
LGBTQ+ community 145–146, 176–178, 212, 214, 215, 236n30; and Hungary 123
Libera, Antoni 146–148
liberal-humanist values 204, 228–229
liberatura (liberation + literature) 160
Life is Elsewhere (Kundera) 27
Liga Polskich Rodzin (LPR) (League of Polish Families) 169
Lipiński, Edward 78
Lipska, Ewa 200, 204
Lipski, Jan Józef 116
literacy 45
'Literary Life, The' (Borun-Jagodzińska) 215
literature and politics 11, 13–16, 22, 24, 137–138; and censorship 135–136; and Hungary 124, 131–132; Jewish-Polish 79–80; and lustration 180; and Poland 16–17, 66–71, 142–143, 151, 160; and post-socialist intellectuals 133–134; and post-WWII Poland 102; and tradition 95; and UK 17–19, 42; and the 'West' 20–21
Lloyd George, David 89

Index 263

'Long Live Europe! (From the Memoirs of an Ex-European)' (Wat) 77
Lord Jim (Conrad) 55
'Loyalty' (Kornhauser) 115
Lubiewo (*Love Town*) (Witkowski) 215–216
lustracja 162
lustration laws 166, 167
Luttwak, Edward 199–200
Luxemburg, Rosa 11
Lynn, Jonathan 18

Machej, Zbigniew 149–150
Macierewicz, Antoni 166, 180
Madame (Libera) 146–148
mafia and football 201
magazines and journals 55, 76, 144–145; Catholic 97; and culture 43, 47; Hungarian 124, 222, 224; Jewish-Polish 73, 75; and lustration 184–185; and poetry 149; and the Underground resistance 94–95
'Maggots and Angels' (Michnik) 116
Magyar Demokrata Fórum (MDF) (Hungarian Democratic Forum) 124, 130, 134, 138, 140n2
Magyar Nemzet (*Hungarian Nation*) (newspaper) 224
Maleszka, Lesław 168
Mándy, Iván 132–133
Marks, Laurence 18
Martha, Stefan (Herbert alias) 113
Martial Law in Poland 7, 15, 116, 144; and fake police reports 183; and Fiszbach 24n4; and literature 115; in novels 146, 148; and poetry 149
Marx, Karl 50
Masaryk, T.G. 32, 34
Masłowska, Dorota 155–156
mass culture 45
Matka-Polka (Mother-Pole) 67
Mazowiecki, Tadeusz 164, 165, 196
Medaliony (*Medallions*) (Nałkowska) 98
media suppression in Hungary 222, 224
Mendel, Hersh 75
Mennonite communities 152
Merkel, Angela 226–227, 228
Mészáros, Lőrinc 222–223
Michalowski, Aleksander 109
Michnik, Adam 10, 29, 116, 117, 142, 165, 196, 204; and Herbert 214; and lustration 168–169, 175, 179–180

Mickiewicz, Adam 51–52, 59, 103
Międzyrzecki, Artur 11, 23
Miesiecznik Literacki (*Literary Monthly*) 76
Mikołajczyk, Stanisław 92–93
milicja 3–4
Miłosz, Czesław 11, 16, 66–67, 81, 82n12, 95, 115; and communism 119n12, 168; and Herbert 111–112; and State disinformation 183; on tradition 71
Mitteleuropa 32, 34
Młoda Polska movement 57–58, 105
Młodzież Wszechpolska (MW) (All-Polish Youth) 213, 229
Moczulski, Leszek 180–181, 189n14
Modelski, Izydor 88, 118n1
modernism 36–37, 57–58, 70
modernity, transition to 194–195, 197
Modzelewski, Karol 107, 196
'Mona Lisa' (Herbert) 110–111
Morawiecki, Mateusz 220
Morvai, Krisztina 122
Mościcki, Ignacy 85
Mróz, Daniel 120n19
Mrożek, Sławomir 102–103, 120n18, 120n19
'Mr Schmetterling thinks about a United Europe' (Lipska) 200
Mullin, Chris 18
Musil, Robert 39
Myśliwski, Wiesław 113, 118n5

Nad Niemnem (*On the Niemen*) (Orzeszkowa) 53
Nałkowska, Zofia 67–69, 98, 214
Naródnyy Komissariát Vnútrennikh Del (NKVD) (People's Commissariat for Internal Affairs) 79, 91; and Katyń massacre 94
Narodowe Siły Zbrojne (NSZ) (National Armed Forces) 91, 95, 118n6, 119n13
Narutowicz, Gabriel 61, 229
national debt in Poland 193–194
National Heritage of the Republic of Poland 158
nationalism 34–35, 65, 67, 68, 199, 212, 216, 221, 226–232; and Catholicism 184, 187n6; and culture 38; and EU 202–203; and romanticism in Polish literature 52
NATO 46, 204, 227
Naumann, Friedrich 32, 34

264 *Index*

Nazism 11–12, 32, 150; and Central
 Europe 35; and culture 37–38; and
 inteligencja 94; legacy of in Germany
 227; in post-communist novels
 151–152; *see also* Holocaust, the
Neighbours (Gross) 144, 175, 209
neo-Nazism: Hungary 122–123; Poland
 165–166, 212–213
neo-positivism 96, 101–106
Népszabadság (*Liberty of the People*)
 (newspaper) 222
Netanyahu, Benjamin 234n17,
 236n25
New Hungarian Quarterly (magazine)
 124
newspaper industry 136
Newsweek and Kapuściński 178
Nienasycenie (*Insatiability*)
 (Witkiewicz) 70–71
Niezabitowska, Małgorzata 183,
 191n18
Nine (Stasiuk) 149
'Nobody Will Laugh' (Kundera) 26
nomenklatura 166, 170, 171, 187n4,
 199
Nord Stream 228, 236n28
Norwid, Cyprian 52
Notes Herbertowski (Herbert) 24
novels and novelists: and anti-
 Semitism 109–110; and communism
 98; and German-ness 151–153;
 Jewish-Polish 73, 77–78, 143–146;
 Kundera 26–27, 44, 48; and
 LGBTQ+issues 215–217; Polish 36–
 37, 54, 67–71, 146–149; political
 21; popular 120n22, 157–158;
 reactions to World War II 99–100;
 Roth 34; Strugatsky 25n7; and
 Western culture 17–21, 104; women
 writers 154–156
Nowa fala (*new wave*) 112, 115
nuclear-free zones 31
nuclear weapons 30–31, 40

Obama, Barack 234n15
Obóz Narodowo-Radykalny-Falange
 (ONR) (National Radical Camp)
 64–65, 82n11, 186n2–187n2
'Ode to Youth' (Mickiewicz) 51
O'Farrell, John 18
O'Harists 149
oil price crisis 193–194
'An Old Prophecy' (Machej) 149–150
Olszewski, Jan 166
'On a Journey' (Mrożek) 103

Open Letter to the Party, An
 (Modzelewski and Kuroń) 107
Open Society Foundations (OSF)
 223
Orbán, Viktor 222–225, 228, 230,
 236n25, 237n33
Organization for Security and
 Cooperation in Europe (OSCE) 224
Orwell, George 17
Orzeszkowa, Eliza 53, 55
ostalgia 22–23, 191n21

Pacłowski, Wacław 200
Palę Paryż (*I Burn Paris*) (Jaseiński)
 77
Palestine, Jewish emigration to 79–80,
 83n22, 93
Pamiętki (Bobrowski) 54–55
Pamiętnik Antybohatera (*The Memoir
 of an Anti-Hero*) (Filipowicz) 99–100
Pamiętnik z Powstania Warszawskiego
 (*A Memoir of the Warsaw Uprising*)
 (Bialoszewski) 114–115
Pan Cogito (*Mr. Thinker*) (Herbert)
 114, 215
Pan Tadeusz (Mickiewicz) 52
Pani Intuita (*Ms. Intuition*) (Filipiak)
 215
pan-Slavism 29
Partition of Poland 1772–1918 51, 53,
 59, 193, 198, 218, 235n20
Paszkiewicz, Gustaw 88, 118n7–119n7
PEN 125, 133, 140n1, 206
Penguin Modern Poets series 2
People's Republic of Poland 1, 103
people trafficking 202
Perechodnik, Calel 75
Peretz, I.L. 73
philosophy of labour (Brzozowski) 58
Pianist, The (film) 169
'Pigeons' (Krynicki) 114
Pilch, Jerzy 218
Piłsudski, Józef 60, 61–63, 64, 67, 84,
 86
Piwowska, Anna 215
Platforma Obywatelskie (PO) (Citizens'
 Platform party) 203, 207
Plato 206
poets and poetry: and feminism 215;
 and German-ness 153–154; Herbert
 110–114, 164; Jewish-Polish 75, 76;
 and lustration 186; Polish 51–52,
 65–66, 94, 115, 149–150; romani
 126–127; and the Underground
 resistance 95

Index 265

Pogotowie Patriotów Polskich (Aid for Polish Patriots) 86
Poland, author's experience of 1–10, 23, 133
Polish culture: and inter-war years 36–37, 105–106; and Russia 34; and *tradycja* 56; *see also* positivism in Poland; romanticism in Poland
Polish identity 51, 53, 60, 65–66, 80–81, 147–148, 154, 219–220; and banned literature 206; and EU 200–201, 204; and German-ness 151–153, 156; and the internet 158; and Jews 74; and military code of honour 71; and Młoda Polska 58; post communist 141–142, 208; post independence 60–61, 68; post-War 95, 96, 150–151; and Sanacja 62–63; and *szlachta* culture 56–57; and tradition 159–160
Polish independence 59–65, 81; and Skamander movement 66–67; and women's rights 69
Polish-Jewish: history 143–146; literature 72–80
Polish Literary Fund 158
Polish Ministry of Culture 158
Polish Parachute Brigade 93, 119n9
Polish Uprisings 53; failure of 56; in 1863 54, 55; and Jews 78
political assassinations 236n31–237n31
political science 14
politics and literature 13–16, 22, 24, 137–138; and censorship 135–136; and Hungary 131–132; Jewish-Polish 76–77, 79–80; and lustration 180; and Poland 16–17, 66–71, 142–143, 151, 160; and post-socialist intellectuals 133–134; and post-WWII Poland 102; and tradition 95; and UK 17–19, 42; and the 'West' 20–21
Pollena 196
Polonisation of minorities 53, 60, 219; and Jewish *inteligncja* 72; and Ukranian nationalists 64
Polska Partia Socjalityczna (PPS) (Polish Socialist Party) 57, 62, 67, 86
Polska Zjednoczona Partia Robotnicza (PZPR) (Polish United Workers Party) 164, 171, 189n14; and Kapuściński 178; and *nomenklatura* 187n4
Polski kodex honorowy (*The Polish Code of Honour*) (Boziewicz) 71, 82n14

Polskie Radio 183
Polskie Stronnictwo Ludowe (SL) (Polish Peasant Party) 86
Pomer, Stefan 72
Poniatowski, Prince Józef 52, 200
popular culture 44, 131, 141, 157–158; and novels 120n22
Pornografia (Gombrowicz) 70
Portrait of the Artist as a Young Man (Joyce) 146
positivism 53–54, 59
post-colonial writers 20
post-communist literature 13, 22
post-communist society 129–130, 133–134, 141–142, 159, 160, 169, 197, 199–203, 231–232; in Hungary 122–124, 126, 131–132; and lustration 162–163, 166–172, 184–186; and translated literature 158–159; and writers 217
post-modern literary theory 21
Pound, Ezra 135
poverty 63, 64, 70, 79, 184, 191n20
'Power of Taste, The' (Herbert) 112
Pożegnanie z Marią (*Farewell to Mary*) (Borowski) 98
Prague Spring 40, 108
Pravda (Brenton and Hare) 136
Prawo i Sprawiedliwość (PiS) (Law and Justice party) 169, 186, 190n17, 206, 207–208, 234n11, 237n34; and EU 220, 237n36; and right wing politics 210–213, 220, 229
'Prevention of Literature, The' (Orwell) 17
privatisation and multinational corporations 196, 197
Protestantism 33–34, 218
Prus, Bolesław 53–54, 55, 102, 103
Przedwiośnie (*The Coming Spring*) (Żeromski) 69–70, 148
Przybyszewski, Stanisław 106
publishing and privatisation 132, 137, 231, 237n35
puns 154
Putin, Vladimir 227
Pyjas, Stanisław 168
Pyzik, Agata 82n13, 219, 228

Quo Vadis? (Sienkiewicz) 54

racism 10, 126; in Hungary 212–213, 224
Raczkiewicz, Władysław 85–86, 88, 89

266   Index

Radio Maryja 169, 174, 180, 187n7–188n7, 206
Rapacki, Adam 30–31
Reagan, Ronald 29, 31
Rebirth of History, The (Glenny) 198
'Reflections on the Problem of the Nation' (Herbert) 110
regime-change world-wide and transitional justice 162
religious warfare 33–34
Report from a Besieged City (Herbert) 164
'Republics' division of Polish history 188n8
'Retrotopia' 230
right wing politics 220, 228–231; and Hungary 221–225; and the West 226–227
Roadside Picnic (Strugatsky) 25n7
Robinson, Tommy 212
Rołecki, Michał 177
Romania 129, 133–134
romani community in Hungary 126–127
Romans in Britain, The (Brenton) 135
Romans Teresa Hennert (*The Romance of Teresa Hennert*) (Nałkowska) 68
romanticism 51–53, 54, 58, 59, 62–63
Rondo (Brandys) 104–105
Roth, Joseph 34
Rowling, J.K. 18, 21
Różycki, Tomasz 154
Ruch Narodowy (National Movement) 212
Rudnicki, Adolf 95
Russia 227–228; and Europe 28–29, 34–35; and the West 35; *see also* Soviet Union
Russianisation 34
Russian Revolution 35, 36
Rydzyk, Fr. Tadeusz 169, 174, 187n7–188n7
Rymkiewicz, Jarosław 144
Rywin, Lew 168–169, 180

'Salvation' (Krall) 145
Samoobrona (Self-Defence party) 169, 182, 200–201
Sanacja regime 62–63, 81; and anti-Semitism 78–79; and armed forces 85–86, 87; suppression of minorities 64; and the Underground resistance 90–91

Sanatorium Pod Klepsydrą (*Sanatorium under the Sign of the Hourglass*) (Schulz) 77
Sandauer, Artur 76, 100
Sapkowski, Andrzej 157–158, 186
Sarmati people 82n13
Schindler's List (film) 146, 168
Schneider, Peter 22
Schulz, Bruno 36, 70, 77–78, 115
Schwarzbart, Isaac 88
Schweitzer, Andras 223
Segal, Harold B. 72
Sejm (Polish parliament) 61, 63, 192n22; and anti-Semitism 108; and Moczulski 180; and Polish-Jewish writers 73; post-communist 164, 166–167
Shakespeare 20
Shaw, G.B. 17
Shielding the Flame (Krall) 143–144
Shoah (film) 144
shtetl and Jewish culture 72, 74, 75, 77, 80
Sielatycki, Mirosław 176
Sienkiewicz, Henryk 54, 105
Sikorski, Władysław 86–88, 89, 90, 91–92
Simicska, Lajos 224
Singer, Isaac Bashevis 73
Singer, Israel Joshua 73
Skamander group 62, 66–67, 106
skinhead culture 39
Sklepy Cynamonowe (*Cinnamon Shops*) (Schulz) 77
Śliwiński, Piotr 200
Słonimski, Antoni 62, 74, 76, 80, 120n25
Słoń (*The Elephant*) (Mrożek) 102–103
Słowacki, Juliusz 52, 112
Służba Bezpieczestwa (SB) (Polish Security Service) 168, 183–184; and Boni 182; and Catholic Church 175; and Jarosław Kaczyński's homosexuality 175–176, 177; and Kapuściński 178; and Wałęsa 174
Smallholders Party 130, 134
'small' nations 39–40
Śmigły-Rydz, Edward 64–65, 84
socialism 57, 129; and communism 45; and culture 44; and literature 17–18
social structure of East-Central Europe 34
society and commercialism 46–47
Socjaldemokracja Rzeczpospolita Polski (SdRP) (Social Democracy of the Republic of Poland party) 171

Index 267

socrealizm (socialist-realism) 97, 100, 159
'Soiree at the Czar's Plenipotentiary' (Lars) 215
Solaris 203
Solidarność 4, 6, 31; electoral victory 164–165; and Polish literature 15
Solzhenitsyn, Aleksandr 29
Sól ziemi (Salt of the Earth) (Wittlin) 78
Soros, George 223, 224, 236n25, 237n33
Sośnicki, Dariusz 150
Sosnkowski, Kazimierz 86, 88, 90, 92–93
Soviet Union 2, 7, 8, 12; and Chernobyl disaster 40–41; collapse of 45, 171, 198; and Czechoslovakia 29–30; and East-Central Europe 29; and glasnost 194; and *inteligencja* 94; invasion of Poland 88; and World War II 93
Sowińska, Ewa 177
Spender, Stephen 17
Staff, Leopold 66
Stalinism 26, 29, 34, 35, 102; and Jews 107; and uniformity 38
Stalin, Josef 13, 89, 94, 132, 193
Stasi 167, 190
Stasiuk, Andrzej 148–149, 206, 218
Staszewski, Stefan 120n25
Steel, Mark 18
Steiner, George 37, 50, 150
Stempowski, Jerzy 99, 115
Stolica (newspaper) 181
Strategic Defence Initiative (SDI) 29, 31
Stronnictwo Narodowe (SN) (National Alliance) 86–87, 88, 118n2
Stronnictwo Pracy (Labour Alliance) 86
Strugatsky, Boris and Arkady 25n7
Struna światła (Chord of Light) (Herbert) 113
Stryjkowski, Julian 74
Styliński, Adam 183
Sublokatorka (The Subtenant) (Krall) 109–110, 144–145
Subotić, Milan 173
Świat nie przedstawiony (The World Un-represented) (Zagajewski and Kornhauser) 113, 114
Swietlicki, Marcin 150
Syrian refugee crisis 2015 205, 208, 226
Syruć, Jan *see* Miłosz, Czesław
Szabad Demoktraták Szővetsege (SZDSZ) (Alliance of Free Democrats) 124, 129–130, 138, 140n2

Szaruga, Leszek 151
Szczedrzyk village, Poland 2
Szczypińska, Jolanta 188n10
Szechter, Symon 107
Szelényi, Iván 133
Szewc, Piotr 144
Szigliget writers' retreat 134–135
szlachta society 52, 56, 81n2, 82n4
szmalcownicy 210, 234n16
Szymborska, Wisława 164, 167, 186, 206
Szymel, Maurycy 72
Szymiczkowa, Maryla 216

'Table, The' (Huelle) 152
Tajemnica domu helcelów (The Secret House of Helcel) (Szymiczkowa)) 216
Tales of Galicia (Stasiuk) 149
Tango (Mrożek) 103
Tarczyński, Piotr 216
Targowiczanin 219, 235n20
Taylor, John 31
Teletubbies banned 177–178, 206
Testament (Gombrowicz) 101
Thatcher, Margaret 18, 41, 135
'thaw' of 1956 16, 36, 97, 100, 102; and Herbert 113; and Kundera 26
theatre of the absurd 36
Third Reich 12, 35
Thomas, Mark 18
Thompson, E.P. 30
Tokarczuk, Olga 156–157, 219
Torańska, Teresa 116
totalitarianism and post-communist Europe 48
Tóth, Eva 125–126
tradition 21–23, 50, 77, 80–81, 95, 120n27–121n27; and Herbert 111; Jewish-Polish 76, 77–78, 79–80; and neo-positivism 102–104; and Polish literature 24, 50–51, 71, 115–116, 159–161, 217–220
tradycja (Polish = tradition) 50–51, 56
'Tragedy of Central Europe, The' (Kundera) 33, 49n1
Trainspotting (Welsh) 155
transitional justice 162
translation of Polish literature 158–159
Transylvania 125
Treaties of Riga and Versailles 60
Trump, Donald 225
Trylogia (Sienkiewicz) 54
Trzech Kumpli (Three Pals) (film) 168

268 Index

Tusk, Donald 203, 212
Tuwim, Julian 65, 76
TV-Niepokalanów 206, 233n10
Tygodnik Powszechny (*Weekly Universal*) (Catholic newspaper) 97, 119n15, 121n29
Tymiński, Stanisław 165–166
Tyrmand, Leopold 96, 97
Tysiąc spokojnych miast (*A Thousand Peaceful Cities*) (Pilch) 218

Ukraine 25n6, 40, 219, 235n22; *see also* Chernobyl nuclear melt-down
Ukrainian migrants 235n22
Ukrainian nationalists 64, 83n20
Umschlagplatz (Rymkiewicz) 144
Unbearable Lightness of Being, The (Kundera) 27
Underground 90–91, 94
United Kingdom (UK): and Brexit 19, 226, 228; and culture 19–20, 42, 48; and European elections 122; and Polish Government-in-Exile 88, 89, 91, 93; and Polish migration 155, 202; and Russian espionage 227–228
United States of America (USA) 44, 48, 159, 225
Urban, Jerzy 179
Urząd Kultury Fizycznej i Turystyki (UKFiT) (Department of Physical Culture and Tourism) 201
Urząd Ochrony Państwa (UOP) (Department of State Protection) 201, 233n5
USSR *see* Soviet Union

Vajda, Miklós 124, 136
Vashem, Yad 119n11
Vaterland (Różycki) 154
Velvet Prison, The (Haraszti) 129
Very British Coup, A (Mullin) 18
victimhood, Polish cult of 57, 190n17, 209–210; and economic 'shock therapy' 197; and Jewish-communist conspiracy theories 211–212, 221; and lustration 184, 186; and refugee crisis 205
Victory (Conrad) 147
'Village Wedding, The' (Dąbrowska) 120n18
Volksdeutsche 120n17

Wajda, Andrzej 120n24
Waldstein, Bronisław 168

Wałęsa: człowiek z nadziei (*Wałęsa: Man of Hope*) (film) 188n9
Wałęsa, Lech 129, 151, 165, 198; and homosexuality 177; and lustration 174
Walicki, Andrzej 56
Wannsee Conference 84
Warsaw Gay Pride 176
Warsaw Ghetto 89, 118n3, 145
'In Warsaw' (Miłosz) 95
Warsaw University 108
Warsaw Uprising 94, 95, 110, 112, 114–115, 119n9
Waszczykowski, Witold 190n17, 220, 235n21
Wat, Aleksander 67, 76–77, 104, 115
Ważyk, Adam 80
Webb, Beatrice and Sydney 17
Webb, Charles 146
'Wedding at Atomics' (Mrożek) 120n18
Weiss, Peter 101
Welsh, Irving 155
Wesele (*The Wedding*) (Wyspiański) 58
Western society and culture 43–44, 225
'What do Men Bring?' (Piwowska) 215
White and Red (Masłowska) 155–156, 161n7
White Raven (Stasiuk) 148–149
Who was David Weisser? (Huelle) 152, 153
Wiadomości Literacki (*Literary News*) (magazine) 75, 78
Wiatr, Sławomir 168
Widdicombe, Ann 18
Wielgus, Stanisław 174–175, 180
Wielki Tydzień (*Holy Week*) (Andrzejewski) 106–107, 120n24
Wieniawa-Długoszowski, Bolesław 85
'Wilco Girls, The' (Iwaszkiewicz) 69
Williams, Raymond 17, 50
Wiskemann, E. 81
Witkiewicz, Stanisław Ignacy 36, 70–71, 85, 153, 202, 206
Witkowski, Michał 215–216
Wittlin, Józef 78
Wojskowe Służby Informacyjne (WSI) (Military Information Service) 170
Wołoszański, Bogusław 173
Woman from Hamburg, The (Krall) 145
women's rights 67, 69, 155
women writers 154–157, 214–215
work and tradition 55
Worker in a Workers' State (Haraszti) 129
World War I 36, 60

Index   269

World War II 11, 41, 95; and Austria 39; and cultural wars 33; and culture 38; and Poland 13; Polish armed forces, Underground resistance and Government-in-Exile 85–93; writers' reactions to 98–99; *see also* Holocaust, the; Nazism; Third Reich

W pustyni i w puszczy (In Desert and Wilderness) (Sienkiewicz) 54

Writers' Union: Hungarian 125, 126, 137; Polish 120n25

Wrocław 3

Wyspiański, Stanisław 58, 105

Wyszynski, Stefan 174

xenophobia 212–213, 224

Xięga Bałwochwalcza (The Book of Idolatry) (Schulz) 78

Yiddish 73

Yugoslavia 34, 133

Zagajewski, Adam 112–113, 114, 115, 121n28, 218

Zakaria, Fareed 234n14

Zambrowski, Roman 120n25

Zapis (Record) (underground journal) 113

Żegota (*Rada Pomocy Żydom*/Council Aiding Jews) 89

Żeleński, Tadeusz 'Boy' 65, 71, 94

Żeromski, Stefan 55, 69–70, 105–106, 147–148, 161n2

Zeszyty Literackie (magazine) 231

Zionism 37, 75, 78, 79–80, 83n18, 83n21, 108

Żółkiewski, Stefan 108

Związek Walki Zbrojnej (ZWZ) (Union of Armed Struggle) 90

Zycie Warszawy (magazine) 144

Żydokomuna (Judeo-Communism) 170–171

Zygielbojm, Szmul 88, 118n3